D1758971

THE M MANUAL
2008

EIGHTY-THIRD
ANNUAL ISSUE

Edited by Lee McGlone

BICENTENNIAL
1807
WILEY
2007
BICENTENNIAL

EDITORS OF THE MINISTER'S MANUAL
G.B.F. Hallock, D.D., 1926–1958
M.K.W. Heicher, Ph.D., 1943–1968
Charles L. Wallis, M.A., M.Div., 1969–1983
James W. Cox, M.Div., Ph.D., 1984–2007
Lee McGlone, Ph.D.

Translations of the Bible referred to and quoted from in this book may be indicated by their standard abbreviations, such as NRSV (New Revised Standard Version) and NIV (New International Version). In addition, some contributions have made their own translations and others have used a mixed text.

Published by Jossey-Bass
A Wiley Imprint
989 Market Street, San Francisco, CA 94103-1741   www.josseybass.com

Library of Congress Cataloging Card Number

25-21658
ISSN 0738-5323
ISBN-13 978-0-7879-8571-4

Printed in the United States of America
FIRST EDITION
HB Printing
10 9 8 7 6 5 4 3 2 1

CONTENTS

SECTION I

GENERAL AIDS
AND
RESOURCES

Civil Year Calendars for 2008 and 2009

2008

January	February	March	April
S M T W T F S 　 　 1 2 3 4 5 6 7 8 9 10 11 12 13 14 15 16 17 18 19 20 21 22 23 24 25 26 27 28 29 30 31	S M T W T F S 　 　 　 　 　 1 2 3 4 5 6 7 8 9 10 11 12 13 14 15 16 17 18 19 20 21 22 23 24 25 26 27 28 29	S M T W T F S 　 　 　 　 　 　 1 2 3 4 5 6 7 8 9 10 11 12 13 14 15 16 17 18 19 20 21 22 23 24 25 26 27 28 29 30 31	S M T W T F S 　 　 1 2 3 4 5 6 7 8 9 10 11 12 13 14 15 16 17 18 19 20 21 22 23 24 25 26 27 28 29 30
May	June	July	August
S M T W T F S 　 　 　 1 2 3 4 5 6 7 8 9 10 11 12 13 14 15 16 17 18 19 20 21 22 23 24 25 26 27 28 29 30 31	S M T W T F S 1 2 3 4 5 6 7 8 9 10 11 12 13 14 15 16 17 18 19 20 21 22 23 24 25 26 27 28 29 30	S M T W T F S 　 　 1 2 3 4 5 6 7 8 9 10 11 12 13 14 15 16 17 18 19 20 21 22 23 24 25 26 27 28 29 30 31	S M T W T F S 　 　 　 　 　 1 2 3 4 5 6 7 8 9 10 11 12 13 14 15 16 17 18 19 20 21 22 23 24 25 26 27 28 29 30 31
September	October	November	December
S M T W T F S 　 1 2 3 4 5 6 7 8 9 10 11 12 13 14 15 16 17 18 19 20 21 22 23 24 25 26 27 28 29 30	S M T W T F S 　 　 　 1 2 3 4 5 6 7 8 9 10 11 12 13 14 15 16 17 18 19 20 21 22 23 24 25 26 27 28 29 30 31	S M T W T F S 　 　 　 　 　 　 1 2 3 4 5 6 7 8 9 10 11 12 13 14 15 16 17 18 19 20 21 22 23 24 25 26 27 28 29 30	S M T W T F S 　 1 2 3 4 5 6 7 8 9 10 11 12 13 14 15 16 17 18 19 20 21 22 23 24 25 26 27 28 29 30 31

2009

January	February	March	April
S M T W T F S 　 　 　 　 1 2 3 4 5 6 7 8 9 10 11 12 13 14 15 16 17 18 19 20 21 22 23 24 25 26 27 28 29 30 31	S M T W T F S 1 2 3 4 5 6 7 8 9 10 11 12 13 14 15 16 17 18 19 20 21 22 23 24 25 26 27 28	S M T W T F S 1 2 3 4 5 6 7 8 9 10 11 12 13 14 15 16 17 18 19 20 21 22 23 24 25 26 27 28 29 30 31	S M T W T F S 　 　 　 1 2 3 4 5 6 7 8 9 10 11 12 13 14 15 16 17 18 19 20 21 22 23 24 25 26 27 28 29 30
May	June	July	August
S M T W T F S 　 　 　 　 　 1 2 3 4 5 6 7 8 9 10 11 12 13 14 15 16 17 18 19 20 21 22 23 24 25 26 27 28 29 30 31	S M T W T F S 　 1 2 3 4 5 6 7 8 9 10 11 12 13 14 15 16 17 18 19 20 21 22 23 24 25 26 27 28 29 30	S M T W T F S 　 　 　 1 2 3 4 5 6 7 8 9 10 11 12 13 14 15 16 17 18 19 20 21 22 23 24 25 26 27 28 29 30 31	S M T W T F S 　 　 　 　 　 　 1 2 3 4 5 6 7 8 9 10 11 12 13 14 15 16 17 18 19 20 21 22 23 24 25 26 27 28 29 30 31
September	October	November	December
S M T W T F S 　 　 1 2 3 4 5 6 7 8 9 10 11 12 13 14 15 16 17 18 19 20 21 22 23 24 25 26 27 28 29 30	S M T W T F S 　 　 　 　 1 2 3 4 5 6 7 8 9 10 11 12 13 14 15 16 17 18 19 20 21 22 23 24 25 26 27 28 29 30 31	S M T W T F S 1 2 3 4 5 6 7 8 9 10 11 12 13 14 15 16 17 18 19 20 21 22 23 24 25 26 27 28 29 30	S M T W T F S 　 　 1 2 3 4 5 6 7 8 9 10 11 12 13 14 15 16 17 18 19 20 21 22 23 24 25 26 27 28 29 30 31

Church and Civic Calendar for 2008

January

1	New Year's Day
6	Epiphany
7	Orthodox Christmas
10	Muharram (Islamic New Year)
14	Orthodox New Year
18	Confession of St. Peter
21	Martin Luther King Jr. Day
25	Conversion of St. Paul

February

2	Presentation in the Temple
5	Shrove Tuesday
6	Ash Wednesday
10	First Sunday in Lent
14	Valentine's Day
17	Second Sunday in Lent
18	Martin Luther's Birthday
18	Washington's Birthday
24	Third Sunday in Lent

March

2	Fourth Sunday in Lent
9	Fifth Sunday in Lent
9	Daylight Savings Time Begins
16	Palm Sunday
17	St. Patrick's Day
20	Maundy Thursday
20	Prophet's Birthday (Islamic)
21	Good Friday
22	Holy Saturday
23	Easter Sunday
25	Annunciation Day

April

4	Martin Luther King Jr. Birthday
9	Dietrich Bonhoeffer Birthday
20	First Day of Passover
27	Orthodox Easter
25	St. Mark the Evangelist
27	Last Day of Passover

May

1	Ascension Day
2	Yom HaShoah
5	Cinco de Mayo
8	Yom HaAtzmaut
11	Pentecost Sunday
11	Mother's Day
18	Trinity Sunday
22	Corpus Christi
26	Memorial Day

June

9	Shavuot
15	Father's Day
24	Nativity of St. John the Baptist
29	St. Peter and St. Paul

July

1	Canada Day
4	Independence Day

August

6	Transfiguration Day
10	Tisha B'Av
15	Mary, Mother of Jesus

September

1	Labor Day
2	Ramadan begins (Islamic)
7	Grandparents Day
27	Lailat Ul Qadr (Islamic)
30	Hashanah (Jewish New Year)

October

2	Eid-ad-Fitr (Islamic)
5	World Communion Sunday
9	Yom Kippur
13	Columbus Day
14	First Day of Sukkot
20	Last Day of Sukkot
24	United Nations Day
31	All Hallow's Eve (Halloween)
31	Reformation Day

November

1	All Saints' Day
2	All Faithful Departed Day
2	Daylight Savings Time ends
4	Election Day
11	Veterans Day
27	Thanksgiving Day
30	First Sunday in Advent

December

7	Second Sunday in Advent
9	Eid-al-Adha (Islamic)
14	Third Sunday in Advent
21	Fourth Sunday in Advent
22	First Day of Chanukah
25	Christmas Day
26	Kwanzaa (until Jan. 1)
28	Day of the Holy Innocents
29	Last Day of Chanukah
31	New Year's Eve

The Revised Common Lectionary for 2008

The following Scriptures are commended for use by various Protestant churches and the Roman Catholic Church and include first, second, and Gospel readings, and Psalms for 2008.

New Year's Day
    Jan. 1: Eccl. 3:1–3; Ps. 8; Rev. 21:1a; Matt. 25:31–6

Season of Epiphany
    Jan. 6: Isa. 60:1–6; Ps. 72:1–7, 10–14; Eph. 3:1–12; Matt. 2:1–12
    Jan. 13: Isa. 42:1–9; Ps. 29; Acts 10:34–43; Matt. 3:13–17

Jan. 20: Isa. 49:1–7; Ps. 40:1–11; 1 Cor. 1:1–9; John 1:29–42

Jan. 27: Isa. 9:1–4; Ps. 27:1, 4–9; 1 Cor. 1:10–18; Matt. 4:12–23

Feb. 3: Exod. 24:12–18; Ps. 99; 2 Pet. 1:16–21; Matt. 17:1–9

Season of Lent

Feb. 6 (Ash Wednesday): Joel 2:1–2, 12–17; Ps. 51:1–17; 2 Cor. 5:20b–6:10; Matt. 6:1–6, 16–21

Feb. 10: Gen. 2:15–17, 3:1–7; Ps. 32; Rom. 5:12–19; Matt. 4:1–11

Feb. 17: Gen. 12:1–4a; Ps. 121; Rom. 4:1–5, 13–17; John 3:1–17

Feb. 24: Exod. 17:1–7; Ps. 95; Rom. 5:1–11; John 4:5–42

Mar. 2: 1 Sam. 16:1–13; Ps. 23; Eph. 5:8–14; John 9:1–41

Mar. 9: Ezek. 37:1–14; Ps. 130; Rom. 8:6–11; John 11:1–45

Holy Week and Easter Season

Mar. 16 (Palm Sunday): Liturgy of the Palms: Matt. 21:1–11; Ps. 118:1–2, 19–29; Liturgy of the Passion: Isa. 50:4–9a; Ps. 31:9–16; Phil. 2:5–11; Matt. 26:14–27:66 or Matt. 27:11–54

Mar. 17 (Monday): Isa. 42:1–9; Ps. 36:5–11; Heb. 9:11–15; John 12:1–11

Mar. 18 (Tuesday): Isa. 49:1–7; Ps. 71:1–14; 1 Cor. 1:18–31; John 12:20–36

Mar. 19 (Wednesday): Isa. 50:4–9a; Ps. 70; Heb. 12:1–3; John 13:21–32

Mar. 20 (Thursday): Exod. 12:1–4 (5–10), 11–14; Ps. 116:1–4, 12–19; 1 Cor. 11:23–26; John 13:1–17, 31b–35

Mar. 21 (Good Friday): Isa. 52:13–53:12; Ps. 22; Heb. 10:16–25; John 18:1–19:42

Mar. 22 (Holy Saturday): Gen. 1:1–2:4a; Ps. 136:1–9, 23–26; Isa. 55:1–11; Rom. 6:3–11; Matt. 28:1–10

Mar. 23 (Easter): Acts 10:34–43; Ps. 118:1–2, 14–24; Col. 3:1–4; John 20:1–18 or Matt. 28:1–10

Mar. 30: Acts 2:14a, 22–32; Ps. 16; 1 Pet. 1:3–9; John 20:19–31

Apr. 6: Acts 2:14a, 36–41; Ps. 116:1–4, 12–19; 1 Pet. 1:17–23; Luke 24:13–35

Apr. 13: Acts 2:42–47; Ps. 23; 1 Pet. 2:19–25; John 10:1–10

Apr. 20: Acts 7:55–60; Ps. 31:1–5, 15–16; 1 Pet. 2:2–10; John 14:1–14

Apr. 27: Acts 17:22–31; Ps. 66:8–20; 1 Pet. 3:13–22; John 14:15–21

May 1 (Ascension Day): Acts 1:1–11; Ps. 47; Eph. 1:15–23; Luke 24:44–53

May 4: Acts 1:6–14; Ps. 68:1–10, 32–35; 1 Pet. 4:12–14, 5:6–11; John 17:1–11

May 11 (Pentecost): Acts 2:1–21; Ps. 104:24–34, 35b; 1 Cor. 12:3b–13; John 7:37–39

May 18 (Trinity Sunday): Gen. 1:1–2:4a; Ps. 8; 2 Cor. 13:11–13; Matt. 28:16–20

May 25: Isa. 49:8–16a; Ps. 131 or Ps. 62:5–12; 1 Cor. 4:1–5; Matt. 6:24–34

June 1: Gen. 6:9–22, 7:24, 8:14–19; Ps. 46; Rom. 1:16–17, 3:22b–28 (29–31); Matt. 7:21–29

June 8: Gen. 12:1–9; Ps. 33:1–12; Rom. 4:13–25; Matt. 9:9–13, 18–26

June 15: Gen. 18:1–15; Ps. 116:1–2, 12–19; Rom. 5:1–8; Matt. 9:35–10:8 (9–23)

June 22: Gen. 21:8–21; Ps. 86:1–10, 16–17 or Ps. 17; Rom. 6:1b–11; Matt. 10:24–39

June 29: Gen. 22:1–14; Ps. 13; Rom. 6:12–23; Matt. 10:40–42

July 6: Gen. 24:34–38, 42–49, 58–67; Ps. 45:10–17 or Ps. 72; Rom. 7:15–25a; Matt. 11:16–19, 25–30

July 13: Gen. 25:19–34; Ps. 119:105–112 or Ps. 25; Rom. 8:1–11; Matt. 13:1–9, 18–23

July 20: Gen. 28:10–19a; Ps. 139:1–12, 23–24; Rom. 8:12–25; Matt. 13:24–30, 36–43

July 27: Gen. 29:15–28; Ps. 105:1–11, 45b; Rom. 8:26–39; Matt. 13:31–33, 44–52

Aug. 3: Gen. 32:22–31; Ps. 17:1–7, 15; Rom. 9:1–5; Matt. 14:13–21

Aug. 10: Gen. 37:1–4, 12–28; Ps. 105:1–6, 16–22, 45b; Rom. 10:5–15; Matt. 14:22–33

Aug. 17: Gen. 45:1–15; Ps. 133; Rom. 11:1–2a, 29–32; Matt. 15:10–20, 21–28

Aug. 24: Exod. 1:8–2:10; Ps. 124; Rom. 12:1–8; Matt. 16:13–20

Aug. 31: Exod. 3:1–15; Ps. 105:1–6, 23–26, 45c; Rom. 12:9–21; Matt. 16:21–28

Sept. 7: Exod. 12:1–14; Ps. 149:1 or Ps. 148; Rom. 13:8–14; Matt. 18:15–20

Sept. 14: Exod. 14:19–31; Exod. 15:1b–11, 20–21; Rom. 14:1–12; Matt. 18:21–35

Sept. 21: Exod. 16:2–15; Ps. 105:1–6, 37–45 or Ps. 78; Phil. 1:21–30; Matt. 20:1–16

Sept. 28: Exod. 17:1–7; Ps. 78:1–4, 12–6; Phil. 2:1–13; Matt. 21:23–32

Oct. 5: Exod. 20:1–4, 7–9, 12–20; Ps. 19; Phil. 3:4b–14; Matt. 21:33–46

Oct. 12: Exod. 32:1–14; Ps. 23 or Ps. 106:1–6, 19–23; Phil. 4:1–9; Matt. 22:1–14

Oct. 19: Exod. 33:12–23; Ps. 99; 1 Thess.1:1–10; Matt. 22:15–22

Oct. 26: Deut. 34:1–12; Ps. 90:1–6, 13–17; 1 Thess. 2:1–8; Matt. 22:34–46

Nov. 1 (All Saints' Day): Rev. 7:9–17; Ps. 34:1–10, 22; 1 John 3:1–3; Matt. 5:1–12

Nov. 2 (All Saints' Sunday): Josh. 3:7–17; Ps. 107:1–7, 33–37; 1 Thess. 2:9–13; Matt. 23:1–12

Nov. 9: Josh. 24:1–3a, 14–25; Ps. 78:1–7; 1 Thess. 4:13–18; Matt. 25:1–13

Nov. 16: Judg. 4:1–7; Ps. 123 or Ps. 76; 1 Thess. 5:1–11; Matt. 25:14–30

Nov. 23 (Christ the King): Ezek. 34:11–16, 20–24; Ps. 100; Eph. 1:15–23; Matt. 25:31–46

Nov. 27 (Thanksgiving Day): Deut. 8:7–18; Ps. 65; 2 Cor. 9:6–15; Luke 17:11–19

Advent and Christmas Season

Nov. 30: Isa. 64:1–9; Ps. 80:1–7, 17–19; 1 Cor. 1:3–9; Mark 13:24–37

Dec. 7: Isa. 40:1–11; Ps. 85:1–2, 8–13; 2 Pet. 3:8–15a; Mark 1:1–8

Dec. 14: Isa. 61:1–4, 8–11; Ps. 126; 1 Thess. 5:16–24; John 1:6–8, 19–28

Dec. 21: 2 Sam. 7:1–11, 16; Rom. 16:25–27; Luke 1:26–38, 47–55

Dec. 24 (Christmas Eve): Isa. 9:2–7; Ps. 96; Titus 2:11–14; Luke 2:1–20

Dec. 25 (Christmas Day): Isa. 52:7–10; Ps. 98; Heb. 1:1–4 (5–12); John 1:1–14

Dec. 28: Isa. 61:10–62:3; Ps. 148; Gal. 4:4–7; Luke 2:22–40

Four-Year Church Calendar

	2008	2009	2010	2011
Ash Wednesday	Feb. 6	Feb. 25	Feb. 17	Mar. 9
Palm Sunday	Mar. 16	Apr. 5	Mar. 28	Apr. 17
Good Friday	Mar. 21	Apr. 10	Apr. 2	Apr. 22
Easter	Mar. 23	Apr. 12	Apr. 4	Apr. 24

Ascension Day	May 1	May 21	May 13	June 2
Pentecost	May 11	May 31	May 23	June 12
Trinity Sunday	May 18	June 7	May 30	June 19
Thanksgiving	Nov. 27	Nov. 26	Nov. 25	Nov. 24
Advent Sunday	Nov. 30	Nov. 29	Nov. 28	Nov. 27

Forty-Year Easter Calendar

2008 March 23	2018 April 1	2028 April 16	2038 April 25
2009 April 12	2019 April 21	2029 April 1	2039 April 10
2010 April 4	2020 April 12	2030 April 21	2040 April 1
2011 April 24	2021 April 4	2031 April 13	2041 April 2
2012 April 8	2022 April 17	2032 March 28	2042 April 6
2013 March 31	2023 April 9	2033 April 17	2043 March 29
2014 April 20	2024 March 31	2034 April 9	2044 April 17
2015 April 5	2025 April 20	2035 March 25	2045 April 9
2016 March 27	2026 April 5	2036 April 13	2046 March 25
2017 April 16	2027 March 28	2037 April 5	2047 April 14

Traditional Wedding Anniversary Identifications

1	Paper	7	Wool	13	Lace	35	Coral
2	Cotton	8	Bronze	14	Ivory	40	Ruby
3	Leather	9	Pottery	15	Crystal	45	Sapphire
4	Linen	10	Tin	20	China	50	Gold
5	Wood	11	Steel	25	Silver	55	Emerald
6	Iron	12	Silk	30	Pearl	60	Diamond

Colors Appropriate for Days and Seasons

White.   Symbolizes purity, perfection, and joy and identifies festivals marking events in the life of Jesus, except Good Friday: Christmas, Epiphany, Easter, Eastertide, Ascension Day; also Trinity Sunday, All Saints' Day, weddings, funerals. Gold may also be used.

Red.   Symbolizes the Holy Spirit, martyrdom, and the love of God: Good Friday, Pentecost, and Sundays following.

Violet.   Symbolizes penitence: Advent, Lent.

Green.   Symbolizes mission to the world, hope, regeneration, nurture, and growth: Epiphany season, Kingdomtide, Rural Life Sunday, Labor Sunday, Thanksgiving Sunday.

Blue.   Advent, in some churches.

Flowers in Season Appropriate for Church Use

January: carnation or snowdrop	July: larkspur or water lily
February: violet or primrose	August: gladiolus or poppy
March: jonquil or daffodil	September: aster or morning star
April: lily, sweet pea, or daisy	October: calendula or cosmos
May: lily of the valley or hawthorn	November: chrysanthemum
June: rose or honeysuckle	December: narcissus, holly, or poinsettia

Quotable Quotations

1. The sum of the whole is this: walk and be happy; walk and be healthy. The best way to lengthen out our days is to walk steadily and with a purpose.—Charles Dickens

2. When your friends begin to flatter you on how young you look, it's a sure sign you're getting old.—Mark Twain

3. He that waits upon Fortune, is never sure of a Dinner. —Benjamin Franklin

4. Cromwell, I charge thee, fling away ambition. By that sin fell the angels. How can man, then, the image of his maker, hope to win by it?—Shakespeare

5. We can refute assertions, but who can refute silence?—Charles Dickens

6. The penalty of backsliding is not something unreal or vague . . . but something already marked within the structure of the soul. —Henry Drummond

7. The man who does not read good books has no advantage over the man who can't read them.—Mark Twain

8. Within that awful volume lies the mystery of mysteries! Happiest they of human race to whom God has granted grace to read, to fear, to hope, to pray . . . and better had they not been born who read to doubt or read to scorn.—Sir Walter Scott, written in his Bible

9. Tact is the ability to describe others as they see themselves.— Abraham Lincoln

10. God heals, and the doctor takes the fee.—Benjamin Franklin

11. To worship is to quicken the conscience by the holiness of God, to feed the mind with the truth of God, to purge the imagination by the beauty of God, to open the heart to the love of God, to devote the will to the purpose of God.—William Temple

12. The reputation of our enemies must be as sacred from our gossip as the reputation of our dearest relatives.—F. W. Faber

13. Man is the only animal that blushes. Or needs to.—Mark Twain

14. Tolerance means reverence for all the possibilities of truth. —John Morley

15. It is a tremendous moment when first one is called upon to join the great army of those who suffer.—George John Romanes

16. I destroy my enemy when I make him my friend.—Abraham Lincoln

17. There is no limit to human suffering. When one thinks, "Now I have touched the bottom of the sea—now I can go no deeper," one goes deeper.—Katherine Mansfield

18. Culture, like a mountain, should be broad-based, as it is to rise to a lofty height.—Edmond Holmes

19. Reflect on your present blessings, of which every man has many; not on your past misfortunes, of which all men have some. —Charles Dickens

20. It ain't those parts of the Bible that I can't understand that bother me, it is the parts that I do understand.—Mark Twain

21. Is not our want the occasion of our brother's charity, and thus does not good come out of that evil?—William Makepeace Thackeray

22. Character is like a tree and reputation like its shadow. The shadow is what we think of it; the tree is the real thing.—Abraham Lincoln

23. You cannot run away from a weakness; you must some time fight it out or perish.—Robert Louis Stevenson

24. Adam and Eve had many advantages, but the principal was that they escaped teething.—Mark Twain

25. Charity begins at home, and justice begins next door.—Charles Dickens

26. Labor is prior to and independent of capital. Capital is only the fruit of labor, and could never have existed if labor had not first existed.— Abraham Lincoln

27. Be sure your sin will find you out. It does not say your sin will be found. It says it will find you out in the deep and secret places of the soul.—G. H. Morrison

28. There is only one sin, and it is characteristic of the whole world. It is the self-will which prefers "my" way to God's, which puts me in the center where only God is in place.—William Temple

29. The most frequent impediment to men's turning the mind inward upon themselves is that they are afraid of what they shall find there.—Samuel Taylor Coleridge

30. To sin by silence when they should protest makes cowards out of men.—Abraham Lincoln

31. One reason why we meet so few people who are reasonable and agreeable in conversation is that there is scarcely anybody who does not think more of what he has to say than of answering what is said to him.—Lord Chesterfield

32. Methuselah lived to be 969 years old. . . . You boys and girls will see more in the next fifty years than Methuselah saw in his whole lifetime.—Mark Twain

33. If I had my life to live over again, I would make it a rule to read some poetry and listen to some music at least once a week. —Charles Darwin

34. Resolve to perform what you ought; perform without fail what you resolve.—Benjamin Franklin

35. A loving heart is the truest wisdom.—Charles Dickens

36. Freedom is the last, best hope of earth.—Abraham Lincoln

37. A man will hardly ever be awkward in public, who in secret pay habitual reverent court to God.—F. W. Faber

38. The highest proof of virtue is to possess boundless power without abusing it.—T. B. Macaulay

39. I say fearlessly respecting repose, that no work of art can be great without it, and that all art is great in proportion to the appearance of it.—John Ruskin

40. I believe that remorse is the least active of all a man's moral senses— the very easiest to be deadened when wakened; and in some never wakened at all.—William Makepeace Thackeray

41. A man who has wrapped his will in God's will, put his life consciously in the stream of divine life, for such a man there is an over-ruling Providence which guards and guides him in every incident of his life.—George Seaver

42. The fact of progress is written plain and large on the page of history; but progress is not a law of nature. . . . The thoughts of men may flow into channels which lead to disaster and barbarism.—H.A.L. Fisher

43. The one kind of pride which is wholly damnable is the pride of the man who has something to be proud of.—G. K. Chesterton

44. I believe that the root of almost every schism and heresy from which the Christian church has ever suffered, has been the effort of men to earn, rather than to receive their salvation.—John Ruskin

45. There is nothing that makes us love a man so much as praying for him.—William Law

46. Among the smaller duties of life, I hardly know any one more important than of not praising where praise is not due.—Sydney Smith

47. Doubtless, peace of mind, a quiet conscience, and a cheerful countenance are the gift of the Gospel, and the sign of the Christian.—John Henry Newman

48. History is a voice for ever sounding across the centuries the laws of right and wrong. . . . Justice and truth alone endure and live. Injustice and falsehood may be long-lived, but doomsday comes to them at last.—J. A. Froude

49. Martyrdom . . . is often a battlefield where no clash of earthly combatants is heard. . . . To have the spirit of a martyr . . . is to be true at all costs to the best and highest things you know.—F. W. Faber

50. We have more moral, political, and historical wisdom than we know how to reduce into practice.—Percy Bysshe Shelley

Questions of Life and Religion

1. What is the will of God and how does one know it?
2. Does providence rule one's life, or is there authentic human freedom to choose?
3. How does a Christian reconcile patriotism and loyalty to Christ?
4. In what ways does Christian faith encourage the role of parenting?

5. Can youth learn from the elderly? How?

6. What are the unexplainable mysteries to your personal faith?

7. Who teaches us morality, and how is it taught?

8. Is money the root of all evil?

9. Do miracles happen in the modern world?

10. What virtue is there in meditation and contemplation?

11. How is a martyr to be defined?

12. What are the values of a Christian marriage?

13. What is meant by justification by faith and not by law?

14. How important is ecumenical thought in our day?

15. Laughter is said to cure a thousand ills. Do you agree?

16. Is sin personal or is it corporate?

17. How are Christians to view war?

18. If death is our entry into heaven, why do we so fear it?

19. Is justice a possibility in a world filled with hate?

20. How do we reconcile pluralism with the mandate to be of one mind?

21. Do we still worship idols today?

22. How do you define a hypocrite?

23. What place do historic hymns have in present-day worship?

24. What are the "high ideals" that claim your life?

25. Why is the Christian family so important to modern society?

26. Hope is defined as the assurance of things not seen. What does that mean?

27. Are "gifts of the Spirit" still active in our modern day?

28. What does heaven look like? Are there really "streets of gold?"

29. We all fail at some time. How does God encourage us in such times?

30. Can Christian faith make families stronger? How so?

31. What does "being called" by God mean? How would one know?

32. My friend's church has times of fasting. Why don't we?

33. Do we control our own destiny, or is our fate already determined?

34. What is the limit to an appropriate premarital sexual relationship?

35. Is it a sin to make bad grades?

36. Why do we need to go to church each week?

37. I'm confused. Which is the best translation of the Bible?

38. How can I know God's will for my life?
39. What does the word *gospel* mean? How does it affect my life?
40. I have Muslim friends. How can I share my faith with them?
41. How do I overcome my fear of death?
42. Are all religions the same?
43. Can good and evil coexist forever?
44. What is servant leadership? How is humility a motivator?
45. What did Jesus mean when he said little children were "like unto the Kingdom of God"?
46. Can all sin, regardless of its severity, be forgiven?
47. I read a book that said I had a purpose for living. How can I find my purpose?
48. Is it wrong for a Christian to pledge loyalty to the American flag?
49. The book of Revelation frightens me. What does it mean?
50. I am a Christian, but I don't understand why I need to be baptized. What is that about?

Biblical Benedictions and Blessings

The Lord watch between me and thee, when we are absent from one another.—Gen. 31:49

The Lord bless thee and keep thee: the Lord make his face to shine upon thee, and be gracious unto thee; the Lord lift up his countenance upon thee, and give thee peace.—Num. 6:24–26

The Lord our God be with us, as he was with our fathers; let him not leave us, nor forsake us; that he may incline our hearts unto him, to walk in all his ways, and to keep his commandments, and his statutes, and his judgments, which he commanded our fathers.—1 Kings 8:57–58

Now the God of patience and consolation grant you to be likeminded one toward another according to Christ Jesus; that ye may with one mind and one mouth glorify Christ. Now the God of hope fill you with all joy and peace in believing, that ye may abound in hope, through the power of the Holy Ghost. Now the God of peace be with you all.—Rom. 15:5–6, 13, 33

Now to him that is of power to establish you according to my gospel, and the preaching of Jesus Christ, according to the revelation of the mystery, which was kept secret since the beginning of the world, but now is manifest, and by the scriptures of the prophets according to the commandment of the everlasting God, made known to all nations for the obedience of faith: to God only wise, be glory through Jesus Christ for ever.—Rom. 16:25–27

Grace be unto you, and peace, from God our Father, and from the Lord Jesus Christ.—1 Cor. 1:3

The grace of the Lord Jesus Christ and the love of God, and the communion of the Holy Spirit, be with you all.—2 Cor. 13:14

Peace be to the brethren, and love with faith, from God the Father and the Lord Jesus Christ. Grace be with all them that love our Lord Jesus Christ in sincerity.—Eph. 6:23–24

And the peace of God, which passes all understanding, shall keep your hearts and minds through Christ Jesus. Finally, brethren, whatsoever things are true, whatsoever things are honest, whatsoever things are just, whatsoever things are pure, whatsoever things are lovely, whatsoever things are of god report; if there be any virtue, and if there be any praise, think on these things. Those things, which you have both learned, and received, and heard, and seen in me, do; and the God of peace shall be with you.—Phil. 4:7–9

Wherefore also we pray always for you, that our God would count you worthy of this calling, and fulfill all the good pleasure of his goodness, and the work of faith with power, that the name of our Lord Jesus Christ may be glorified in you, and you in him, according to the grace of our God and the Lord Jesus Christ.—2 Thess. 1:1:11–12

Now may the Lord of peace himself give you peace always by all means. The Lord be with you all. The grace of our Lord Jesus Christ be with you all.—2 Thess. 3:16–18

Grace, mercy, and peace, from God our Father and Jesus Christ our Lord.
—1 Tim. 1:2

Now the God of peace, that brought again from the dead our Lord Jesus, that
great shepherd of the sheep, through the blood of the everlasting covenant,
make you perfect in every good work to do his will, working in you that which
is well-pleasing in his sight, through Jesus Christ, to whom be glory for ever
and ever.—Heb. 13:20–21

The God of all grace, who has called us unto his eternal glory by Christ Jesus,
after that you have suffered a while, make you perfect, establish, strengthen,
settle you. To him be glory and dominion forever and ever. Greet one another
with a kiss of charity. Peace be with you all that are in Christ Jesus.—1 Pet.
5:10–11, 14

Grace be with you, mercy, and peace, from God the Father, and from the Lord
Jesus Christ, the Son of the Father, in truth and love.—2 John 3

Now unto him who is able to keep you from falling, and to present you as faultless before the presence of his glory with exceeding joy, to the only wise God
our Savior, be glory and majesty, dominion and power, both now and forever.—
Jude 24–25

Grace be unto you, and peace, from him which was, and which is to come; and
from the seven Spirits which are before his throne; and from Jesus Christ, who
is the faithful witness, and the first begotten of the dead, and the prince of the
kings of the earth. Unto him that loved us, and washed us from our sins in his
own blood, and has made us kings and priests unto God and his Father; to him
be glory and dominion for ever and ever.—Rev. 1:4–6

LECTIONARY RESOURCES FOR 2008

*Sermons, Illustrations,
Congregational Music,
Children's Sermons,
Worship Aids*

SUNDAY, JANUARY 6, 2008
Epiphany

LECTIONARY SERMON TOPIC: "The Servant's Great Work"
TEXT: Matt. 2:1–12; Eph. 3:1–12
OTHER READINGS: Isa. 60:1–6; Ps. 72:1–7, 10–14

We read this morning of the Wise Men coming to find the Christ child. In the history of the Christian Church, this story is not emphasized as part of the Christmas story. It stands alone and comes after the celebration of Christmas. In history, we have remembered the coming of the Wise Men with a unique celebration called the Feast of the Three Kings, or Epiphany. Its date each year is January 6th. It's an important date for us, but one we all too often pass over.

The Wise Men represent that noble spirit of curiosity that searches for truth and goes the distance to find it—and having found it, recognizes its deity and bows before it in worship and praise. The men could have been satisfied with research and speculation on the nature of the stars, but they were not. Their search led them to the fulfillment of life. There are two things I want to say about the Wise Men and what they mean to us:

I. The presence of the Wise Men proclaims God's salvation to all people.
These men were outsiders. They did not "belong" at the manger. They came from a foreign place and returned to a foreign place. They were Gentiles, not Jews, and thus were outside the ancient covenants between Abraham's people and God. What they knew about God may have been very little. Yet there they were, standing with the Christ child, bowing before him with gifts of gold, frankincense, and myrrh. With their worship ended, they returned to the place of their origin, taking with them the message: God's unique Son—hidden, secret, obscure—was hidden, secret, and obscure no longer. In a way greater than the angels, the shepherds, or even Mary and Joseph, the Wise Men tell us what the coming of Jesus was about. It was about God's all-inclusive love.

In fact, the Wise Men are our representatives. Why? Because, like most people in the Christian Church, they were Gentiles, not Jews. Except for the mercy of God, they would have had no place there. This idea of a Messiah, coming as fulfillment of prophecy, was pretty much of Jewish origin. Except for God's mercy, there would be no room in Bethlehem for us either. This Feast of the Three Kings, or Epiphany—God's revealing of himself to the entire world—is about us. It is our feast. Without it, we are on the outside looking in; with it, we are starring players in the greatest story ever told. It is indeed "good news of great joy to *all* people."

At the heart of the book of Ephesians (the location of our second text) and at times in the strongest terms possible is the unity of all persons under the Lordship of Christ. This secret, or "mystery" as he called it, is no longer a secret. It had been hidden until the time of Christ, but his Incarnation, Crucifixion, and glorious Resurrection opened up the mystery to all. Every person—Jew, Gentile, bond or free, male or female, black or white, rich or poor, American or foreigner—is to share in God's eternal peace, love, and power. How easily we forget that Jesus died for all, that our Lord tore down the walls of separation and bitterness, that there is one Lord, one faith, one baptism—one God and Father over all. We know that. The Wise Men told us so.

II. **The Wise Men challenge us to share that good word with others.** Here is where the story of the Epiphany comes closest to us. It is one thing to acknowledge the history behind Epiphany, to give thanks for the presence of the Wise Men at the side of the Christ child, and even to acknowledge the debt we owe Paul, whose preaching included those of us in the Gentile world. But what about our sharing with others the word of grace that has come to us? That is another thing—a different and demanding thing.

In our age of tolerance and diversity, it seems almost rude to some folks to suggest that we have something that should be shared with others, not just because sharing it makes us feel good about ourselves but because the message we share is good. Think about how you became a Christian. You, more than likely, had the opportunity to not only see his star but to see him. Not one of us is a Christian because we simply chose to be; we responded to some influence, at God's direction, that awakened faith within us. Salvation is not about the power of the human will to decide its way. We are Christians because God worked through others to bring us to the point of grace. Either someone thought enough of us to show us the way, or else we saw in someone else something of great consequence that we wanted for ourselves and, by their example, were led to Christ. Isn't it so that most of us came to Christ, not so much through the rigors of some abstract truth or doctrine but through the power of a life in love with Christ?

I suppose for most of us, family served as that conduit of grace. That's why family is such a vital part of God's plan for the world. More of the gospel is taught and learned in the home than anywhere else. It was that way for me. I didn't discover the gospel on my own. I became the recipient of grace passed down through the ages. For you, the messenger of grace could have been a pastor, or teacher, or friend. You may be able to name a specific person who influenced you; you may not be able to. But as sure as life itself, we depend on others to show us the way.

III. **Our calling today is to express, in belief and in vital action, the overwhelming love of God for the entire world.** Numerous national opinion polls indicate that the Christian Church is losing influence in the lives of many people. In the same polls, it is clear that the same people truly want a deepening spiritual life. But they are unconvinced that the institutional Church can lead them to it. I wonder why. Can it be that we are scratching where people don't itch—answering questions people aren't asking? But we can take a clue from the Wise Men. There was something within them—an ache that had to be attended, an emptiness that had to be filled, a goal to be accomplished—that drove them on the two-year search for the Christ child. That same drive belongs to each of us and to the entire world. They were not disappointed in the discovery of joy they found. Neither are we.

Let's *be* an epiphany—a manifestation of Christ to the world; may our lights so shine that the entire world may see our good works and glorify our Father in heaven.—Lee McGlone

ILLUSTRATIONS

A Prayer for the New Year: "Therefore your servant found it in his heart to pray this prayer to You." (2 Sam. 7:27)

> Father, as we begin the cycle of years again,
> Let each day belong to you.
> Let us look forward and not backward.
> May grace see us through.
> Grant peace to our hearts,
> And courage your will to do.
> Give us gentle and kind spirits.
> May grace see us through.
> In these days of terror and fear,
> We stand on Your Word that is True.
> Your strength our comfort still.
> Your grace sure to see us through. Amen.
> —Lee McGlone

Inclusiveness. Dr. F. Russell Bennett (a former faculty member at Southern Seminary and a longtime friend) and I were at lunch one day in downtown Louisville. The restaurant was housed in a building that, some years earlier, had been a church. Judging from the size of the building, it had been a significant church in that great city. The community changed. Over time, the church lost membership and eventually died; its assets were given to the remaining members. The restaurant bought the property and converted it into a robust business. Some of the pews were still there, propped up against the walls. The stained-glass windows were still in place. The chancel and altar area had become the bar.

During the meal, I couldn't help but notice the wide array of clientele the restaurant attracted. There were businessmen in suits and college students in cut-off jeans. There were old and young, male and female, black and white, Latinos and Chinese—people of all kinds. I remarked to Dr. Bennett about the great variety of people there. He leaned over close to me and said, "Most of these folks should be glad this is not still a church. If it was, they couldn't be here today." It is truly a difficult thing to recognize the all-inclusive love of God!—Lee McGlone

Musical Selections Appropriate to the Day

Hymn suggestions for lectionary texts:

Isa. 60:1–6	*Arise Your Light Is Come; Shine Jesus Shine*
Ps. 72:1–7, 10–14	*Jesus Shall Reign Where're the Sun*
Eph. 3:1–12	*Ye Servants of God Your Master Proclaim*
Matt. 2:1–12	*As with Gladness Men of Old; We Three Kings of Orient Are*

Children's Lectionary Sermon

TITLE: You're Invited

SCRIPTURE: Eph. 3:1–12

KEY VERSE: *This is that secret truth: that the non-Jews will receive what God has for his people, just as the Jews will. The non-Jews are together with the Jews as part of the same body. And they share together in the promise that God made in Christ Jesus. The non-Jews have all of this because of the Good News.* (Eph. 3:6, International Children's Bible, New Century Version)

KEY CONCEPT: Jesus came for all people, everywhere.

MATERIALS: One large birthday party invitation, plus enough small invitations to hand out to each child; Bible

PREPARATION: A special invitation for each child that says, "You are all invited!"

(*Greet the children, then begin playing the role of a bragging, show-offy child.*) Hey, look what I have. (*Show children large party invitation.*) Isn't it fantastic? I got an invitation to this great party. I am so excited. I can hardly wait. So, did you get one? No? (*Ask a few children if they got an invitation like yours.*) I thought everyone got one, but I guess only some people, like me, have been invited to this super-incredible-extra-fantastic party. Well, I am sorry you didn't get one, but I did, so I guess I'll be going without you.

(*With a rueful look*) Wow, it doesn't feel very good to know everybody didn't get invited to the same super-cool party I am going to, does it? In the passage of Scripture we are looking at today, the apostle Paul is reminding us that we are not the only ones who got an invitation from Jesus. Paul is telling us that the party Jesus has planned for us includes everyone from everywhere. It is an invitation Jesus wants everyone to accept.

Today, we begin the season of Epiphany. This is the season in the life of the church when we celebrate that Jesus came for all people. Today, we look at this truth. Jesus Christ came for every person from every nation in the whole world. Jesus has given each one of us an invitation. It is an invitation to join him in a relationship that will last forever. You and I are personally invited. Would you like to come along? (*Pass out the invitations, one to each child.*)—Lizette Hunt

WORSHIP AIDS

Call to Worship: On the first Sunday of the New Year, we gather to proclaim God's presence and power among us. As with the prophet of old, we enter worship to declare, "The Lord is in his Holy Temple: let all the earth keep silence before him" (Hab. 2:20).

Invocation: Father, we recall your promise that where two or three are gathered in your name, you are with them. We rejoice in that promise and pray that we may be fully aware of your presence, for you know our needs, whether personal challenges or larger world matters. Help us, O Lord, that we shall be all that we can be, wiser than we believe, and stronger than we can conceive.

Offertory Sentence: "This is what the Lord commands: 'Take from among yourselves an offering to the Lord: whoever has a willing heart, let him bring . . . an offering unto the Lord'" (Exod. 35:4–5).

Offertory Prayer: Lord, as we begin a New Year, may this first offering reflect our gratitude for the blessings of the past year, our joyful anticipation of the year ahead, and of our unyielding loyalty to you as stewards of all you have entrusted to our care. Bless these tithes and gifts for the building of your Kingdom.

Morning Prayer: Even though the courses our lives have taken during the past week have occasionally led us away from your presence, Lord, we have nonetheless been drawn back to you today. Much as the needle of a compass cannot resist being always drawn toward the North, neither can we resist the steady pull of your grace. In the midst of the uncertainty and tension that fills our world and the confusion and indecisiveness that mark our lives, you remain at the center, calling us to hope, promising us life, giving us peace, and blessing us with your presence when we are willing to walk with you.

We know that the way to your Kingdom is narrow and that few really find it. So be our guide, O Lord, that we may never lose our way or stray from the path. Give us strength to endure when the journey is more difficult or takes longer than we expected. Give us courage to face all the temptations and problems that frighten and perplex us. Give us wisdom to make the right choices in all our decisions. And give us humble spirits, ready to admit our helplessness, our sinfulness, our complete need of you.

Help us to be true followers of our Lord Jesus Christ, who taught us to live every day as if the Kingdom were already here. Help us to live as he lived, sharing what we have with other persons and loving each other for no reason at all except that you first loved us, and Christ died to redeem us from our sin and to draw us into eternal fellowship with you. In his name we pray. Amen.—Gary C. Redding

Benediction: Now as we go out into the week that lies ahead and into all the weeks of this New Year, may we go in the power and goodness of the Lord, whom we name as Father, Son, and Holy Spirit. May his peace be with you. Amen.

SUNDAY, JANUARY 13, 2008

LECTIONARY SERMON TOPIC: "A Voice out of the Congregation"
TEXT: Acts 10:34–43
OTHER READINGS: Isa. 42:1–9; Ps. 29; Matt. 3:13–17

Here in Acts 10, with the Church still in its infancy, is the moving, powerfully dramatic account of a double conversion: that of a Roman centurion named

Cornelius and the conversion of the Church itself. The high, noble descriptions of the Church—Body of Christ, People of God, Temple of the Holy Spirit—are to be honored, but in its early days the Church needed to define its direction. Here the Church latched on to the Spirit of Jesus. Here the Church discovered its mission.

It all happened in the prayer-filled, spiritually directed, conversation between Peter and Cornelius. First there is Peter—the apostle, Jewish-born, son of the Old Testament promise, personal disciple of Jesus, and perhaps the most significant leader in the early Church. One would anticipate his presence here. Then there is Cornelius—a Roman, a Roman soldier, a Roman soldier of influence, stationed in Caesarea (Caesar-ville) there along the Mediterranean Sea, apparently introduced to the God of the Old Testament and a God-fearer but not yet a believer. He was a man of prayer. We would call him a seeker in our world today. Although we could expect to see Peter in such a scene in the Bible, a man like Cornelius may be a bit of a surprise. God speaks to Peter. God speaks to Cornelius. God brings them together with their own entourage of friends and followers. It looks something like a church congregation. Peter says, "I'm here just as you asked. Now what am I here for?" And Cornelius, a voice rising out of the congregation, speaks plainly: "We are all here in the presence of God to listen to everything the Lord has commanded you to tell us" (v. 33). Think about this voice.

I. **It is a voice of anticipation: "We are all here in the presence of God."** All across this chapter is the sense of expectation, for our God is a God of expectation. People are praying—Cornelius during his hours of worship, Peter on his rooftop. When people pray, we should expect something to happen. The Kingdom is expanding, and this is an exciting time. But no one knows exactly what will happen. God is not willing to leave well enough alone and challenges us to move ahead into the future.

We are not to loathe the past but instead to appreciate it. Likewise, we are not to be fearful of the future, for God goes before us. Ours is a life of expectancy. We are all here present before God and don't want to be anywhere else.

II. **It is a voice of readiness. They were there to hear "what God says."** This is a seeking voice that wants to hear the voice of eternity. No human words will do. This is not a question about the relative merits of Jewish, as opposed to Roman, law or a quaint discussion on philosophical existentialism or personal opinion. This is a seeking question. We want to hear from God, from beyond ourselves.

We arrive at this readiness often in desperation. The Great Awakening Revivals came about as people by the thousands sensed the great need for renewal and broke forth in massive camp meetings and prayer gatherings. It began with a pleading. Often we arrive at the place of readiness in times of utter despair: the angularities of life, illness, death, loss of job security. In such times, we truly want to know, "What does God say?"

III. **It is a voice of challenge**: "All that God has commanded you"—this the hard work of the Christian faith. We seek to put aside the noise of a busy world and the cultural bends that tell us we are on our own. We intend to listen to what God says, and that is hard. It was hard for the disciples. The Great Commission's demand that they go into the entire world would require some attitudinal changes. "Jesus, are you sure you mean the entire world?" And Jesus said, "Yes, the entire world."

It was hard for Peter. When he came to declare that God was no respecter of persons, he didn't arrive there on his own. God said, "Arise and eat." "No," said Peter, "I will never eat anything unclean." This was painful hearing for him, for it was not about unclean meat but about people he considered unworthy of God's grace.

It is a hard word for all of us. Some years ago, my wife and I drove through a small rural town and saw a church marquee that gave the name of the church and beneath it and, in larger print, these words: "independent, fundamental, Bible believing, charismatic, pre-millennial, dispensational." And beneath that, in even larger lettering, this: "Everyone Welcome." As we drove past, my wife said, "I'm not sure that sign is accurate. I suspect you would need to be at least four out of those six to be welcome there." Hearing all that God has commanded is hard.

IV. **It is a voice of surrender: "We are here to hear what God has to tell us."** What they said was this: we are on the receiving end of this message, and we want to hear so we can respond. And we are ready to respond! And they did! Look what happened. They heard what God was saying, that God loved all people everywhere, regardless of their ethnic or religious background. Then they yielded to faith in Jesus Christ—and then Pentecost came again! And all who believed were baptized in Jesus' name. The miracle of saving grace rolled in like a tidal wave. The barriers were broken down. The wall of separation was destroyed.

It all came about as they surrendered themselves to the Word they heard from God. Years later, Paul the apostle called those of his day (and calls to us today) to the same matter of ultimate surrender: "I beg you by the mercies of God to present yourselves as living sacrifices, holy and acceptable unto God, which is your spiritual worship. Do not be conformed to this world but be transformed by the renewing of your mind—for this is the good, accept-able, and perfect will of God" (Rom. 12:1–2). The call to surrender is still heard clearly today. And when we hear it, will we heed it?—Lee McGlone

ILLUSTRATIONS

Cost of Discipleship. About three years ago, we were blessed to share in our worship a marvelous choir composed of a number of the lost boys from Sudan. These are young men who had escaped under the most difficult circumstance from the genocide in their homeland, some by walking a thousand miles. They were with us for worship dressed in native dress. They sang native songs. They danced the native dances. I loved it. The most moving moment was toward the end when they sang a hymn I knew: "I have decided to follow Jesus." But that very familiar hymn took on new meaning that day as they sang, "I have decided," because, for the first time, I experienced believers for whom the words they sang—"no turning back, no turning back"—were matters of life and death.—Lee McGlone

Freedom. Maya Angelou grew up in the 1930s, in Stamps, Arkansas, forty miles from my hometown. Her autobiography—*I Know Why the Caged Bird Sings*—was a best seller. She tells openly, honestly, of her experience of grow-ing up black in the Deep South. She speaks of racism, sexism, the haunting poverty, the exploitation, and the grace that guided her along the way. Why does the caged bird sing? She answers the question in a poem:

... the caged bird sings with fearful trill
of things unknown but longed for still
and his tune is heard on a distant hill
on a distant hill
and the caged bird sings for freedom.

My friends, we are all caged birds. So was Peter. So was Cornelius. And
we want to hear from God. What God is doing is meeting our deepest need.—
Lee McGlone

Musical Selections Appropriate to the Day

Hymn suggestions for lectionary texts:

Isa. 42:1–9	*I'll Praise My Maker While I've Breath; O God Your Constant Care and Love*
Ps. 29	*To God Be the Glory*
Acts 10:34–43	*Good Christians All Rejoice and Sing*
Matt. 3:13–17	*When John Baptized by Jordan's River; When Jesus Came to Jordan*

🐾 Children's Lectionary Sermon

TITLE: One of a Kind

SCRIPTURE: Matt. 3:13–17

KEY VERSE: *And a voice spoke from heaven. The voice said, "This is my Son and I love him. I am very pleased with him."* (Matt. 3:17, International Children's Bible, New Century Version)

KEY CONCEPT: Jesus revealed as God's beloved Son

MATERIALS: Bible, a tray, and three objects—a collectible coin, an award won at a banquet or celebration, and a collectable doll or toy

PREPARATION: Gather the tray and the three objects. Cover the tray and objects with an opaque cloth. Show them at appropriate times.

I brought some things to show you this morning. These are some of my most valued possessions. These are rare, valuable, and one of a kind. Let me reveal them to you. (*Remove the cloth and show the tray.*)

This coin is valuable because it is very rare. There are just a few around. This award is special to me because I received it at an awards banquet when I used to play soccer. I won the Most Improved Player Award. And this doll is valuable because I have kept it in mint condition. Someday it will be worth more money than I paid for it.

(*Open Bible.*) In the passage for today God has done something incredible. God did it so everyone in the whole world would make no mistake about it. John the Baptist was baptizing Jesus. As Jesus came up out of the water the Holy Spirit came to Jesus like a dove and landed on him. Then God's voice said, "This is my Son—and I am very pleased."

(*Hold the items as you make these statements.*) This coin is one of many that were made that year, but Jesus is the only Son of God. This year hundreds of kids in Dickinson, North Dakota, will win an award just like this one, but Jesus is unique because God sent only him to pay the price for our sin. This doll and all the other ones like it might be very valuable one day. But in God's perfect timing, God has revealed to us all, God's uniquely valuable, one-of-a-kind Son, Jesus.

This season of Epiphany is about understanding that God sent God's only Son, Jesus, at just the right time, for just the right reason, for everyone, every-where.—Lizette Hunt

༺ WORSHIP AIDS ༻

Call to Worship: We gather in this place to worship in spirit and in truth. We come to express devotion to the one who declared, "From the rising of the sun to its setting, my name is great among the nations" (Mal. 1:11).

Invocation: O almighty God, who pours out on all who desire it the Spirit of grace and of supplication; deliver us, when we draw near to you, from coldness of heart and wanderings of mind, that with steadfast thoughts and kindled affections, we may worship you in spirit and truth. (Book of Common Prayer)

Offertory Sentence: "Give unto the Lord the glory due his name; bring an offering, and come before him. Worship the Lord in the beauty of holiness" (1 Chron. 16:29).

Offertory Prayer: Kind and gracious Heavenly Father, accept these gifts as our effort to return to you a portion of the bounty that you have lavishly poured out on us. Multiply these gifts for the building of your Kingdom here and around the world. Give us wisdom and compassion, as well as generous and glad hearts, in our giving and receiving. For the sake of Jesus Christ, the Lord.

Morning Prayer: O Lord, our God, we know how many ways we have fallen short. Grant us assurance of your forgiveness and assurance of new beginnings and new possibilities. We know that none of us can avoid the trials and tribulations, nor the anxieties and the heartaches of life. Give us understanding now as we pray for those in situations of stress, those facing a new situation in their relationships; young people away from home; a new baby; a husband or wife recently widowed; a couple in the difficulty of separation or divorce; those just retired—help them to find their bearings again and to discover what changes in themselves you want them to make. We think of children who are caring for elderly parents and of single adults on the road of life whose family is the church and loyal friends.

We know, O Lord, that what happens to us is a great test of character, and our trials and difficulties may leave us worse or better, depending on how we respond. We thank you for all who have come through some hard experiences and proved their faithfulness. Help us today to remember the ideals and the celebrations that make our memories of love so treasured. In the name and spirit of the Lord, we pray. Amen.—George L. Davis

Benediction: We go out now with hearts gladdened by the good news we believe and share. May our lives in the days of this week be reflections of the nature of God our Savior, Father, Son, and Holy Spirit, who lives and reigns through us. Amen.

SUNDAY, JANUARY 20, 2008

LECTIONARY SERMON TOPIC: "A Witness to Christ"

TEXT: John 1:29–42

OTHER READINGS: Isa. 49:1–7; Ps. 40:1–11; 1 Cor. 1:1–9

The question about purpose in life is often raised in times of fear and depression. "Why am I here? What difference does my life make?" These are difficult questions for which there are no easy or single-factor answers. But the text helps us here by pointing to a unique personality: John the Baptist, the wilderness character who came to the direct attention of Jesus Christ. His purpose in life is expressed simply and clearly: "He came for testimony. He came to bear witness."

I. **He was a man who had identified himself.** "Who are you?" they asked. That's good. It's a question we all need to ask. Is there a way to describe who we are? Is personhood related to what we do? Is it defined by who we used to be? Is the answer related to God? Am I somehow related to eternity? Who am I?

   The good news is that John knew who he was. He stated it plainly: "I am not the Christ, but a voice crying in the wilderness." The wilderness was not a pleasant place. In Hebrew history it was a place of wandering and aloneness. For Jesus it was the place where he met Satan face to face for forty days. Perhaps we've all been there in the times of our upheaval, sickness, family disintegration, or spiritual darkness. At times, it is where we discover ourselves.

II. **His life had contentment.** He was crying in the wilderness but not crying about just anything. There are many today whose lives are obsessed with crying about everything. But John became intent in his heart "to make straight the way of the Lord." He was to turn the consciousness of the people toward God, for God was about to do a new thing.

   How do you do that? How do you turn the consciousness of people toward God? John shows us by his example. We are to speak plainly the

Word of God as it comes to us. We are to become witnesses—martyrs—and to live our faith courageously. And herein lies our contentment. Opportunities for ministry approach us, and we can let them pass us by, or we can move to claim the opportunity and allow God to do through us a brand new thing.

III. **His life depended on God's grace.** It wasn't John who was at work. It was God at work in John. His message was demanding but at best only an image of something greater. "I baptize with water, but the one who comes after me will baptize you with the Spirit." John pointed beyond himself to Christ. Redemption is in Christ. And it still is.

The greatest need of human life is to relate deeply, personally, intimately with the living Christ. Our need is not met in opinions, creeds, laws, and so on, but in our personal experience with Christ. John discovered that life had purpose and that purpose was found within his own arena of testimony, in his sphere of witness. Even so, we have our own opportunities for service and witness. We can let that possibility pass by, or we can today yield completely to its claim.—Lee McGlone

---

ILLUSTRATIONS

Our Niche. When growing up on a small farm, we had an old milk cow named Betsy. As Mother milked her each day, this trouble-making little boy would crawl under her stomach, pull at her tail, and climb on her neck. And Betsy never moved! Betsy was the epitome of a contented cow, until the day I put a saddle on her back and tried to ride her. Then she lost all sense of humor. She was never intended to be a horse. God made her to be a cow. I suspect that the unhappiest people in the world are those who have never found their place. They've never discovered their niche.—Lee McGlone

Commitment. I'm reminded of C. S. Lewis's *The Lion, the Witch, and the Wardrobe*. The children are being told of Aslan, the great lion who is the king. One asks another: "The king is a lion. Is he safe?" The leader replies, "Is he safe? My, no, he's not safe. He's not safe, but he's the king—and he's good."—Lee McGlone

Musical Selections Appropriate to the Day

Hymn suggestions for lectionary texts:

Isa. 49:1–7	*Great Is Thy Faithfulness; O Splendor of God's Glory Bright*
Ps. 40:1–11	*New Songs of Celebration; Sing a New Song to the Lord*
1 Cor. 1:1–9	*Like a River Glorious*
John 1:29–42	*Behold the Lamb; Am I a Soldier of the Cross?*

❧ Children's Lectionary Sermon

TITLE: I Know You!

SCRIPTURE: John 1:29–42

KEY VERSE: *Then John said, "I saw the Holy Spirit descending like a dove from heaven and resting upon him. I didn't know he was the one, but when God sent me to baptize with water, he told me, 'When you see the Holy Spirit descending and resting upon someone, he is the one you are looking for'. . . I saw this happen to Jesus, so I testify that he is the Son of God."* (John 1:32–34, New Living Translation)

KEY CONCEPT: Trusting God

MATERIALS: Bible

Have you ever met someone you have never seen before? I remember going to meet my Grandma Morris. We traveled to visit her when I was four years old. My family knew what my grandma looked like, but I had never seen her before. When we got to her house, I saw her for the first time. Until that day, I would never have known her. I needed someone to show me who she was and what she looked like. Since all my family knew her, I could depend on them to show me my grandma.

In today's passage we read about a man named John the Baptist. John was doing what God told him to do. John was to prepare the people for the Son of God. He was preaching to the people about turning away from sin and turning back to God. John was not sure who the Son of God was, but God told John to look for a sign. God told John he would know the Son of God, because he would see the Holy Spirit touch this person.

(*Have Bible open.*) One day John was baptizing the people at the river Jordan. And Jesus came to the water with John. Then something incredible happened. When Jesus came up out of the water, the Holy Spirit came to Jesus and touched him. This was the sign God told John to look for. The Son of God would be touched by God's Spirit. John knew Jesus was the Son of God. Now John could tell everyone about Jesus.

We know Jesus. Each one of us can tell our friends about Jesus, just as John did. This week tell a friend about Jesus and invite that person to church with you. We want everyone to say, "I know you, Jesus."—Lizette Hunt

WORSHIP AIDS

Call to Worship: We gather in the joy of God's presence and in the profound fellowship we share as God's children—sons and daughters all. "I was glad when they said unto me, 'Let us go into the house of the Lord'" (Ps. 122:1).

Invocation: Father of all life, who spared not your own Son for our salvation, grant that today our worship will reflect the true devotion of our hearts. Encourage us to pray, to praise, to confess our sin, to hear your Word, and to surrender life to you. Reveal to us the presence of your dear Son, Jesus, who is the Christ. Amen.

Offertory Sentence: "And he said to them all, 'If any man will come after me, let him deny himself, and take up his cross daily, and follow me'" (Luke 9:23).

Offertory Prayer: Bless what we give O Lord and shape it after your will that it may benefit many and honor the Christ. Amen—E. Lee Phillips

Morning Prayer: Heavenly Father, as we draw aside from the busyness of life, grant that today we will find here a time of renewal, a quiet refreshing, the gentle breath of the Holy Spirit blowing across our human spirits. Come to us, we pray, with the strength and insight that we need. Grant that we may search the priorities of life and determine again what matters most and what doesn't matter at all. We admit that it is far too easy to trust in ourselves, in our abilities, in our strength, and to blame troubles on others. Give to us clear insight into our personalities, our strengths and weaknesses, and great wisdom that we may know how best to live.

Give to us a full measure of the compassion of Christ. Help us to see others as you do—each person made in your image, after your likeness, and worthy of all dignity and respect. Involve us in the needs of our fellow man so that we will not become complacent or self-centered. Help us to relate closely to your church that we may know fullness of life.

Father, help us to be sensitive to those who are today touched by trouble, whose lives know challenges and despair, frustration and defeat. As you lift these up, grant that we may seek to be helping people, to stand by friends and family, to love, to help, to encourage. Grant that we will rejoice with those who rejoice, weep with those who weep, as we bring good news to the poor, release to the captives, recovering of sight to the blind, and liberty to the oppressed, just as Jesus said. Lord, again we place our lives in your hands. Have your way with us. In Jesus' name. Amen.—Lee McGlone

Benediction: Let us depart in the joy of Christ's Spirit and go forth into the days of this week, in our times of labor and leisure, to speak lovingly his Holy Name and to live in his power. May his peace be yours. Amen.

SUNDAY, JANUARY 27, 2008

LECTIONARY SERMON TOPIC: "Jesus Came Preaching"
TEXT: Matt. 4:12–23
OTHER READINGS: Isa. 9:1–4; Ps. 27:1, 4–9; 1 Cor. 1:10–18

They say first impressions mean a lot. First impressions are lasting impressions. Very often, the length of a relationship depends on the first encounter. It can be a good impression. It can be bad. One thing for sure, you only get a first impression once. You try, therefore, to make it a good one. Matthew did something like that in his Gospel. Following Jesus' baptism and wilderness temptation, his ministry began in earnest. His preaching was robust, stirring, challenging, and often confrontational. His preaching was not topical. He had but one message—the divine inbreaking of the rule of God. We can learn much from his approach to the preaching life.

I. **First, he tied his hearers back into their own tradition.** Once we are capable of looking back with appreciation for a common heritage, we are better equipped to deal with present-day needs and to press forward to the future. Here Jesus called up the memory of the prophet Isaiah, even mentioning the common geography ("land of Zebulon and Naphtali"), shared by the prophet and Jesus' hearers. The Lord helped the people to reflect upon their heritage and to reinterpret it in light of the current day.

And when he did so, the Word of God came to life. Isaiah spoke of his people living in great darkness. Indeed they were. But a light came. A call out of the dismal conditions of the day, out of their awkward "nobodiness," rose in the land. A leader ascended who could restore the people to the land of promise and offer a bright and new day. It was truly a glorious and hopeful word of promise. Jesus' very presence, so filled with wonder and intrigue, was enough to encourage the people to believe: he was truly the fulfillment of Isaiah's promise.

II. **Then he spoke forcefully the Kingdom demand for repentance.** It is the same sermon John the Baptist had preached earlier: "Repent, for the Kingdom of God is at hand." Perhaps these very words were what so caught Jesus' attention that he felt compelled to identify with John's message and was so identified through baptism in the Jordan River.

There is little doubt that Jesus was misunderstood. His message was not so generalized that it had no meaning. It was quite frank and clear: "You have been going in the wrong direction. If you continue on the current path, you will come to your own undoing. You have an option before you. Choose to go in the other direction, the direction of faithful and joyful participation in grace, and instead of your coming to nothing, you will find fullness of life." Changing direction! That's repentance. That's what the word means. And it offers to each of us, over and again, a new beginning. Even now as we walk through the days of Epiphany, we are encouraged by the delightful design of God's grace that reaches out to all people and draws us to fullness of life.

III. **There is then about him a sense of authority, based on his intimacy with the Heavenly Father, that commanded the attention of others.** He had a vital connection, and that connection could not go unnoticed. Some have lamented that preaching is often manipulative, that its persuasive techniques are exaggerated and, as a result, it is not an "honest" discipline. Let's sadly accept the critique, admitting that abuse of persuasive powers has surely laid victim many a trusting soul. But while we lament the abuse of persuasive powers, let's not ignore the clear directive of Scripture: the gospel is inherently persuasive! And Jesus' influence on the lives of others is the clearest example.

What else can we make of the calling to discipleship of these four fishermen? They were busy about the normalcy of life when, suddenly it seems, an intrusion came that would rock their worlds. The conversation seems strangely limited. Jesus simply "saw" them casting and repairing their nets. His words of challenge were brief: "Follow me and I will make you fishers of men." But the words were enough to compel a change of life's vocation! "They dropped their nets and followed him."

My supposition (and it is only that) is that it was our Lord's "ethos"—the sense of credibility that he carried in his being, put there by God's own design—that immediately convinced the fishermen to commit to a life of fealty. The truth is (again my supposition) that each of us who proclaims the gospel message, if we are to carry any weight at all in the lives of others, must, like our Lord, deliver the message through the vessel of our own personalities, which are energized by a life of intimacy with the Father. Jesus showed us the way.

IV. **But let's not forget this: his preaching ministry was filled with compassion.** "He went about all of Galilee . . . teaching, preaching the good news of the kingdom, and healing every disease and sickness among the people." There was no sense of aloofness about our Lord. He was vitally connected to the common people, the people of the land, and they loved and followed him because of it. His ministry of healing was not separated from his preaching.

Perhaps we are who and where we are today for this same reason. The work of God's grace has come to us all in unique ways. At some point in our lives, God in Christ made himself known to us. The Lord spoke our names, placed his hand upon our shoulders, and made himself and his will known to us. In short, he had compassion on us! However that act of grace arrived, it was the single most significant event in all of life. It is the event that becomes the guiding force—the directing light—that moves us into the work of the gospel with sureness of heart. We have known the compassion, the eternal compassion, of Another, spelled with a capital A. What has then come to us is intended to go through us to touch the lives of others.

May we never forget that Jesus came preaching. His message of long ago is still our message today. His methods of declaration and persuasion will not be improved on. And as we go out in the days of our ministry, may we carry with us his resolve for clear thinking and speaking and his heart for all people everywhere be our heart, too.—Lee McGlone

ILLUSTRATIONS

Caring. In the film *Jerry Maguire,* the character played by Tom Cruise is a greedy sports agent who has a change of heart. He writes a mission statement declaring that agents should be less concerned about money and more concerned about their clients. He is promptly fired. After being fired for this conviction, he lives out his beliefs through starting his own company.

In one scene he slouches down to the floor with a far-away look in his eyes. He turns on his laptop computer and writes from his heart. The words flow freely. Memories of simpler days capture the moment as he once again determines the high priorities of his life. The key to life, business, and otherwise, he knows to be interpersonal relationships. Suddenly it is all very clear. The answer is fewer clients, less money, more attention, more care for the clients—and for all people!—Lee McGlone

Encouragement. The young son on the *Little House on the Prairie* series was outside the school one day. The boys were all showing off their chin-up skills—in front of all the girls. The champ could do ten chin-ups, but the best the Ingalls boy had ever done was seven. On that day he was determined. He made seven, and then with a struggle he made eight. Exhausted though he was, he hung onto the limb and refused to let go. With all his strength, he drew himself up to the bar for number nine. The crowd was quiet. Could he do it? Could he match the champ? Out of the quiet, his sister spoke, "Come on, you can do it. One more time!" And that was all he needed. Over the top for number ten he went.—Lawrence Vowan

Musical Selections Appropriate to the Day

Hymn suggestions for lectionary texts:

Isa. 9:1–4	*Comfort, Comfort Now My People; Let All Mortal Flesh Keep Silence*
Ps. 27:1, 4–9	*We Are Singing for the Lord Is Our Light; Leaning on the Everlasting Arms*
1 Cor. 1:10–18	*At the Cross*
Matt. 4:12–23	*Dear Lord and Father of Mankind; Jesus Calls Us, O'er the Tumult*

✒ Children's Lectionary Sermon

TITLE: He Is Finally Here!

SCRIPTURE: Matt. 4:12–23

KEY VERSE: *These people who live in darkness will see a great light. They live in a place that is very dark. But a light will shine on them.* (Matt. 4:16, New Century Version)

KEY CONCEPT: Jesus' presence

MATERIALS: A picture Bible—one with pictures of people from the Bible stories

PREPARATION: Mark several pictures of people from the Old Testament. When you say, "They were waiting for God to send someone to . . . show them the way," hold the Bible so the children can see the pictures.

Have you ever had to wait for something to happen? Maybe your birthday is coming up, or you have a special day planned with your family, or maybe your most favorite aunt or uncle is coming for a visit. But you have to wait, because that day is not here yet.

(*Open Bible.*) When Jesus came along the beach and saw Peter and Andrew, he said, "Come follow me." And right away the two men dropped what they were doing to go with him. They were waiting. They were doing what they needed to do while they waited. But when Jesus called to them, they were ready to follow him; the waiting was over.

It was like that for all the people who had lived before Jesus came. They were waiting and waiting for a Savior. They were waiting for God to send some-one to help and to show them the way. (*Show pictures from the Bible, such as pictures of Isaiah, Jeremiah, or other prophets.*) These are pictures of some of the people who were waiting for Jesus to come.

When the time was right, God sent Jesus to the world. God sent him as a tiny baby who grew into a man. God revealed Jesus to the world as our Savior and Lord. It is like that for you and me, too. When the time is right, the wait-ing is over. We know who Jesus is. Jesus is the One we have all been waiting for. Jesus is here with us and wants us to worship him.—Lizette Hunt

﹌ WORSHIP AIDS ﹌

Call to Worship: For God alone we gather to worship. Our hearts and minds are fixed on the Eternal. Our words, yea all that we are, we offer as praise. "Let the words of our mouths, and the meditations of our hearts, be accept-able in your sight, O Lord, our strength and our redeemer" (Ps. 19:14).

Invocation: Lord God of all eternity, we delight in meeting you here today. In this place, in the hour, may your Word be heard and heeded. Speak to our hearts from your kind affection and draw us near to you. Grant that we may know the fullness of your grace. Amen.

Offertory Sentence: "And he said unto them, 'Take heed what you hear, with the measure you give it shall be measured to you: and unto you that hear shall more be given'" (Mark 4:24).

Offertory Prayer: Father, you have very graciously given to us. From the bounty of your mercy we have received the gifts of life, family, friends, daily bread, challenges that keep us on our toes—and on our knees—and the great purposes of life for which you created us. Now, as we have freely received, may we freely give. Bless and multiply these tithes and gifts for your King-dom's sake. Amen.

Morning Prayer: Lord of all life, as we gather here in this sacred place this morning, we pray that you will grant us lips to speak the truth and to speak it always in love. Grant us minds to seek the truth and grant that we may face the truth, even when it hurts and condemns us. Grant that we may never shut our eyes to that which we do not wish to see. Grant unto us hands that work with diligence and that still have time to help others in their struggles and tasks. Grant unto us the resolution needed to stand for principle, but save us from stubbornness and from magnifying trifles into principles. Grant us the grace to conquer our temptations and to live in purity, but save us from the self-righteousness that would look down on anyone who has fallen by the way. Move mightily among us now we pray, meeting us in our need and guiding us to your purpose. We pray in Jesus' name. Amen.—Henry Fields

Benediction: As we depart from this place, let us go in the knowledge and power of the gracious God we know as Father, Son, and Holy Spirit. May we live the truth declared from God's Word today. And may we gather again next Lord's Day as God's children, full of joy and hope. God's peace be with you. Amen.

SUNDAY, FEBRUARY 3, 2008

LECTIONARY SERMON TOPIC: "Windows on the Heart of the Universe"
TEXT: Matt. 17:1–9
OTHER READINGS: Exod. 24:12–18; Ps. 99; 2 Pet. 1:16–21

In the Transfiguration event, Peter, John, and James gained a new perspective on Jesus. What really happened we don't know, but we can be assured that something truly significant occurred. Matthew tries to tell us something he can transmit in no other way.

So let's extend the tableau for just a moment. You'll remember at Caesarea Philippi, Jesus tells his friends he carries with him none of their national hopes or political expectations. He might have said something like this: "The world has seen enough messianic power plays and scrambling for domination. Our mission is to conquer no one, but rather to invite them to put their lives on the line for their neighbor and, yes, even their 'enemies.' And in Jerusalem where so much is at stake in power and privilege, my style, my vision, my behavior can lead only to rejection and execution."

The disciples refuse to believe it. Peter insists, "No Lord, you go in triumph, not to die; to mount not a Cross but a throne." The disciples refuse to offer allegiance to the mission of Jesus as he understands it.

Enter now, if you will, the Transfiguration. The evangelist tells us in this brilliant narrative that God is confirming our Lord's understanding of what he must do. On that mountain, with three skeptical disciples as witnesses, there is a recasting of Jesus in such a manner as those who see it can only say, "Yes! This way is God's way! Yes! Suffering love, not political acumen or military arsenals, will finally save the world. No pageantry, no trumpets, no canons, just life available and for Love's sake, given to others." Jesus transfigured: the disciples glimpse for the first time the Source of our Lord's commitment to heal the world through a readiness to be broken in it; to reconcile its divisions by submitting himself to them. Jesus' ministry is no longer a scheme to be debated; it provides a window on the heart of the universe.

I. **As we reflect on this passage, it is clear we often suffer the spiritual myopia of the disciples.** There is so much going by us that could serve as windows to the heart of the universe—windows of the Spirit. Take our families, for instance. Heaven knows, there are some very sad things going on among our modern families. One in every two marriages in the United States breaks up. But there is another reality, too. It is the family many of us search for: a family of nurture and encouragement—a family where fairness, kindness, and empathy carry the day. Lives can be transfigured in loving families, and for all the cynicism that is abroad, we need to affirm time and again that families can be colonies of heaven—windows on the love at the heart of the universe.

II. **Churches are not immune.** Heaven knows that they, as well as families, can be disappointing, discouraging, selfish enterprises. We in the churches are no more immune to the rudeness and failure of human nature than any other association of men and women. Indeed, perhaps we are less immune because we make higher claims. We are no less tempted by status, inclined to exclusivity, mistaken in our priorities, or deceived about our goodness. Those are the human facts. But they are not the only reality. Heaven forbid! There is a reality of people giving their best day by day to become more like Christ. Who dares count the acts of kindness and sacrifice offered anonymously for the sake of love alone. Many people pour their lives into our churches—into this church—in order that they and we may be faithful, courageous, creative, compassionate, prophetic—windows on the love at the heart of the universe.

III. **We can be transfigured.** Paul uses the startling image of the Transfiguration and its continuing implication for us. He prays we will reflect in ourselves, as a mirror does, the character of Christ. But he does not stop there. He says that our goal is to be more than a reflection of Christ. Our goal is to live so closely with him that the reflection itself changes—it becomes transfigured into the one it reflects. For Paul, that is what the Christian life is all about.

Can it be so—that you and I are transfigured into the image of Christ, that we can become windows on the love at the heart of the universe? Such transfiguration is not the result of a sudden change of heart or spirit. It is not something we gain. It is something we are given. Like that memorable "great stone face" that used to brood over Franconia Notch, New Hampshire, shaped by wind, ice, and avalanche, our conforming to the image of Christ is a lifetime of courage, risk, and self-abandonment. To be that way is never a simple proposition, especially in an age when we are battered from every quarter with invitations to pamper ourselves, to have our feelings massaged, and to assume that what "number one" wants, "number one" gets. To be conformed to the image of Christ is to offer ourselves for the ministry that he described and pursued and to which he surrendered. Our transfiguration will take place on a pilgrimage of loving, risking, praying, serving. Life itself will take on a new shape: the shape of the cross— that clearest window on the love at the heart of the universe.—James W. Crawford

ILLUSTRATIONS

New Perspective. In the gift shops around Washington, you will find for sale a unique copy of the U.S. Constitution. You will see it transcribed in such a manner that on a normal reading, it appears to be a replica of the original document. But if one holds the Constitution at arm's length, the particularity of the letters and words disappears, and what becomes apparent in the shadows of penmanship is a portrait of George Washington. Similarly, a painting by Ralph Pallen Coleman hung in my church school. The picture includes the faces of people, young and old, a melting pot of races, nations, and dress. On close investigation it simply pictures human diversity. But at arm's length, it becomes the face of Jesus Christ.

In both these pictures what appears to be there at first glance veils a deeper, more profound reality. Seen at the proper distance, each picture becomes transfigured. In the U.S. Constitution, the written words become the person behind the founding of our nation. In the second, we see the people of the world as beautiful human community, radiant in the face of Jesus Christ.—James W. Crawford

Image of Christ. Walter Russell Bowie has written a profound and beautiful hymn: *Lord Christ, When First Thou Cam'st to Men.* The hymn includes a verse perhaps capturing the essence of our own transfiguring pilgrimage toward the image of Christ:

O wounded hands of Jesus, build
In us Thy new creation . . .
We bring our hearts before Thy Cross
To finish Thy salvation.[1]
—James W. Crawford

---

[1]Walter Russell Bowie, "Lord Christ, When First Thou Cam'st to Men," Hymn 325, *Pilgrim Hymnal* (Boston: The Pilgrim Press, 1958).

Musical Selections Appropriate to the Day

Hymn suggestions for lectionary texts:

Exod. 24:12–18	*The God of Abraham Praise*
Ps. 99	*How Great Thou Art*
2 Pet. 1:16–21	*Christ Whose Glory Fills the Skies*
Matt. 17:1–9	*Jesus on the Mountain Peak; We Have Come at Christ's Own Bidding*

❧ Children's Lectionary Sermon

TITLE: Because God Says So!

SCRIPTURE: 2 Pet. 1:16–21

KEY VERSE: *No prophecy ever came from what a man wanted to say. But men led by the Holy Spirit spoke words from God.* (2 Pet. 1:20, New Century Version)

KEY CONCEPT: God's Word

MATERIALS: Bible

Have any of you ever said the phrase, "Because my mom said so!" or, "Because my dad said so, that's why!" Why would anyone say, "Because my mom said so!"? (*Let the children answer with examples. Reflect the children's answers.*)

Maybe someone needed to pass on some important information, like telling your little brother it was time to turn off the TV and get back to finishing his after-school chores, because your mom said so. Maybe your dad told you to stop teasing your big sister. We say these words because our parents—people who are very important to us—say so!

Even at school or here at church we might say things like, "Oh, that is because Pastor said to do it that way," or, "Mrs. Johnson asked me to tell you to come back to class, now." We know it is important to respect what our teachers and parents say to us. We know it is right to do what we are told to do by these important people in our lives.

This passage of Scripture reminds us to pay close attention to what Scripture tells us (*open the Bible*). In 1 Peter 1:16 it says, "No prophecy ever came from what a man wanted to say." But men led by the Holy Spirit spoke words from God. God has spoken through God's people. Peter, one of Jesus' first followers, wrote this book of the Bible. Peter is telling us to remember that God's Word comes from the Holy Spirit. The stories are real and can help us to understand how much God loves us. We need to believe it because God said so!

This season of Epiphany, we remember that Jesus came for all people because God said so! God's Word tells us this, and we can believe.—Lizette Hunt

WORSHIP AIDS

Call to Worship: In worship, we declare our full dependence and joyful intimacy with the One who is greater than all. Hear his Word: "For thus says the high and lofty One who inhabits eternity, whose name is Holy; I dwell in the high and holy place, and with those also who are contrite and humble, to revive the spirit of the humble and the heart of the contrite" (Isa. 57:15).

Invocation: God of peace, you have taught us that in coming to you we shall be saved and that in quiet confidence we shall know strength. In this hour and by your Spirit, be present to us. Help us to be still and to know that you are God. Amen.

Offertory Sentence: "Therefore, my beloved brothers, be steadfast, unmovable, always abounding in the work of the Lord, forasmuch as you know that your labor is not in vain in the Lord" (1 Cor. 15:58).

Offertory Prayer: Gracious Father, whose loving hand has provided all that we possess, grant us grace that we may honor you in our giving. May our tithes and offerings reflect a deep commitment of faith, and may they be given with glad and joyful hearts. Remembering the account that we will one day give, may we be faithful stewards of your bounty. Amen.

Morning Prayer: O God, lean toward us now and grant us the grace to lean toward you. On those days when we feel most alone in the world, please make your presence felt and help us to reach out and widen our friendships. Work through us to shore up what is good about our world and to remake what has gone wrong, for we know there is much that is good, and there is too much that is not. Give us the eyes to see what you would have us do, the strength to do our part, and the faith to know that each of us does have a part and that our part matters.

On this day and gathered as we are in this place, we ask your special consideration for the families among us who have suffered the loss of someone close and dear in recent weeks. Help them find whatever solace and peace is possible, and help the rest of us to reach out to them in just the right ways.

Hear also this morning our prayers of thanksgiving for cool morning mist and golden evening light, for the changing of seasons and time with family and good friends, for children who love us anyway, for a friend who listens, for the fortune to have what we need, and for the grace to give away what we don't. Unite our church, not in cheap agreement but in a deep and enduring desire to share a common adventure of ideas and action, always pursuing those truths that lie beyond dictionary definitions, in the sure and certain faith that on the road ahead, your light will shine and not be dimmed. Amen.—Roger Paine

Benediction: People of God, go forth into the days of this week full of confidence and hope, knowing that God goes before you. God's Presence, known to us as Father, Son, and Holy Spirit, will guide you, keep you, and strengthen you for the living of these days. May you be a powerful presence in the world, bringing peace to those whose lives you touch. Amen.

SUNDAY, FEBRUARY 10, 2008
First Sunday in Lent

LECTIONARY SERMON TOPIC: "On Making Crucial Choices"
TEXT: Matt. 4:1–11
OTHER READINGS: Gen. 2:15–17, 3:1–7; Ps. 32; Rom. 5:12–19

Each of us, probably as we were sitting down to dinner with some friends in a restaurant, has faced the challenge of a varied and exotic menu. Overwhelmed by all the goodies, we find ourselves remarking under our breath, "Decisions!

Decisions! Decisions!" We enjoy making these kinds of decisions, because whatever the choice, we come out a winner. Who really suffers over oysters on the half shell or filet mignon?

Nonetheless, we face choices in our lives that are far more crucial. They point toward vocation; they deal with personal relationships, and they include the use of money and time. These decisions touch on our ambitions, our religious convictions, how we handle trouble, manage suffering, and just plain survive. These choices usually say much about our ultimate loyalties, the depths of our faith, and the quality of our hope. This kind of choice faced Jesus in this marvelous passage from Matthew. We need to remember that the New Testament never considers Jesus more exempt from critical ethical choices than you or me. A classical misunderstanding of our Lord assumes he was programmed always for the right and the good and that he strode through the drama of life as one who diligently rehearsed his lines and danced at the end of celestial strings.

Not so! Jesus' struggle for faithfulness was no less a struggle than yours or mine. The dilemmas he faced in his wilderness experience were no less baffling than the dilemmas we face in our wilderness.

I. **Matthew's first critical choice lies in turning stones into bread.** Here we find a test of using our own unique gifts, strengths, and powers. Some of us, for instance, can turn deadly relationships into trusting ones. Others of us can transform confused data into useful information. Still others can transform considerable wealth into philanthropic, life-saving ends. Many of us are gifted in some ways, and these gifts and powers lead to critical choices. As with Jesus, they are the ones put first to the critical test. Our discipleship comes under its most severe test precisely at the point we consider ourselves deepest in resources. It is not necessarily the squandering of our power; the problem is the exploitation of our resources, excessive trust in them, overdependence on them to accomplish what we want.

Here, for instance, is a gifted physician whose patients are devoted to her. She inspires confidence, knows the way around the hospital, and is a broad gauge and splendid professional. She possesses power to turn stones into bread, and she does. Yet she is so consumed by her work that her domestic life turns to stone. She leaves the house before the family rises and gets home after they've gone to bed. She reads mostly professional journals and socializes mainly with her colleagues. Her practice flourishes, but relationships that make life whole fail to thrive. Bread is available, yes. But maybe the bread has turned to stone! We need to assess carefully our strengths and unique gifts. They may well be of such magnitude as to turn stones into bread. But we need be careful that we do not turn bread into stone.

II. **The second of our Lord's tests lies in the challenge to leap off the parapet of the Temple and be saved by God from injury.** It tests our relationships. How do we treat others? It has to do with the manipulation of relationships to prove their reliability. We frequently try this test ourselves. Our feelings about ourselves are such that we often seek signs that others really do love us. We contrive our little games so that other people (and sometimes even God) will in some way offer proof of their love and concern.

You surely know of people who seek a permanent relationship, and as soon as one with a future develops, they begin to play the game, "How much do you love me?" They test, probe, and sometimes sulk or pout about a subtly created or imagined slight. The tests are frequently, in some way, fabricated.

We play these games with God, too. "How much do you love me?" we may ask. We want God to satisfy our needs, to answer our prayers, to do our will. When things don't go our way, we are tempted to say, "There is no God." And what we ask him to do on our behalf, or because we think we deserve it, is almost like jumping off the parapet of the temple and asking him to save us.

And our Lord's response? "You shall not tempt—you shall not test—the Lord your God" (Matt. 4:7). That answer emerges from perfect trust. That conviction lies with one who is persuaded that through the breadth and depth of life, the mercy and grace of one who loves us is present. To play the game of, "How much do you love me?" with others, or with God, is a betrayal of love. The choice is this: Shall we manipulate others—and God—or shall we trust them?

III. **The last testing of our Lord is the opportunity to rule over a world laid at his feet.** It is a critical choice at the level of values. More than anything else, Jesus wanted our world to accept the quality of his life as its norm. As witness to our suffering and conflict, our self-deception and moral myopia, Jesus wished more than anything else to mend a broken world. And he could have done it, for a price!

Jesus faced this test of values. The Tester challenged him to move toward a new world of justice and peace, by shaving off a little integrity here, negotiating his alliances, urging him to pursue noble ends with less than noble means.

And our Lord's answer? "You shall serve the Lord your God and him only will you worship" (Matt. 4:10). A simple answer keeps our Lord's values intact. Jesus does not mistake his own ends for God's. He does not pursue his own vision to the point it corrupts him. Our career purposes, for instance, may be noble, but if we sell ourselves to gain them, we cripple our integrity. If we make our own ambitions supreme, if we place ultimate value there, then we give way to the risk of using ungodly means to gain selfish ends. To be loyal to God is to maintain humane and divine perspective on our own objectives. That loyalty shrinks the possibility of mistaking our own sense of what is important with God's vision of what is crucial and important.

Thus, my friends, there are critical choices we have to make in our lives. Some of them have to do with our gifts; others with how we handle human relationships, and still others with what we believe to be important. God grant that these choices may be informed by faith and exercised in love, always bearing hope.—James W. Crawford

ILLUSTRATIONS

A Biblical Footnote. We would be closer to the essence of this passage if we understood that the words and expression pointing to "tempt" and "temptation" were closer to "testing." Rather than calling this passage "The Temptations of Jesus," we might call it "The Testings of Jesus." The mood of this passage is not so much seduction as it is challenge. It suggests not so much subversive persuasion as it does moral opportunity; not so much tumbling into moral traps as hammering out moral choices. It calls for moral maturity—that of Jesus and that of you and me.—James W. Crawford

Values. Remember Floyd Landis in the summer of 2006? He wanted to win the Tour de France so badly that he cheated with drugs! Or Barry Bonds? All those home runs? Deceit. A wrecked reputation. Of what value is the education of your children? What price will you pay to get them into the "right schools" with the "right people"? What price to be popular, to be successful, to get results? Whatever price it is, we find ourselves tested at the critical junction of our values.—James W. Crawford

Musical Selections Appropriate to the Day

Hymn suggestions for lectionary texts:

Gen. 2:15–17, 3:1–7	*For the Beauty of Meadows*
Ps. 32	*Jesus, What a Friend of Sinners; Jesus Lover of My Soul*
Rom. 5:12–19	*Grace Alone; Wonderful Grace of Jesus*
Matt. 4:1–11	*Lord, Who Throughout These Forty Days*

❧ Children's Lectionary Sermon

TITLE: How to Fight Temptations

SCRIPTURE: Matt. 4:1–11

KEY VERSE: *But Jesus told him, "No! The Scriptures say, 'People need more than bread for their life; they must feed on every word of God.'"* (Matt. 4:4, New Living Translation)

KEY CONCEPT: Temptation, God's Word

MATERIALS: Bible, stones (optional), picture of the Temple (optional), picture of a very high mountain (optional)

Does anyone know what *temptation* means? (*Give the children a chance to answer. If you have older children, they may be able to tell you. Examples are a good way of communicating this. Use an example of something that would be tempting to you.*) It is hard to resist those things we want, especially if a parent or a teacher has told us we can't have what we want.

In our Gospel lesson today, we are hearing the story of Jesus' temptation. Now Jesus was out in the wilderness for forty days and nights. He was getting pretty hungry. The Devil came up to him and said, "If you are God's Son, then you can turn these stones to bread. You don't have to be hungry." Jesus could have done that because he was hungry. But instead he answered the Devil's temptation with a verse of Scripture (Matt. 4:4) (*open the Bible and read: But Jesus told him, "No! The Scriptures say, 'People need more than bread for their life;*

they must feed on every word of God.'") Jesus knew we need more than food for life; we need the Word of God in us.

Did you know that the Devil tempted Jesus again, but the second time the Devil was slick—the Devil tempted Jesus using Scripture from Psalm 91:11–12 (*read the passage*). Jesus answered the Devil again with a Scripture passage from Deuteronomy 6:16 (*read the passage*). The Devil tempted Jesus a third time, and again, Jesus resisted the temptations using a verse of Scripture.

We sometimes have temptations come our way. We can learn from Jesus that knowing God's Word is important in helping us to resist those things we know we shouldn't do.—Marcia Thompson

WORSHIP AIDS

Call to Worship: God's goodness and mercy draw us to worship. We gather joyfully to speak praise and adoration. We pray, as did the psalmist of old, "O send out your light and your truth: let them lead us; let them bring us unto your holy hill, and to the tabernacles" (Ps. 43:3).

Invocation: Dearest Father, who guides the meek and humble, who gives light to the darkened paths we travel, grant to us grace that we may truly rise above our doubts and uncertainties. May our worship today be such that your Spirit will teach us the way to right choices and that in the light of your countenance, we shall walk the straight paths. Amen.

Offertory Sentence: "So then every one of us shall give account of himself to God" (Rom. 14:12).

Offertory Prayer: Lord, accept these gifts we offer in the name of your Son, Jesus Christ, who is our Savior. Empower us through faith in the living Christ to use these resources for the proclamation of the gospel and the healing of the nations. Amen.

Morning Prayer: Eternal Spirit, we give thanks for your abundant blessings that make it possible for us to be together this morning in the company of friends and neighbors whom we love and trust. We give thanks that our stomachs are full, that the room is warm, that we can meet in peace. Outside these windows, we watch with anticipation as the days gradually lengthen, and the promise of new life trembles just beneath the icy ponds and snow-blanketed fields.

But the long winter has brought suffering to so many. We ask your forgiveness, Oh God, that we are so occupied with our daily concerns—rushing from car to supermarket, paying our bills, wiping our children's noses—that we often forget those who need our help and prayers. Dear God, we ask especially that you watch over the homeless men and women who huddled last night on street grates and in subway stations, as the bitter cold bore deep into the marrow of their beings. Help us to know what we may do to allay their suffering. In these lingering days of ice and snow, may we also remember the many who are shut in because of illness or infirmities. And for those who are silently bearing burdens of depression or grief or loneliness or fear in these dark days, we ask you, God, to bring the light and cheer of the coming spring into their hearts. Amen.—Janet Boynton

Benediction: Now as we go out, may we know that the God of grace—Father, Son, and Holy Spirit—will guide us in our way. We walk not alone but in the strength of God. And so, with joy and peace in our hearts, we depart to serve in his name and to live at peace with all mankind. Amen.

SUNDAY, FEBRUARY 17, 2008
Second Sunday in Lent

LECTIONARY SERMON TOPIC: "Life"
TEXT: John 3:1–17
OTHER READINGS: Gen. 12:1–4a; Ps. 121; Rom. 4:1–5, 13–17

Nicodemus belongs to the religious elite. He's intelligent, thoughtful, and eager to sustain the religious and national tenets of his people. But Nicodemus comes to Jesus, not really alone. He comes representing his colleagues in the religious establishment. He expresses their concern. They watch Jesus. They wonder about him. They're intrigued and troubled by what they see. They discern a casual attitude toward orthodox religious practice. They witness an acceptance of apparent blasphemous behavior. They blanch as crowds hang on every heresy. They perceive a challenging and dangerous, a bewildering and threatening figure. So at night, in the darkness (John's description, not so much a moment in time but rather of a spiritual condition), Nicodemus attends his appointment with Jesus.

I. **Nicodemus initiates the conversation and sends out a friendly probe.** "Rabbi," he says, "we know you are a teacher who has come from God, for no one can do these signs that you do apart from the presence of God."

Nicodemus approaches Jesus with no condescension, no insults, and no put-down. Nicodemus seeks to draw Jesus out. Today, he might sound something like this: "Say Reverend: where do you stand on this matter of gay men and women presiding at denominational communion tables?" or "Good Doctor: if a political leader's personal morals are more or less impeccable, but he countenances poverty and initiates wars, how shall we make judgments about his virtue?" Nicodemus wants to kick off a religious bull session. And Jesus? Remember his reply? His words carry the ring and profundity of an oath: "In very truth, I tell you no one can see the Kingdom of God without being born from above."

Nicodemus steps back, stunned and confused. "Reverend," he says, "what are you talking about? I want a thoughtful opinion about the appropriate presence of gay people in the Christian ministry. I seek your perspective on questions of an executive's personal morals and their relation to public policy. Your references to new birth lose me. They are beside the point."

The new birth—beside the point? Or does Jesus, in fact, speak directly to the point. This encounter between Jesus and Nicodemus always make me uncomfortable. Speaking to Nicodemus, Jesus seems to say, "Nicodemus, you seem to be the ultimate open-minded religious type—a mind open to everything and closing on nothing. You want your religion intellectually manageable. You resonate to ideas. You like to wrestle with doctrine, but at arm's length. You seek to debate truth claims. Sorry; that's not enough. I am compelled to ask, in what, in whom do you claim your deepest identity?

The crucial religious questions facing us have little to do with sparring over ecclesiastical legalism or the morals of public servants. These matters are but symptoms of a more crucial question: *Nicodemus, who and what defines your life?* Is your true birthplace a geographical setting, or are you really born a child of my healed, reconciled future? The key question you face, Nicodemus, is this: Where do you find yourself rooted, grounded, nourished, claimed, identified. Who you are, in mind, soul, heart, and spirit and, as a consequence, how you treat, how you serve, how you succor and sustain—how you love others—answers the crucial question of your identity.

II. **What identifies you or me?** John knows most of us are born into the world of the "flesh," by which he does not mean the world of vice, desire, gluttony, and all the rest of the seven deadly sins. He means life in the world as we know it. When asked where we come from, we begin with little shards of autobiography. "I'm from Rochester, Bismarck, or Jasper. My father teaches first grade, my mother is an engineer, my brother is a magician, and I was baptized in a Methodist Church." If we find ourselves rooted in a world of entertainment, snowed by celebrity, blown away by sports, intrigued by the latest spin or buzz, seeking the highest market share, up on the latest in trendy food—if these are our milieus, interests, and venues, then, as John writes, we are "once born of the flesh."

But John offers an alternative. He asks if we come from a reality where the joy of self-surrender, the peace of self-investment in a healed and renewed humanity saturates the totality of our being and purpose, where service is the order of the day. That kind of selfhood demands from most of us a new beginning, a new start, a fresh grounding. Indeed, it demands what, for lack of a better analogy, we can only call a new birth, from a new place—new birth from above.

III. **To be reborn means to invest in others.** Nicodemus still fails to get it. He is dissatisfied with our Lord's cryptic, nonsequitur of an answer. "Look," he exclaims, "I am an old man. I can't return to my mother's womb in an old age. Your suggestion is absurd." Jesus plunges again into the core of the old man's life. "In truth I tell you, no one can enter the Realm of Heaven without being born of water and Spirit."

What? Another disconnect? What's Spirit got to do with the realities of the world? Cyclones in the South Pacific, mutual slaughter in the Middle East, nuclear threats, urban crime? Is he talking about what we usually call conversion—an ecstatic experience we frequently see coming at the hands of a well-heeled televangelist, an experience labeled in popular parlance, "born again"? I doubt it. To John the Spirit transmits life, communication, love—all taking the shape we see in the mission and ministry of Jesus. To be reborn in the Spirit—to discover our identity from above—means life lived out of the love that never lets us go, life and love that this side of heaven may run into dead ends, betrayals, rejection, and manipulation—but life and love never giving up.

Life in the "realm born of the Spirit" means life invested, right now, in encouraging and building up the lives of others. It means life rooted, grounded, claiming as its birthplace the peace and compassion that risks everything, as did our Lord, to save this beautiful world as it muddles and stumbles after justice and true community. It means identifying with a source of life leading to the possibility of a destiny on the cross. That's life in the realm of the Spirit; that's existence in the Dominion—the Kingdom—of God. There lie the true sources of our life that we might call Christian: our real birthplace, our true home.—James W. Crawford

---

ILLUSTRATIONS

New Birth. Most of us know of Dorothy Day, the founder of the *Catholic Worker,* a person who spent her later years in soup kitchens, picket lines, prison cells, houses of hospitality, and "the street." She called herself "a fool for Christ." She tells us, quoting the Archbishop of Paris, Cardinal Suhard, "To be a witness does not consist in engaging in propaganda, or even stirring people up, but in being a living mystery; it means to live in such a way that one's life would not make sense if God did not exist." Of course. Living in such a way that one's life would not make sense if God did not exist. Now that's being born from above.—James W. Crawford

Christian Life. "God has no hands but our hands to do his work today; God has no feet but our feet to lead others in his way; God has no voice but our voice to tell others how he died; and, God has no help but our help to lead them to his side."[2]—Annie Johnson Flint

---

[2]Annie Johnson Flint, *Best Loved Poems* (Grand Rapids: Zondervan, 1962), p. 81.

Musical Selections Appropriate to the Day

Hymn suggestions for lectionary texts:

Gen. 12:1–4a	*My Faith Has Found a Resting Place*
Ps. 121	*I Lift My Eyes to the Quiet Hills*
Rom. 4:1–5, 13–17	*Standing on the Promises*
John 3:1–17	*Blessed Assurance; Give to Our God Immortal Praise*

Children's Lectionary Sermon

TITLE: Help Will Come

SCRIPTURE: Ps. 121

KEY VERSE: *My help comes from the Lord, who made the heavens and the earth!* (Ps. 121:2, New Living Translation)

KEY CONCEPT: God's faithfulness and love

MATERIALS: Bible, large piece of chart paper, marker

PREPARATION: Prior to Sunday, write the key verse large on the chart paper. You will use it on Sunday with the children.

We are in the church season called Lent. During Lent, we come to God and ask him to help us and forgive us. The person who wrote Psalm 121 knew this (*open Bible*). He wrote, "My help comes from the Lord, who made the heavens and the earth!" The psalmist even wrote about how God was faithful to God's people—God *watches over you.* God watches over all of us. Isn't it good to know God is trying to help us all the time, even when we are having a hard time following God's way!

I want us to do something a little different this morning. I brought this chart paper, and at the top I have written in large letters the verse I read you from Psalm 121. I want you to think of something God could help you with, and then I want you to raise your hand when you have it in your head. (*Ask the children who volunteer to tell you how they would like God to help them this week. Write the sentence or phrase on the chart paper under the verse.*)

Now we have written these things we want God to help us with. We are going to invite the congregation to join us in a prayer. I will say your name and read what you want God to help you with this week. Then we will say the verse above together. We will do this until we have done everyone's requests. It will be our prayer to God who watches over us and loves us so much. We can be sure God will help us, too. (*Begin with name and the request, then have the children and congregation read the verse together.*)—Marcia Thompson

❧ WORSHIP AIDS ❧

Call to Worship: Worship draws us into God's presence and requires us to hear and heed God's Word: "With what shall I come before the Lord, and bow myself before the High God? . . . He has shown you, O man, what is good; and what does the Lord require of you, but to do justly, to love mercy, and to walk humbly with your God?" (Mic. 6:6, 8).

Invocation: Hear our prayers and bless our worship today, O Lord, that growing in grace we might become children of light and faith as you intended. Amen.—E. Lee Phillips

Offertory Sentence: "For every beast of the forest is mine, and the cattle upon a thousand hills" (Ps. 50:10).

Offertory Prayer: We are yours, O Lord. You have created us and redeemed us. You have given us the ability to attain the fruits of our labor. For all your gifts we are truly grateful. We now bring to you as offerings of gratitude and love that which is already yours. Amen.

Morning Prayer: Lord, we have a hard time trying to understand. Your thoughts are not our thoughts, your ways are not our ways, and we struggle to hold on. Lord, we believe in you; help us in those moments when we find it hard to believe. Through fears and tears, we yet confess that you alone are our refuge and that underneath us are your everlasting arms. Thank you, Lord, for giving us voice and hope to sing your praises in the nighttime of our despair. Through Christ our Lord we pray. Amen.—Thomas Smothers

Benediction: As we go, we are led by the gracious God who loved us first. In these days, let us remember that our Savior set his face toward Jerusalem and bore there the weight of eternity for us. May we go from this place in the joy of God's love, and may we serve in love all the days of this week. Amen.

SUNDAY, FEBRUARY 24, 2008
Third Sunday in Lent

LECTIONARY SERMON TOPIC: "Unity"
TEXT: John 4:5–42
OTHER READINGS: Exod. 17:1–7; Ps. 95; Rom. 5:1–11

When Linda and I go to the movie theater close to our home, especially when a Bill Murray film is showing, we find the theater packed. We move through tons of people, hundreds of teenagers out on a Friday night at the flicks stocking up on popcorn, soda, Snickers—meeting, greeting, and looking each other over. That theater provides ambience, access, and availability, triggering social electricity, designed, as well as chance, connection. What a hangout!

It's just like that well in Sychar where Jesus encounters a woman who had come to draw water. A well in that scorching desert land provides the equivalent of our neighborhood theater. At the well, drawn by the necessity of water, the citizens of Sychar, by chance or choice, encounter one another. The well provides not only a source of water; the well serves as the village hangout.

And at that well, we participate in a dramatic, world-changing event. Remember? When Jesus meets a Samaritan woman they engage in conversation; she beginning with antagonism, wondering how he, an alien Jewish male, dares speak with her, a foreign, Samaritan female. As the conversation progresses, she addresses Jesus as "teacher," then "prophet," and finally as "Christ." Beneath this conversation, amid this encounter at the well, flowing from the confrontation with the townspeople and the disciples in this vivid and glorious narrative—John illuminates the ultimate unity of humankind; he embraces us all in the arms of the God who, through Jesus Christ, meets the woman— the God who meets *us*—at the well.

I. **We ask first of all, who do we see at the well?** We see a Galilean and a Samaritan. From John's point of view they represent not simply two individuals; they represent ethnic siblings—Semites—both of them. They share turf, tradition, culture. But years ago the Samaritans went their own way; they turned their backs on their Jewish heritage; they sliced and diced their religion; they hooked up with military enemies; as a result, Jews and Samaritans treated one another with virulent contempt and hatred. John sees the initial meeting of that Samaritan woman and that Jewish man as an explosive mixture of ethnic dynamite.

And what happens at this meeting? How does the conversation take place? We see our Galilean operate as if no breach exists. We see this Galilean, Jesus, who John understands to represent "all-embracing community"—we see the Galilean treat the Samaritan with neither condescension nor contempt. Jesus approaches this apparent antagonist with neither prejudice nor disdain but with a deep recognition of her full humanity. "May I have a drink?" he asks. No hostility; no superior bearing—a monumental breakthrough: ethnic and national barriers treated as irrelevant!

Can you imagine what a difference we might see if the united presence we witness at Jacob's well were operative in our world today? As people in the Middle East—Persians and Arabs and Jews—express their ethnic identities with violence, it seems at the very spot where Jesus meets the Samaritan woman with respect now rings with the imperative, "Hate Thy Neighbor!" In our own country, the conflicts over immigration, with all the fear and contempt meted out to others, flies in the face of our Lord's encounter at Sychar. Our own city, with its tribes of Brahmins, blacks, Irish Italians, Jews, Haitians, Vietnamese, Latinos, all scrapping and scrambling, reflects the condition John describes surrounding that well in Sychar.

It's sad. We still live with our equivalent of the Galilean-Samaritan division in the twenty-first century. We see it in struggles over who will attend our schools; we witness it in housing patterns; we glimpse it in suburban zoning and tax structures, in gated communities, in club memberships, and in health care. Whoever we are, regardless of our heritage, we know the condescension we can hold for the so-called "them," who are ostensibly of inferior breeding, cruder culture, more primitive traditions. Or vice versa, we can feel the contempt that so-called "they" may hold for us and our peculiar traits, cultural habits, religious traditions, racial characteristics. At the well of Jacob, we see Christ, evident as dynamic love embracing different nations, binding us into one human community.

II. **We see more at the well.** We see a Galilean man and a Samaritan woman: a male and a female. Watch carefully, for here again, John interprets the Christ as the source of inclusive community. Remember? Late in John's narrative our Lord's disciples arrive at the well bringing lunch from downtown. They discover Jesus talking to the woman. They stand stunned at what they see. They yearn to challenge the woman. "Who do you think *you* are? What do *you* want? They look at Jesus, shocked, appalled. They can't believe their eyes: "What good is *she*? What do you want with *her*?"

Do you see what John does? He, first of all, dissolves cultural contempt and inferiority. Here he takes on gender disparities. Women in the surrounding culture count for nothing. Men and women do not speak in public. Women take second place. When they're born, the family mourns their birth, praying for a son. That's the world John and Jesus know.

But John and the community he writes from confess: man and woman, female and male in the realm of the inclusive Christ, exist in their full humanity with and for one another. Traditions, cultures, social structures, ideologies providing deference to anyone because of gender—all collapse where the inclusiveness we call Christ permeates the life of the community. We know of national and religious cultures where the heresy of male supremacy reigns supreme—a heresy working itself out in sexual tyranny, abuse, and condescension, continuing to deprive our churches, our universities, our procession, and commerce of the infinite gifts of half the human race. "No more!" says Jesus in this passage. When Jesus meets that woman at the well, we understand misogyny is dissolved, and the heart of the universe affirms the dignity of every woman and man in the mutuality of human community.

III. **John points beyond the parochialism of both Mt. Gerazim and Jerusalem toward a new loyalty described as "worship in spirit and in truth."** Do you know what John does here? He abolishes religion. He takes our pious "isms," our liturgical rites, our church institutions, our sacred terminology, our devout theologies, our glorious anthems and our hallowed words—and walks right through them. In this encounter at the well, John exposes religious alienation for what it is—pious illusion driving human fragmentation. John sees in the literal commitment of Jews to Jerusalem and the Samaritans to Mt. Gerazim the figurative commitments all of us make to holy places, religious rituals, and sacred buildings, wedging us from one another. John sees our routine religious practice as diversion from the investment that the loving Christ invites us to make in a suffering, divided, splintered humanity. John tells us our jealous guarding of hierarchies, doctrines, prayer books, hymn texts, bylaws, and priesthood demonstrates primarily the continued fracture of humankind. When John announces that "the hour is coming and now is when the true worshiper will worship . . . in spirit and in truth," he means we surrender all our sectarian, parochial, ethnic, ideological cause-oriented sovereignties, whether, Congregational, Presbyterian, Episcopalian, Baptist, Roman Catholic, or Pentecostal, and invites us to the sovereignty of outgoing, healing re-creative love. Worship and mission operate in the unity of Spirit and truth.

Do you remember how the woman concludes her encounter with Jesus? She asks, "Can this be the Christ?" Really now. With the breakdown of ethnic barriers, gender division, and religious boundaries—"Could this be the Christ?" Of course! Who else?—James W. Crawford

ILLUSTRATIONS

Companionship. I believe that we are placed here to be companions—a wonderful word that comes from *cum panis* (with bread). We share the bread.—Robert McAfee Brown

Friendship. We often overlook the power of relationships. One of the most telling novels is Ernest Hemmingway's *The Old Man and the Sea*. It's the story of an old and poverty-stricken fisherman. He is befriended by a young boy who stands by him and loves him—and whom he loves. His great dream, however, is to make the catch of his life.

Finally, he hooks the prize. He fights it day and night, through fatigue and hunger, and finally lands the giant fish. He tethers the fish to the side of his boat and heads back to the shore. He would be the hero of the day. His villagers would shower praise upon him. On his way home, sharks tear away at his prize. When he arrives, all that is left is a skeleton and a few chunks of bloody meat.

In the end, he is back in his little village, still a poverty-stricken old fisherman, but along his side is the boy, his friend, who gives meaning to life when all else is gone.—Lee McGlone

Musical Selections Appropriate to the Day

Hymn suggestions for lectionary texts:

Exod. 17:1–7	*All the Way My Savior Leads Me*
Ps. 95	*Come Christians Join to Sing*
Rom. 5:1–11	*And Can It Be That I Should Gain*
John 4:5–42	*O Master Let Me Walk with Thee*

◈ Children's Lectionary Sermon

TITLE: Friends of God

SCRIPTURE: Rom. 5:1–11

KEY VERSE: *So now we can rejoice in our wonderful new relationship with God— all because of what our Lord Jesus Christ has done for us in making us friends of God.* (Rom. 5:11, New Living Translation)

KEY CONCEPT: Lent, Jesus as Savior

MATERIALS: Bible, stickers with a cross on them

I want us to talk about friends. How would you describe really good friends? (*Let the children answer. Reflect back the answers they give you.*) I like the ways you have described really good friends.

Did you know that Paul in the letter to the Romans tells us how we have become friends of God? (*Open Bible.*) In Romans 5:11, Paul writes, "So now we can rejoice in our wonderful new relationship with God—all because of what our Lord Jesus Christ has done for us in making us friends of God." What do you think Paul was talking about when he says, "what our Lord Jesus Christ has done for us"? (*Give the children an opportunity to answer. If they are too young to know, give them a hint.*)

Jesus died on the cross for our sins. During this time of Lent, we need to think about those things we do that are against God's way. We can have joy and be happy because we know that because Jesus died for the wrong things we have done, we can be God's friends, even though we don't always do the things God wants us to do.

I am going to give each of you a sticker with a cross on it to remind you that you are God's friends. We can be happy and joyful, thanking God, because God loves us so.—Marcia Thompson

WORSHIP AIDS

Call to Worship: The power and intimacy of God's love draw us into worship. Jesus said, "If a man love me, he will keep my words; and my Father will love him, and we will come unto him, and make our abode with him" (John 14:23).

Invocation: Grant, dear Father, as we gather to experience your presence as brothers and sisters in Christ, a deepening love for you. Open our hearts to receive a fuller measure of your indwelling Spirit, and may we then, in turn, share with the world the joy of faith, which is the good news of your salvation. Amen.

Offertory Sentence: "The silver is mine, and the gold is mine, says the Lord of hosts" (Hag. 2:8).

Offertory Prayer: The gifts of tithes and offerings we bring, O God, are reflections of our love for you and as expressions of our responsible stewardship. May every aspect of our living, our working, our leisure, our saving, our planning, be lived mindful of your grand intentions for us, and may our giving be multiplied for the building of the Kingdom. Amen.

Morning Prayer: O God, teach us to hate evil and to love the good, to be willing to take the hard and difficult way when it is your way and not the easy path if it is the popular or softer way. Forgive us for not trying when the way is hard and the obstacles are difficult. May we remember the way of the crucified Christ. Give us courage to take up our crosses and follow him in the war against evil, in the battle of truth over ignorance, justice over inequity, and righteousness over corruption. Help us, O God, to bring light where there is darkness, hope where there is fear, concern where there is apathy, victory where there is defeat, and redemption where there is division.

Guide us to draw upon the strength of your abiding presence that can enable us to become what you have created us to be. Let us not grow weary, then, in well-doing. Inspire us with confidence to continue to follow the way of Christ wherever it leads us. For we pray in his strong name. Amen.— William Powell Tuck

Benediction: As we go, we are blessed by the presence of Almighty God, Father, Son, and Holy Spirit. May our lives this week be useful for the Kingdom and, as we gather next Lord's Day, may it be with testimonies of praise to you. Amen.

SUNDAY, MARCH 2, 2008
Fourth Sunday in Lent

LECTIONARY SERMON TOPIC: "The Business of Light"
TEXT: Eph. 5:8–14
OTHER READINGS: 1 Sam. 16:1–13; Ps. 23; John 9:1–41

I got a flashlight for Christmas when I was nine years old. In those days our family lived in a house that was lighted by a solitary kerosene lamp. At night if you left the room where the lamp was located, you were enveloped in darkness. You can imagine how amazed and pleased I was when that flashlight permeated the oppressive darkness around me. That light made it possible for me to see what would have been impossible to see in the darkness and probably gave me a boldness that was terribly superficial.

Isaiah knew something about darkness—a darkness of spiritual ignorance. He compared the people's ability to comprehend to that of stolid oxen and mulish donkeys, saying even "the ox knows his master, and the donkey his master's crib, but Israel does not know, my people do not understand" (Isa. 1:3). Yet looking down the long road of the future, despite this, he saw that "people walking in darkness have seen a great light; on those living in the shadow of death, a light has dawned" (Isa. 9:2). Thus light became one of the most eloquent and expressive metaphors found in the Bible. Among all the symbols used in the Bible, no other carries more meaning than the word *light*.

I. **Light is the symbol for revelation.** Nothing else helps one see reality more clearly. In the beginning, the redemptive purposes of the Coming One were seen only in faint outline. Yet in those early chapters of the Bible, God began nudging the human spirit toward something so entirely new, something so scandalously divine that it had to dawn incrementally on the human mind. His sovereign power was being manifested by flood and freedom. He moved from messianic promise to prophetic vision, from tribe to the triumphant, his redeeming love inexorably and clearly unfolding.

A singularity of revealed religion is that God always meets people where they are. God came to Abraham in the city where he lived and in the situation that surrounded him; God called him to go out from every known human security and depend entirely on a promise. That very thing is the distinguishing mark of revealed religion, and it is "the straight gate and narrow way" of the gospel that, according to Jesus, few ever find (Matt. 7:14).

In revealing his love for sinners, God became like us. It was necessary for the revelation to be personified in order to put God within the range of our knowing powers. Humans learn from and understand other humans best. When Jesus said he was the light of the world, he was saying that he was the embodiment of God's revealed truth. The apostle Paul, grasping the significance of this aspect of revelation said, "God made him who knew no sin to be sin for us, so that in him we might be made [or declared to have] the righteousness [a right standing with] of God" (2 Cor. 5:21). Jesus said to Nicodemus, "Just as Moses lifted up the serpent in the wilderness, so must the Son of Man be lifted up" (John 3:14). The serpent on the pole was a replica of the snake that had bitten the Israelites, so the answer to human frailty and "self-help" arrogance was to come from a human expression of that love and forgiveness. The writer of the Hebrew letter affirms this truth: "For surely it is not angels he helps, but Abraham's descendants. For this reason he had to be made like his brothers in every way, in order that he might become a merciful and faithful high priest in service to God, and that he might make atonement for the sins of the people" (2:16–17).

As in a symphony, the personality of the composer becomes more vivid and pronounced until, with an ending crescendo, she or he is revealed. So divine revelation moves from serpents and suffering until God will command the light (his revelation) to shine out of darkness and then "a gladness breaks like morning" in the face of Jesus Christ (Gal. 4:4).

II. **Another symbolic function of light in the Scriptures is illumination.** This light not only enables one to see but also to interpret or understand what is seen. Isaiah reached back to remind Israel of how God had cared for them, yet Israel's behavior indicated that the people were not living out— nor did they even understand—the compelling force that this love should have on their lives. The necessity for insight and appropriation is heightened by Jesus in his conversation with Nicodemus when he said, "I tell you the truth, no one can see the Kingdom of God unless one is born again" (John 3:3). The verb *see,* used here, is not for physical sight, but it refers to perception, for seeing into, for seeing the reality and value of the Kingdom of God. Spiritual illumination begins with being born from above.

When asked why he spoke in parables, Jesus responded, "This is why I speak in parables: though seeing, they do not see, though hearing, they do not understand" (Matt. 13:13). Jesus came into a world where travelers were on "the broad way that leads to destruction" into a muddled milieu where existed an impudent feeling of adequacy, a fatal conceit that assumed that one could obtain salvation through self-righteousness. The Israelites believed the way to God's acceptance and forgiveness was through keeping the Law of Moses. Jesus spoke to the fallacy of "compliance" by referring to the futility of the righteousness of the scribes and Pharisees who subscribed to the Law with meticulous care (Matt. 5:20). They were missing the acceptable righteousness, which is by faith in Jesus Christ. There was a tragic misreading of God's plan of redemption. This was the darkness into which the light came. And this light would give interpretation and understanding.

Before he ascended, Jesus promised that his illuminating presence would continue on and on in the person of the Holy Spirit, which is God's invisible presence. The illuminating ministry of the Holy Spirit would have these facets: "When he comes, he will convict the world of guilt in regard to sin and righteousness and judgment. In regard to sin, because men do believe in me" (John 16:9–10). One work of the counselor is to help persons understand why they need to be saved. It is not because they are wicked or criminal; it is because they have never believed on the name of Jesus Christ (John 3:18).

III. **Once more, light is the symbol for animation.** It is the business of light to shine. This characteristic of light transforms the darkness with its energy. The darkness melts in the path of light. How grateful we should be that light is stronger than darkness, that knowledge is better than ignorance (John 1:5). Generally, the unknown and unseen generate the most fear and dread. As Emerson said:

Some of your hurts you have cured,
Others you still have survived
But what torments of grief you have endured
From evils that never arrived.

As "the light of the world," Jesus came to dispel the darkness of our mis-understanding about God. For reasons that will never be clear, our forebears listened to one in the Garden of Eden who said that God was not to be trusted (Gen. 3:4). Then centuries ago this mistrust began to take root in the deepest places of our hearts, and ever since, people have been living out of a totally false perception of God, namely, that God is *not* essentially good and, moreover, has a problem with attitude. God's image has been distorted; he has been perceived—contrary to reality—as angry and vengeful.

The light was the revealing of God's unconditional love that seeks to redeem. Also revealed was the problem that lies at the door of persons: "All have sinned and come short of the glory of God" (Rom. 3:23). It is we who need to be reconciled to God (2 Cor. 5:20). Jesus stands at the door and knocks with the message that God is love and that forgiveness is above all.

Do you remember the apostle Paul saying that "no one will be declared righteous by observing the law, rather through the law we become conscious of sin" (Rom. 3:20)? It is helpful, then, to recall that the Law is not some relic relegated to the dustbins of the past; the Law is the basis of every "good" work that we seek to do. It is comprehensive. The Law of Moses gives birth to all honesty, purity, charity, kindness, or any other act of good-ness known to humankind. When we do those "good" works that we hope will win acceptance with God, we are simply observing the Law that the Bible says fails to justify us in the sight of God. It is so important that people understand their "coming short" is due entirely to the fact they are depending on "my way" for salvation. Jesus himself said that the work of God is this: "to believe in him whom he has sent" (John 6:29). Have you believed in him? Jesus said, "I am the light of the world; he that follows me shall not walk in darkness but shall have the light of life" (John 8:12)! "Come to the light 'tis shining for thee!"—John C. Huffman

ILLUSTRATIONS

Spiritual Illumination. Jim Murray, the Los Angeles sports writer, said of Charles Whittingham, one of the best race horse trainers: "Those blue eyes always seemed to be looking at what no one else could see." Likewise with spiritual illumination—the believer understands more and more of the work of the Mysterious One. When I told my parents that I felt I had been called to preach, my dad, who wasn't a Christian at the time, said to me, "I'd rather you be a fruit tree salesman!" That was the image of a horseback rider with a few seedlings in his saddle bags, riding across the countryside, hoping to make a sale while living in near poverty. As far as I know, that was a reference to the least worthwhile occupation he knew. But later, when he became a believer, he had a different viewpoint: he felt that I was investing my life in the greatest cause. Afterward, he could "see" with more empathy or understanding; he was looking finally from the inside.—John C. Huffman

Repentance. An erroneous view of God caused people to erect an elaborate system of "self-helps" to cajole and humor God, and, they hoped, change his attitude. The people would present "blood of bulls and the ashes of a heifer" (Heb. 9:12, 10:4) before God in the Temple as sacrifices aimed at winning appeasement. It was into this dispirited darkness that the light of God's grace was presented on the altar of the cross before us! Repentance, then and now, is about giving up the false perception that God must be placated by our intended acts of goodness and at the same time accepting the truth that God came in the form of our Lord Jesus and is the author of our personal salvation. This animating power of light is encapsulated in the statement of the Apostle Paul to the Corinthians: "For God who commanded the light to shine out of darkness has shined in our hearts to give the light of the knowledge of the glory of God in the face of Jesus Christ" (2 Cor. 4:6). Carlyle Marney said, "Humankind never could stand a redemption it didn't deserve!" Religiosity is the story of this fatal conceit that hopes at last to win God's approval, but sadly to no avail.—James W. Crawford

Musical Selections Appropriate to the Day

Hymn suggestions for lectionary texts:

1 Sam. 16:1–13	*We Are Called to Be God's People*
Ps. 23	*The Lord Is My Shepherd, I Shall Not Want;*
	The Lord My Shepherd Guards Me Well
Eph. 5:8–14	*Trust and Obey; This Little Light of Mine*
John 9:1–41	*Amazing Grace; Praise the One Who*
	Breaks the Darkness

✍ Children's Lectionary Sermon

TITLE: Appearances

SCRIPTURE: 1 Sam. 16:1–13

KEY VERSE: *The Lord doesn't make decisions the way you do! People judge by outward appearance, but the Lord looks at a person's thoughts and intentions.* (1 Sam. 16:7b, New Living Translation)

KEY CONCEPT: Judging others

MATERIALS: Bible, blown-out egg, super-size candy bar wrapper, a $20 bill

PREPARATION: Blow out an egg making a very small hole. Let it dry. Stuff the egg with the $20 bill. Make the hole as small as you can so when you hold the egg you can cover the hole. Get a piece of cardboard the same size as the candy, and make it look like a real candy bar.

I brought an egg and a super-size candy bar. If you had to choose one of these, which one would you choose? Raise your hand if you would choose the egg? (*Most will probably not choose this.*) Raise your hand if you would choose the super-size candy bar. (*Most will probably choose this one, but be prepared that some child might choose the egg. Then base your next words on the fact that most children chose the candy bar.*)

Most (*or all*) of you chose the candy bar. It would really be good to eat. Let's open it and see if it looks good. (*Open the bar to find the cardboard.*) That doesn't look like chocolate, does it? Let's check out the egg. (*Crack the egg to find the $20 bill.*) Would you have guessed there would be a $20 bill in the egg?

Sometimes things look one way on the outside but are different on the inside. In the Old Testament (*open the Bible*), Samuel learned this. God told him to go and anoint a person to be King of Israel. He went to see Jesse's sons, and Samuel thought the one who was the oldest and strongest would be the one God would choose, but he was wrong. God told him, *The Lord doesn't make decisions the way you do! People judge by outward appearance, but the Lord looks at a person's thoughts and intentions.* Samuel found out that God had chosen David, the shepherd, to be the King of Israel, because David loved God. That is not something you can see when you just look at someone. It comes more from looking at what a person does and says.

Don't look at the way someone looks or dresses, but look at their actions. Our actions tell about who we are. We need to make sure our actions show our love for God.—Marcia Thompson

❧ WORSHIP AIDS ❧

Call to Worship: Our Lord's words declare the spirit in which we gather: "The hour comes, and now is, when the true worshippers shall worship the Father in spirit and in truth: for the Father seeks such to worship him" (John 4:23).

Invocation: Father of life and light, you declare that you do love us all, that you forgive our sins, and that you welcome us into your presence. Grant that today we may admit our human plight, our sin and inadequacies, and reach out to you for mercy and strength. Amen.

Offertory Sentence: "Seek first the Kingdom of God, and his righteousness, and all these things shall be added unto you" (Matt. 6:33).

Offertory Prayer: Lord God, take what we share this day and multiply it by the Holy Spirit to do great deeds, the worth of which only heaven can fully measure. Amen.—E. Lee Phillips

Morning Prayer: God, you are present in each one of us, and your Spirit sweeps around us, and yet we are so uncertain where to find you. We can sense your face in the red and purple evening skies and the glow of the crescent moon. Yet somehow, God, we can feel so alone. We struggle to find you, understand you, and listen to you.

We thank you for the support of our families, for the love and joy they bring to us. Help us to find strength in each other and ourselves, so we all may overcome adversity and be the best we can be. We ask you for understanding and forgiveness. Help us to listen to each other, despite our differences.

We pray, God, for those who are struggling, whether it is through sickness, loneliness, or sadness. May they hear our prayers and find the strength to go on and find a glimpse of the light at the end of the tunnel. Let us also keep in our prayers those who are distraught inside and covering their pain with a smiling face and a confident aura. Let us remember to always be good to all people.

We pray for peace, for health, for happiness, for understanding, for knowledge, and most important, for love. So we may be held together in this world of uncertainty, stay with each of us, God. Keep us humble and ever grateful. Amen.—Eliza O'Neil

Benediction: People of God, go out today fully assured that life lived according to the high priorities of faith matters forever. Guided by the Faithful One—Father, Son, and Holy Spirit—live this week in confidence—and power. Amen.

SUNDAY, MARCH 9, 2008
Fifth Sunday in Lent

LECTIONARY SERMON TOPIC: "Two Choices for Life"

TEXT: Rom. 8:6–11

OTHER READINGS: Ezek. 37:1–14; Ps. 130; John 11:1–45

A sea change had occurred in his life. The plates had suddenly moved under Paul's religious world, and he would never be the same. Jesus had broken into his neat, legalistic world unexpectedly, like an intruder, but really we shouldn't be surprised; the divine never appears to be a part of ordinary reality. Rudolph Otto's "totally other" would become the passion of Paul's life and epistles. This is the point he keeps hoping to make as he contrasts "living in the flesh" with "living the Spirit." Mere words, singly or in combination, or aroused from sleeping beds of rhyme have difficulty carrying the weight of this life-altering difference, but Paul sums it up in two deafening words: *death* and *life*. There are two choices for your life, just two: you can set your watch by the town clock, or you can live with a sense that life is always decisive. It's the "broad way" or "the narrow way"; it's the "wide gate" or the "straight gate."

I. **The prominence of the word *flesh* in Paul's letters is likely because it is a synonym for one's orientation to this physical world.** And this has different facets, as we will see. It stands for a kind of elemental existence, where the assumptions of culture are thought to be guides for living without much, if any, examination. Every culture has its own body of officially accredited wisdom—the beliefs and values that most people take for granted as self-evidently true. There are institutions and functionaries whose work is to perpetuate these evident truths. As my friend Carlyle Marney would express it: "The temple is always downtown." This to Paul was the "wisdom of the world." Many, at least vicariously, partake of this "wisdom."

Since *flesh* is used in our text to illustrate the narrow boundaries of a life that is confined to the limits of this world, it can be said that such a person remains like an animal for life, and that is the plane of her or his existence. This person lives in oblivion to anything but bodily functions and procreation and perhaps an ambition that issues into greed or dereliction. Such is the embodiment of the "wisdom of the world." Such people live with a doubt that help is available from beyond the human faculties. In this state life usually evolves downward and dangerously.

Among the corrosive effects of being oriented toward the material world was the conception that one's relationship to God was brought about by something someone did. The negative nabobs, if I may borrow that term, who dogged Paul's steps through his epistles insisted that circumcision not only enhanced one's Christian belief but was actually efficacious. Talk about something being of the flesh, for the flesh, and by the flesh—circumcision for Paul became the equivalent of "flesh" in all efforts to rectify one's relation to the Lord. A primacy was placed on physical birth, and John the Baptist warned those who came to his baptism not to depend on the fact that they were descendants of Abraham. It seems that in Paul's writing, if the want-to-be Christian resorted to circumcision, he disqualified himself for the atonement of Christ (Gal. 5:3–4). I doubt it is taking liberties to wonder if anything else done by human agency—any ritual or ceremony—that is made a mandatory addition to what Christ has done could be put in the same category with circumcision.

Living in the flesh, or secularism, where salvation is concerned produces a "do-it-yourself" attitude and impudent feeling of adequacy with regard to religion. For example, when the crowd finally caught up with Jesus (sixth chapter of John), they wanted to know what they could do "that they might work the works of God." Jesus replied, "This is the work (the whole nine yards of revelation) of God, that you believe on him who he has sent" (v. 29). What accounts for the urge to add to the gospel other than the insufferable egotism imbibed from the secular world? I have come to the conclusion that living in his Word, we can hardly stand openness and the uncertainty of promise, so we are inclined toward our own, seemingly "guaranteed," agendas. Likely, a great many of us are disquieted by Paul's certainty that the end result of living according to the flesh would be death.

II. **The change in Paul's life occurred when "the law of the Spirit of life in Christ Jesus had made him free from the law of sin and death."** When this happens to him and to all others, there is no condemnation. Surely, he wanted us to know that the antithesis of "flesh" was "Spirit."

What is "living in the Spirit"? As you know well, there are multitudes of opinions and concepts. In addition, in a material-spiritual universe there is the risk that "Spirit" may drown in "stuff." Nearly every denomination of Christians represents a particular view of how one's relation to the Almighty is rectified. Many who sit in the pews of our churches do not know the biblical basis on which one can claim to be Christian. When asked if one is saved, a variety of answers come back: "I am not sure" or "I try to be"—all betraying uncertainty about what makes one a Christian. There is an indefatigable idea that one's daily behavior is a deciding component in the experience of conversion. Years ago I visited in a Sunday school class, where the teacher said, "God forgives your sins up to the moment you confess your faith, but from there on it's up to you to keep saved." Bizarre? It's more surprising how many subscribe to that thinking. To prove that point, I was in a large church in the South recently, and the preacher's topic was baptism. In his sermon he said, "When you are baptized, God gives you an A. Then it's up to you what grade you have at the end of the way." Really? What grade is required? Jesus saved me because I couldn't make the grade (Rom. 8:3)!

Lest you think that lifestyle is unimportant to me in the Christian experience, let me disabuse you of that notion. Paul wrote to the Ephesians that after "being born from above" (his words are "renewed in your mind"), there is a lifetime of "putting off the old person and putting on the new person which after God is created in righteousness and true holiness" (Eph. 4:24). We are never finished with that here. Early on I learned that the fruit doesn't create the tree; it's the other way around.

III. **Life in the Spirit by Christ Jesus references, among other things, that your life is unfolding in a spiritual realm.** Those who accept Christ as Savior enter God's family and are transformed in such a way that the world is no longer their home.

In the church I attend, the offertory prayer is led by a layperson, and it seems the prayer is always well spoken. But how often I wish I could hear that a purpose of the offering was for more than paying the utility bill or some amorphous reference to preaching the gospel around the world. Sometime I would like to hear it said that the congregation, at that moment especially, is before the judgment seat as to whether one believes in a world beyond this one. Jesus spoke of "laying up treasure in heaven." The writer of Hebrews talks to us about "tasting of the heavenly gift" (Heb. 6:4). Even though the Church possesses ultimate truths to be found nowhere else, it troubles me that in our worship there is little cognizance that we are dealing with something from another world.

"Living according to the flesh" creates a mentality that is unaware of the condemnation that has already set in. So in his mercy, God sends his Holy Spirit to overcome this insulation and to awaken a sense of lostness and need. As a barefoot boy of nine years, I wandered under the tent of an evangelistic meeting in our town and, listening with an attention that surprised me, I left that place feeling condemned for the first time. So, for me, God began to "make foolish the wisdom of the world" (1 Cor. 1:20).

From the biblical viewpoint, becoming a Christian is truly a cataclysm of change where one's relationship to God has been dramatically altered so that one begins to live in a new realm. As I was growing up, I was familiar with an old gospel song that began with, "There is a land that is fairer than day, and by faith I can see it afar." How true! But also how lamentable! Why defer that realm to some indefinite time beyond history? Why not celebrate now your freedom in Christ Jesus from all condemnation? Why not live empowered by the Spirit in that "land that is fairer than day" here and now?—John C. Huffman

---

ILLUSTRATIONS

Human Nature. In an unpublished sermon, Carlyle Marney describes the unredeemed potential and most likely direction of this earth-borne creature who seeks coherence and meaning by organizing life around some temporal object:

> The most dangerous animal is not the lion, nor the tiger, nor the elephant. The
> most dangerous animal is man. His bite is poisonous, his hand is a club and his

foot is a weapon. His brain that triples in size the first six months of life is a literal storehouse for pain making. His legality opens the door to illegality. His ability to reason between this and that gives him the ability to conspire and murder and wage war. The most dangerous animal is man.

And Marney concluded that all the world's great civilizers have failed to move this human spirit toward wholeness. I would add that such a human is the classic and ultimate example of "flesh" and nothing but! Everything is visceral, and only that is real which can be seen.—John C. Huffman

Transcendence. In his book, *A Far Glory*, Peter Berger, a sociologist of Boston University, laments the absence of transcendence in our contemporary worship. He says, "If an individual wants to pretend to certitude that he does not possess, he badly needs an authority to validate his vulnerable posture. . . . Very often the object of faith shifts from the transcendent to the authority that purports to represent it."[1] It is far more acceptable to "worldly wisdom" to substitute authority for the element of "transcendence" in our worship. Does that have the ring of familiarity?—John C. Huffman

Musical Selections Appropriate to the Day

Hymn suggestions for lectionary texts:

Ezek. 37:1–14	*Breathe on Me, Breath of God*
Ps. 130	*Out of the Depths; Rain Down*
Rom. 8:6–11	*God Is Here; Sweet, Sweet Spirit*
John 11:1–45	*I Am the Bread of Life; O for a Thousand Tongues to Sing*

---

[1]Peter Berger, *A Far Glory* (New York: Anchor, 1992), p. 137.

🐟 Children's Lectionary Sermon

TITLE: Fearing God

SCRIPTURE: Ps. 130

KEY VERSE: *But you offer forgiveness, that we might learn to fear you.* (Ps. 130:4, New Living Translation)

KEY CONCEPT: Meaning of fear of God

MATERIALS: Bible, night light

(*Show the night light.*) I brought this night light today. It belongs to my youngest son, who is afraid when it gets really dark. Just a little light helps him to go to sleep. His fear of the dark makes it hard for him to go to sleep without it.

What do you think the word *fear* means? (*Let the children answer. If you have older children, they will probably think of words such as* afraid *or* scared. *Restate what they say about fear and then continue.*) If we think fear is to be afraid or scared of something, can you name things you are afraid of? (*Readily accept the answers the children give to this question.*) We are all afraid of different things.

Did you know that in the Bible, the word *fear* has a different meaning? (*Open Bible.*) In Psalm 130:4, it says, "But you offer forgiveness, that we might learn to fear you." This verse tells us how God forgives us—not so we will be afraid or scared of God but so we will honor and respect God and God's power. So when we read Scripture that speaks of fearing God, it doesn't mean we are to be afraid or scared; rather, we are to honor and respect God and God's power.

So when you read or hear the phrase, "the fear of the Lord" or "fear" used with God's name, remember this means honor, awe, and respect.—Marcia Thompson

🐟 WORSHIP AIDS 🐟

Call to Worship: During Lent, we are called to repentance and renewal of faith. Hear God's call from the prophet Joel: "Rend your heart, and not your garments, and return to the Lord your God: for he is gracious and merciful, slow to anger, and of great kindness" (Joel 2:13).

Invocation: Father, during these holy days of Lent, encourage within us such spiritual insight that the life and labor of our Lord Jesus will be remembered— not, Lord, as something from long ago, buried in history, but living and vital among us now. Stir within our hearts the same Spirit who in Christ showed us the glory of your love and who, on Calvary's Cross, declared it forever. Amen.

Offertory Sentence: "To whom much is given, much shall be required. And to whom men have committed much, of him they shall ask the more" (Luke 12:48).

Offertory Prayer: Father, we are thankful that in our day many have truly been given much. Your bounty has been great toward us. Yet often we are untrusting stewards of that bounty. Increase our faith, remove from us the fears of calamity, open our hearts that they may be springs of life-giving refreshment. And may we discover the joy of giving. Amen.

Morning Prayer: To the Creator God, who gave us a world that in this season is beautiful beyond all words, we join our voices in thanks and praise: for fertile fields, spring rains, new life, and old memories; for work that fulfills, time that renews, and people who care; for the freedom to pray together here in this sanctuary, for the sense of community we find here, and for the ideals we profess here in word, deed, and song. We join in giving thanks for all of these things and ask that we may never take any of them for granted. Remind us that from those to whom much is given, much is expected. Forgive us for those moments when we betray the best that is in us, whether with a kind word left unspoken, an angry outburst we wish we could take back, or a lack of generosity toward someone in need.

Grant to all of us the desire and determination to lead with love as often as we possibly can, to be disturbed by thoughts beyond ourselves, to stand ever and always against intolerance and prejudice, and to remember that we are not owners but only keepers of this earth.

O God, who is the poet of the world, always reaching out to touch us, may we have the confidence, the faith, and the courage to reach back and touch you, for we know that is also how we will touch all that which is best in ourselves. Amen.—Roger Paine

Benediction: We go out with the words of the psalmist declaring our way: "Glory in His holy name; let the hearts of those rejoice who seek the Lord! Seek the Lord and His strength; seek His face forevermore!" (Ps. 105:3–4). Amen.

SUNDAY, MARCH 16, 2008
Palm Sunday

LECTIONARY SERMON TOPIC: "Who Is Your Jesus?"
TEXT: Matt. 21:1–11
OTHER READINGS: Ps. 118:1–2, 19–29; Isa. 50:4–9a; Ps. 31:9–16; Phil. 2:5–11; Matt. 26:14–27:66; Matt. 27:11–54

Plaudits of people are often based on false premises. The choruses of adulation, the praise expressed in shouts and carrying the heavy accent of palm branches that met Jesus' entrance into Jerusalem rose from the throats of those deliriously happy folk who thought that they had another Moses on their hands, who would furnish them lots of bread, or some other miracle worker who would surely defy death. If something bad happened to him in this hostile place it wouldn't really be so bad. If he died, he wouldn't die like you and me. He would pull rank on death. So many of us on this Palm Sunday want to bootleg Resurrection into this picture to sustain the celebration a while longer.

It is regrettable that some modern worldview is always becoming the yardstick by which Jesus' identity is measured. As in the picture of the triumphal entry, Christ, and now his Church, is being constantly submitted to the judgment of the culture rather than the other way around. Is this acceptable? This quandary gave Harvey Cox a market to write about the Church being the captive of the culture. Of course, opinions differ about Wordsworth's "world being too much with us late and soon." My evaluation is based on the following premises:

I. **The Church should not partake of the culture.** Jesus prayed for his followers to be in the world but to be kept from evil (John 17:14–15). If the action of the crowd on Palm Sunday leaves you at a loss and more than a little confused, then the effects of the miasma of culture described by the Scripture referred to here would seem conclusive. When I apologized to my doctor for calling him at home, he responded by saying, "This is what I do"; similarly, I maintain that this is what culture does. It takes little imagination to know that it distorts the picture. Yet despite the probable danger that lurks, the culture has a powerful fascination and gravitational pull for those who feel they must be "with it."

Writing in the *U.S. News and World Report* a few years back, John Leo, an editor, wrote that a soccer coach had been forbidden to refer to non-starting players as "subs" because that term was hierarchical and demeaning to those who sat on the bench. Political correctness is a form of cultural captivity. This week a new presiding bishop was elected for the Episcopal Church, with the assurance that the bishop would abide by the cultural totems of being inclusive and inoffensive. The Bible be hanged!

Our Roman Catholic friends have put an Italian word into our religious vocabularies with their word *aggiornamento,* which means to bring the Church up-to-date. Isn't this the voice you hear on every hand? Those who have devoted themselves to the high calling of being critical cutworms claim the Bible is woefully out of date, that it is a patriarchate in nature. I suppose those people think it needs to be rewritten. We have an incurable itch to make Christianity relevant. The good news of the gospel is that it is already relevant! Just preach it.

II. **The Church in tension with culture is in its native habitat. Therefore, the Church should not forsake the culture.** There is little doubt that culture (the carnal mind) is a powerful contagion that by its very definition would vitiate the gospel if it is allowed. However, I am suggesting that there is a middle ground between the "liberal" or "progressive" surrender to the age and the fundamentalist denial of it. I think the Church should allow modernity to yield true pictures of the human condition, for it seems the Church has permitted culture to mitigate the gravity of the human predicament.

Our social context is surprisingly similar to the situation of the early Christians. In the face of a Corinthian culture that was suffocating in the odors of their own flesh, Paul, not the least bit intimidated by "a common grayness that silvers everything," said, "Your faith should not stand in the wisdom of men, but in the power of God" (1 Cor. 2:5). Without foolhardiness, and certainly I would hope without arrogance, I join the many who think the gospel should engage the culture. In fact, we will engage or seek to escape it.

And escape the anxiety created by a raucous culture that is so sure of itself, we can. It is precisely those churches that are so sure about everything, that exude certainty from every pore, that enforce strict doctrines and make demands on behavior, offering a false certainty—those churches are building larger buildings to house those who flock to them. And to understand this requires no white light of omniscience, for the uncertainties generated by the prevailing culture become burdensome; the relief is quite intense if we can find it in ourselves to surrender to this or that "orthodox group" and acquiesce into their lump. On the opposite end of the escape continuum are those who glibly believe that religious affirmations are nothing more than subjective exclamations. There is no problem for those with this mind-set.

III. **Our culture needs and perhaps unconsciously longs for a fresh vision of full manhood, which Jesus demonstrated.** Without going over to humanism that runs out at the edge of death, it seems that sensual, sensate culture that depends only on the senses for perceiving reality would be open to this out-of-the-ordinary manhood. Jesus did such extraordinary things that the people questioned his identity by asking, "Is this not the carpenter's son?" It will be helpful if we remember that he was fully God, yet he was a man and, as such, he was showing our unrealized potential, though never to his extent. Because he lived here as a man, I know I can do better! Many times I have failed to assess the contagions of this to infect culture for the better.

But wait! How do we come into this kind of full manhood? How is it possible for our manhood to be redemptive? Do we blow on our hands and then, with some prodigious effort, convince society that this is the way? No. We must hear again Jesus' question: "Who do you say that I am?" The middle ground that I believe exists is an answer to the questions that people still are asking about Jesus: "Who is this?" I could wish with all my heart the crowd had known that fateful day we call Palm Sunday.

The center around which we organize our lives tells who we think he is. Could it be that things are as they are because we have said who we think he is and our answer has been less than he is? Jesus gets to be known by who we say he is. Who is he to you?—John C. Huffman

ILLUSTRATIONS

Church and Culture. In his book, *A Far Glory,* Peter Berger developed an interesting insight for the problems afflicting the Corinthian Church. Although none of the students of this passage venture what the heresies were, according to Berger, the folk in the church there were troubled by the discrepancy between what they believed about the gospel and the assumptions that operated in the world. I'm encouraged that they at least recognized that an antithesis existed. The apostle said they wanted to relieve some of the starkness of the gospel and make it less a "folly." The "wisdom of the world," with its self-assurance, must have been giving the church the business!—John C. Huffman

Docetism. In his Perkins Lectures, Carlyle Marney makes the point that we are liable to become Docetists in our view of Christ's identity because for so many years we have emphasized his divinity. Doceticism believes that Jesus did not partake of humanity but "that he passed through Mary's womb like water through a tube." So the fact of Jesus' manhood has been diminished for us. And with that conception of manhood has gone the glorious potential of it.—John C. Huffman

Musical Selections Appropriate to the Day

Hymn suggestions for lectionary texts:

Liturgy of the Palms:

Matt. 21:1–11	*Hosanna, Loud Hosanna*
Ps. 118:1–2, 19–29	*This Is the Day*

Liturgy of the Passion:

Isa. 50:4–9a	*O Sacred Head, Now Wounded*
Ps. 31:9–16	*God of the Ages*
Phil. 2:5–11	*All Hail the Power of Jesus' Name*
Matt. 26:14–27:66	*Hallelujah, What a Savior* [or]
Matt. 27:11–54	*Were You There When They Crucified My Lord?*

◈ Children's Lectionary Sermon

TITLE: Palm Sunday Praise

SCRIPTURE: Matt. 21:1–11

KEY VERSE: *Praise God for the Son of David! Bless the one who comes in the name of the Lord! Praise God in highest heaven!* (Matt. 21:9b, New Living Translation)

KEY CONCEPT: Palm Sunday

MATERIALS: Bible, palms, cloaks for the floor, verse written out on a piece of poster board, costume for an adult

PREPARATION: Enlist an adult to do the following monologue, acting as Jesus on Palm Sunday.

Today, we are celebrating Palm Sunday. I brought some cloaks and palm branches for you to help us reenact Palm Sunday. I want to teach you what you need to say as Jesus comes to Jerusalem. It is from Matthew 21:9 (*open Bible and begin reading*). "Praise God for the Son of David! Bless the one who comes in the name of the Lord! Praise God in highest heaven!" (*Hold up the poster board with the verse for those who can read. Explain to the children that they will line up; place the cloaks down on the floor on the aisle; they are to say the verse as Jesus makes his way down the aisle and follow him.*)

(*Recite this monologue*): As I came toward Jerusalem with my disciples, I asked a couple of them to go ahead and get a donkey and a colt that I knew were up at the village. I told them if anyone asked them about taking the animals to say that the Lord needed them. My disciples did as I asked them and threw their cloaks over the colt and I sat on it. As we continued down the road, people gathered on the side, and they said (*children say the verse and follow him down the aisle*). We made our way to Jerusalem, and I could hear people saying, "Who is this?" and the people following said, "It's Jesus, the prophet from Nazareth in Galilee."—Marcia Thompson

◈ WORSHIP AIDS ◈

Call to Worship: On this holy day, we enter worship to declare our fealty. What does God seek from us? "The sacrifices of God are a broken spirit: a broken and contrite heart, O God, you will not despise" (Ps. 51:17).

Invocation: Lord, let us this day lay down every encumbrance that holds us back from the worship of our Savior, that with palms of delight and shouts of hosanna we proclaim the King of the Jews, Lord of our hearts. Amen.—E. Lee Phillips

Offertory Sentence: "It is required of stewards, that we be found faithful" (1 Cor. 4:2).

Offertory Prayer: Kind Father in heaven, grant that we may lay our offerings joyfully before you and not with reservations or doubt. Help us to remember your gift to us, O Lord, that which came in Christ Jesus, the Lord. May any reluctance in giving perish as we recall the magnitude of your loving sacrifice for our salvation. Amen.

Morning Prayer: O God, whose presence is Light, hear the praise of your people. For we who have known the darkness of despair find it difficult to adjust to the Light of Promise. Teach us to sing before we see and to hope before we are healed. We are thankful that hope is not rooted in statistics, win-loss records, performance ratings, or bank statements. Thankful are we that in the midst of hopelessness, even the hopelessness of Gethsemane and the cross, Christ says to us: "I have overcome the world."

O Lord, deliver us from the convictions that we have been overcome by the conditions of this present age. Be with those in this congregation who know the pangs of separation. May your presence be light and hope to those we love who are in nursing homes, hospitals, and jails, and help us not to forget those who find themselves without loved ones. Renew our ministries, O Lord, to the orphan, the widow, and the poor. Enable us to seek justice for the nameless, as well as for friend or relative. We pray especially for our government. May truth win the day and your justice and mercy go beyond party spirit and narrow nationalism. We pray in the name of Jesus. Amen.—Gary Stratman

Benediction: As we go out into the week we call holy, may we so live that our words, and our deeds, will proclaim hallelujah and hosanna to the King! May the splendor of our calling be matched by the fervor of our living. May God forever be praised! Amen.

SUNDAY, MARCH 23, 2008
Easter Sunday

LECTIONARY SERMON TOPIC: "The Outcome That Overcomes"
TEXT: Matt. 28:1–10
OTHER READINGS: Acts 10:34–43; Ps. 118:1–2, 14–24; Col. 3:1–4; John 20:1–18

This generation is impatient before mystery, but we grasp the obvious fairly quickly. Reality for most consists of what can be experienced with the senses. The transcendent is a little spooky for us, so we don't hear much about it in our churches. We seem to be more comfortable with exploring the mental health of Mary Magdalene. When Saul sets out for Damascus, he was a perfect example of just such impatience. He was armed with names and places, and he intended to put an end to this nonsense about Resurrection. Yet while he was "breathing out threatening and slaughter," a light from heaven shone around him, and the voice of Jesus said to him, "Saul why do you persecute me?"

There are times when my morale ebbs. When that happens, I go back to Saul's experience and ask myself some questions: How can one account for the change that came over Saul that transformed his life into one obsessed with his mission and into an unbending and endlessly aggressive preacher of the gospel that he once ridiculed? Why was he willing to face the same persecution that he once meted out and death at the hands of the Romans, unless he had been confronted by the Risen Christ?

I. **In the ministry of Jesus, sin is the prime enemy to be overcome.** The call of Jesus and John the Baptist for repentance is not a summons to a better behavior; it is a summons for an acknowledgment of Jesus as God's Son, the Messiah, and the Savior of the world—even of oneself. First there is the tree, then the fruit. Those who reverse this sequence live to regret it.

Paul S. Fiddes in his breakout book, *Past Event and Present Salvation*,[2] defines *sin* as the refusal to trust in the resources that are offered from beyond ourselves. We ignore a righteousness that is provided for us as an unconditional gift through faith in Jesus Christ as Savior (Rom. 3:20) and turn to our own solutions by making some object or person in this world our absolute security. This is the perpetual lure of idolatry.

The apostle Paul says to the Roman Church that there is a righteousness of God (standing in right relationship) that is made known without any commandment for doing this or that; it is God's righteousness (a rectified relationship) that is freely given to the believer, simply because such a one puts entire dependence in Christ for salvation. The gospel waxes soundly our impudent feelings of spiritual adequacy! Could this be the "straight gate" Jesus spoke about being hard to find?

I hear what you are saying. "If I believed that, I would go out and rob, kill, and commit all the atrocious acts that I wanted." Well, an African American preacher with his linguistic skills intact said, "Grace works on the wanter." These antinomians came against Paul's preaching of grace, but his conclusion was "that if by grace, it is no more of works, if by works it is no more by grace" (Rom. 11:6). You can't have a little of both!

II. **The Resurrection that declared "Jesus to be the Son of God with power" (Rom. 1:4) has delivered us from the bondage of the fear of death (Heb. 2:15).** The writer does not imply, I think, that we are so paranoid that we think about dying all the time. But I remember that Richard Lovelace sang, "Stone walls do not a prison make, nor iron bars a cage."

Thus servitude takes many different forms and shapes, and some of those formations are so subtle that they guide our actions before we know it. Even though the fear of dying does not haunt our days and nights, it can plunge its victims into a bondage that is so commonplace that it begins to say who we are. Someone has said that "death has taken over from sex as the taboo subject of the day."

---

[2]Paul S. Fiddes, *Past Event and Present Salvation* (Louisville, KY: Westminster John Knox Press, 1989), pp. 4–5.

The Christian believer does not have to fear death. In the Resurrection of Jesus, God did an incredibly new thing. Death is the transition to something entirely new; it is not a continuation of life here. Yet the dread is pardonable because, for some of us, the different, the new, can be frightening. Some years ago, Dr. Ernest Ligon, the director of a child research project in Schenectady, New York, spoke to us about the methodology of learning and said that life is made up of many rooms. After living and learning in one room for a time, we are reluctant to leave "our comfort zone," but finally we do, to discover that the new room we enter is larger and better than the one we hesitated to leave, and so on it goes. For the believer, some reluctance to leave the earth-room where "the devils we know are preferred to those we don't know," where ties to loved ones bind us, is understandable, but the final exit here will lead to another room graciously prepared by the One who said, "In my father's house are many rooms" (John 14:2), and, to our amazement, among all the rooms of experience this is the best room of all! The Resurrection of Jesus Christ not only assures our resurrection, it delivers us from slavery to the fear of dying.

III. **The Resurrection pledges the power of future salvation in the present:** "If you will confess with your mouth the Lord Jesus and believe in your heart that God has raised him from the dead, you will be saved" (Rom. 10:9). Not only saved eternally—sometime in the distant future, somewhere beyond history, at the end of time—but saved with eternal life now! Being raised in baptism that pictures the Resurrection, we are to walk (live) here each day in the newness of life (Rom. 6:4); to me, this means claiming the promise of that which is not yet for that which already is.

Am I too harsh in saying that the Christian faith has all but banished from its life the mobilizing, revolutionizing, and critical effects of this future hope that is its very essence to some far-off shadowy, nebulous "sweet forever"? The dynamic of the future hope, transported back from "the end of time" and applied to his daily life in the here and now, helped Paul to exclaim, "We are more than conquerors" in all these "things" (Rom. 8:37).

I have been helped in this by Jurgen Moltmann's *Theology of Hope*,[3] where he laments relegating the stimulating dynamics of the end of time

---

[3]Jurgen Moltmann, *Theology of Hope* (New York: HarperCollins, 1967).

to some date beyond history that robs us of its creative power to change things as they are now, especially in light of biblical testimonies that emphasize that this future hope of ultimate triumph is brought back to energize the present.

Let the word go forth: "He is not here, he is risen and if you be risen with him, then seek those things which are above where Christ sits on the right hand of God" (Col. 3:1). He is our refuge and our present help! "Don't you hear those bells now ringing, don't your hear the angels singing?" Yes, but don't relegate the power of that victory to energize your life now to some "far-off sweet forever"! When we can comprehend that "the worse things are not the last things" and that crystallizes into hope, it will have a transforming effect of the present. This is the outcome that overcomes! Lift up your hearts!—John C. Huffman

ILLUSTRATIONS

Easter Power. The Lord's Church began with a few uneducated fisherman and tax gatherers, but it swept across the known world in the next three centuries. This peaceful revolution is unparalleled in history. It happened as believers said boldly to inquirers: "Jesus is alive. He surely died for you but he is alive! Meet him and discover for yourself the living Christ." They did. And the Church, birthed at the Easter grave, spread everywhere.—Lee McGlone

Discipleship. One of the most moving scenes of my life has been to watch the streams of persons moving to the platform in the Billy Graham meetings to confess Christ as Savior. But I wonder how many have done this before and how many will do it again and again. When a person "confesses with the mouth the Lord Jesus and believes with one's heart that God has raised him from the dead," that person is saved. "For with the heart man believes unto righteousness and with the mouth confession is made for salvation" (Rom. 10:9–10). All one can ever do for salvation is receive it, but what one does with salvation is another matter for a lifetime (Eph. 4:22).—John C. Huffman

Musical Selections Appropriate to the Day

Hymn suggestions for lectionary texts:

Acts 10:34–43	*There's a Wideness in God's Mercy*
Ps. 118:1–2, 14–24	*He Has Made Me Glad*
Col. 3:1–4	*Rejoice the Lord Is King*
John 20:1–18	*Christ the Lord Is Risen Today* [or]
Matt. 28:1–10	*He Lives*

✎ Children's Lectionary Sermon

TITLE: He Is Risen

SCRIPTURE: John 20:1–18

KEY VERSE: *Mary Magdalene found the disciples and told them, "I have seen the Lord!"* (John 20:18a, New Living Translation)

KEY CONCEPT: Resurrection, Easter

MATERIALS: Bible

Today is a special day for all Christians everywhere. It is Easter Sunday, when we celebrate Jesus' Resurrection. Three days after Jesus died, he rose from the dead, and now he lives.

Have you ever wondered what it would have been like to be there on the first Easter? (*Open Bible.*) The disciples of Jesus must have been sad because Jesus had died. They weren't sure what to do. Mary Magdalene was one of Jesus' friends. She went to the tomb early in the morning while it was still dark. When she got to the tomb, the big stone had been rolled away. She ran back and told two of the disciples. Can you imagine her, out of breath, saying, "They have taken the Lord's body out of the tomb, and I don't know where they have put him!" (*Be dramatic in your reading of the quotes.*)

Peter and the other disciple ran to the tomb. Peter went into the tomb and found the linens that had been wrapped around the body. The other disciple came in, too, and saw that Jesus was gone. What do you think they thought about this? The book of John says, "Then the other disciple also went in, and believed—for until then they hadn't realized that the Scriptures said he would rise from the dead."

The two disciples went home, but Mary stuck around. She was very upset and she was crying. Then she saw two angels, and they asked her why she was crying. She was worried someone had taken Jesus away. Then she saw another person behind her. At first she didn't recognize him, but it was Jesus. *Mary Magdalene found the disciples and told them, "I have seen the Lord!"*

We can be thankful today, because Jesus is alive! We can say it together: "Jesus is alive!" (*Repeat and let the children say it with you.*)—Marcia Thompson

WORSHIP AIDS

Call to Worship: We gather today in joy and celebration! Along with the angels, we declare, "You seek Jesus of Nazareth who was crucified; he is risen. The Lord is risen indeed" (Mark 16:6; Luke 24:34).

Invocation: O Lord of our Risen and victorious Savior, rise up in every seeking soul, in every needy heart, that the love of God may save and edify and reign supreme. Amen.—E. Lee Phillips

Offertory Sentence: "Jesus sat over against the treasury, and beheld how the people cast money into the treasury" (Mark 12:41).

Offertory Prayer: We rejoice on this day that you take death and make from it life. You take the darkness of Good Friday and make from it the brightness of Easter. In your power, the desert rejoices and blossoms like a rose. We lay before you our offerings and pray that you will multiply them for the cause of your Kingdom, like the loaves and fishes that fed the multitude. Amen.

Morning Prayer: Father, before whom graves open, the dead are raised, and the wicked confounded, break the glow of Easter across our brows

and shine the Resurrection light into our lives that we may rejoice in
newness of life and sing the songs of praise and thanksgiving due
your name. In Resurrection you have called forth forever light out
of sinful darkness and given us Easter Sunday, replete with the shimmer of
eternal life.

Father, only you can create emptiness to proclaim fullness. Only you
can take an empty cross and, through it, forever proclaim pardon and
forgiveness. Only you can, through an empty tomb, proclaim complete
salvation and powerful, eternal life. Only you can take our empty lives
and make them whole and complete in Christ Jesus.

As we come to celebrate this sacred day, we come like those followers
of the Lord who first encountered the Resurrection. We come with
longings like theirs. With them, we gather behind the locked doors of our
fears and doubts. We hide behind the doors of our hurts and sorrows,
our distrusts and misunderstandings. O this morning let us hear and
experience again your blessing of, "Peace be with you," as you slip into
our midst as you did so long ago. Like Peter we wait in the anguish of
betrayal, seeking forgiveness and another chance. As you sought him
out, so seek us the favor of the invitation to feed your sheep. As you
called Mary by name, call us tenderly by our names that we, too, shall
surely know that it is you. Like Thomas, we wrestle with our doubts.
Gently touch us and allow us to touch your presence. As you made confused, sad, and lonely hearts rejoice by your resurrected presence, so
make us rejoice this morning. Then as we walk our Emmaus roads, share
the journey with us and instruct us in your truths that we may be able to
look back, remembering with joy and understanding the burning within
our hearts. Then will our alleluias sound with vigor, along with those long
ago.—Henry Fields

Benediction: We have worshipped in the presence of the Resurrected
Christ. Now we go in Christ's strength that fills our lives and replenishes
our souls. May our efforts for the Kingdom bring to Christ glory and
honor, now and forever, world without end. Amen.

SUNDAY, MARCH 30, 2008

LECTIONARY SERMON TOPIC: "The Preaching Event"
TEXT: Acts 2:14a
OTHER READINGS: Acts 2:22–32; Ps. 16; 1 Pet. 1:3–9; John 20:19–31

The Sunday after Easter seems often to be a letdown. I am not suggesting that Christianity is relegated to certain periodic events, but attendance at these special events, compared with that of each Lord's Day thereafter, gives me a measure of anxiety. However, I am an enthusiastic participant in these "special" events, even if there is some risk of sending the wrong message, for I believe that a little is better than nothing. Yet the spiral of passionate enthusiasm after the incredible events of the Crucifixion and Resurrection was upward in the New Testament rather than downward toward listlessness and business-as-usual. We can learn valuable lessons from Peter's preaching.

I. **If a story is compelling enough, it will be told.** I can envision Peter unable to restrain himself any longer, literally jumping to his feet rather than merely standing up to face the blasphemous insolence of those who intimated that the new enthusiasm of the one hundred twenty persons was due to new wine. It is somewhat amusing to me that Peter's stout defense rested on the time of day! "Why it's only nine o'clock in the morning. Nobody is drunk at that time of day!" But I'm not surprised, for if I have learned anything in my considerable years, it is that God uses the weak to confound the mighty!

Peter had undergone a dramatic experience of change. The reorganization of his life was leading to something even better than when he enjoyed the personal company of Jesus. Transformed from a fearful fellow, he began preaching about the same Jesus whom he had previously said he didn't know. The compulsion that propelled Peter to his feet is likely what Paul felt after being confronted by the Risen Christ. As soon as his sight was restored, the Scriptures tell us that after spending some time with the disciples, "at once he began to preach in the synagogues that Jesus is the Son of God" (Acts 9:20). I notice here with some interest that he began where the opposition was the greatest! And also the need. In fact, the "fire that burned in his bones" was so intense that when the apostles sent Paul and Barnabas on a preaching mission, they sent along Silas, "the chair of the board," to equalize their passion. We all tend to be skeptical of people who are a little too wrought up. We don't like the organ music too loud or a preacher who hollers.

The location of the pulpit in churches may indicate the primacy and value that is placed on preaching. In the New Testament, Paul enjoins Timothy to "Preach the word!" (2 Tim. 4:2). To the Romans, who were urbane, sophisticated, and sinful, the Church would rest its case on "the foolishness of what is preached" to convert the souls. Yet in my lifetime, preaching generally has been degraded to something of an aside in the churches. The preacher is tempted to become a manager or the chief executive of the congregation, with a key to the washroom and a desk on mahogany row. Worse still, he is told by a few seminary professors that his highest calling is into counseling, where he can be titillated by listening—a kind of sanctified voyeurism. But there are encouraging signs on the horizon that churches are discovering the necessity of preaching the gospel. And alongside, there is the insight that there is a mysterious efficacy in gospel preaching.

II. **Pentecost is the prophetic result of God's willingness to prepare the tellers.** God always shows up with help to do his work, not to hand out help for our whimsical desires. So the Great-Commission-doing-kind-of-help came at Pentecost, when those present were seized, but not with a seizure; they were being possessed, not given a possession; they were not given propositions to which they had to assent but were being offered relations they accepted! It was as if they were compelled by a tsunami force. It is no wonder that when Peter stood up to preach, temerity had replaced timidity, and the preaching event was weighted with a new ability and a new urgency and a new message.

In his sermon, Peter reflected on some of the back roads of prophecy that now have become so obvious and have become the basis of a new confession. Of course, they should have recognized at the time that the miracles and wonder and signs were so scandalously out-of-this-world that only the Messiah could do them. But they were sure that the Messiah would be a kind of Mosaic prophet, who would give them bread, or some kingdom builder who would break the shackles of Rome; in this preoccupation they missed the main event. For us, like them, often the good is the enemy of the best.

III. **We cannot afford to dismiss a sense of the transcendent in our preaching.** It is not done with main strength and awkwardness, although I have tried that a lot of times. In the Corinthian correspondence, Paul counterposed "the wisdom of the world" with the gospel and found that the gospel was "foolishness" to the pluralistic culture. There was an alien quality about the "word of the cross" that went over their heads, yet in that "foolishness," the worldly must have sensed something of the disturbingly extraordinary rather than the ordinary, hence their aggressive efforts toward oppression.

Students of the Corinthian correspondence are reticent about what heresies had divided the different camps, and the Bible doesn't tell us. However, could it have been that they were attempting to make the gospel more compatible with the "worldly wisdom"—the standard by which the gospel was being judged? In your church, is the wisdom of the world the yardstick by which any proposition about reality is assessed? By doing so, we, like the Corinthians, are reducing the spiritual qualities of the gospel to bring it more in line with the assumptions that operate in conventional wisdom. It is imperative that we recover the conviction that the gospel is not of this world! Unless we do, the Church not only loses its redemptive power; if this "folly" is surrendered, the Church loses its reason for being.

In the preaching event, the divine sovereignty that has drawn near becomes a live issue in Christ's gracious communion with publicans and sinners—all who need the gospel. Preaching is not handing on something to be preserved, but it is an event that summons the dead and godless to life.—John C. Huffman

---

ILLUSTRATIONS

Celebration. To begin his sermon on the Sunday after Easter, Ernest Campbell of Riverside Church in New York looked around and asked: "Where are the trumpets?" You couldn't miss his point. They'd had a week of it—the pageantry, the once-a-year celebration of death and Resurrection, the trumpets and great choir that raised goose bumps. But now, thanks be to God, it was over. They could go back to Wall Street and Dow Jones averages. How we have sullied divine realities by efforts to keep them alive!—John C. Huffman

   Preaching. Carlyle Marney once said that your church is no bigger than your Christ! If the story is compelling, we'll find a way and a place to tell it.—John C. Huffman

Musical Selections Appropriate to the Day

Hymn suggestions for lectionary texts:

Acts 2:14a, 22–32	*Christ Is Risen! Shout Hosanna*
Ps. 16	*You Are My All in All*
1 Pet. 1:3–9	*O How I Love Jesus*
John 20:19–31	*Thine Is the Glory*

🐾 Children's Lectionary Sermon

TITLE: Believe in What You Cannot See
SCRIPTURE: John 20:19–31
KEY VERSE: *Then Jesus said, "Because you have seen me, you have believed; blessed are those who have not seen and yet have believed."* (John 20:29, New International Version)
KEY CONCEPT: Belief
MATERIALS: Bible, flip chart, white chalk
PREPARATION: Place the chart in easy view of the children.

Boys and girls, have you ever written someone a message they could not read? Maybe it was a secret code. You knew what the message said, but they didn't. Today I'm going to write you a message. (*Use the chalk to write a greeting to the children.*) Now, who can read what I wrote? Anyone?

You can't because I used white chalk on white paper. You can't see the letters I wrote, but yet, you saw me writing. You believed I was writing on this flip chart, because you saw me use the chalk on the paper.

After Jesus was crucified, he rose from the tomb on the third day. He appeared several times to the disciples and friends. Thomas, one of the disciples, doubted the person who had entered the locked room was really Jesus of Nazareth. Jesus knew Thomas would need more evidence that he was really alive. Jesus asked Thomas to put his hand to his side and to see the nail marks in his hands. Thomas touched Jesus and believed.

(*Open Bible.*) "Then Jesus said, 'Because you have seen me, you have believed; blessed are those who have not seen and yet have believed.'" We believe in a God we cannot see, but we feel God's presence in our lives. We know God is real and God watches over us.—Carolyn Tomlin

✿ WORSHIP AIDS ✿

Call to Worship: Each day brings delight and opportunity. Our worship declares, "This is the day which the Lord has made; we will rejoice and be glad in it!" (Ps. 118:24).

Invocation: Father, while the high and holy experiences of recent weeks are now memories, grant that this day our joy shall be that of the Risen Christ. May we now seek the things that are above, where Christ reigns, seated at the right hand of the Father. Amen.

Offertory Sentence: "Every one shall give as he is able, according to the blessing of the Lord your God as he has given to you" (Deut. 16:17).

Offertory Prayer: Kind and gracious Father, we have asked and you have given us from the rich measure of your goodness. Now open our hearts to the partnership we share in the work of the gospel. May our giving help bring hope to the hopeless and light to the dark places on earth. Multiply these gifts and use them as you intend, that nothing should be wasted. Amen.

Morning Prayer: Father, we approach you knowing that you welcome us into your presence, and we praise you for the glorious invitation. Through the life, death, and Resurrection of Jesus, the curtain of the Temple that separated us from you was torn from top to bottom. Now, in this instant, by faith we approach you boldly, yet not arrogantly.

Lord, you have made yourself known to us through change—the changing of the seasons, the changing seasons of life, the new life that comes through faith, our salvation, and the making of us to be your people—not perfect people, but yours. In you, the tired are refreshed, the weary find new strength, the disillusioned find hope, and the dead are raised to walk in newness of life.

Give to us, O Father, eyes of faith that see visions of what may open before us in the fullness of time. Give us listening ears that we may hear the gentle, hushed tone of your still, small voice. Give us expectant hearts that we may long for the Kingdom's rule within us and around us. Give us willing spirits that we may yield ourselves to you and surrender our all today.

Father, revive us again, not alone for our sake but for the cause of your Kingdom. May the Kingdom, begun long ago, come to completion, on earth as it is in heaven. In the name of Jesus, the eternal Christ, we pray. Amen.—Lee McGlone

Benediction: By the power and the grace of Almighty God, Father, Son, and Holy Spirit, we go out today bearing the spirit of truth. Into homes and businesses and schools and neighborhoods, we carry the heart of faith, made glad by the comradeship we share with God and with one another. Go in peace. Amen.

SUNDAY, APRIL 6, 2008

LECTIONARY SERMON TOPIC: "A Walk to Remember"
TEXT: Luke 24:13–35
OTHER READINGS: Acts 2:14a, 36–41; Ps. 116:1–4, 12–19; 1 Pet. 1:17–23

Death comes to us all. Resurrection comes to all who believe. Connecting Christ's Resurrection to our own life, death, and destiny is the fulfillment of faith.

I. **Faith takes us on a journey.** It is a journey not as much of miles as one of heart and soul. In Christ, God makes bold moves that are revealed by signs that do not leave us alone. Christ's power makes average-but-willing persons into faith heroes who go with God's call to do what needs to be done. Faith heroes get involved. For us, like the Emmaus companions, where we have been and what we have done can be used by God to help people live the gospel. Gradually, the Emmaus twosome realized they were uniquely positioned by God to share with people what had just been grown in their lives. By how they followed the signs given by Jesus, they could show others the way of Resurrection.

II. **What one believes about eternity is challenged when standing by an open grave of a loved one.** We do not play games or give false platitudes at the cemetery. Is the gravesite the final resting place for a loved one whose casket is about to be lowered in the ground? Or is the grave a historical location where we recall the person's earthly life, grieve that the person will no longer walk with us on earth, then celebrate that our loved one now shares in the promise of Christ's Resurrection? Resurrection is the transforming work of God by which believers enter the space and time of heaven. At physical death, believers fulfill the baptismal promise of resurrection "buried with Christ in the tomb, and raised to walk in newness of life" (Rom. 6:4).

Easter fits the size of God at work. Touched by the power of the One who created the heavens and the earth, comes the miracle we sing: "Up from the grave He arose, a mighty triumph over His foes." With Christ's Resurrection comes our resurrection. With Christ's Resurrection comes Satan's ultimate defeat. With Christ's Resurrection is the victory of heaven over hell, love over hate, hope over despair, forgiveness over sin. Like the early believers, we are to share the joy of Easter's promise. Christ is risen. Christ is risen, indeed!

Promise means "for mission." A promise is given to prepare one for the adventure of traveling into the future. God's promises prepare us to travel into his future (1 Cor. 2:9–10). When these Emmaus disciples remembered Jesus' promise to be raised again on the third day, they realized that they were in the midst of that miracle of miracles. Looking back, they could see forward. They responded with a confidence that only comes with Easter. Emboldened, they went to tell the Eleven.

III. Doubt becomes belief. Not until Clops and the "other disciple" witnessed Jesus' presence in Emmaus, did Simon Peter's experience become clear to him. The references of Luke 24:12 and 24:34 are to the same person. Upon hearing the witness from Emmaus, Simon Peter's belief caught up with his sight. Earlier, he had been with the Resurrected Christ.

In an earlier attempt to walk through the stormy waters to Jesus (Matt. 14:26–32), Peter learned a faith-lesson that he again needed to recall. Seeing things from only his point of view meant he missed God's promise. Failure in faith stems from our only seeing circumstances from a human vantage. Succeeding means to see the same circumstances from the wider angle of God's point of view. The size of the gap between the two is the size of belief required to turn failure into success. At first, trusting God's promise may seem like a failure to others, but to God we look like what we actually are—a stunning success being shaped by his ability to calm our fears and release his greatness from within us.

While the Eleven and other gathered disciples were still talking about the Emmaus experience, "Jesus entered their conversation by standing among them and saying, 'Peace be with you.'" His words were more than a mere phrase. Throughout his ministry, Jesus spoke of the peace that believers could experience with themselves and in God. By being at peace with Christ, believers were connected to the One who could give them peace in all circumstances. "Peace be with you," was his invitation for them to be at peace with his Crucifixion so they could now experience his Resurrected presence.

Jesus asked the Eleven, as he had asked the two walking toward Emmaus, "Do doubts arise in your minds?" This Greek word for "doubt" denotes stressful reflection. Jesus called out to their troubled hearts and minds to trust that he—the Resurrected Christ whom they loved—was in their midst. To help them move beyond their doubt, Jesus appealed to their sense perceptions of sight ("look at my hands and feet" and see the marks of crucifixion), touch ("determine that I am not a ghost since a ghost does not have flesh and bones"), taste and smell ("They gave Him a piece of broiled fish which He ate in their presence"), and hearing (Jesus said, "It is I myself"). Through this demonstration, Jesus engaged each of their senses to witness the reality of his Resurrection.

IV. **Changed lives show power of Christ.** The trustworthiness of Luke's witness, as well as that of the Bible, has undergone serious review by believers and skeptics. No book has been placed under more scrutiny than the Bible. No witness from the Bible has been examined more than the life, death, and Resurrection of Jesus. The written accounts by Luke, in particular, and the Bible as a whole, have proven themselves to be true. Like a twenty-first-century Theophilus, you "may know the certainty of the things you have been taught."

Christ's Resurrection gives us the ultimate reference point to determine the direction our life is headed. On a shelf in my office rests a shotgun shell that was given to me by a man who was going to use it to kill himself. He called me shortly before midnight on Easter Eve. He agreed to meet me at my office. We talked through the events that had caused his crisis. He then let me show him how those same circumstances would look different if he trusted in Christ's Resurrection. He prayed to receive Christ. We then walked to his car and removed the shell from his shotgun.

I believe in Easter because of the truthful historical witness of Christ's Resurrection. The witness began on the first day, not months or years after it was claimed to have happened. Christ's Resurrection did not originate as a bit of wishful thinking, looking back to a supposed event. The historical witnesses gave understanding to what had already happened. I believe in the Resurrection because it deals with unbelief straight up. The male disciples only believed when they saw Christ firsthand. Two of them on the day of the Resurrection had already left Jerusalem and were walking to Emmaus—the wrong direction. They weren't believing until Jesus showed up in their midst as a historical witness to their unbelief.

I believe because I have been with believers as they died. I have seen the look of Resurrection in the eyes of those who were leaving this world. If they were able to speak, I heard it in their voices. I have seen the power of Resurrection in the transformation of people who were breathing one moment and in the next moment their bodies were declared dead. You don't play games when you are dying. Believers give witness as they pass on from this world into the arms of Jesus. I believe in Easter because seekers today, like the Emmaus companions, become believers by conscientiously following Christ as Savior and Lord. Changed lives give witness to the power of Christ.—D. Leslie Hollon

ILLUSTRATIONS

Resurrection. *Egeirein* is a Greek term for "resurrection" that emphasizes the concrete nature of Resurrection—the Risen Body of Jesus with material and spiritual features. This term stresses the physical restoration of life (Matt. 11:5, 27:53; Mark 5:42; John 11:25–26; Acts 9:40).

Though filled with joy and amazement, most of the disciples did not believe until Jesus connected his earlier teachings to what they were experiencing. Through this, "He opened their minds so they could understand" the Law of Moses, the Prophets, Psalms, and all his teachings. As everything from the past came into view for the disciples, they trusted that they were now with the Resurrected Jesus.—D. Leslie Hollon

Testimony. One summer, while working with Christian leaders in Switzerland, I spent some free time exploring the Alps. The highest peak in Europe—the Jungfrau—stands majestically over lakes and villages. The day before our conference began, I left my hotel at dawn and rode three trains to the last stop, where a research center and restaurant are located. "Achtung" (the German word for danger) caught my attention, as I saw an exit sign while meandering through the buildings. "Go beyond this point at your own risk" was the essence of the sign's various warnings. So I decided to give it a look. Walking onto a glacier to see the stunning beauty of Europe from twelve thousand feet was worth the risk. Catching my breath, I realized there was a dog-sled team ahead of me and a handful of people. Then I noticed tall, thin poles standing in the snow, spaced sixty-five feet apart. They marked a snow-covered trail that gave no sign that I would fall through a crevice or cause an avalanche. So I started hiking, not sure how far I could—or would—go.

After making it to the end, a funny thing happened as I started hiking back to the place of my departure. Once I descended the slope and walked past the same Swiss flag I had passed earlier, I came across some adventurers who were walking in the direction from which I was returning. Amidst our huffing and puffing, they asked what lay ahead. Though I had been there only once, I had been there. Therefore, I had something to offer them. Having been there and done that, it was now my responsibility to show others the way.—D. Leslie Hollon

Musical Selections Appropriate to the Day

Hymn suggestions for lectionary texts:

Acts 2:14a, 36–41	*He Is Lord; Come Be Baptized*
Ps. 116:1–4, 12–19	*For the Beauty of the Earth; What Gift Can We Bring?*
1 Pet. 1:17–23	*I Lay My Sins on Jesus*
Luke 24:13–35	*Open My Eyes That I May See; Open Our Eyes Lord*

Children's Lectionary Sermon

TITLE: Thankfulness for God's Goodness
SCRIPTURE: Ps. 116:1–4, 12–19
KEY VERSE: *How can I repay the Lord for all his goodness to me?* (Ps. 116:12, New International Version)
KEY CONCEPT: Thankfulness
MATERIALS: Bible, candy corn
PREPARATION: Give each child a small bag of candy corn.

In Psalm 116, David's soul overflowed with thankfulness. David praised God for God's goodness and mercy to him throughout life. He knew God showed love in dealing with him. David knew that God had been faithful to him in the past and that God would continue to be faithful in the future. (*Open Bible.*) In Psalm 116:12 David says, "How can I repay the Lord for all his goodness to me?" Do you ever wonder how you can repay God for all he has done for you?

Open your bag of candy. We can use these candies to represent ways God has been good to us. As I read each statement, hold up one piece of candy.

- The first piece of candy reminds us God loves us.
- The second piece of candy reminds us God provides for our needs.
- The third piece of candy reminds us God keeps his promises.

- The fourth piece of candy reminds us to be thankful for family and friends.
- The fifth piece of candy reminds us God hears our prayers and answers them.

Now, it's your turn. Who would like to hold up a piece of candy to represent something God has blessed you with? What are you thankful for today? (*Allow several children to participate.*) We can thank God by accepting Jesus as Savior of our life and living as God has shown us, through Jesus, how to live.—Carolyn Tomlin

❧ WORSHIP AIDS ❧

Call to Worship: We experience in worship God's kind affection and share it with the family of faith, declaring, "Grace to you, and peace, from God our Father, and from the Lord Jesus Christ" (Phil. 1:2).

Invocation: Our Father, we give thanks for the fellowship of the gospel in which we share, for your work among us in which we so joyfully labor, and for the promise of its fulfillment, according to your purpose. May this hour of worship encourage and strengthen our hearts that we may so serve you that your will shall be done among us on earth as it is in heaven. Amen.

Offertory Sentence: "If you are eager to give, God will accept your gift on the basis of what you have to give, not on what you do not have" (2 Cor. 8:12).

Offertory Prayer: Gracious God, may we know that no true offering is so small that it goes without your notice or so large that it requires more than is possible. Help us to remember both the widow's mite and the yielding of Jesus' entire life to the Father's will. Accept our gifts today as the fruit of our labor and the product of your grace. In the name of him who loved us and gave himself for us. Amen.

Morning Prayer: Most Holy Father, as we gather in your presence this morning, remind us that it is you who created us in love as your children and who now sustains us in all walks of life, even when we do not acknowledge your presence and power and love. Remind us again this morning that it is from you that we receive every good and perfect gift that makes life bearable and lovely. Keep us aware that it is by your grace that we are healed from those diseases of the heart and soul that destroy in us the joy of life and the meaning of living.

As we turn to you this morning, we pray that you will dwell in us as power of love and soundness. Touch us with divine insight that we might be healed from discord in the depths of our souls. Pluck from our memory the sorrow rooted there, even as you cleanse our overcharged heart from its misery and pain. Grant to us the boon of peace for a troubled conscience. Put out the fires of evil that rampage within us, and let the sunrise of holy love break like dawn on the beginning of a new day, that our lives may be warmed and purified, even as our souls are saved by the grace and power of Jesus Christ, in whose name we pray. Amen.—Henry Fields

Benediction: As we go, may we go in the power and under the guiding hand of the God who created us, sustained us, redeemed us, and now walks by our sides day by day. Father, Son, and Holy Spirit—three in one—lead us into the days of this week and bring us back together next Lord's Day. Amen.

SUNDAY, APRIL 13, 2008

LECTIONARY SERMON TOPIC: "Prayer and the Abundant Life"
TEXT: John 10:1–10; Ps. 23
OTHER READINGS: Acts 2:42–47; 1 Pet. 2:19–25

Jesus revealed himself as the Good Shepherd so we could experience abundant life. By knowing Jesus, we discover ourselves as though for the first time. Jesus lived among us to be known, understood, trusted, and believed. Jesus performed miracles so people would see his authority and trust themselves to his care. Jesus taught so people would understand and apply his message. Jesus related in love so he would be known in mercy and justice as Savior and Lord. Jesus acted so those who had "eyes to see" would believe in him.

Jesus' words from John 10 were given from his heart of love, shortly before he died on the cross. They warn us. They direct us. They implore us to trust him. Only through trust in him as the Good Shepherd can we get through this world without our souls being destroyed. Only through him can we know the abundant life. As we live with the Good Shepherd, we experience abundant living and are given permission to pray in his name. And as his authority is at work in us, we will pray in a way that the best prayers will be blessed and the others will be discarded.

I. **What comes from prayer.** Prayer is conversation with the Shepherd. This conversation of listening and talking with Christ is provided as a gift—one for our benefit and for the world. The poet Tennyson had it right when he wrote, "More things are wrought by prayer than this world dreams of." More things need to be born from prayer as we now live in the twenty-first century. The world needs our prayers. *We* need our prayers.

II. **Psalm 23 can calm and guide us.** *"The Lord is my Shepherd, I shall not want."* Stay near the Shepherd. Circumstances affect us but do not control us, as we follow the Shepherd. God is the resting place for our fears. Bringing our fears to the Shepherd places us in the care of the One who holds together our lives, our universe.

 • *"He makes me to lie down in green pastures. He leads me beside the still waters. He restores my soul."* We absorb the shock of life through prayer, through worship, through still moments alone with God, through tender moments with friends and family. Our grief works itself out through the comfort and counsel of the Holy Spirit. Our souls are restored like David's in Psalm 51.

 • *"He leads me in the paths of righteousness for His name's sake."* God does not leave us alone to muddle in uncertainty. We are not left adrift. Aimless is not our direction. God calls us to action through his righteousness. Evil is defeated by the sustained actions of God's people "doing justice, loving mercy, and walking humbly with our God." When we said we would be forever different because of September 11, 2001, it meant our normal routine would become different because we would measure what we do by asking, "Does this matter in light of life's fragile nature?" And by feeling God's presence and purpose in our return to routine, we feel power in knowing that what we do—small as it may seem—serves a purpose in God's larger scheme.

• *"Yea, though I walk through the valley of the shadow of death, I will fear no evil. You are with me. Your rod and staff do comfort me."* Putting one foot in front of the other is the key to getting through the valley of the shadow. Trusting God with each moment of every day during this valley walk means that the Shepherd, not evil, will see us through. Fear paralyzes us in the grip of the shadow. Faith frees us to walk with enough light to see and feel God's rod and staff.

• *"You prepare a table before me in the presence of my enemies. You anoint my head with oil. My cup runs over."* Enemies win by frightening us. Jesus, the Good Shepherd, said for us to only fear ones who can harm our souls. Therefore, we are freed from our enemies' threats by praying for them, spiritually confronting them, and dealing with the issues that formed enmity— freed by changing ourselves as we need to be changed and then conquering our enemies by converting them into walking a common pathway with the Shepherd.

• *"Consequently, goodness and mercy shall follow me all the days of my life and I shall dwell in the house of the Lord forever."* We end our lives by how we live our lives. If we lived with the Shepherd, then we know that our earthly shelter becomes a heavenly shelter. The Shepherd's ways keeps us near to him by making our character good and our actions merciful. Evil's defeat is assured. There is a price we must all pay in this campaign, but the victory celebration makes worthy every sacrifice.

III. **We recognize that Jesus is the Good Shepherd.** During a pivotal period of Jesus' ministry, he took the apostles, the way a shepherd would take sheep, to the northern sector of Israel. Near the border, Jesus stopped at Caesarea Philippi. Having taken them to the edge, where the familiar greets the unfamiliar, he asked them two questions: "Who do people say the Son of Man is?" and "But what about you, who do you say I am?" Then was the time and that was the place Jesus chose to call out the faith commitment of those who were ready to give it. With mounting expectation, Jesus seemed to be asking, "What about yourselves? You have been with me. You have heard my teachings, seen my miracles, walked with me, asked me questions, calmed your fears by my presence, been shocked, humbled, and bewildered by me. We have prayed and worshiped together. You need to know that you know who I am! So give me your best answer."

The best of the rest in that moment was Peter. He spoke with a faith that he knew was true: "You are the Christ, the Son of the Living God." There. It was said. Peter was glad and proud that he could boldly speak what the others were thinking but were unable or unwilling to say. "You, Jesus," Peter was saying, "are the anointed Messiah, and you are doing this as the sign of the Lord's living presence. You are the Shepherd."—D. Leslie Hollon

ILLUSTRATIONS

Prayer. P. T. Forsythe said, "Prayer is to the Christian as the laboratory is to the scientist." Prayer is the place of discovery—and intrigue. Prayer nourishes us into habits of holy excellence, connects us with the comfort and counsel of the Holy Spirit, inspires us into the Scriptures' holy inspiration, gives us boldness to stand up for God's ways, guides us into Christian community, makes us sensitive to the need of others so our faith-sharing is given as acts of love, and shapes our life skills into Christian purpose. Praying beyond where we are today positions us to where God can take us tomorrow.—D. Leslie Hollon

Morning Renewal. When the alarm clock goes off, I hit the snooze button. Half awake and half asleep, while turning over in bed, I utter, "God, I give you my life this day." Renewed by a night of rest and moments of meditation, I am ready to get up. Touched from heaven, I am ready to live on earth. And thus I pray for God to bless all the people I will see. With feet on the floor, I set the alarm to "off" and live the day before me. "He makes me lie down in green pastures, He leads me beside quiet waters, He restores my soul. He guides me in paths of righteousness for His name's sake." This purposeful prayer positions us into God's abiding presence as we begin each day.—D. Leslie Hollon

Musical Selections Appropriate to the Day

Hymn suggestions for lectionary texts:

Acts 2:42–47	*How Firm a Foundation; Let Us Break Bread Together*
Ps. 23	*The King of Love My Shepherd Is; The New 23rd*
1 Pet. 2:19–25	*Revive Us Again; In Water We Grow*
John 10:1–10	*Savior, Like a Shepherd Lead Us; You Satisfy the Hungry Heart*

Children's Lectionary Sermon

TITLE: God Provides for Our Needs

SCRIPTURE: Psalm 23

KEY VERSE: *The Lord is my shepherd; I have everything I need.* (Ps. 23:1, New Living Translation)

KEY CONCEPT: God's care

MATERIALS: Bible, shepherd's staff, robe

PREPARATION: Dress in a shepherd's robe, and walk in carrying a staff and a Bible.

Hello boys and girls. I'm holding a shepherd's staff. Does anyone know what a shepherd's staff was used for? (*Pause and allow a response.*) In Bible days, the job of a shepherd was to watch over the sheep. In order to find grass and water for the flock, the shepherd might guide the sheep to new places to find food and water. This meant the shepherd would be away from home for long periods of time. People who cared for sheep had a difficult job. They were outside during all kinds of weather. Wild animals, sickness, and lost sheep were constant dangers.

It was the shepherd's job to keep his flock safe from harm. If an animal fell into a deep hole or became trapped in a thorn bush, the hook on the staff could rescue the animal. The shepherd had to be near his flocks at all times. He was on duty all day and all night.

When I think of a shepherd watching his flock, I think of God watching us. David, the shepherd boy, understood the life of keeping the sheep safe. As he watched the stars at night, David prayed. (*Open Bible.*) In Psalm 23:1 it says, "The Lord is my shepherd; I have everything I need."

David realized God could supply all his needs. Like the shepherd who watches continually over his sheep, God will care for those who follow him. God cares for us, just as God cared for David. We can ask God to help us because God is always there for us—because God cares for us.—Carolyn Tomlin

WORSHIP AIDS

Call to Worship: "Behold, I stand at the door and knock: if any one hears my voice and opens the door, I will come into him, and will eat with him, and he with me" (Rev. 3:20).

Invocation: Dearest Father, in worship we open ourselves to you individually. We open to you our collective praise, the joy of our lips. We open the heart of our fellowship and do seek to open the hearts of people everywhere. Grant that the splendor of our communion with you will so transform us that we shall serve you faithfully. Amen.

Offertory Sentence: "Give unto the Lord the glory due his name: bring an offering, and come into his courts" (Ps. 96:8).

Offertory Prayer: Lord, let our gifts this day, whether large or small, reflect faithful hearts that give joyfully and point to our Lord Jesus Christ. Amen.— E. Lee Phillips

Morning Prayer: Dear God, as we gather in this place of simple beauty and serenity, we give thanks to you for bringing us safely to this day, with the feel of spring looming in the air and in our hearts and, at least for today, for another day of fragile peace. May you bring us many more such days, as we strive to find ways to keep peace in this world. Give voice to our concerns and courage to our convictions, while always remembering to be tolerant, patient, understanding, and forgiving of others.

Here, surrounded by the warmth of friends and neighbors, let us find comfort for our grief and sorrow and shelter from the storms of life. Lord, be our guide through life's deep valleys, and lift us up to a higher place, where we may come to find your deep love and peace in our hearts. Bring healing to our friends and loved ones who may be sick or in despair, and shower down your love on them, like a warm spring rain.

God, just as you embrace each of us, let us embrace each other. Let us embrace both our common desires and our differences, remembering that we are all God's children, and let us embrace this church community of love, care, and concern, for we need each other more than ever. Lord, may we find in you a calm and a stillness our hearts long for, and may you grant us thy peace. Amen.—R. L. Smith

Benediction: By the power, and in the Spirit of our Lord we go forth to honor his Holy Name—Father, Son, and Holy Spirit—and to declare in the days of this week the reign of truth under which we live. Go in peace. Amen.

SUNDAY, APRIL 20, 2008

LECTIONARY SERMON TOPIC: "Who Can Show Me My Future? Jesus, the Way"
TEXT: John 14:1–14
OTHER READINGS: Acts 7:55–60; Ps. 31:1–5, 15–16; 1 Pet. 2:2–10

Christ is present, even when he seems to be absent. How can that be? The John 14 narrative challenges us to experience Christ in the way he is actually with us and not be blinded by our preferences. The disciples were suffering from separation anxiety as Jesus spoke of his coming death. The future looked dismal. To see the future that Christ is creating, we must know that trusting in God shows us how to be secure in an insecure world, that a better future is created by loving the people we are guiding and the cause we are leading, that Christ shows us the future as we follow in his way, believe his truth, and receive the life he offers. The size of the challenge, however, fits God at work through you.

I. **Christ shows our Father in heaven.** A sign at a place I work out reads: "If you lead a good life, go to Sunday School & church, and say your prayers every night, when you die you will go to Kentucky." Well? As great as Kentucky is, even when we sing, "My Old Kentucky Home," I am glad to know there is a heaven greater than the beauty of our bluegrass, horses, rivers, mountains, fields, and people. Knowing this helps us to be a follower of the One who is "the Way, the Truth, and the Life."

The following is a portion of a pastoral column I wrote after tragic news rippled through Kentucky.

> Forty-nine people died in Lexington last Sunday morning. A plane filled with people of promise, who were set for destinations of service and celebrations, was set to depart before dawn. Their take-off became a crash landing. In the span of seconds their earthly lives came to an end. The importance of each individual, connected by this deathly tragedy, unites everyone affected into a community of grief. The anguish still ripples with sadness as awareness of who was on the plane becomes known. As the news broke shortly before Sunday's morning service, we prayed during worship for the families and friends of those whose loved ones died from the crash. One life affects so many lives. A death multiplied 49 times touches so many people. The tragedy forever changes how thousands of people will be able to live.

From such stark news we are grateful for the good news of God's goodness, which steadies us during unsteady times. As Jesus said, "Do not let your hearts be troubled. Trust in God, trust also in me. In my Father's house are many rooms; if it were not so, I would have told you. I am going there to prepare a place for you. And if I go and prepare a place for you, I will come back and take you to be with me that you also may be where I am. You know the way to the place where I am going."

II. **Heaven is God's unshakable Kingdom.** We are Kingdom seekers. We search for a Kingdom where we are known and loved. We search for a Kingdom possessing the treasures of our happiness. Whether in places, people, or purpose, we search for a Kingdom that will grant us full citizenship. And in this citizenship, with all the privileges and responsibilities thereof, we hope to fill our "soul pockets" with everlasting joy.

Heaven is more real than earth itself. Earthly life ends. Heaven is eternal. Heaven shows that God's vision for our lives is more than this world can contain.

By taking heaven seriously, we can see this world more clearly for what it is and is not. What happens here is important, but the importance is measured by heaven's values and standards. If we think this world is all there is, it may be that the reward we receive on earth is the only one we will ever receive.

Warning! Heavenly immortality is not determined by earthly "celebrity" status but by the heavenly decisions we make and fulfill while on earth. Knowing this truth, we become spiritually disciplined. We then "hunger and thirst" for a righteousness, which is fulfilled. If we want to make a lasting difference on earth, we've got to get a realistic view of heaven. C. S. Lewis, who lived through two world wars, put it this way: "Aim at heaven and you will get earth thrown in. Aim at earth and you get neither."

III. **Heaven is a reality that reveals and reminds us that earth is too small to contain the vastness of God.** What happens in heaven is bigger than any one of us. The size of heaven fits God. Thomas's honest question to Jesus revealed how eternal life requires change, and change makes us uncomfortable. When presented with God's bigness and the accompanying responsibilities, we get tempted to shrivel God to our own size, and we flee from the Kingdom's call.

Through a combination of bold and subtle efforts, the resistance to letting God be God comes as we attempt to limit God to our own set of experiences, our own way of reasoning and feeling, our own realm of ambitions; it approximates our wanting to make God over in our own image, to make God into a god—an idol we can control. Christian disciples stand in the earthly place of God's Kingdom while knowing that only in heaven will perfect bliss be found. As one friend who had ministered for fifty years said, "Walk with your head in heaven and your feet on earth." We are to live in the tension of the "already" and the "not yet." Through trusting God, we learn how *not* to get enslaved by mortgage payments, food consumption, sexuality, book learning, spectator sports, materialism, or racism. We are to be converted and made disciples by following what God promises.

The Christ in us shines through in proportion to our allowing that likeness to shape our character. And our character is the consummation of our decisions and experiences. Because what we do with our heads, hands, and hearts shapes us and reveals us, we are not to conform to idols of this world but to be transformed by Christ's renewing our minds. Disciples are, as Martin Luther said, "little Christ-ians." As people redeemed in Christ, disciples stand in an unshakable Kingdom that is present and future, earthly and heavenly. We are as Jesus was, between baptism and crucifixion-resurrection. Living at the in-between puts us on life's cutting edge and keeps us from being dulled by the forms of this world.

Paul warned "that the god of this world blinds unbelieving minds and keeps them from seeing the light of the gospel of the glory of Christ, who is the likeness of God." William Wordsworth, the great Romantic poet, explained the dulling process this way: "The world is too much with us, late and soon. Getting and spending we lay waste our powers." Heaven's hope is there for us all. Let God's heaven come to you and fill your soul with heavenly happiness.

When we've been there ten thousand years,
Bright shining as the sun,
We've no less days to sing God's praise
Than when we'd first begun.
—D. Leslie Hollon

ILLUSTRATIONS

Heaven. The Greek word for heaven (*ouranos*) is used 284 times in the New Testament.

Heaven is: a relationship, an eternal way of life, a space and time created by God that is more than earth.
Heaven reveals: God's sovereignty, God's mercy, God's rewards.
Heaven means: God's vision for our life is more than earth can contain. There is a connection between our earthly life and our heavenly life. We are confronted by two realities. All of us will die. All of us must trust God.
Heaven humbles us because: "Now we can only know in part, as looking in a mirror dimly . . . then we will know fully even as we are fully known."

Only that which we do with faith, hope, and love lasts forever.—D. Leslie Hollon

Assurance. John Oxenham was the poet, novelist, and hymnist who composed one of our most cherished hymns: *In Christ There Is No East or West*. He lived through the troubled and promising years of 1861–1941. Through knowing the heights of God and the depths of human nature, he helped bridge the chasm between the two by his undying faith in Christ Jesus. He wrote of how we are on a journey, a journey to an eternal home that is welcoming and inviting. Life is hopeful for our future is secure.

He knew through faith, seasoned by experience, that no force can defeat God. No force can keep us from getting to our eternal home. No force can turn out the home lights God has turned on for us nor bar the door God has opened for us. Oxenham knew, as Jesus promised, "the gates of Hades can not prevail against" God.—D. Leslie Hollon

Musical Selections Appropriate to the Day

Hymn suggestions for lectionary texts:

Acts 7:55–60	*Faith of Our Fathers*
Ps. 31:1–5, 15–16	*God of Our Life*
1 Pet. 2:2–10	*Christ Is Our Cornerstone; We Are Called to Be God's People*
John 14:1–14	*I Know That My Redeemer Liveth; 'Tis So Sweet to Trust in Jesus*

ᕦ Children's Lectionary Sermon

TITLE: Jesus Will Comfort You

SCRIPTURE: John 14:1–14

KEY VERSE: *Don't be troubled. You trust God, now trust in me.* (John 14:1, New Living Translation)

KEY CONCEPT: God's comfort
MATERIALS: Bible, poster of children playing
PREPARATION: Set up the easel for displaying the poster.

We know God is good. God made us. God created us and the world in which we live. Did you know God gives us comfort when we are sad? God can help us when bad things happen that make us feel sad.

Playing together is something we all enjoy. Look at the picture of these children at play. What are some problems you have had when playing with other children? Has someone taken a toy you were playing with? Who would like to share some problems? (*Wait for response. If you have really young children, guide them through this by giving examples.*)

Sometimes when we play with friends, they do things that make us sad. This is a time we can know God is with us. (*Open Bible.*) In John 14:1, Jesus says, "Don't be troubled. You trust God, now trust in me." We can pray to God. We can talk to Jesus. We can pray for our friends. It is important to be a friend, too. We have to think about how others feel and make sure we are helpful.

Another problem may be getting along with brothers and sisters in your home. Let's think of ways we can share, take turns, and be a helper at home. Could you include a younger brother or sister in your games? Could you offer to play with a toddler while parents perform other household work? (*Ask these types of questions, aware of the age of your children.*)

Let's remember that God wants us to know about our problems. God is our comforter, which means God can make us feel better because God always loves us.—Carolyn Tomlin

WORSHIP AIDS

Call to Worship: As we enter worship, God invites us into his presence, and we tremble. "Holy, holy, holy, is the Lord of Hosts; the whole earth is full of his glory" (Isa. 6:3).

Invocation: Almighty God, whose Kingdom extends from the East to the West, from the North to the South, we gather in your name. Come this day and reign over this little portion of planet earth and over our hearts and lives. Help us to glorify you, thrice-holy God. Amen.

Offertory Sentence: "Honor the Lord with your substance, and with the first fruits of your labor" (Prov. 3:9).

Offertory Prayer: Father, you love and care for all things. Not even a falling sparrow is hidden from you. Grant that we, in our giving, may become extensions of your love to all creatures, especially to the creation made in your image. May these gifts be blessed and multiplied to touch others and to meet their deepest needs. Amen.

Morning Prayer: Dear God, in our habits and moods please free us from clinging. It's time for spring cleaning. Please give us the focus and time to take stock—to sort out and maintain our hearts. May our hearts and souls be lightened by forgiving. May your abode in our hearts be filled with thanksgiving and light.

Grant that we all learn the meaning of "enough" by putting our faith in you, who have carried us in abundance all our days. As we wipe winter's smudges from our windows, clean the soot from our mantels, sweep the grit from our porches, may each chore become an act of purification for our hearts, brightly polishing the mirror of our souls so we may reflect outward your all-pervading light in our actions, words, and thoughts.

We ask that your presence and strength be felt in the lives of those who are living with loss, illness, or heartache today. We ask that we may be vessels of your compassion and kindness and pour forth gentle support for all those in need of any kind. May our hands reach out freely and often, knowing that we are instruments of your great goodness, and may your love be a constant source of guidance and comfort. In all humility, we ask these things. Amen.—Carolyn Montie

Benediction: Now may our holy and gracious God guide us from this place and into the activities of the coming week. Be to us, O Lord, our hands, and feet, and voices, that we may speak and live the gospel. Amen.

SUNDAY, APRIL 27, 2008

LECTIONARY SERMON TOPIC: "Sharing Our Faith"

TEXT: Acts 17:22–31

OTHER READINGS: Ps. 66:8–20; 1 Pet. 3:13–22; John 14:15–21

The Bible is God's storybook. God wants us to know his story, not because he thought everyone would love him because of the stories, though that was his hope; not because he thought everyone would get it, though that was his aim; not that he thought everyone would live better lives because of lessons learned from the stories, though that motivation moved him. He had the stories recorded because they give witness to his glorious acts of salvation and that whosoever had "eyes to see and ears to hear" would personally experience salvation by the stories delivered.

Paul's story illustrates God's amazing grace. Saul, the terrorist, became the apostle Paul, who shared God's open promise of salvation for all seekers. On a walk to remember toward Damascus, he was converted and called. His call gave him his nickname, "Apostle to the Gentiles." God would use his life experiences to shape his future opportunities of service. The same is true for you and me.

I. **Paul preached in Athens.** A later Church father, Tertullian, would ask: "What did Athens have to do with Jerusalem?" What did the academy of learning have to do with Christ's life, death, and Resurrection? Tertullian, who was trained in Greek thought, distrusted the philosophical approach to evangelism. Paul knew how to avoid the pitfalls of this approach and thereby maximize the effect of helping people to think through their faith so each could spiritually move from being an atheist *to* an agnostic *to* a theist *to* a seeker of Jesus *to* (finally) a believer.

On Athens's acropolis, he engaged people by teaching Christ. In the shadow of Athena's Parthenon, and Nike's temple of champions, and the Areopagus debating societies, Paul saw a stone column bearing the inscription, "To an Unknown God." There he connected with people who believed in many gods but were confused by their plethora of choices. He scratched their itch for clarity by telling them about the abiding truth of Jesus Christ.

II. **Everyone has the right to know about Christ.** God sees more than we see, always. God sees everything everywhere. We see, as Paul said, "only in part." But God's love, made perfectly known in the life, death, and Resurrection of Christ, is how we see enough to know enough to believe. Everyone has the spiritual right to know about Christ. Why? Because in Christ "there is neither Jew nor Greek, slave nor free, male nor female" (Gal. 3:28). How is this possible? Because anyone in Christ is "a new creation where the old passes away and the new has come" (2 Cor. 5:17). Paul made clear that Jesus' death validated his life. Through his death, believers can know "at-one-ment" with God. This ultimate act of sacrifice meant that our sins are known, dealt with, and forgiven by God.

Shortly before his Crucifixion, Jesus talked to a friend in crisis. To Martha he explained that death, in God's hands, becomes life: "I am the resurrection and the life. He who believes in me will live, even though he dies; and whoever lives and believes in me will never die. Do you believe this?" Jesus' promise ends with an invitation. Either you do or do not believe (John 11:25–26). To this question there is no middle ground. This promise becomes known by personally trusting in Christ.

When designing our family cemetery plots, I chose these verses to be chiseled in stone on a meditation bench. Recently, I sat on that bench and stared at the ground where one day my body will be buried. In such moments we get really honest with ourselves. I felt renewed gratitude that Jesus went toward Calvary and not away from it. Faith takes us toward, not away from, salvation.

A great Christian writer, Søren Kierkegaard of Denmark, first coined the phrase "leap of faith." The words describe what is required to be in a trusting relationship with God. Reason, research, and analysis can take us a long way but only so far. Then we must take another step—sometimes a leap into what can only be known by experience. To leap into life's experience requires faith. Without faith we cannot go forward. Kierkegaard also said, "Life is lived forwards but understood backwards." Only by experiencing life can we really know life. Only by loving can we know love. Only by trusting God can we know trust. Only by believing in Christ can we know Christ.

III. **In current-day Macedonia, God gave witness to a seeker who wanted to know the unknown God of her dreams.** Her name is Eleza and she had a dream. Standing in the middle of a lake was a man, and around him were drowning people. From the dream he called out to Eleza, "Help me." She woke from the dream wondering what it all meant. She asked a friend, who did not know. She asked the mullah. He did not know. She inquired of another local Islamic leader, who could not explain the dream. Then someone in the Macedonian refugee village told her about someone else who knew how to interpret dreams.

   She took her dream to him. After hearing the dream, he said he thought he knew the identity of the man calling out to her from the middle of the lake. But the dream interpreter wanted more information from Eleza. The stories of a refugee flowed from her—stories of bigotry, massacres, rape, and financial ruin cried from her soul as she explained what happened to her friends and family in Kosovo during the 1999 war. She told all of this and more to a person of love and faith. That person was Rick Shaw, a missionary serving in Kosovo and Macedonia. Rick took my wife and me to meet Eleza. No longer a refugee, she had returned to her hometown to fulfill the meaning of her dream.

   From Rick she came to understand that the man in her dream was Jesus and that he was asking her to help him rescue people from drowning in the world's pain. Eleza then accepted Christ and was baptized. Living in the shadow of supporters of ethnic cleansing, as well as Muslims who resented her conversion, Eleza shows herself to be a Christian of courageous faith. Arriving in her Kosovar home, we saw miracles under way, as we met her sons, daughters-in-law, grandchildren, and friends. All these people had loved ones slain during the war. Many of these people now know the grace of Christ, and we felt their joy. From her home we went to a storefront on Main Street. There we gathered for worship. We sang. We prayed. We shared. We danced. Testimonies were shared. Jesus was fulfilling the dream he gave to Eleza.

IV. **Here are four approaches to sharing your faith.** Evangelists are "good news" tellers of Christ. We labor for other people to know the joyous salvation made available by God's grace. We do so voluntarily. We should want people's decisions to be made voluntarily, whatever they might be. A mutual respect for the dignity of every human being and every group of people means that faith-sharing should be pursued with respectful love.

A variety of approaches exist. Learn the styles so you may know when to use which one and how to speak with words and actions so other people will understand.

Personal approach: Tell how you became a Christian and what has happened in your life since you began following in the ways of Jesus. Personal experience carries passionate persuasion. Paul frequently told his story.

Relational approach: Build trust into each of your relationships. This positions you to share convincingly about Jesus. Ask questions about the seeker; listen and apply what you learn. Paul listened and observed before he preached.

Actions of servanthood: Use kindness to care for the seeker's mind and body, and let it be an entrée to talk about things spiritual.

Intellectual approach: Guide the person's curiosity or doubts about Christ to the point where reason merges into faith. This flip-flops a person's perspective from this: "I have to know for sure by reason and observation before I will believe," to this: "I believe in order to understand."

Biblical verses: Verses such as the Roman Road to Salvation (Rom. 3:23, 6:23, 10:13), the Woman at the Well encounter (John 4), the Prodigal Son (Luke 15:11–32), and Zacchaeus (Luke 19:1–10) carry the conviction of Scripture for those seekers who believe the Bible is God's unique book.

Teachable moments: Be present when major life events happen in seekers' lives because then they are distinctly open. The soul, at such times, is open to the real Christ for their real-life situation.

Our worried world is in need of the gospel. For such a time as ours, we serve as ambassadors for Christ.—D. Leslie Hollon

ILLUSTRATIONS

Evangelism and Persuasion. Here are principles that help guide our ministry in personal evangelism: (1) We are all made in God's image, and each person is to be equally valued. The dignity and human rights of all persons are affirmed. (2) We must be truthful about our essential beliefs, such as the centrality of Christ, and recognize our difference with others. This is a principle of respectful communication. (3) In light of our differences, there are still common concerns we can mutually pursue. (4) Liberty of choice is valued for all people and guarantees a free marketplace for the peaceful exchange of contrasting and competing perspectives. Evangelism and missions, therefore, become the legitimate enterprise of effectively taking the gospel to local and global communities.—D. Leslie Hollon

Our Stories. Laurens Vander Post, a South African explorer who lived among the bushmen of the Kalahari desert, realized that they would only tell "their stories" to him after months of his living in their midst. First they had to trust him; to them, their stories possessed the secrets of their soul. To tell their stories was to risk their lives. If an enemy came to possess their stories, they would be destroyed. Like them, most of us are only willing to tell our personal stories to people we believe are trustworthy. We don't want to be made fun of. We don't want our stories to be distorted and spread around for others to trample on. We are vulnerable as we share our stories.—D. Leslie Hollon

Musical Selections Appropriate to the Day

Hymn suggestions for lectionary texts:

Acts 17:22–31	*All Creatures of Our God and King*
Ps. 66:8–20	*To God Be the Glory*
1 Pet. 3:13–22	*At the Name of Jesus; Put Peace into Each Other's Hands*
John 14:15–21	*Because He Lives; Love Divine All Loves Excelling*

∾ Children's Lectionary Sermon

TITLE: God Listens

SCRIPTURE: Ps. 66:8–20

KEY VERSE: *But God did listen! He paid attention to my prayer.* (Ps. 66:19, New Living Translation)

KEY CONCEPT: Prayer

MATERIALS: Bible, megaphone

(*Start out whispering to the children.*) Can you hear what I am saying? What is it? You can't hear me? Can you hear me now? (*Repeat this whispering again. As the children complain they can't hear you, stop and try the megaphone. Use the megaphone and say the same thing again, very loud. When the children say, "It is too loud," stop talking.*)

When I whispered, you couldn't hear me very well. When I was speaking very loud, you covered your ears because it was so noisy. It is easier to hear me when I just speak to you in my regular voice.

I was wondering how we should speak when we talk to God through prayer. How do you speak to God when you pray? (*Let the children respond.*) There are so many ways we can speak to God. (*Reflect back the ways the children responded.*) We can close our eyes and think in our heads what we want to say to God. We can use our regular voice to pray to God. We can even shout a prayer to God.

(*Open Bible.*) This is what the writer of Psalm 66 did. This writer was so excited about God listening to his prayer that he shouted, "*But God did listen! He paid attention to my prayer.*"

We can be sure God listens to our prayer, too. God wants us to tell God what we need help with, what we are sorry we did, and how much we want to thank God for all the things God has given us. I am so glad God listens to us, and we can pray together now to God. (*Have a prayer with the children.*)—Marcia Thompson

∾ WORSHIP AIDS ∾

Call to Worship: In worship we are called to attention: "He who has an ear, let him hear what the Spirit says to the churches" (Rev. 2:29).

Invocation: O Lord, speak to us that we may hear. Tell us of your loving judgment that comes like a tender parent's discipline, which makes life better for us all. Tell us of your unending love that rekindles the fire of faith within. And grant that we may carefully listen as you speak. Amen.

Offertory Sentence: "Bring all the tithes into the storehouse, that there may be meat in my house, and prove me now, says the Lord. See if I will not open the windows of heaven, and pour out a blessing on you, that there shall not be room enough to receive it" (Mal. 3:10).

Offertory Prayer: Kind, divine Heavenly Father, bless these gifts as expressions of our renewed dedication to your service. May they be multiplied and used in ways that declare your glory. Make steadfast our resolve to love you more deeply and to serve you more fervently, that we may live faithfully and bear much fruit. Amen.

Morning Prayer: Spirit of beauty, shining in the golden glory of the sun and in the silver fire of the stars, laughing in the rippling streams, lifting your voice above the mighty breakers of the sea, crowning the mountain peaks with majesty sublime, open our eyes that we might behold you, inspire our souls to enjoy you and our hearts to share your loveliness.

This morning, Father, may your grace come like the floodtide to wash us clean and lift us from the grip of our past failures to be all that we have been called to be. May your guiding power drive us on with a renewed and deeper purpose that will give us new confidence and sure direction amid the swirling currents of the day. And may we here today recommit our lives and souls and hearts to following your will, serving your church, and fulfilling its ministries in the home, in the workplace, and in all our walks through the world, even as did those early followers who, by so doing, changed the world.—Henry Fields

Benediction: Lord God, whom we know as Father, Son, and Holy Spirit, walk with us in the days ahead. Inspire us to noble living, in word and deed, and bring us back again next Lord's Day. Amen.

SUNDAY, MAY 4, 2008
Ascension Sunday

LECTIONARY SERMON TOPIC: "John Prays for His Disciples"

TEXT: John 17:1–11

OTHER READINGS: Acts 1:6–14; Ps. 68:1–10, 32–35; 1 Pet. 4:12–14, 5:6–11

What crosses your mind when people say they will be praying for you? Sometime when we face sickness, difficult experiences, or tough decisions, someone will say, "I will be praying for you." For me that brings a warm, special feeling of concern and care. It is uplifting.

Now in this Scripture we read about Jesus saying to his disciples, "I will pray for you." He was talking to his disciples, who were present. But could he also be speaking to us—his disciples of today? Sometimes we have a picture, a concept of Jesus pointing a finger at us like a stern parent, telling us to straighten up. But the picture here of Jesus praying for his disciples is more fitting. What does he pray for?

I. **He prays that as we immerse ourselves in everyday living, we will have victory.** Jesus preferred that his disciples, including us, involve ourselves in the issues of life. We are to be involved in what is going on in our world, working to make a difference, working for change. Sometimes in doing that, we get "beat up" and want to quit; we take a "What's-the-use?" approach. Someone once said that the church is like a field hospital; we go out to work, sometimes do battle, sometimes get beat up, and then we come to church to have our wounds healed, be hugged and loved, made ready to go back out again. Jesus did not pray that we would be taken out of the world. Sometimes we get to the place where we want to be taken out of the issues of life, but it seems we are to stay in, and the promise is that he will be with us. We recall Scripture that reminds us that we are "the salt of the earth" and the "light of the world." How are we doing?

There is a certain seduction the world offers us, and it usually involves letting go some of our values for the sake of acceptance. But scarcely anyone calls for Christians to be so separated from the world that we have little or no witness. Sometimes that almost seems too easy. At the same time the prayer of Jesus reminds us that we do sometimes come in conflict with societal values, and we are to be "leaven."

There have been times in recent days when the Church fought societal values and refused to be taken in. One great battle the Church led was in the area of civil rights. Sadly, however, it seems that the Church has become so identified with some societal values in politics and social practices that it is difficult to determine the witness of the Church.

II. **The second subject of Jesus' prayer is for unity.** In verse 1, Jesus prays that we may be as one. Now, there is more than one way we could go with this. The history of the Church has, at times, not been a pleasant one when it came to unity. One can go back to New Testament times and see the schisms and difficulties, even in the early Church. God has been able to take some of these difficult times and bring something good from them. So we could focus on the larger Church, as well as on the local church. Although there are some difficulties still between church bodies (denominations), it does appear that in some ways Jesus' prayer is being answered. That is to say, there is more tolerance and understanding among many groups than at previous times. There are some who believe they have a corner on the whole truth, but most seem willing to learn, dialogue, and explore where work can be done together.

Although this may not be the answer to the prayer of Jesus, there does seem to be movement. Just as with an individual, we in the wider Church must have enough humility to admit that we do not have all the answers or know all the truth, but we do have a willingness to learn and consider. Another area of unity to consider is within the local church. Most of us have experienced conflict within the church body. These are painful and difficult times for families, individuals, and the body as a whole. Unity does not mean agreement on every issue brought up, but it does involve listening to each other, praying for one another, and being open to considering another way. Far too often, we have seen churches become so politicized in opinions, ideas, and directions that the mission is hampered. This is something we have to work at on an ongoing basis. We learn to listen, share, be willing to grow, keep our eyes open to new truth, and not become stuck in ways we have "always done it." We must learn that often the unity of the body is of utmost importance to us and our witness.

I recall one time while I was pastoring a church while a student at the seminary. The church was considering buying a piece of property, and the vote was in favor by one vote. One of the deacons said to me later, "Pastor, this is not good; we are not a political organization where if you win by one vote, you win. This is a church!" That stuck with me to this day.

This sermon is very simple and straightforward, yet has dealt with some difficult issues. Jesus wanted us to be involved in the world but also to try to change it. He wanted his disciples to be united in purpose and mission.—Louis Twyman

---

ILLUSTRATIONS

Who Gets Credit? I was reading a short article about the nineteenth-century British nurse, Florence Nightingale. She was asked one time how she was able to do so much in her life to help others. And this is what she said: "If I could give you information on my life, it would be to show you how a woman of ordinary ability has been led by God in extraordinary ways. God has done it all. He should get the credit. Not me."—Jackie Little

What's up There? Have you ever considered how the ancients understood the mystery that surrounded them? What if those wandering nomads, as they sat by a campfire, gazed into the night sky, were amazed by the twinkling of the stars, and wondered, "What's up there?" Or better still, "Who's up there? Be ye friend or be ye foe?" The Bible's message is that the God who is up there and out there, who created all this, is a God of love who wants to know us intimately and that this God is made known to us through his Son, Jesus the Christ.—Lee McGlone

---

Musical Selections Appropriate to the Day

Hymn suggestions for lectionary texts:

Acts 1:6–14	*Crown Him with Many Crowns; Alleluia! Sing to Jesus*
Ps. 68:1–10, 32–35	*Rejoice Ye Pure in Heart*
1 Pet. 4:12–14, 5:6–11	*God Will Take Care of You*
John 17:1–11	*The Bond of Love; O Love, How Deep, How Broad*

Children's Lectionary Sermon

TITLE: What Are You Afraid Of?

SCRIPTURE: 1 Pet. 4:12–14, 5:6–11

KEY VERSE: *Cast all your anxiety on him because he cares for you.* (1 Pet. 5:7, New International Version)

KEY CONCEPT: Dealing with anxiety

MATERIALS: Bible, dry-erase board, marker

PREPARATION: Place the dry-erase board near the children.

I want us to start this morning reading a very special verse from the New Testament. (*Open Bible.*) In 1 Peter 5:7 we read, "Cast all your anxiety on him because he cares for you." Let's talk about this Scripture for a few minutes. First, do you know anxiety is? (*Let children respond, especially if you have some older children who may know.*) The dictionary says anxiety is also fear, worry, concern, and unease. If you have felt afraid or worried, raise your hand for me. (*Give them a chance to respond.*)

Of course, everyone experiences these feelings at some time or other. Next, let's list some of the things that cause us to feel anxiety, to be afraid or worried. (*As children call out things that cause anxiety, write them on the board. Use some of the following causes. Give the example of a bad storm, if they need help.*)

It is okay to be afraid. God made us this way, so we would know when there is danger. But not everyone is afraid of the same things. Those things we are afraid of are very real, and we should not make fun or laugh at our friends for having these fears.

There is something we can do. We can let God help us. We can tell God our fears. We can pray when we are afraid, because God is a loving God, who cares for us.—Carolyn Tomlin

WORSHIP AIDS

Call to Worship: As we gather to worship, we proclaim the Lordship of Jesus Christ over all and stand with those in days of old who stood gazing up into heaven. "For this same Jesus who was taken up into heaven shall so come in like manner" (Acts 1:11).

Invocation: Lord, God, we know the Risen Savior who ascended into glory will one day come again. Keep us ready, expectant, and watchful, for in such an hour as we know not, the Christ of the universe returns, as triumphant as when he left. Hallelujah! Amen.—E. Lee Phillips

Offertory Sentence: "He whose giving shows mercy does so cheerfully" (Rom. 12:8).

Offertory Prayer: Merciful God, recognizing that it is you who entrusts us with what we have and what we are, we give you thanks, asking that you lead us to use these resources wisely. In thought and word, in deed and planning, help us to be architects of your just and loving realm. For as you first loved us, so we seek to now love you, through Christ, our inspiration and foundation. Amen.—Lael P. Murphy

Morning Prayer: Spirit of Power, that each spring brings us such an array of beauty and color, we give thanks. After a long stretch of winter we bask in the glory of forsythia, the blush of red maples in the swamps, and the yellow clumps of daffodils along the roadsides. How reliable these sights and sounds are of your seasonal love. We give thanks for them and your reassuring faithfulness. May we never take them for granted. Hear our praise and appreciation.

Around the rest of the world are heard sounds of war, of new respiratory diseases, of sorrows and ills of every sort. We ask, Father, for our leaders who struggle to find solutions to so many issues, that they be patient and steadfast in their pursuit of solutions and give thanks for their service to our country and the welfare of her people. We pray that hope shall rise like the brilliance of the full moon, and shall give way to the reign of universal peace and justice for all. Amen.—Martha DeNormandie

Benediction: As we go, may our obedience to Christ make clear our surrender. Eternal One, whom we name as Father, Son, and Holy Spirit, guide our steps, enrich our days, and lead us in the way everlasting. Amen.

SUNDAY, MAY 11, 2008
Pentecost

LECTIONARY SERMON TOPIC: "Change"

TEXT: Acts 2:1–21

OTHER READINGS: Ps. 104:24–34, 35b; 1 Cor. 12:3b–13; John 7:37–39

We often talk of change that happens in our lives, society, and the world. Sometimes, we feel the change is for the worse; other times change is for the better. We have often bemoaned some of the changes, feeling that we have lost some of our values, ideals, principles, and moorings. At other times we feel the change is for the better, and we have become energized, renewed, and invigorated. Today's Scripture reading is about change. What changes come about when God's Spirit gets hold of us? This is one of the key lessons of Pentecost.

You know the story of how people of different tongues were gathered in Jerusalem. The words of Jesus concerning the Holy Spirit seem to have made little impression on these sorrowing disciples. They were about as down as you could get. But then they were filled with the Holy Spirit, and although they spoke in different languages, they all understood as though they spoke the same language. This brought about amazing changes in their understanding and perceptions. Could it still be true that when God's Spirit comes upon us, there will be changes similar to the changes at Pentecost?

I. **There are changes in how we experience God working in our lives.** When does God's Spirit begin working in us? It begins the moment we recognize and allow the Spirit to work! Note the emphasis on the fact that the Spirit was given to the whole group; it was poured out on the whole fellowship. There were no first- and second-class Christians. What was the new thing that happened at Pentecost? The Spirit was given in a new way, as never before. Never in the Old Testament was the Spirit poured out on all people—only to the chosen leaders. Also, the fit was temporary for a crisis; when the crisis was over, the Spirit departed.

Jesus taught us how people filled with the Spirit respond to others. The Sermon on the Mount is an indication of God's Spirit working the change through us—how we view and experience each other! Someone has said that it is not so much what we experience with the coming of God's Spirit in our lives, but what matters is what other people experience coming through us. For example, if we are hurt by the words of another, we choose to let go of the incident. When we are lied to, we choose to forgive. When someone breaks our trust, we choose not to dwell on their shortcoming. The more we choose such responses, the stronger and more visible the Spirit of God becomes.

II. **Something new is created when God's Spirit comes into our lives and the life of our church.** Some of the results are that our differences fade away, and we realize we are one in Christ Jesus. We need to create a habitat for God's Spirit—one that encourages the divine creativity and innovation within.

Steve Shoemaker points how we create this habitat for God's Spirit. We take delight in our work. We stick to our calling. We enjoy solving problems inherent in our work. We love beauty. What we do seeks to find a way to fit into the larger scheme of life. We have to be willing to walk on the edge of chaos in order to create something new. Creativity requires that we take chances and be willing to make mistakes. Inspiration is rooted in the past. The new has the sense of reaching for something that has always been. Creativity honors the past without being bound by it. Inherent in creativity and innovation is a kind of suffering—the pain of failure, failed experiments, criticism, rejection. Unless we are willing to suffer, we will never enter into divine creativity.

Jesus said that the Spirit anointed him to preach good news to the poor, to proclaim release to captives, to open blind eyes—to set at liberty and to proclaim now as the year of God's favor. The Spirit is upon us to do the work of Christ. What is that work? It is the work of reconciliation. All through the Scriptures we hear this call to the work of reconciliation. The Spirit is making us one. Old distinctions, race, gender, class, nationality, the way we look, talk, walk—these make no difference any longer. The Spirit is to make us holy, make us joyful. What goes on in the church and in the name of God must be about righteousness, peace, and joy. That is what the Spirit of God is all about.—Louis Twyman

---

ILLUSTRATIONS

Spirit of God. Richard Stetler said in a sermon, "There is a difference between those who seek spiritual ecstasy of being in God's presence and those who seek to teach others about the pearl of great price. This difference is not about earning our own way into God's favor by becoming well disciplined in Jesus' teachings, rather it is about getting ourselves out of the way so that the Spirit of God becomes visible. God is always ready and eager to reveal his nature to the world. It is we who must open our doors and thrust open our windows so that the light of God can be seen."—Louis Twyman

Measuring Spiritual Growth. In the late 1820s, a New England farmer named William Miller became convinced that the Second Coming of Christ was soon to occur. He became obsessed with certain Scripture texts and predicted that Christ would return on March 21, 1843. So convinced was he of his own extraordinary spiritual insight that he gave up his farm and became an itinerant preacher, traveling up and down the Eastern states warning people of the imminent return. His sensational appeal was so convincing that thousands of people became followers. As the March 21, 1843, date approached, many of his disciples sold their own homes and gave away their belonging; they believed these would no longer be needed. They donned white robes and waited to meet Christ.

A problem arose, however. Christ didn't return on March 21 or on any of the other suggested dates Miller had set. He was wrong, at least about that. But in his day people revered him as a spiritual giant. His movement was later called Millenarianism, his followers called Millerites. I wonder, was he really a spiritual giant? Were those who followed him with such fanaticism spiritually mature? Was their zeal alone a true measure of their maturity?—Lawrence Vowan

Musical Selections Appropriate to the Day

Hymn suggestions for lectionary texts:

Acts 2:1–21	*Come, O Spirit, Dwell Among Us; Spirit, Working in Creation*
Ps. 104:24–34, 35b	*O Worship the King*
1 Cor. 12:3b–13	*One Bread, One Body*
John 7:37–39	*I Heard the Voice of Jesus Say*

ᔑ Children's Lectionary Sermon

TITLE: Pentecost

SCRIPTURE: Acts 2:1–21

KEY VERSE: *And everyone present was filled with the Holy Spirit and began speaking in other languages as the Holy Spirit gave them this ability.* (Acts 2:4)

KEY CONCEPT: Pentecost

MATERIALS: Bible, red balloons (or cupcakes with a candle)

PREPARATION: If you have people in your church who can speak various languages, have them read Acts 2:17–21 in the language they know at a cued time.

Today, we celebrate Pentecost. It is what we could call the birthday of the Church. This first Pentecost happened a long time ago. It was fifty days after Easter morning—Jesus' Resurrection.

Now, what you need to know is that Pentecost was actually a Jewish celebration. It took place fifty days after Passover. There were Jewish people from all over the world in Jerusalem for this celebration.

Then something amazing happened. Some of Jesus' followers were together. A loud sound came toward them from above them and then flames of fire settled on each of them. (*Open Bible.*) And in Acts it says, "And everyone present was filled with the Holy Spirit and began speaking in other languages as the Holy Spirit gave them this ability." (*At this point if you have people in your con-*

gregation who can speak different languages, have them do this now from where they are sitting.) The people from all the different countries could not believe what they were hearing or what they were seeing.

Peter came forward and spoke to the crowd. He told them how everything that had happened was what the prophet Joel said would happen. "I will pour out my Spirit upon all my servants, men and women alike and they will prophesy" (v. 18).

On this special day, when the Holy Spirit came to the disciples, the Church began to grow and spread. The believers of Jesus had the help of the Holy Spirit to go out and tell the world about Jesus.

Today, we celebrate Pentecost as the birthday of the Church. The Holy Spirit guides us today, just as the Holy Spirit did in Bible days. (*The next is optional.*) Here is a (*balloon or cupcake*) to celebrate the coming of the Holy Spirit and the beginning of the Church long ago. We have come to believe in Jesus because of those early believers who followed Jesus. We should celebrate and be thankful for all those followers of Jesus who have come before us.—Marcia Thompson

WORSHIP AIDS

Call to Worship: We share with believers through the ages the joy of Pentecost. As the Spirit came in power on that day, may again we experience something like tongues of fire resting on us. "Since we live in the Spirit, let us also walk in the Spirit" (Gal. 5:25).

Invocation: Rain down upon us, O God, in grace and glory and power that as on that first Pentecost we may respond and go forth to share in every language the power of God to save and secure forever through the Holy Spirit. Amen.—E. Lee Phillips

Offertory Sentence: "The earth is the Lord's, and the fullness thereof; the world and all that dwells therein" (Ps. 24:1).

Offertory Prayer: Gracious Lord, we acknowledge your ownership over all the earth and we who live within it. With the Spirit's help, we confess our love and loyalty to you and, with the Spirit's help, dedicate these gifts to your eternal purpose. Through him who gave his life for us. Amen.

Morning Prayer: Lord God of life, hope, and joy, breathe your Spirit upon us. Enable us to feel the strength and the power of your breath and the possibilities that are within us. Throw open the windows of our lives and let the breeze of your Spirit rush in and overcome our stale thinking, so that we can have new hopes, new dreams, and new possibilities. Remove blinders from our eyes that keep us from seeing those around us who have needs and sorrows, those who ache, who are hungry, tired, weary, frustrated, disillusioned, depressed, and hopeless. Breathe within us the breath of your joy. Well up within us that living water that comes from Jesus Christ, our Lord. Free us from the shackles that bind us to the past, to bad habits and broken dreams. Open our eyes this day to what we can become through Jesus Christ, who suffered and died for us and lives again. For we offer this prayer in his strong name. Amen.—William Powell Tuck

Benediction: People of God, go forth today in the power and the presence of the Holy Spirit, boldly declaring by word and deed the joy that resides within. May we be reminded that the Church is the work of the Spirit and that through God's Spirit we live and move and have our being. Holy Spirit, lead us. Amen.

SUNDAY, MAY 18, 2008
Trinity Sunday

LECTIONARY SERMON TOPIC: "The Majesty of God"
TEXT: Ps. 8
OTHER READINGS: Gen. 1:1–2:4a; 2 Cor. 13:11–13; Matt. 28:16–20

If you were going to take a trip to the moon and leave something there, what would it be? My understanding is that this psalm is the first biblical text left on the moon. The Apollo mission left a disk containing messages from seventy-three nations. The Vatican contributed this psalm. It speaks of the grandeur of the sovereignty of God and also the high status of being human. One commentator calls this psalm the Majesty of God and the glory of man.

I. **God's majesty in creation.** The psalmist expresses great excitement. He is saying that God brings order out of chaos. This is for us to understand regarding the Creation; later, we will see it is God's continuing work and purpose. God brings light from darkness, again reminding us that God continues working in creation with us. Clyde Francisco points out that to the Hebrews, the world was never just so many sticks and stones. Its every wonder testified to the glory of God who made it.

Picture David sitting on a hillside looking out at the vastness of the universe and contemplating the majesty of God. Ever done that yourself? Try it sometime. Studying astronomy brought to my attention the vastness and wonder of God's universe. Lie down and look up at the stars in the sky. Remember that each of those stars is about the size of our earth, and there are many others beyond what we can see. It is very difficult to come away without awe and wonder of God's creation. Yet in all the great wonder and splendor of the universe, the psalmist declares that creation of mankind is the crown of all God's creation. In an unpublished sermon, Steve Shoemaker reminds us that when God made humankind, God did not look and say (as he had said of the rest of creation) that it was good. God said, "It is very good, exceedingly good!" It is not an evil material world as some have avowed over the years. It is not the result of blind chance, a random accident. It is creation, the good and purposive work of a good God.

II. **Man's significant purpose.** The psalmist expresses great excitement, almost beyond himself, when he considers the wonder of God's creation. Who am I, and why am I here? We have asked that question one time or another. Some would have different answers. For instance, Karl Marx would probably define man in economic terms. Darwin would have said man is essentially a highly developed animal. Freud may have said man is an underdeveloped child. The psalmist describes man's significant purpose. In verses 5–8, God has placed us over all creation. Dominion over creation! How are we doing?

This dominion is a gift of God and with this comes responsibility. How have we handled it? Sometimes we tend to think the Bible focuses first on sinfulness of man. But the universe began, not in original sin but in "original blessing." And this must be word of hope to the world today that we have been blessed and are to be a blessing to all mankind. Those of us who believe we are biblical people must take that as primary in what it means to be "God's people." We are all loved, cared for, significant, special.

III. **Partners with God in caring for the earth.** To leave God out of the partnership invites disaster; indeed, frightening ecological disasters are all around us. This psalm is a reminder that those God-praising and earth-caring communities are one. There is indication that to be part of God's creation may also involve suffering. Yet we also are mindful that having a partnership with God also means that God is involved in our suffering. One writer points out that this psalm figures prominently in the book of Job. Job's suffering first causes him to deny the high status of mankind, but later he comes to change his mind and comes to conclude that the high status of being human involves both suffering and glory. We see this best in Christ Jesus—One who was most holy, but suffered. Yet in his suffering he pointed to God, who cares for each of us.—Louis Twyman

---

ILLUSTRATIONS

Glory and Dignity. In Today's English version of the Bible, this psalm has a heading titled, "God's Glory and Man's Dignity." That expresses, in a succinct way, what we are about. When we recognize man's dignity and attempt to restore dignity to our fellow man, we are glorifying God. At the same time, we cannot do so without recognizing the dignity of our fellow man. We, as Christians, have a special calling to recognize this in ourselves and each other but also share this concept in our everyday lives. As we care for the earth—God's creation and humankind—we are living out God's purpose.—Louis Twyman

Nature of Christ. "What do you think of Christ, the one who will come as the Anointed One, the Messiah?" is the question Jesus asked the Pharisees. "Whose son is he?" The Pharisees knew the easy answer: "The son of David."

Everyone knew that. Then Jesus complicated their thinking. "Well, how is it then that David, in Psalm 110:1, speaks by divine inspiration and refers to the coming Christ as his 'lord?'" How can Christ be the son of David and simultaneously be the Lord over David? Jewish families, out of respect, understood that fathers were lords over the sons, not sons over the fathers. And so the question, "The Christ: who is he?" goes unanswered by the Pharisees. But it's a question that cannot go unanswered by us. The clear implication of this text is that the Christ was more than just a special human being, despite his lineage to the house of David. This one, Jesus declares, uniquely manifests the presence of God. He is God's Son, known to us as Jesus of Nazareth.— Lawrence Vowan

Musical Selections Appropriate to the Day

Hymn suggestions for lectionary texts:

Gen. 1:1–2:4a	*This Is My Father's World; For Beauty of Meadows*
Ps. 8	*How Majestic Is Your Name*
2 Cor. 13:11–13	*May the Grace of Christ Our Savior*
Matt. 28:16–20	*Lord You Give the Great Commission; Jesus Saves*

❧ Children's Lectionary Sermon

TITLE: Being Together

SCRIPTURE: 2 Cor. 13:11–13

KEY VERSE: *Dear brothers and sisters, I close my letter with these last words: Rejoice. Change your ways. Encourage each other. Live in harmony and peace. Then the God of love and peace will be with you.* (2 Cor. 13:11, New Living Translation)

KEY CONCEPT: To accomplish God's work there must be unity.

MATERIALS: Bible, a letter

I brought a letter with me today. At the end of this letter from my friend, there is a special wish for me. At the end of the letter it says, "I hope you have a great day. Write soon!" The closing of this letter told me what my friend wished for me.

In the New Testament we have letters Paul wrote to different churches. He had wishes for these people he had been with. He had taught them about Jesus. (*Open Bible.*) In the letter we know as 2 Corinthians, Paul gives the believers at this church some wishes he has for them. Here is what Paul writes to them: "Dear brothers and sisters, I close my letter with these last words: Rejoice. Change your ways. Encourage each other. Live in harmony and peace. Then the God of love and peace will be with you."

What do you think he meant when he said, "Rejoice"? (*Let the children respond, reflecting back the answers they give.*) What do you think he meant by "change your ways"? (*Let the children respond, reflecting back their answers. Guide them as they need it.*) What does it mean to "encourage each other"? (*Let the children respond and reflect back their answers.*)

All these things Paul wished for the church in Corinth. We can listen to these wishes for our church, too. We can rejoice together through worship and through having times of fun together as followers of Jesus. We can change our ways if they are not pleasing to Jesus. We can encourage each other by saying kind and loving words or sending a card to tell someone you are happy you know them. We can worship, work, and play together in peace as God's people. We then know that God is with us and God's love and peace are in us.—Marcia Thompson

WORSHIP AIDS

Call to Worship: We joyfully gather in worship to experience again God's presence among us and to go forth prepared to serve. May we declare, along with the apostle, "in nothing I shall be ashamed, but with boldness, as always, so now also Christ will be magnified in my body, whether by life of by death" (Phil. 1:20).

Invocation: We ask, O Lord, how can it be that we have knowledge of an unfettered love, of a living Savior, of power over sin and death? Then we consider the Trinity of creation, conviction, and certitude and worship you anew in the name of the Father, Son, and Holy Spirit. Amen.—E. Lee Phillips

Offertory Sentence: "Even as each person has received God's gift, we are to minister the gift one to another, as good stewards of the grace of God" (1 Pet. 4:10).

Offertory Prayer: Father of life, we have nothing except that which we have received. We give thanks for your gracious provision. Receive these gifts of tithes and offerings as expressions of our gratitude and use them for the benevolent care of your world. We place this offering, and our lives, into your hands. Amen.

Morning Prayer: Almighty God, whom the heavens cannot contain, much less the temples that our hands have built, we stand in your presence this morning, awaiting some strong word, some insight from you for the living of these days. Let your wisdom be fathomed to the degree that we may understand your will for us. Let your truth be understood sufficiently that it may bring nobility to us. Let your Spirit work in us that we may fulfill your purpose for us. It is in you that the mysteries of life are made meaningful. It is in following your leadership and living by your truth that the dulling chains of routine are broken, and we are set free to live with a sense of purpose as we serve those in the world about us.

This morning we confess that there is much in our lives that needs renewal and change. Too often we respond to the motivation of our own selfish desires. We are too slow in giving up ancient prejudices, thereby bringing belittlement and pain to the human family. We so often refuse to accept new insights and stubbornly cling to unenlightened ideas, thereby hindering the progress of mankind, even the progress of those whom we love. Renew in us sensitivity to your ongoing revelation and enlightenment of your children that we may be able to make a worthy response to you and our fellow man, rather than a confused and demeaning answer to the calls for help and understanding sounded all around us.

Father, help us to know that through your guidance, fear can be replaced with courage; spiritual and emotional weakness can be replaced with strength; worry can be overcome by peace; loneliness can lead to closer companionship with you and with others who need us; hate in us and in others can make us more sensitive to the need for the presence of love. And doubt, dealt with, can lead us to a deeper knowledge and faith.—Henry Fields

Benediction: Lord God, whom we know as Father, Son, and Holy Spirit, look with favor upon your people as we go out to serve in the days of this week. May we focus on the power of life given to noble surrender and service. And fill our lives with your peace. Amen.

SUNDAY, MAY 25, 2008

LECTIONARY SERMON TOPIC: "The Antidote to Anxiety"
TEXT: Matt. 6:24–34
OTHER READINGS: Isa. 49:8–16a; Ps. 131 or Ps. 62:5–12; 1 Cor. 4:1–5

Anxiety is a very common word in our vocabulary today. We know of people who suffer from anxiety so severe that it often disrupts life. The psychological symptoms of anxiety would go something like this: excessive worry, tension, restlessness, irritability, inability to relax. Often these are related to health, money, or family issues and are not to be taken lightly. We go to therapy or take anti-anxiety medicine in order to live life. Often we feel guilty about our anxiety because we have been taught that anxiety comes from a lack of faith.

 I. **First, we need to understand that we are not immune from life's difficulties.** Difficulties come to the just and the unjust. Some of us have been "scripted" to worry, to look for bad things to happen. In my family, worrying was a way to show that you cared: "I've been so worried about you." We cannot understand this teaching unless we see that Jesus was deeply concerned that people have the physical necessities of life. Jesus did not withdraw from the world; he paid attention to the material needs of people. At the same time, he warned against making material values the object of trust and affection.

II. **Second, this Scripture is more about the focus of our lives.** Some translations say, "Do not be anxious" or "Take no thought." A better translation may be, "Do not be distracted." Where is our focus? What are our ultimate values? Jesus spoke of laying up treasures for yourself, to be careful of things we trust in or cling to. We must be careful not to hold on to things too tightly. Often we have a tendency to secure ourselves by way of earthly things.

Rick Warren, in his book, *The Purpose-Driven Life,*[1] suggests that each person is driven by a purpose—a focus around which life is centered. Warren mentions five common values and circumstances that drive our lives.

Some people are driven by guilt. For them, the past controls the future. Some people are driven by resentment and anger. They hold on to hurts and don't get over them. Some people are driven by fear, either the result of a trauma or family situation. Some people are driven by materialism—the desire to get and have more and more that often resembles an addiction. Self-worth is often based on possessions. Security is often based on possessions. Some people are driven by the need for approval and spend enormous amounts of time working to please others. The question we ask ourselves is this: Where is our focus?

III. **We stand before the great impossibility.** "No man can serve two masters." Jesus did not say you "should not serve two masters." He said, "You cannot serve two masters." We live in a world where many of us are pulled and pushed one way or another. That is going to be part of the territory of living. In today's world, where the words *stress, anxiety,* and *pulled in all directions* are very common descriptions of living, there is a need to learn where our "center" is. We all know of times when we have been too busy to come to church, too tired to pray, too many obligations to spend time with our families.

What can we do? What is the answer? We return to our Scripture of the morning to find this: we can help each other find our main focus. I believe that we must look closely at Foster's idea of the "Freedom of Simplicity"— simplifying our lives, recognizing our primary focus, as laid out in our Scripture of the day. The Scripture does not indicate that the things of life are bad

---

[1] Rick Warren, *The Purpose-Driven Life* (Grand Rapids: Zondervan, 2002).

or evil. The problem comes when they gain mastery over our lives and usurp God's power and presence. The words of Jesus sound very dogmatic and unbending; as a matter of fact, they are. We are to have only one master in our lives: Jesus Christ. We can serve God and possess some of the world's goods, but we cannot serve God and also let the things of the world possess us.

Some anxiety is the result of a medical issue, but much of it is brought on by our lives being pushed by conflicting loyalties, undue pressure from the inside or outside. The antidote is to get our priorities straight! That is why we need to continue to be supportive of each other as we live life in a stressful, busy, competitive world, reminding each other from time to time about what is really important. We all probably know what that is. We just need to be reminded of it once in a while.—Louis Twyman

---

ILLUSTRATIONS

Stewardship. Richard Foster, in his book *Freedom of Simplicity,* cites reasons we should be careful not to amass earthly treasure but should store up heavenly treasure. The first reason is that the world is a very uncertain place. Moths and rust may break in and steal, meaning no matter how secure things are, if our trust is in those, it will ultimately fail us. The second is that whatever we fix as our treasure will possess our whole life. "For where your treasure is there will your heart be also" (Matt. 6:21).—Louis Twyman

Time Management. I often hear people discuss the pulls and tugs of life, where they many times feel "out of control." They might say, "I would like to do this, but I just don't have time." We in the church need not lay a guilt trip on these folks but instead help them—and each other—center our lives, find our main focus. This is no easy task; some of the difficulty is self-imposed; some is due to trying to meet the expectations of others or following a family script. We often hear folks talk about getting out of the rat race, getting caught up in others' expectations. It would also do us well as churches to be sure that we are not playing into the game of expectations that often only adds to the stress and guilt.—Louis Twyman

Musical Selections Appropriate to the Day

Hymn suggestions for lectionary texts:

Isa. 49:8–16a	*I Love Your Kingdom, Lord; He's Got the Whole World in His Hands*
Ps. 131	*Be Still My Soul* [or]
Ps. 62:5–12	*When Peace Like a River*
1 Cor. 4:1–5	*Find Us Faithful; When We All Get to Heaven*
Matt. 6:24–34	*O Master Let Me Walk with Thee; More Love to Thee, O Christ*

❧ Children's Lectionary Sermon

TITLE: I Can Always Trust God

SCRIPTURE: Ps. 62:5–12

KEY VERSE: *O my people, trust in him at all times. Pour out your heart to him, for God is our refuge.* (Ps. 62:8, New Living Translation)

KEY CONCEPT: Trust

MATERIALS: Bible, a picture of a tornado and storm shelter

This is a picture of a tornado. When a tornado comes, it is good to have a storm shelter. This is the picture of an underground shelter. When there is a tornado, this door is opened and there is a stairway into the shelter. Inside you might keep a flashlight and possibly a radio.

You probably don't have a storm shelter at your house. These days, homes are built to be very strong. When a storm comes, we go to a safe place like a basement, hallway, or bathroom until the storm goes away. You practice your storm plans at school, too. You trust your teachers to take you to a safe place.

Sometimes bad things happen. There are accidents, or sickness, or war. We don't understand why these things happen, but we can trust God. (*Open Bible.*) Listen to this verse: "O my people, trust in him at all times. Pour out your heart to him, for God is our refuge." Do you know what *refuge* means? A refuge is a shelter or a safe place. When it says we can pour out our heart to him, it means we can talk to God through prayer. We can trust God is there and will hear us.

Even when we don't understand why things happen, we believe God loves us and would never leave us alone. God is our refuge. Let's pray together now.—Ken Cox

WORSHIP AIDS

Call to Worship: We seek today the close companionship of our Heavenly Father. The One who knows us intimately draws us now to worship. We rejoice in God's favor: "To the Lord our God belongs mercy and forgiveness" (Dan. 9:9).

Invocation: Lord, we are truly aware of the weakness of our faith and the inadequacies of our obedience. We are exceedingly grateful for your mercy and forgiveness. As we draw near in worship, speak clearly to our souls that we may, through word and deed, truly praise you. Amen.

Offertory Sentence: "And the children of Israel brought a willing sacrifice to the Lord, every man and woman, whose heart made them willing to bring for all manner of work, which the Lord had commanded to be made by the hand of Moses" (Exod. 35:29).

Offertory Prayer: Father, we dedicate these tithes and offerings to you, asking that you receive them as expressions of our love and devotion. May the fruit of our labor be given cheerfully and used as channels for blessing to others, and may the gospel message of Jesus Christ go forth to the ends of the earth. Amen.

Morning Prayer: O Lord, you have been our dwelling place in all generations. Before the mountains were brought forth or you had formed the earth and the world, from everlasting to everlasting, thou art God. A thousand years in thy sight are but as yesterday when it is past and is a watch in the night. So teach us, O God, to number our days. We contemplate that we are creatures of time, who sooner or later will come to the end of this life's journey. Help us, Lord, as we live one day at a time, to know that every day is precious, never to be recaptured. It cannot be lived again. We pray, O God, for guidance in living each moment, in living each week, to know that this one week will never be regained.

You have made us free, O God, to love, free to enjoy the moment, the life, the day. And yet we know our days are numbered, and we sense that. O God, we pause on this Memorial Sunday, to thank you for each life now completed. As we read their names, we can picture in our minds the faces of loved ones or friends who have gone before. Accept our gratitude for their lives in our life, and their lives within our church family and in this community, for every way they worshipped and worked and witnessed, in and through this great fellowship we call the church. And as we think about their lives, help us to consider how we are spending our lives. So may we live a little taller, with our faith a little deeper, our hopes and our visions a little brighter, knowing that life gives us another day. For we come together to worship and to catch that vision and the spirit, and in the name of Jesus Christ. Amen.—George Davis

Benediction: We go forth today with ready spirits, O Lord, eager to speak and live in such ways that your love will be seen through us. And in that same spirit of joy and service, bring us back together next Lord's Day. Amen.

SUNDAY, JUNE 1, 2008

LECTIONARY SERMON TOPIC: "The Ultimate Survivor"
TEXT: Gen. 6:9–22, 7:24, 8:14–19
OTHER READINGS: Ps. 46; Rom. 1:16–17, 3:22b–28 (29–31); Matt. 7:21–29

Perhaps you are one of the millions of Americans who got addicted to the popular *Survivor* series on television. On a remote island or in rugged terrain, participants choose to live in the most primitive conditions, using physical strength, imagination, and endurance skills to withstand rigorous activities and to survive. Contestants on the show have had to construct boats that would carry them over the ocean from one island to another, eat creepy-crawly critters to stay alive, and endure physical challenges that would do most of us in. Not everyone who sets out to win the prize is able to survive the challenges of the wilderness. Many drop out along the way.

I. **Evidently, there is something about being a survivor that strikes a common chord in the human psyche.** Indeed, the survivor motif can be a metaphor for our lives. We all want to be survivors in the game of life, do we not? We all want to be safely carried over the flash floods of life that wash our way. When life sends us trouble and heartache, we want to be strong enough to stand and do what we must. We want to overcome and endure. We want to survive.

But deep down in our souls we realize that a "life-preserver faith" will not do. That is, we cannot expect to sail along through life, giving no thought to God or faith or things spiritual and then, when trouble strikes, latch onto faith like a life preserver tossed into the sea. Yet, this is exactly what many are tempted to do—have no active prayer or contemplative life, not give time to searching for spiritual truth, or give little thought to active church attendance or community involvement.

But then when there is a death in the family and a funeral is needed, or a son or daughter is ready to be married and a church wedding is called for, or a marriage is on the rocks and counseling is needed, an SOS goes out for help, and faith becomes an emergency response. Sometimes a faith cry as a last-minute, emergency attempt will suffice. But oftentimes it will not.

Preparations for life's flash floods really need to be made far in advance. Those persons who participate in the survivors' competition don't just one day decide they want to sail off to a deserted island to become a survivor. Most likely they have spent weeks or months in disciplined training so they are prepared for the rigorous ordeals that confront them.

II. **At this point enter Noah, the first true survivor.** Noah had the character and personality traits that qualified him to become the first true survivor. In other words, Noah was inwardly prepared—deep in his soul—for the great test that lay before him. And Noah commenced preparing the ark for the salvation of his family months in advance of the flood that would cover the earth. We are not really told how far in advance Noah began constructing the ark prior to the flood's beginning. However, a boat about 450 feet long, approximately five times the length of the *Mayflower* that brought the Pilgrims to America, would take several months—probably even years—to complete. As one biblical commentator has pointed out, "Noah . . . not only foresaw the crisis; he also did something about it, and he did it ahead of time. He began to build his ark before there was any obvious evidence it would be needed."[1] Noah made preparations—both inward and outward—far in advance of his ultimate survival challenge.

Proper preparations for being a survivor today include making adequate spiritual provisions. It means being in covenant (or right relationship) with community, and in fellowship with God and others. It means striving to be blameless and just in the way that one lives in relation to God and others. And it means living in truthfulness and faithfulness.

Being adequately prepared means foreseeing inevitable crises ahead of time, as Noah did. It is building your life, knowing full well that storms will come—testing, sorrow, unexpected trouble, possible financial loss, serious illness—and being somewhat prepared for whatever life sends our way. The point of the story is not that Noah was perfect or sinless; no one is. Rather, Noah had an unusually close relationship with God; he sought to do justice and act blamelessly, and he tried to be a person of high integrity. Such are attributes of the ultimate survivor in today's difficult world: right living, or doing what we know is the right and just thing to do, and living in fellowship or community, and having favor with the world. Then when the floods of life come pouring down upon us, we are prepared. We are spiritually strong. We can, in good conscience and confidence, call out to others and the Force of life to help us.

III. **Jesus also drew upon the flood imagery and survivor motif when he taught the parable of the two men who built their houses, one on sand and one on rock.** In that time and place, houses would sometimes be built in the sandy valleys (we might call them flood plains), which were

---

[1]George Buttrick (ed.), *The Interpreter's Bible Commentary*, Vol. 1 (Nashville: Abingdon Press, 1952), p. 540.

mostly dry and flood-free. But occasionally a hard rain would cause these low-lying areas to flood. Some would build their houses right down on the sand, without laying any type of foundation. So when the low-lying valley filled with rushing floodwaters, the houses were washed off the sand and destroyed. But the wise builder dug down deep into the sand and laid or poured a rock foundation. The rock foundation was built up off the ground several inches, so when the floodwaters came, the house was firmly grounded on solid rock.

Such it was with the house that my maternal grandparents lived in. My grandparents lived beside a stream that began high up in the mountains. Every now and then, hard rains would cause that stream to rise and wash from its banks. On more than one occasion, I saw my grandparents' house completely surrounded with floodwaters. But the floods never washed the house away because the builders had dug down in the earth and laid a rock foundation and then positioned the floor of the house about two feet off the ground on limestone rocks.

Jesus' emphasis in the parable is that the wise ones will build their lives properly by *hearing* and *acting upon* the words that he taught, as summarized in the Sermon on the Mount (Matt. 5–7). In summary, Jesus teaches right living, humility, mercy, peacemaking, purity, truthfulness, generosity, love, compassion, forgiveness, and kindness. To build one's life on the teachings of Jesus, as revealed in the Sermon on the Mount, is to make oneself spiritually strong and prepared to survive whatever storms life may send our way. I have heard it said more than once by people who were enduring troubles: "My faith is all that is keeping me going; I don't know what I would do without my faith."

In the end it will not matter how many churches we have belonged to, or how many creeds or confessions we have recited, or how many offices we have held in the church. It will not matter how much wealth we accumulated, how large our house was, or how many automobiles we owned. In the end all that will matter is whether or not we have built our lives upon sound teaching, upon spiritual truth. In the final analysis, the character that we are building—righteousness, justice, and faithfulness—is important. And our relationship with the Divine and all of life will enable us to withstand the floods of life that come our way. The faith that we have, the character that we build, and the relationships that we nurture are the things that will enable us to be the ultimate survivor in today's turbulent world.—Randy Hammer

ILLUSTRATIONS

Firm Foundation. A couple of years ago we were vacationing at the beach. I sat in a beach chair at the water's edge and watched kids build giant castles in the sand. Before long a renegade wave came in much further than all the rest and dashed against the wall of the sandcastle. Thinking about this Scripture in Matthew, I said to the kids: "You built your house upon the sand." And so it is with so many of our time. They are building their house (their lives) upon the sand and have no firm foundation against the floods of life that sooner or later are bound to come. Those who build their lives upon the sand, so to speak, are not necessarily bad people; they may just be thoughtless, living a careless and unexamined life.—Randy Hammer

Character. A letter from Pliny, governor of Bithynia, to Trajan the Roman Emperor, written about 110 A.D., complains of the difficulties he has been having with the Christian sect. Pliny saw that the early Christians refused to worship the Emperor. He went on to explain the reason why: "They sing to Christ as though to a god."—Lawrence Vowan

Musical Selections Appropriate to the Day

Hymn suggestions for lectionary texts:

Gen. 6:11–22, 7:24, 8:14–19	*Guide Me, O Thou Great Jehovah; How Firm a Foundation*
Ps. 46	*O God Our Help in Ages Past; A Mighty Fortress Is Our God*
Rom. 1:16–17, 3:22b–28 (29–31)	*I Love to Tell the Story; Amazing Grace*
Matt. 7:21–29	*The Solid Rock*

☙ Children's Lectionary Sermon

TITLE: Be Silent

SCRIPTURE: Ps. 46

KEY VERSE: *Be silent, and know that I am God!* (Ps. 46:10a, New Living Translation)

KEY CONCEPT: Faithfulness

MATERIALS: Bible

I want us to play a game this morning. Here is what I need you to do. I am going to say "Ready, set, go," and then I want you to be as still and silent as you can. Don't move and don't say a word. I want to see who can be the quietest. "Ready, set, go!" (*Some children will start to laugh, and some might be serious. If they take it seriously, then try to make them laugh.*)

Sometimes it is hard to be quiet and still. Your parents ask you to be still and quiet during worship time. We need to take quiet moments to be with God. (*Open Bible.*) This is what the writer of Psalm 46 said: "Be silent, and know that I am God!" Sometimes we get busy with all our activities. We have on the television or our video games. We don't take time to just be still and silent with God. But we need to make time. Being still shows we honor God and we love God.

Can you think of times during your day you could be silent and still and be with God? (*Let the children respond. Reflect back their responses.*) I like to be in my room by myself to be still and silent with God. It is a time I can pray. It is a time I can wonder about all the beautiful things God has made. It is a time to be thankful.

I know it might be hard to be silent and still, but give it a try this week. Find a quiet place and be silent with God. Honor God by just praising him silently.—Marcia Thompson

☙ WORSHIP AIDS ☙

Call to Worship: As we gather to worship, the joy we know in Jesus Christ is expressed as praise that rises from our hearts and in our words. With the psalmist of old, we declare, "Lift up your hands in the sanctuary, and bless the Lord. The Lord who made heaven and earth bless you" (Ps. 134:2–3).

Invocation: Kind Divine Father, we enter into your presence with grateful hearts. You have given us life, and family, and friendship, and a host of other blessings, and most important is a true sense of comradeship with you. Meet us here this day that we may be strengthened for the living of our days. Amen.

Offertory Sentence: "Give, and it shall be given to you; good measure, pressed down, and shaken together, and running over. . . . For with the same measure that you measure shall it be measured to you again" (Luke 6:38).

Offertory Prayer: Gracious God, we express thanks for your overflowing generosity. Give to us, we pray, gracious hearts like your own. Let not fear or selfishness cause us to hold back from giving as you call us to give. May our gifts of tithes and offerings be given with glad hearts, and may they be used for the building of your Kingdom. Amen.

Morning Prayer: Our Father, Creator of the universe, Father of our Lord Jesus Christ, we come to you with hearts filled with praise. You are to us the gracious and caring God of the Bible. You have shown your marvelous deeds in days past and are showing them again. You have revealed to us yourself, through the person and work of Jesus Christ, the Lord. We stand in awe in your presence and yield our hearts to you in trust and love.

We confess that we often vacillate between faith and doubt. We see your handiwork and rejoice. Then some experience baffles us, some pain injures us, some cloud comes over us. O Lord, give us such commitments of love that the night and the day will be the same, that our obedience will be sure, so that even in the darkness we shall be led, as it were, by a pillar of fire. May no duty be left undone, no word of witness left unsaid, because of a wavering heart.

Let now your gracious blessings be poured out on us. We pray not for selfish blessings that may lift us up but for the blessings of your Spirit that forever point us to those purposes of life that are greater than ourselves. To you, O Lord, we offer ourselves, all that we know ourselves to be, to all we know you to be. In Jesus' name, Amen.—Lee McGlone

Benediction: God of all creation, author of life and light, made known to us in Scripture as Father, Son, and Holy Spirit, lead us as we step into a new week. Let our walk be your walk. Amen.

SUNDAY, JUNE 8, 2008

LECTIONARY SERMON TOPIC: "Friends in Low Places"
TEXT: Matt. 9:9–13, 18–26
OTHER READINGS: Gen. 12:1–9; Ps. 33:1–12; Rom. 4:13–25

A few years ago, before he slowed down and went into semi-retirement, Garth Brooks was one of the hottest country singers around, selling more records and grossing more ticket sales than practically any other artist. In 1991, his song titled "Friends in Low Places" received the Country Music Association award as the nation's number-one single. We laughed at the song at our house when we first heard it, having no idea that it would be voted number one. Here's how it goes:

> I've got friends in low places,
> Where the whiskey drowns and the beer chases
> All my blues away; and I'll be okay.
> I'm not big on social graces
> Think I'll slip on down to the oasis
> Oh, I've got friends in low places.

As I first listened to the lyrics, I wondered what Jesus would think of this song if he were here on earth now. And I decided that Jesus might jump right in with Garth Brooks and sing along. For you see, Jesus, too, had friends in low places—a *lot* of friends in low places. Some of them are mentioned in today's Gospel reading.

I. **The chief character in this passage is Matthew, a tax collector for the despised Roman government.** Usually, tax collectors were Jews who excised taxes from their own people on behalf of their foreign oppressors. Being a tax collector was a bought position—one you paid for. The position of tax collector had much latitude for abuse. The Roman government didn't care how much tax a man collected as long as they got their share. Thus one could collect two, three, or four times what was really due, and no one could do anything about it. As a tax collector for an oppressive foreign government, Matthew was despised by his own people; he was viewed as an outcast, and he was looked upon as a defiled man by the religious establishment. Yet it was this type of man that Jesus called to follow him.

Why did Jesus choose such a man to be one of the twelve? We can only conjecture. Perhaps it was because Matthew was a businessman, wise to the ways of the world, and a good manager of money. But more important, perhaps Jesus chose Matthew because he saw in him, as he sees in each of us, the great potential that lay within him—potential that could be tapped and harnessed for the Kingdom of God.

II. **Upon hearing the call, Matthew immediately got up, left his good-paying profession, and followed Jesus.** In celebration of his new calling, perhaps, and wanting to introduce Jesus to his friends, Matthew planned a dinner party. He called in all his friends: other tax collectors, embezzlers, thieves perhaps, maybe even some ladies of the evening. All these "sinners" or outcasts came to Matthew's house and gathered around Jesus, the guest of honor. As they lounged around on the floor, they broke bread together, one of the most intimate things friends can do. With whom one chose to eat was a matter that was taken quite seriously in first-century Judaism. Now, there were those who could not understand this. They would not associate with or sit at table with anyone who did not keep the ritual purity laws, for fear that they might defile themselves. "Why does your teacher eat with tax collectors and sinners?" they demanded from Jesus' disciples (Matt. 9:11). Does he not know with whom he is associating? Does he not care that he could defile himself? Is he not concerned that people will talk about him for being seen with these people?

Jesus heard this questioning. His reply was that it was for this reason that he came into the world, to love and minister to all those in low places—those down on their luck, those in the gutter, those at the bottom of the scale of self-esteem. "Those who are well have no need of a physician, but those who are sick," Jesus said (Matt. 9:12).

As I said, Jesus had lots of friends in low places; in addition to tax collectors, there were cursing fishermen, former prostitutes, and those considered unclean and untouchable. I don't think we can really understand to what extent Jesus reached out to those on the lowest rungs of society's ladder. But the truth is, the early Christian movement was founded by a small group of mostly poor peasants who lived on the fringes of society and acceptability. But they didn't stay in low places very long. Through Jesus' presence and grace, they were lifted up and given a new vision of what they could be and do.

III. **Further down in our Gospel reading, we are told about another person down on her luck—the woman who had suffered a flow of blood, a constant hemorrhage, for several years.** It is important to note that the woman's affliction was not only physical (which was bad enough in and of itself), but it was social, for according to religious law she was unclean, and everything she touched was made unclean. But the good news is that through Jesus, God's mercy and compassion, was—and is—extended to all humanity and that mercy or compassion takes precedence over everything else. "But go and learn what this means: 'I desire mercy, not sacrifice'" (Matt. 9:13) Jesus said, quoting from the Hebrew prophet Hosea.

Indeed, Jesus' example of compassion is also our purpose and calling in coming together as a church—to show mercy (compassion) to each other and the world. To help people get back on their feet, to be the hands of Christ to help pull people up from their low places of life and give them a new vision of what they can be through God's power and grace—this is our high calling.

A question we might consider this morning is this: Do we have friends in low places? As a church certainly we should. Now, when I refer to friends in low places, I don't necessarily mean "bad people," although they certainly would be included. Rather, I mean those who are low down on their luck. I think of those who are struggling with any sort of addiction (and addiction takes many forms today). I think of the abused or neglected child who has to get out of the home, the battered wife who is being held prisoner in her own house. I think of the poorest of the poor in the Dominican Republic that medical missionary Alan Kerr is serving; those living with HIV-AIDS being served by the Damien Center and Support Ministries in Albany, New York; those who have had to live on the streets but are trying to better themselves and are being served by places like the Capital City Rescue Mission. The low places of life can take many different forms, and all of us could be there at one time or another.

The good news for those who are feeling low, those who are down on their luck, is that God cares. And for the church to be true to Christ and to follow his example, the church also has to care and befriend those in low places.—Randy Hammer

---

ILLUSTRATIONS

Tradition. Marcus Borg points out that in the religion of Jesus' day, there were two primary interpretations or traditions of what it meant to be a good, religious person.[2] One was the "purity" interpretation. To be in right standing with God, one had to become and remain pure, holy, undefiled. This position is based on the biblical verse where God is quoted as saying, "You shall be holy as the Lord your God is holy" (Lev. 11:44). The other position was the "compassion" tradition that says true religion is showing love and compassion to God and neighbor. It is based on the biblical verses, "Love the Lord your God with all your heart, soul and mind," and "love your neighbor as yourself" (Deut. 6:5; Lev. 19:18). The dominant and ruling class in Jesus' day emphasized the purity laws. The reason Jesus got into so much trouble was that he came emphasizing the compassion tradition. Today there are those in America

---

[2]Marcus Borg, *Meeting Jesus Again for the First Time* (San Francisco: HarperSanFrancisco, 1994).

who would fall into the "purity position," whereas others with their emphasis upon inclusiveness would fall into the "compassion camp."—Randy Hammer

Trust. There is the old story about a man who was walking along a narrow path, not paying much attention to where he was going, and slipped over the edge of a cliff. As he fell, he grabbed a branch growing from the side of the cliff. Realizing that he couldn't hang on for long, he called out for help: "Is there anybody up there?" When a voice answered, the man said, "Who's that?" The voice replied, "It's God, do you trust me?" The man said, "I trust you completely, Lord." God replied, "Good. Let go of the branch." After a short pause the man cried out, "Is there anybody else up there?"—Lawrence Vowan

Musical Selections Appropriate to the Day

Hymn suggestions for lectionary texts:

Gen. 12:1–9	*The God of Abraham Praise*
Ps. 33:1–12	*Sing Praise to God Who Reigns Above*
Rom. 4:13–25	*I Worship You, Almighty God*
Matt. 9:9–13, 18–26	*Jesus! What a Friend for Sinners*

Children's Lectionary Sermon

TITLE: God's Plans

SCRIPTURE: Ps. 33:1–12

KEY VERSE: *But the Lord's plans stand firm forever; his intentions can never be shaken.* (Ps. 33:11, New Living Translation)

KEY CONCEPT: God's plan

MATERIALS: Bible, blueprints

These are blueprints for a house. Here is a picture of where the roof goes. Here are the different rooms in the house. When construction workers build new houses, they have a plan to give them directions. The bathroom goes here, and the closet goes there. (*Show the children the plan as you point to the various areas of the house.*)

God makes plans, too. God's plans are based on love, wisdom, and right-eousness and are full of good intentions for us. (*Open Bible.*) Listen to this verse: "But the Lord's plans stand firm forever; his intentions can never be shaken."

What God wants for us and from us doesn't change. God wants us to obey what we have learned from God's Word. God wants us to make good choices. God wants us to pray. God wants us to love God and others. God shows God's love to us through all the things God created and through the loving people we have around us. Most important, God showed God's love by sending Jesus.

Now, I have a tough question for you. Do you think when bad things hap-pen that God wants changes? (*Let the children respond.*) Sometimes bad things happen because people make wrong choices. God is sad, but what God wants does not change. Sometimes bad things happen and we don't know why. They make us sad and God sad, too. But even when those things happen, God still is the same. God loves us and can help us not feel so sad.

The building plans for a house show we need wood, metal, and various plastics. We are involved in God's plan. Our greatest happiness comes as we live obeying God and discovering ways God can use us to share God's message with others. No matter who we are, God wants us to follow and live as God has taught us to live. Then God's love can spread all over the world.—Ken Cox

☙ WORSHIP AIDS ☙

Call to Worship: Worship is a call to life—to fullness of life through the love of Jesus Christ. How do we know what this love is? "This is how we know what love is: Christ gave his life for us. We too, then, ought to give our lives for our brothers" (John 3:16).

Invocation: Loving Father, make yourself known to us as we gather in your name. May your Word teach us the truth of your way, and may your presence inspire us to live it out each day. Give us strength to be faithful to you and to every person for whom Jesus died. Amen.

Offertory Sentence: "They gave according to their own means, as I can testify, and beyond their means, of their own free will" (2 Cor. 8:3).

Offertory Prayer: God of grace and mercy, we know the certainty of your care for us. You have loved us all our days. Who we are, your grace has made us. What we have, your provisions have supplied. We offer these gifts of tithes and offerings to express our love to you. Take them, we pray, and work your grace in others. Amen.

Morning Prayer: God of all mercy, help us to rejoice as readily when times are difficult as when things are running smoothly. Keep us from looking at the momentary events of our lives and treating them as if they are the final scene. So often that is how we view things. The present overwhelms us with its pains and its struggles, and we can see no bright ray of hope penetrating the future. This morning, enable us to walk along the Pilgrim's Road, endowed with sufficient faith to generate trust, which will be indicated by your love and guidance. Let us see the banes of today become the blessings of tomorrow. Let us experience the sorrows turned to joy, the pains turned to healing, our lostness turned to salvation. Above all, we pray that we will not let the uncertainties of today and the miseries of the moment cause us embarrassment in our giving or reluctance in committing our material wealth for the causes of the Kingdom of Christ. Lead us to give as you have prescribed, even though what we may have to give is meager. Then we pray that all we offer to you at this alter of giving will be touched with the power of the Lord so that it will be as the loaves and fishes for the good of others. This we pray in the power and name of Jesus. Amen.—Henry Fields

Benediction: With glad hearts we go forth to the opportunities that lie before us. May we, with the strength of compassion and the certainty of faith, reach out beyond ourselves to touch and to bless the lives of others. Dearest God, whom we know as Father, Son, and Holy Spirit, go with us. Amen.

SUNDAY, JUNE 15, 2008

LECTIONARY SERMON TOPIC: "When God Makes Us Laugh"

TEXT: Gen. 18:1–15

OTHER READINGS: Ps. 116:1–2, 12–19; Rom. 5:1–8; Matt. 9:35–10:8 (9–23)

If you have ever witnessed a human birth, then you know that laughter is a natural response. The mood of the event is so spontaneous, so unique, and so joyous. I remember when our daughter was born. We almost did not make it to the hospital in time. My wife had suffered false labor for weeks, and we had already made a couple of premature trips to the hospital. So we wanted to be sure that when pains started, it was the real thing. When the right time finally did arrive, our daughter arrived just twenty-five minutes after we pulled up to the Emergency Room door. We had attended Lamaze natural childbirth classes, and I was supposed to be in the delivery room helping. But as soon as my wife was checked by the doctor, two of the nurses came running down the hall after me. One nurse was on each side of me, trying to dress me in that paper gown, cap, and little paper booties, as we were running down the hall together. No sooner had I stepped in the delivery room than our daughter made her appearance. Immediately after the birth, as I saw all that was going on, I began to feel faint. My wife had to tell the nurse to make sure I didn't pass out. All she could do was laugh. It was a natural and uncontrollable emotion of joy at an event so unique, so spontaneous, so joyous. So it often is when God astounds us by sending blessings our way. God makes us laugh.

I. **A wonderful story about laughter is in the biblical account of Abraham and Sarah.** As seen in this story, God sometimes makes us laugh when we are recipients of good news. We did not read the passage in Genesis 17 today, but another tradition states that Abraham laughed when God informed him that he would have a son by his aged wife, Sarah. Abraham "laughed to himself in disbelief," the Scripture says. "How could I become a father at the age of one hundred?" (Gen. 17:17). Likewise, when Sarah heard the news that she would bear Abraham a son, she also laughed silently to herself. "How could a worn-out woman like me have a baby?" she thought (Gen. 18:12).

Now, we have to understand Sarah's plight. Sarah was barren; she was ninety years old and had no children. She lived with the reality of barrenness day in and day out. All a woman really had going for her in those days was her children. If a woman bore her husband no children, he could divorce her and marry a "more fertile" woman. In those days, being barren was looked upon as the woman's fault, and it was often seen to be a curse from God. So we can see why Sarah laughed when told she would have a son. Some nine months later, after she had conceived and her son was born, Sarah proclaimed, "God has brought me laughter! All who hear about this will laugh with me" (Gen. 21:6). Abraham and Sarah appropriately named their son Isaac, which means "laughter" or "he laughs." Laughter often is an uncontrollable emotion of joy when good news comes to us unexpectedly.

II. **If we would only stop and think about it, we may have many reasons to laugh.** We are often delivered from tragedy or trouble. The Divine has often astounded us by entering our lives unexpectedly. Good news constantly enriches our days. We are blessed in so many ways.

So I submit to you that laughter is a gift from God. It is as much a gift from God as is faith, joy, or love. There have been a number of times when I have been reading a good book, studying the Scriptures, or listening to a sermon or lecture when a word of good news seemed to jump right off the page or be directed at me personally, and I reacted by smiling or maybe even chuckling out loud.

III. **But the gift of laughter becomes the greatest gift when it comes wrapped up in the gift of a child.** Today—Father's Day—we can celebrate that great gift. Consequently, we should remember to give thanks often for the great gift of laughter and for the children who bring laughter and joy to our lives.

So how long has it been since you had a good God-inspired laugh? Since you laughed at some good news that came your way? Since you were astounded by and laughed over divine providence at work in your life?

Since you laughed because God, through another person, blessed your day? Since you laughed with a joyful child?

If it has been too long since we last laughed, then perhaps messengers of God have passed by our tent, in a manner of speaking (as they passed by Abraham and Sarah's tent in the heat of the day), but we were not expecting them, and we let them pass right on by. Perhaps it is time for us to be on the lookout for messengers of laughter and to be ready to invite them in.—Randy Hammer

---

ILLUSTRATIONS

Laughter. It has been proven that laughter is healthy. It is good for both body and soul. Laughter causes the body to release chemicals that combat disease and promote healing. In fact, *Reader's Digest* for years had a section called "Laughter Is the Best Medicine." Perhaps you have heard about the man who was diagnosed with a terminal illness, who went to the movie store and bought several boxes of old slapstick comedies. The man then checked into a motel and for weeks did nothing but laugh at those corny movies. The story goes that the man laughed himself back to health. He was cured of his illness that had been diagnosed as terminal. Now, I am not advocating that someone with a serious illness forego medical treatment and trust old movies to bring about a cure. But it has been proven that laughter aids in the healing process.—Randy Hammer

Love of God. The writer Fredrick Buechner was converted under the preaching of George Buttrick at the Madison Avenue Presbyterian Church in New York City. Buechner says he gave his life to God when Buttrick said that a Christian is someone who has the right to fall down before the throne of Christ "with tears and great laughter." When he heard that, Buechner understood for the first time in his life, just as Sarah did when she laughed after the birth of Isaac, what it means to be loved by God.[3]—Randy Hammer

---

[3]Quoted in James W. Cox (ed.), *The Minister's Manual 1999* (San Francisco: Jossey-Bass, 1999), p. 152.

Musical Selections Appropriate to the Day

Hymn suggestions for lectionary texts:

Gen. 18:1–15	*Great Is the Lord; Nothing Is Impossible*
Ps. 116:1–2, 12–19	*Shout to the Lord; My Lord of Light*
Rom. 5:1–8	*Lift High the Cross; What Wondrous Love Is This*
Matt. 9:35–10:8 (9–23)	*Freely, Freely*

Children's Lectionary Sermon

TITLE: The Harvest

SCRIPTURE: Matt. 9:35–10:8

KEY VERSE: *He said to his disciples, "The harvest is so great, but the workers are few. So pray to the Lord who is in charge of the harvest; ask him to send out more workers for his fields.* (Matt. 9:37–38, New Living Translation)

KEY CONCEPT: We should not delay in our service for the Lord.

MATERIALS: Bible, a ripe tomato or other garden produce

Summer is nice because gardens produce delicious vegetables. This is a ripe tomato from a local garden. Gardens produce tomatoes just a few weeks during the year. The gardens are planted in the spring after the cold winter ends. The plants begin to grow in the warm sunshine of summer and must be protected, watered, and weeded. After several weeks of tender loving care, the plants produce flowering buds and then ripe tomatoes.

After the tomatoes get ripe and red, there is only a day or so to pick them. If the tomatoes are left on the plants, eventually the birds will fly up and peck them. If not gathered, the tomatoes become so heavy that they fall to the ground and rot. So gardens are great, but there is a small time period the tomatoes may be picked—harvested and enjoyed.

Jesus said that the same thing can be said about sharing Jesus' message with others. (*Open Bible.*) Listen to these verses: "He said to his disciples, 'The harvest is so great, but the workers are few. So pray to the Lord who is in charge of the harvest; ask him to send out more workers for his fields.'" Jesus wants us to tell everyone his message. There are a lot of people who have not heard.

So how do we do this? First, we have to love and know Jesus. We have to know the stories of the Bible to share with our friends. We have to know there are people who have not heard about Jesus. We have to tell others about Jesus and his love. We can't put it off. We must be Jesus' harvesters—those who go out and tell everyone how Jesus can change their life forever.—Ken Cox

❧ WORSHIP AIDS ❧

Call to Worship: We gather as God's people to worship and to proclaim the grace that has come to us: "How beautiful on the mountains are the feet of him who brings good tidings, who publishes peace . . . who says unto Zion, your God reigns" (Isa. 52:7).

Invocation: We thank you, Father, that you have given us the privilege of declaring your goodness and mercy. Give to us full confidence that you hold us—and the whole world—in your hands. May your presence in this place challenge our spirits and encourage our hearts, to the end that our joy may be complete. Amen.

Offertory Sentence: "For you know that the grace of our Lord Jesus Christ, that, though he was rich, yet for your sakes he became poor, that you through his poverty might be rich" (2 Cor. 8:9).

Offertory Prayer: Father, you have so graciously gifted us with good things that we find joy in returning a portion of your abundance as tithes and offerings. For the gift of salvation we are truly thankful and dedicate these gifts for the work of the Kingdom, and pray that people everywhere may come to know and love you. Amen.

Morning Prayer: Father, we so often crowd into your presence and make demands before you that we have no right to make. But this morning we come in a different spirit. We want now to think of your wonder and majesty, and to speak words of gratitude for the untold and often unrecognized blessings.

We are thankful for the majestic things of life—for the winds that sweep across the landscape, for gentle rains that quench our thirst, for dawn and night and for each passing season. We are thankful for the homey things of life, for an open door at evening, for laughter in the family, for the clasp of a child's hand, for warmth and security, and for the people who enrich our lives. We are thankful for the helping things of life—truths from the Bible, encouraging words from friends, caring acts in times of trouble and hardship, and the almost endless stream of grace gifts that parade across our lives. We are grateful for the healing things—large medical centers and small clinics, caring doctors and skilled nurses, and shoulders to weep on. Mostly, we are thankful for the saving things of life—the Lord Jesus Christ, without whose sacrifice salvation would be unknown, his Church though yet imperfect that echoes his saving grace, for the gospel message and its power, and for sacred moments when we are faced with crucial decisions. You have given the priceless gift of yourself, and we give thanks this morning with our words, our emotions, and with our dedication to Christ, in whose name we pray. Amen.—Henry Fields

Benediction: Dearest God, Father, Son, and Holy Spirit, be to us the light that directs our path. In our going forth, guide our way. Keep us safe from harm, and brighten our minds that we may speak by word and deed your glorious grace—all the days of this week. Amen.

SUNDAY, JUNE 22, 2008

LECTIONARY SERMON TOPIC: "If We Had Known Then What We Know Now"
TEXT: Gen. 21:8–21
OTHER READINGS: Ps. 86:1–10, 16–17 or Ps. 17; Rom. 6:1b–11; Matt. 10:24–39

Abraham. *Father* Abraham. Father of many nations. Father of our Judeo-Christian faith. Father of at least two children—Ishmael and Isaac. So from all indications, the lectionary passage we have read involving Abraham is a good passage for thinking about the "ideal" father. But we all know that there are no perfect fathers. All have their weaknesses, and all fathers sometimes err in their judgment. So it is, I believe, even with Father Abraham.

I. **After years of trying to have a child, Abraham's wife Sarah finally gave up and gave her servant Hagar to her husband as a second wife in hopes that she could bear him a son.** Hagar conceived and bore Abraham a son they named Ishmael, a name meaning "God hears." Some thirteen years later, according to God's promise as the biblical writer tells it, Sarah finally conceived and also bore a son whom they called Isaac. It was inevitable, I suppose, that jealously would develop between the mothers of the two sons who would both vie for Abraham's attention and blessing. And so, Sarah—Abraham's first and natural wife—considering Ishmael to be a threat to her own son, Isaac, asked that her servant Hagar and her son, Ishmael, be sent away.

At this point the story gets complicated and a little disturbing; Abraham doesn't want to send Hagar and Ishmael away. He has love for Ishmael just as he has love for Isaac. The point that disturbs me is that the biblical writer states that God went along with Sarah's demand that Hagar and Ishmael be driven away. Honestly, I find that hard to digest, as the God revealed by Jesus Christ would not seem to be the kind of God that would find pleasure in sending a mother and her son away with nothing but a meager amount of food and a water bottle strapped to her back. I have learned to read with caution biblical passages that say God spoke to such and such in a way that goes against God's nature as revealed by Christ. Sometimes the biblical writers, who often wrote hundreds of years after the fact, wrote their own interpretation into the ancient stories, attributing to God words and deeds in order to rationalize the outcome of history. At any rate, Abraham (I believe, in a temporary lapse of judgment) gave in to Sarah's whim and sent Hagar and his son Ishmael away into the wilderness.

Even though Abraham was told that a great nation would come from Ishmael, too, I don't think he fathomed how history would play itself out. Both Jews and Christians trace their faith history back to Father Abraham through the line of Isaac. But let us not forget that nearly one billion Muslims also trace their roots back to Father Abraham, but through the line of Ishmael. For centuries there has been discord between the descendants of Isaac and the descendants of Ishmael. A question for us is how will we seek to relate to our "cousins in the faith" who are also children of Father Abraham? Have we not arrived at a place in our world when all of us need to learn to love each other and get along, so that no one is cast out?

II. **Had Abraham been able to see into the future, do you think he might have done things differently?** He might have tried to deal with Ishmael and Isaac in such a way that there was no jealously, but rather, mutual understanding and respect. How might history have played out differently? If only Abraham could have known then what we know now.

But isn't that the way with human nature and with being a parent? As we look back on the years of being a parent, if we could have only known then what we know now. How often have we said it: "If I only could have known then what I know now." As a father myself, I know I have said it many times. Our children are now ages thirty and twenty-six and have children of their own. There have been many times when I have wished that we could go back to when they were young, knowing what I know now. Though I feel I was somewhat successful as a father, there are some things I would do differently if I could go back, knowing what I know now:

- Letting my studies slide and spending more time playing with my kids when they were young
- Being more patient with our kids and trying to understand things from their perspective
- Spending more time talking with our kids and learning from them what they had to teach me

But we can't go back. We can only start where we are right now and go forward.

And so, as we think about fathers realizing that all fathers are imperfect, what might we need to do?

- Those of us who are fathers (or grandfathers or parents in general, for that matter) can make the changes in our lives and relationships that we wish we had made years ago—changes like spending more time with our children, regardless of their age.

- We can strive to be more understanding and try to see things from our children's perspective.
- We can be ready and willing to listen and learn from what our children have to teach us.
- We can be careful not to favor one child over another.
- You could probably add some things to the list of your own.

III. Some here may feel the need to forgive their fathers for their imperfections and shortcomings. To forgive does not mean that one condones any wrongs that were done, but sometimes we may need to forgive others not only because everyone is imperfect but also because bitterness and a lack of forgiveness is like acid that eats away at our insides until they are gotten rid of.

Well, all earthly fathers are imperfect. We have determined that. But the good news is that God is good. The God revealed by Jesus is like the *perfect* parent. God is not just the God of the "insiders." God is also the God of all the world's outcasts. When Abraham sent Hagar and Ishmael away, God provided for them in the wilderness and promised Hagar that through Ishmael the world would also be blessed. For, you see, God loved Hagar and Ishmael, just as God loved Sarah and Isaac. And if God is the God of outcasts and refugees, then we are constrained to be the friend of outcasts and refugees as well.

Looking back, we can learn from Abraham's mistakes. We can be more careful as parents in the way we relate to our children. But we can also commit ourselves to working for greater harmony with all our "cousins in the faith."—Randy Hammer

---

ILLUSTRATIONS

Manhood. That man is a man! Not by birth, but life. Not for his stature, but for his heart. Gold doesn't seduce his hands; honor doesn't turn his head; dishonor doesn't turn his feet; fear doesn't curl his backbone; disappointment doesn't crush his heart. He's a man day and night, in the light and in the dark, in prosperity and in adversity; he has quality, and that—not pounds, not inches, not color—makes a man. His grandeur is in his ideals, his beliefs, his practices—and there the world should apply the gauges. For the great hope of our society is in having more people like him.—Author Unknown

A Different Man. James Michener, writing in his book, *The Source*,[4] tells the story of a man named Urbaal, who was a farmer living about 2200 B.C. He worshiped two gods—one a god of death, the other a goddess of fertility. One day, the temple priests tell Urbaal to bring his young son to the temple for sacrifice, if he wants good crops. Urbaal obeys, and on the appointed day drags his wife and boy to the scene of the boy's "religious execution" by fire to the god of death. After the sacrifice of Urbaal's boy and several others, the priests announce that one of the fathers will spend next week in the temple, with a new temple prostitute. Urbaal's wife is stunned as she notices a desire written more intensely across his face than she has seen before, and she is overwhelmed to see him eagerly lunge forward when his name is called. The ceremony over, she walks out of the temple with her head swimming, concluding that "if he had different gods, he would have been a different man." If the kind of God we worship is the kind of persons we will become, we must make sure that the God we worship is the God of the Bible, not one of our own making.—Lawrence Vowan

Musical Selections Appropriate to the Day

Hymn suggestions for lectionary texts:

Gen. 21:8–21	*Borning Cry; God Will Take Care of You*
Ps. 86:1–10, 16–17	*I Need Thee Every Hour; Glorify Thy Name* [or]
Ps. 17	*Lord, Listen to Your Children Praying*
Rom. 6:1b–11	*Praise and Thanksgiving Be to God*
Matt. 10:24–39	*Take Up Your Cross, the Savior Said*

---

[4]James Michener, *The Source* (Greenwich, CN: Fawcett Crest, 1967).

༄ Children's Lectionary Sermon

TITLE: Jesus Knows You

SCRIPTURE: Matt. 10:24–39

KEY VERSE: *And even the very hairs of your head are all numbered.* (Matt. 10:30, New International Version)

KEY CONCEPT: Jesus' children are important.

MATERIALS: Bible, wig on a stand

Hello boys and girls. I have a wig here to help explain our Bible verse for today. How many of you believe I can count the hairs on this wig? Or the hairs on your head? Well, it might be possible, but it would take a long time. The Bible uses this example as a way of saying that Jesus knows all about us, even the number of hairs on our head. If he knows that much about his children, that tells me he loves us and we are important.

(*Open Bible.*) In Matthew 10:30, Jesus said, "And even the very hairs of your head are all numbered." This verse means Jesus knows everything about us. Jesus thinks that we—his children—are so important that he knows even the number of hairs on our head.

Isn't it great to know we are so special to Jesus? Each one of us is special. Older adults, babies, children, and parents are special to Jesus. We can thank Jesus for loving us this much.—Carolyn Tomlin

༄ WORSHIP AIDS ༄

Call to Worship: Lord, we enter worship to meet you. Let there be within us a true sense of confession as we approach the throne of grace. "If we say that we have no sin, we deceive ourselves and the truth is not in us. If we confess our sins, he is faithful and just to forgive us our sins, and to cleanse us from all unrighteousness" (1 John 1:8–9).

Invocation: Father, come to each of us in the hour of worship. Speak to us as you intend. Whether through hymn, Scripture, prayer, preaching, praise, or silence, come and lay your hand upon our shoulder and call our name. We ask in the name of the One who loved us and called us to love one another. Amen.

Offertory Sentence: "It is written, 'He that had gathered much had nothing over; and he that had gathered little had no lack' " (2 Cor. 8:15).

Offertory Prayer: Lord of life, you have bountifully provided all our needs. As we acknowledge your graciousness, may the grace of giving be increased in us. Whether in times of plenty or in times of want, when the harvest is grand or meager, lead us to be faithful stewards. And may our giving reflect our joy in participating in the work of your Kingdom. Amen.

Morning Prayer: Quietly we come into your presence this morning Father, like little children who enter the presence of the unknown with halting step and quiet wonder. For while we have seen something of your love and grace, power, and presence in Jesus Christ, we still stand amazed before you and at times are a little fearful of you.

This morning we pray that you will meet us in our awe and in our wonder and dim our fear and let us experience the acceptance of the loving Father whom Jesus declared and by his life so eloquently showed. Our fear comes because we have allowed our feet to carry us along avenues not in keeping with what we know to be your best and highest will for us. Our divided loyalties, at one moment given to nobility in living and at the next careening to baseness of action, causes us to realize our need for correction and even at times some form of punishment. Yet, like a child we long for forgiveness and an extended hand to lift us from our failures and wrongs yet fear that our wrongs, our baseness, will destroy our possibilities of any relationship with you.

This morning, remind us again of what Jesus did for us and that in his sacrifice shines your unending forgiveness and eternal love. Let such assurance come upon us like a stilling dew at early morning to wash away the gathered dust of our errant journeyings.—Henry Fields

Benediction: We are the salt of the earth, the light of the world, a city set on a hill that cannot be hidden. Lead us, O God, in the days before us to live the gospel message in word and deed and to make a difference in the lives of those around us. Amen.

SUNDAY, JUNE 29, 2008

LECTIONARY SERMON TOPIC: "Being Careful of What We Hear"

TEXT: Gen. 22: 1–14

OTHER READINGS: Ps. 13; Rom. 6:12–23; Matt. 10:40–42

God's voice (leading) is rarely as clear as we would like for it to be. Sometimes it is a challenge to hear God's voice, that is, to discern what God is really saying to us. When I finally made the decision to begin preparing myself for the ministry some twenty-nine years ago, I did so only after a couple of years of intense soul searching and deliberation. Before I took such a huge step, I wanted a sign—a sign not unlike the apostle Paul had when he was converted on the road to Damascus. An audible voice, a bright light—either would have been fine. I *prayed* for a sign. I *longed* for a sign. I *looked* for a sign. But no such extraordinary sign was ever given. Though there were assurances of different sorts that came, in the end I had to step out on faith.

I. **We want to be sure of what we hear, do we not?** It is important that we not get our signals mixed up and our wires crossed. The experience of Abraham serves as a good example of how we need to be sure of what we hear. Of all the passages in the Bible, I (and many others like me) find Genesis 22 to be one of the most challenging.

As one theologian has stated, this passage "is perhaps the most admired and the most troubling of all the stories in Genesis."[5] Because in this passage Abraham is portrayed as the supreme model of one who has faith and is obedient to God, but in order to do what Abraham is convinced (in his own mind at least) that God wants him to do, he must be willing to sacrifice his beloved son of promise. What an inner struggle must have been going on in Abraham's heart and mind.

---

[5]Walter J. Harrelson (ed.), *The New Interpreter's Study Bible* (Nashville: Abingdon Press, 2003), p. 42.

II. **If someone today were to do what Abraham was ready to do with his son Isaac (that is, offer him as a child sacrifice), all of us would be appalled and outraged.** Thus from a contemporary viewpoint and a time when child abuse is in the news almost daily, the text presents a lot of problems. Even from a historical and biblical viewpoint the text is problematic, given that child sacrifice was abhorrent, condemned in Israel. A number of questions have been raised, and a number of explanations have been offered to account for this unusual story:

- Did God *really* tell Abraham to sacrifice his son to test him?
- Was it that Abraham *thought* this is what God wanted him to do, as was the custom among some peoples of that time and place?
- Was the biblical writer who wrote the story hundreds of years after Abraham lived remembering the story in his own way, putting words into the mouth of God?
- Does the story go too far in attributing human characteristics to God or making God in the image of the gods of that time and place?
- Was the story written for another purpose altogether, such as a word of encouragement to Israel in exile several hundred years later about their own test of faith and faithfulness?
- Was the writer trying to say that as Isaac (and hence, the people of Israel as a whole as Isaac's descendants) was saved from extinction by a merciful God, so will Israel be saved from extinction and redeemed from exile?

If God did indeed speak to Abraham, in my limited opinion at least, it was when Abraham raised the knife in the air over Isaac's trembling body and the angel of the Lord called out, "Abraham, Abraham . . . Lay down the knife . . . do not hurt the boy" (Gen. 22:11–12). How tragic the outcome if Abraham had not been listening!

III. **The story of Abraham serves as an encouragement to us to always be sure of what we hear.** As a side note: a lot of false rumors get started, and a lot of people's good reputations are damaged, because someone misheard and wrongly repeated what was being said about someone else. Perhaps you remember the game where someone begins by whispering a complicated story in the ear of one person, who whispers it in the ear of the next, and so on, until the story goes through a couple of dozen ears and mouths. When the last person repeats out loud the story that she heard, it is often much different from the original. It behooves all of us to not only be careful of what we *say* about others but to be careful about what we *hear* about others.

However, regarding hearing God's instructions for our lives, may I suggest some tips that I have found helpful in discerning God's leading? When trying to discern God's voice and God's leading in our lives:

- It helps to live a life of devotion, meditation, and prayer, so that we are attuned to God's leading when it comes to us.
- We need to weigh what we think we are hearing against our God-given reason, as God will not expect us to do the unreasonable.
- We need to judge what we think we are hearing by asking if it is true to the nature of God, as revealed by Jesus Christ.
- We need to decide if what we think we hear God saying to us is compatible with who we are and the person God has created us to be.
- We need to seek guidance from others whose wisdom and insight we cherish and respect.
- We sometimes can look for open doors as signs of divine leading, while seeing closed doors or circumstances with one difficulty after another as signs of the way we should not be trying to go.

"Let anyone with ears to hear listen!" Jesus says (Luke 14:35). We believe in a still speaking God. But in order for God to speak to us, we first have to be careful of how we listen.—Randy Hammer

---

ILLUSTRATIONS

God's Will. How important it is that we are sure of what we hear! Perhaps you have heard the story of the farmer who stepped outside one day and looked up at the sky. The man was one who believed that God gives signs about what one should do and which course of action one should take. As the man gazed up at the clouds, it seemed that they had formed the letters P C. The man thought, and then he said, "God is calling me to *Preach Christ*," the letter P standing for preach and the letter C for Christ. Well, the man announced his call to his church and community and set about trying to preach. But he failed miserably. After a fair amount of frustration and failure, the man prayed earnestly and said, "Lord, when I saw the letters P C in the sky, I took that to mean you wanted me to preach Christ." At which point the man heard the Lord say to him, "What I was trying to say to you was it is time to Plow Corn." The man had misread the signs and had also been wrong about his calling. A faith question that all of us wrestle with is, How do we recognize God's voice? Or to put it another way, How do we discern God's leading in our lives?—Randy Hammer

Choices. Confusion often leads to a quest for meaning that takes us lots of places. We then must choose. We must "stand" somewhere. Winfred Moore, former pastor at the First Baptist Church, Amarillo, Texas, declared that "in west Texas, the only thing in the middle of the road is a yellow line and dead armadillos." We will today choose a stand again before we leave.— Lee McGlone

Musical Selections Appropriate to the Day

Hymn suggestions for lectionary texts:

Gen. 22:1–14	*I Gave My Life for Thee; God Will Make a Way*
Ps. 13	*How Long, O Lord*
Rom. 6:12–23	*I Will Sing of My Redeemer*
Matt. 10:40–42	*Where Cross the Crowded Ways of Life*

Children's Lectionary Sermon

TITLE: Helping Others

SCRIPTURE: Matt. 10:40–42

KEY VERSE: *And if you give even a cup of cold water to one of the least of my followers, you will surely be rewarded.* (Matt. 10:42, New International Version)

KEY CONCEPT: Helping others

MATERIALS: Bible, small cups, pitcher of cold water

PREPARATION: Have in place individual cups and container of water. Ask another person to help serve the children.

Hello boys and girls. Have you ever been really thirsty? If you're like me, nothing satisfies my thirst like water. As we begin our children's sermon, I want to offer each of you a cup of cold water. (*Offer the children water to drink.*) As you sip from your cup, let me tell you a story.

(*Tell this or another personal story you know about missionaries who help other people. Think about the age of the children you are sharing with and what information is appropriate.*) In Africa, there are many areas where clean water is not available. A severe drought has caused many lakes and streams to dry up. Animals cannot find water. Plants do not grow. Water is needed for bathing and washing clothes. Without clean water drinking water, people get sick. AIDS and other serious illnesses take the lives of thousands of people each day. Many children have lost parents to these diseases. Presently, there are projects where mission volunteers and missionaries dig wells and develop a system of irrigation that helps water plants. This provides a safe water supply. They can grow vegetables that will keep many people from starving. In these areas, people have a better life.

(*Open Bible.*) In Matthew 10:42, Jesus says, "And if you give even a cup of cold water to one of the least of my followers, you will surely be rewarded." That tells us that when we give even a cup of cold water to those in need, we will be rewarded. We may not be able to go to Africa now, but we can help our friends at school, our neighborhood, and our families. We can help each other the way Jesus wants us to.—Carolyn Tomlin

☙ WORSHIP AIDS ☙

Call to Worship: Lord God, prepare us just now to experience your presence. Help us to search our deepest motives and, along with the psalmist, to inquire of ourselves, "Lord, who shall abide in your tabernacle? Who shall dwell in your holy hill? He who walks uprightly, and works righteousness, and speaks the truth in his heart" (Ps. 15:1–2).

Invocation: Lord, in our national liberty to worship as we please, we pray. In our freedom from outside interference, we rejoice. In the power to freely share our faith, we join to proclaim the liberating power of the Christ of the Ages. Amen.—E. Lee Phillips

Offertory Sentence: "He who sows sparingly shall also reap sparingly; and he who sows bountifully will also reap bountifully" (2 Cor. 9:6).

Offertory Prayer: Dear God, we stand amazed at the power of your love and the lengths to which you go for us, even to the cross on which our Savior died. May our giving today express our devotion to you, and may it kindle an ever-deepening love. May we give joyfully and cheerfully as partners in the great work of the gospel. Amen.

Morning Prayer: As we journey through worship this morning, we pause a few moments to reflect on our lives in prayer. We realize that the road we travel is much easier, much smoother than that taken by a great many of our fellow travelers. Freedoms, opportunities, and abundance of material wealth all pave the way for us. So we pray that you will guide us as we seek to be grateful and responsible for the goodness that has befallen us. Of all people, we feel that we have been blessed with an unusual abundance.

For some the journey is taken in great difficulty. Nations of people live under restrictions, poverty, and violence. The road they take has shown itself hostile. O Lord, you know those places in our world, those people beset with the unkindness and pain of injustice and war. Our prayer is for you to walk with these, our brothers and sisters, and lead them at least to a safe destination. In the same way we pray for individuals here in this communion of prayer. Perhaps these moments together will be an oasis in their personal desert. We are bold to pray that our Risen Christ will come to the weary and the heavy-spirited ones in our midst. Amen.—Charles F. Hoffman

Benediction: God of all the ages, Father, Son, and Holy Spirit, may we go out today and in the days of the coming week to live in the power of your love. May the grace of the Lord Jesus Christ go with us, guide our steps, keep us from harm, and bring us together again next Lord's Day. Amen.

SUNDAY, JULY 6, 2008

LECTIONARY SERMON TOPIC: "Both Saint and Sinner"
TEXT: Rom. 7:15–25a
OTHER READINGS: Gen. 24:34–38, 42–49, 58–67; Ps. 45:10–17 or Ps. 72; Matt. 11:16–19, 25–30

All of my mature Christian life I have identified more with Peter than any other biblical character. But as I pondered over the seventh chapter of Romans, I found myself identifying more and more with Paul. The honesty of his words and the sincere baring of his soul struck deep chords with my own experience. I, too, at times do not understand my own actions. That which I know to be good, I shun and that which I know to be evil, I embrace. It happens in seemingly trivial matters and in those that are not so trivial.

I. **There is a note of reassurance in reading the words of Paul, found in the seventh chapter of Romans.** Here is quite possibly the greatest of all the saints expressing the same kind of struggle as a sinner that the rest of us do. Saint *and* sinner—how can this be? The fact is that this became a central idea for Martin Luther during the period of the Reformation.

I found it interesting to see how many of the contemporary and past commentators on Romans insist that this passage could not possibly apply to Paul's life as a Christian, so they suggest that Paul is really reflecting on his days before his conversion on the road to Damascus. However, Paul Achtemeier, in his commentary on Romans, makes the point that Paul changes from the past to present tense in verse 14. He maintains that we should see this as "Paul's description of his current existence as a Christian, with the obvious corollary that it would then be applicable to all Christian existence, ours as well."[1]

II. **How do we explain the paradox of being saint and sinner at the same time?** One pastor, Paul J. Nuechterlein, compared it to the experience of a recovering alcoholic: "Even when one wins the victory over drinking by giving it up, it is not a complete cure. The recovering alcoholic learns not to say, 'Gee, I've won. I'm not an alcoholic anymore.' No, the alcoholic is still stuck with the same flesh and blood which reacts to the substance of alcohol in an addictive way. But the recovering alcoholic has won to the extent that alcohol no longer has complete reign over his or her life. It no longer holds the power of death for that person." All of this is accomplished through the power of a higher power—God.[2]

Paul, the saint, admits that he is a sinner. He even admits that he "hates" what he does, but apparently he can't stop doing it. I just came from a convenience store where I observed a young lady buying two packs of cigarettes. Written on the label was the warning that these could cause cancer. It made no difference to her. She knew the risk but proceeded to choose her poison. Addiction is a strong force in our lives, and even though we know better, we give in to the temptation time and time again. The flesh is weak. Anyone who struggles with addiction knows all about doing the very thing we hate and wondering why.

III. **Paul claims that there is a force working within him, which he calls sin.** Is this an evasion of his personal responsibility? I think not. Unlike the comedian Flip Wilson, who dismissed his actions with the rather famous line, "The devil made me do it!" Paul is more than willing to take responsibility for his actions, even though sin abided within his flesh.

A spiritual warfare exists within us: the flesh versus the higher self, which we might designate as the soul. When the flesh wins out, we, like Paul, cry

---

[1]Paul Achtemeier, *Romans* (Atlanta: John Knox, 1985), p. 120.
[2]See the Web site: http://girardianlectionary.net/year_a/proper_9a_1996_ser.htm.

out, "Oh wretched man that I am!" We start beating ourselves up for being such awful people. It is then that we need to hear the continuing words of Paul, when he asks, "Who shall rescue me from this body of death? Thanks be to God through Jesus Christ our Lord."

Paul found his salvation from this sin of the flesh through Christ. Oh, he still had his self-contradictions, but he continued to press toward the high calling of Christ. There he found his freedom from the spiritual battle. He was both saint and sinner. We who believe that Jesus is the Son of God and accept him as our Lord and Savior will still struggle with the sin inside of us until we die. That's just the way it is. But we have the assurance that we exist as saint *and* sinner, and the saint will inherit the Kingdom of God.—John Dever

ILLUSTRATIONS

Inner Conflict. In his novel titled *Godric,* Frederick Buechner retells the story of Godric, a twelfth-century peddler-turned-hermit.[3]

Godric, whose name means "God's wreck," begins his life as a peddler and launches out in his quest for wealth. But his life becomes one long battle with an inner conflict similar to what Paul describes in his letter to the Romans. Godric knew what was right but failed to do it, and he knew what was wrong but did exactly that.

Seeking to redeem himself, Godric becomes a hermit, but even in the midst of this vocational ministry the inner battle continues. Guilt becomes his constant companion. One night he finds himself lying awake, unable to sleep, and he prays: "Lord, God . . . how useless is my life. My flesh is ever prey to lust and pride and sloth. I let folks call me Holy Father though I know myself to be of all God's sinful [children] most foul. . . . Even as I speak to thee, a thousand wanton dreams are set to fall on me when I am done. Oh send some saint to save my soul. Teach me how to serve thee right."[4] Godric's struggle is our struggle, too.—John Dever

[3]Frederick Buechner, *Godric* (San Francisco: HarperSanFrancisco, 1980).
[4]Buechner, *Godric,* p. 143.

Ego. Bruce Sanguin makes an interesting observation when he notes that Paul distinguishes between "me" and "I." One is "his flesh" and the other is his "higher self which knows good and bad and right and wrong."[5]

There is a biochemistry that works within us in the service of pleasure and survival that is neither good nor bad, but it often works against the higher self. There is an egoistic self that seeks short-term gratification and self-perpetuation. It is this ego that is particularly vulnerable to sin.—John Dever

Musical Selections Appropriate to the Day

Hymn suggestions for lectionary texts:

Gen. 24:34–38, 42–49, 58–67	*Happy the Home When God Is There*
Ps. 45:10–17	*Holy God, We Praise Your Name* [or]
Ps. 72	*Jesus Shall Reign*
Rom. 7:15–25a	*Whiter Than Snow; Cleanse Me*
Matt. 11:16–19, 25–30	*Leaning on the Everlasting Arms; Come Ye Sinners Poor and Needy*

❧ Children's Lectionary Sermon

TITLE: Jesus Will Carry Our Burdens

SCRIPTURE: Matt. 11:16–19, 25–30

KEY VERSE: *Then Jesus said, "Come to me, all who are weary and carry heavy burdens, and I will give you rest."* (Matt. 11:28, New International Version)

KEY CONCEPT: Jesus can help us with our problems.

MATERIALS: Bible, cloth sack or pillowcase, three or more bricks

PREPARATION: Prepare a sack filled with bricks before meeting with the children.

---

[5]See the Web site: http://canadianmemorial.org/Sermons/2005Jul03.htm.

Do you boys and girls ever have problems or things that bother you? I need someone to help me. Who would like to try to lift this sack? (*Allow several children to lift the sack.*) It's heavy, because we are going to pretend it contains our problems. As we tell about problems we have, let's remove a brick from the sack. After we talk about the problem, let's pray to Jesus to help us. (*Open Bible.*) Jesus said in Matthew 11:28, "Come to me, all who are weary and carry heavy burdens, and I will give you rest." Does someone want to share a problem you have had? (*Let the children respond. If you don't get any volunteers, use the pressures and problems listed next to start the discussion.*)

- *Making good grades in school.* What can we do? Keep up with daily work. Never miss school unless sick. Ask the teacher for help.
- *Having friends.* How can we be a friend and also have friends? We must treat others the way we want them to treat us.
- *Having enough time for all your activities.* Keeping a monthly and weekly calendar will help you be better organized. Perhaps you have too many activities.

Children have problems just as adults have problems. But we also know Jesus can make our problems easier to deal with because Jesus is always listening to our prayers.

Now, who will lift this sack? Does the sack feel lighter than before? Through prayer we have given our problems over to God. Our problems may not disappear completely, but we know Jesus will help us.—Carolyn Tomlin

WORSHIP AIDS

Call to Worship: In worship we express honor and glory to our God. There is joy in our hearts as we declare, "Delight yourself in the Lord; and he shall give you the desires of your heart. Commit your ways to the Lord, trust also in him, and he shall bring it to pass" (Ps. 37:4–5).

Invocation: Lord of heaven and earth, humble us as we come into your presence. Make soft our hearts that we may worship you in spirit and truth. Encourage us to profound obedience, and give us joy as we lift high your Holy Name. Amen.

Offertory Sentence: "Every person as is purposed in his heart, so let him give; not grudgingly or of necessity: for God loves a cheerful giver" (2 Cor. 9:7).

Offertory Prayer: Holy Father, giver of all good and perfect gifts, may the gifts we offer today go forth in quiet strength to do your work here and around the world. Multiply their usefulness in renewal of the sanctuary and the slum. Bring healing and hope through the good news, which is the gospel, and let it begin in us. Amen.

Morning Prayer: Dear God, we know that praying is something we do with our minds, our hearts, our hands, and our breath. We can use words, or we can be silent. We can dance, or we can sit still. Prayer is our way of remembering that we are not alone in the universe. The universe is much bigger than we are, but it is our friend. Help us, God, to see that you are more than we can ever imagine, and you are as simple as a flower in the field or a butterfly in the air.

Help us to be better people. Help us to be kind, to be good, to be truthful, and to be brave. Help us to care for our parents, our children, our brothers and sisters, our friends and cousins, and the animals who live with us and trust us. Help us to care for those in need, whether they live out in the country, or in the city, in Afghanistan, or anywhere else in the world. Help us to remember that all people are our brothers and sisters and that we are not truly fed when others are starving, that we are not truly safe when others are in danger, that we are not truly rich when others live in poverty, and that we are not truly free when others are not free. We ask for your blessing on this day, as we send blessings out to you. Amen.—Rachele Rosi

Benediction: People of God, go forth into the days of this week, in our business and in our relaxation, in quiet and in the crowd, with renewed joy and steadfastness. May our words and deeds speak lovingly and clearly of the deep commitments that guard our souls. May the peace of God, which passes all understanding, keep your hearts and minds in Christ Jesus. Amen.

SUNDAY, JULY 13, 2008

LECTIONARY SERMON TOPIC: "Sowing Kingdom Seeds"

TEXT: Matt. 13:1–9, 18–23

OTHER READINGS: Gen. 25:19–34; Ps. 119:105–112 or Ps. 25; Rom. 8:1–11

The preceding chapters have made it clear that there was a rising opposition to Jesus' ministry. There was a growing polarization that would lead him to finally leave the Jewish territory and focus on a more responsive audience among various neighboring Gentiles. Matthew 13 contains teachings that explain this polarization. The scene is a Galilean lakeside where a large crowd had gathered to hear this charismatic prophet. In fact, the crowd is so large that Jesus is forced to enter a boat offshore that will serve as his pulpit. He begins his sermon with a parable. The Greek *parabole* means "to throw alongside." It was Jesus' way of helping the people to grasp his message. One can only conjecture, but it is entirely possible that in the distance a farmer was sowing his field in the customary method. As he hand-cast the seed, Jesus saw a perfect example of what had been happening as he spread the seed of the gospel—the good news of the Kingdom of God—among the people who gathered to hear him.

I. **He first noted that as the farmer sowed the seed, some of it fell on the pathways that served as common access to the adjoining fields.** Because these were in constant use by passers-by, they became as hard as pavement. It was no wonder the seed were unable to germinate and take root; they simply lay there for the birds to feast upon. So it was with some of those who heard the words of Jesus. There were those whose minds were so hardened that even the Holy Spirit could not soften them enough for the words to penetrate. And so, to use a modern colloquium, "they ran off like water on a duck's back."

What is it that causes a person's heart to be so hard that not even God's word can penetrate it? I suppose that some would say that God has hardened their heart, and there might be some scriptural testimony to this. But I think there are some other explanations. Prejudice can harden the heart. Pride and tradition can create an unteachable spirit. Often there develops a fear of new truth. This new truth may threaten our comfort zones. The presence of these often leads us to simply refuse to listen to anything that might cause us to change. On several occasions I have heard that accepting the gospel is not a function of the intellect but a function of the will. This sounds good, but I think in reality it is a function of both. Only when both are engaged will the experience ring true for our lives.

II. **Jesus also observed that some of the farmer's seed fell on rocky ground.** I think our first image of this is a field filled with rocks, but that probably is not the case. Rather, it probably refers to ground that was shallow, with bedrock hidden just a few inches under the surface. The seed would fall here, quickly germinate, grow, but soon die out because, with no room to send down roots, the sun became its worst enemy. Jesus saw this as similar to the shallow minds that refused to give his words the thought that they deserved. These are those folks we see today who are always excited about something new. They flit from one craze to another, from one spiritual idea to the next. The enthusiasm wanes rather quickly because there is no depth to their understanding or commitment. Emotion seems to be the driving force in their lives. But no one can exist on emotion alone. Our minds must also be engaged if the experience is to be a lasting one.

   I'm told that only a small percentage of those who make decisions during revival crusades ever follow through with their emotional commitment. For the moment the fire burns brightly, but soon the enthusiasm ebbs and the remaining embers die.

III. **Some seed got mixed in with weed seeds, and when they geminated and began to grow, the weeds won the battle.** They simply choked out the good plants. I think is some ways this must have been the most disappointing result for Jesus. He had seen on many occasions those who heard his word, understood it, and even began to follow him but soon found their lives so involved with other things that they just didn't have time to continue their discipleship.

   If it were true that in an agrarian society things could crowd out one's commitment to Christ, think of how much more true this is in an urban society. Life becomes so hectic that we have no time for prayer, for church, for family, for Christ. This is not only true in the secular world where soccer moms flit from one child's activity to another, and working men and women find their forty-hour week extending into family time. But the institutional church adds its contribution to the rush of life. We can become so active in the institutional life of the church that we really do forget what it is all about. The good becomes the enemy of the best.

IV. **"But some of the seed fell on good ground and grew to maturity and produced fruit, some a hundred fold, some sixty, and some thirty" (Matt. 13:18).** This must have been extremely comforting and encouraging to the disciples who had been with him for some months now. They were not oblivious to the growing opposition, and they must have been wondering if it would all be for naught. Jesus was telling them that the harvest was sure. Difficult times would come, but the Kingdom would grow.

So to those who sow the seed, both ministers and laity, this is a parable of encouragement. Sowing the seed of the gospel is our task. We never really know where it will take root, but we will never see the reaping of the harvest if we do not cast out the seeds of the gospel. One can never tell when, where, or how.

"Coming to Christ" means that we must make him first in our lives. We must commit our hearts, minds, and souls to him. Hearing and obeying the Word of God must come first. Everything else is less important.—John Dever

---

ILLUSTRATIONS

Tenacious Faith. Craig Bomberg summarizes these first three types of responses in this manner:

> Once one realizes that Jesus is talking about preaching the word, it is not difficult to see the first three soil samples as involving those in whom that word took no root, who thus never made any profession of faith; those whose initial commitment proved superficial and temporary; and those who, while first appearing

like true disciples, demonstrated they could not survive competing demands for their loyalty.[6]

Maybe my former professor Dale Moody said it best when he proclaimed, "the faith that fizzles before the finish, had a flaw in it from the first."—John Dever

Clear Decisions. Jim Denison, pastor of Park Cities Baptist Church in Dallas, Texas, tells the story of when, as a college student, he served as a summer missionary in East Malaysia. During one of their worship services, a teenage girl came to announce her decision to follow Christ and be baptized. In this same service, Denison noticed some worn-out luggage leaning against the wall, and he asked about it. The pastor of the small church pointed to the girl and said, "Her father said that if she was baptized as a Christian she could never go home again. So she brought her luggage."[7]—John Dever

Musical Selections Appropriate to the Day

Hymn suggestions for lectionary texts:

Gen. 25:19–34	*Praise the Lord, O Heavens Adore Him; For the Beauty of the Earth*
Ps. 119:105–112	*Thy Word Is a Lamp Unto My Feet* [or]
Ps. 25	*Lord Speak to Me*
Rom. 8:1–11	*And Can It Be?*
Matt. 13:1–9, 18–23	*Long Ago Prophets Knew*

Children's Lectionary Sermon

TITLE: God's Word Can Light the Way

SCRIPTURE: Ps. 119:105–112

KEY VERSE: *Your word is a lamp for my feet and a light for my path.* (Ps. 119:105, New Living Translation)

---

[6]Craig Bomberg, *Matthew, The New American Commentary* (Nashville: Broadman Press, 1992), p. 214.
[7]Raymond McHenry, *Stories for the Soul* (Peabody, MA: Hendrickson Publishers, 2001), p. 48.

KEY CONCEPT: God's Word

MATERIALS: Bible, flashlight

PREPARATION: Ask someone to lower the lights as you begin the children's sermon. This will only work well if your sanctuary is dark during the day when the lights are out.

Hello boys and girls. (*As you begin to speak, ask someone to lower the lights or to turn them off for a minute.*) Look, what has happen to our lights? They are not as bright as before. What happened? But wait, I'll turn on this flashlight, and we can see a small part of the room. The flashlight gives only a little bit of light, while those in our building provided light for the entire room.

We know that our lights are controlled by a switch. We can easily turn the lights off or turn them on. Lights help us see where to go so we won't run into things. What can help us know what choices to make and how to act? (*Open Bible.*) In Psalm 119:105, the psalmist writes, "Your word is a lamp for my feet and a light for my path." What do you think this means? (*Allow children to respond. Reflect back the answers the children give. Help guide them if they are young.*)

Just as lights help us see so we know where to go, the psalmist tells us God's Word can help us know the right choice to make and how to act. The psalmist uses a different word to describe this. The writer chose the word *path*. When we go down a path, we need to have directions so we won't get lost. God's Word is what can help us as we make the right choices each day.—Carolyn Tomlin

☙ WORSHIP AIDS ☙

Call to Worship: Our minds are alert to the call of God upon our lives. Our thinking rises up from the experience of grace. May we, with the apostle, declare: "Whatsoever things are true, honest, pure, lovely, of good reputation, and filled with virtue and praise—let us think on these things" (Phil. 4:8).

Invocation: Father, as we worship grant us great wisdom that we shall experience the true meaning of Jesus' servanthood and give to us courage to follow his way. Teach us the virtues of greatness—the ones Jesus taught and lived—that our living will bring both honor and joy to the Kingdom reign. Amen.

Offertory Sentence: "God is able to give you more than you need, so that you will always have all you need and more than enough for every good cause" (2 Cor. 9:8).

Offertory Prayer: Lord, you have graciously given to us blessings beyond our deserving. We express thanks for the bounty of your favor. Open our hearts that we, too, may be gracious in sharing your favor with others. Deepen our love for you and your world, and help us to know the joy of cheerful giving. Amen.

Morning Prayer: Thank you, O God, from all of us gathered here today for the love of life, for the desire to honestly live. Yes, there are times when we wonder why love comes and then goes, why some friendships do not last. Yes, it's true that some fathers disappear and arguments tear us apart and intolerance leaves us exhausted. And yes, it is true that millions of people live in filth, and millions more die from AIDS and in wars or at the hands of a madman, or because there is not enough medicine. But with all we experience, you keep your faith in us, even more than the most pious men and women keep in you. With all of the wrongs in this world, you gave us our unbreakable spirits.

Now our spirits grow, knowing that a broken heart is best repaired with a new love, that we all have a friend who will stand by, that a mother or a sister is always at our side, that a sunset, sunrise, or summer rain shower can make us smile on a bad day, that an apology, a hug can start rebuilding bridges, that in time people can learn to understand each other's differences, that we feel a need to raise up those people living below us. And that there are so many diseases to cure and so many battles to end. Yes, O God! We know that we have so much to enjoy, so much to fight for, and so much to look forward to. Amen.—Scot McFarlane

Benediction: Precious Lord, take us by the hand and lead us to the Promised Land. Yours, O Lord, is indeed the Kingdom and the power and the glory. And we are yours. Hold us steadfast in faith in the days of this week, and may our witness speak clearly our devotion and love. Amen.

SUNDAY, JULY 20, 2008

LECTIONARY SERMON TOPIC: "God Is in This Place"

TEXT: Gen. 28:10–19a

OTHER READINGS: Ps. 139:1–12, 23–24; Rom. 8:12–25; Matt. 13:24–30, 36–43

I suppose all of us have had an encounter with God at one time or another. For most of us, it came within the confines of a holy place such as a church building or some sacred shrine or in an awe-inspiring experience of God's world of beauty and fascination. But for some, God appears at the most unexpected times. The Bible is full of such encounters. The Genesis text for today records one such moment in the life of Jacob. In fact, as one reads the passage, one wonders why God would have anything to do with this scoundrel. But he does, and the encounter brings a very positive declaration from Jacob: "God is in this place."

That night at the place that from then on would be called Bethel, Jacob was a fugitive from his tribe and his family because of the nasty things he had done to them. By all calculations, Jacob was a died-in-the-wool crook. The preceding chapters in Genesis portrayed Jacob as a cunning rascal who cheats his not-so-swift brother out of his birthright and his blessing from his father, Esau. But momma's boy seems to do no real wrong in the eyes of his parents. Time and time again, they protect him from the consequences of his actions. And when Rebekah hears that Esau has had enough and is out to kill his brother, she goes to Esau and suggests that it would be good for Jacob to have a wife from their ancestral homeland. It just wouldn't be good for the heir to the family blessing to marry a foreign girl.

I. **That is where our story for today begins.** Jacob finds himself out in the hill country north of Beer-sheba. Harried, tired, with nerves frazzled and without home, shelter, or the protection of friends, he pulls up a rock and lies down to rest his weary body. I have a feeling that God was not in his remotest thoughts at this time. And then it happens. Jacob dreams that a ladder was set up on the earth that reached to heaven. Angels were ascending and descending on it. And God stood above it and said, "I am the Lord, the God of Abraham your father and the God of Isaac; the land on which you lie I will give to you and to your descendants; and your descendants shall be like the dust of the earth. . . . Behold, I am with you and will keep you wherever you go, and will bring you back to this land."

Wow! Who would have thought it could happen to Jacob at this time in his life? But it did. I know that as we read on, we find that Jacob doesn't quite understand the full meaning of this encounter. In fact, his old nature continues to rule in his life, as he bargains with God for his future. It will take more such encounters to turn Jacob's life around. But he does realize he has come face-to-face with God, and he knows that this is a significant moment in his life. He arises, builds a stone monument to God, and names the place Bethel, house of God. And in his own words he proclaims: "How awesome is this place! This is none other than the house of God, and this is the gate of heaven."

II. **God was at Bethel, and Jacob experienced God's presence, God's power, God's protection, and God's providence.** Contrary to the famous spiritual, Jacob did not climb the ladder to God. God came to Jacob and ministered to him in a time when he needed it the most. Bethel became a place of worship for Israel in the coming years—it was a constant reminder of God's presence in their midst. It was a reminder that God could and would bind himself with unconditional promises to a trickster and a deceiver. It was a reminder that God could and would meet them at their own Bethel when they least expected it.

Years later, God would come to Moses at a most unexpected time. This wasn't at a time of crisis but at a time of pastoral peace and quiet. There as Moses tended the flock of his father-in-law, Jethro, on the west side of Horeb, the mountain of God, the unexpected happened. God spoke to Moses from a burning bush and gave him a new purpose for his life: "I have seen the affliction of my people who are in Egypt, and have heard their cry because of their taskmasters; I know their sufferings and I have come down to deliver them out of the hand of the Egyptians, and to bring them up out of that land to a good and broad land, a land flowing with milk and honey" (Exod. 3:7–8).

"And guess what, Moses—you have the job." God was in this place, and once again his presence, power, protection, and providence were made known. Moses got a new lease on life.

III. **Sometimes the experience of the biblical characters seems too far in the past to really affect our lives.** It seems like another world, another time—and even a facet of God we don't experience today. So let me ask the question: Have you ever felt and experienced the presence of God in such a way that you, as Jacob did, could say, "God is in this place?" I have. Oh, God didn't speak to me in a dream or commune with me in an audible voice, but I knew he was there.

My teaching colleague and I had taken a group of seminary students to New York to experience inner-city missions. When we arrived, we gave every student five dollars to buy a homeless person something to eat and to encourage the student to engage that person in conversation. We gave ourselves the same amount and took the same challenge. It was the last day of our visit, and I had not followed through. I decided to go to the nearby park and see if God would lead me to someone. Sure enough, there was a bag lady sitting on a park bench. I walked up and asked if I could sit down. She agreed. As she kept one hand on her cart, which held all her earthly belongings, we entered into a rather long conversation. She had been a telephone operator but lost her job to technology. The results eventually led to a life on the streets, sleeping on the grates in the winter and in parks in the summer; five years had already come and gone.

Toward the end of our dialogue, I offered to buy her a meal. "Oh, I just want a hotdog," was her reply. There was a vendor across the street, so I invited her to go with me and I would get a hotdog and a drink. "Oh no, I'll just sit here. You would be embarrassed to be seen with me." I got the hotdog, talked a little while longer, and then as I departed, I said, "Jesus loves you and so do I." She brushed her hair back, sat up a little straighter, and said, "You don't know how long it has been since someone told me they loved me." God was in that place.

IV. **I could relate numerous times when I could truthfully say, "God was in this place."** There were the times I went to the local filling station in a small rural town in Alabama and talked with the good ole boys. The encounter led to the conversion of a town drunk. Years later, as I visited the church there, I met his entire family, who were all active members. Each thanked me for taking the time to share Jesus with their husband, father, and grandfather. God was in that place.

I could relate the more traditional times when God's presence and power were experienced in worship services or spiritual retreats. And then there was the spiritual encounter at my son's funeral, as I wept tears of grief. All of these mountaintop experiences proved over and over again that God ministers to us and through us in a variety of ways and places. Some were expected, but others were not.

I invite you to examine yourselves. I feel certain that if you try, you will recall a time when you, too, could have said, "God is in this place."—John Dever

ILLUSTRATIONS

God's Presence. I was still in seminary when a pastor from Tennessee came for graduate study. This was during the sixties and the time of public school integration. This young man had been a pastor in a small town in Tennessee when the local schools integrated. People had lined the street to jeer and scoff as the lone black girl made her way to the nearby public school to enter the first grade. The pastor felt her hurt and took her hand and walked with her. He was dismissed from his church the next Sunday. I don't know about the church, but God was in that street that day in Tennessee.—John Dever

The Rest of the Story. Saul of Tarsus had a serendipitous experience on the road to Damascus. Saul was intent on stamping out this new sect that had spawned under the leadership of Jesus of Nazareth. Already having experienced some success in Judea, he sought to pursue these heretics to Damascus. The Scriptures say, "Now as he journeyed he approached Damascus and suddenly a light from heaven flashed about him. 'Saul, Saul, why do you persecute me?' And he said 'Who are you, Lord?' And he said, 'I am Jesus, whom you are persecuting; but rise and enter the city, and you will be told what you are to do'" (Acts 9:3–6).

Well, as Paul Harvey would say, "You already know the rest of the story." Paul's life was turned around. Out of this encounter, Paul became a Jewish missionary to the Gentiles. God (Jesus) was in this place. And once again his presence, power, protection, and providence were made known.—John Dever

Musical Selections Appropriate to the Day

Hymn suggestions for lectionary texts:

Gen. 28:10–19a	*Nearer My God to Thee*
Ps. 139:1–12, 23–24	*Search Me O God*
Rom. 8:12–25	*Lord We Hear Your Word; Every Time I Feel the Spirit*
Matt. 13:24–30, 36–43	*Come Ye Thankful People, Come*

৶ Children's Lectionary Sermon

TITLE: A Speaking Spirit

SCRIPTURE: Rom. 8:12–25

KEY VERSE: *For his Holy Spirit speaks to us deep into our hearts and tells us we are God's children.* (Rom. 8:16, New Living Translation)

KEY CONCEPT: Holy Spirit, assurance

MATERIALS: Bible

I want to ask you some questions today. Are you ready? If I flip the light switch, what happens? (*Let the children respond.*) Are you sure? (*Let them respond.*) If you turn on the water faucet at the sink, what happens? (*Let the children respond.*) Are you sure? If you press the "on" button on the TV remote, what happens? (*Let the children respond.*) Are you sure? Are you tired of me asking, Are you sure? (*Let the children answer.*) Are you sure?

Sometimes we just know—we are certain—if we turn on the light switch we get light, or if we turn on the water faucet we get water. There are some things we are just sure of. In the Bible, Paul wrote the Christians in Rome to remind them they were God's children. (*Open Bible.*) He wrote, "For his Holy Spirit speaks to us deep into our hearts and tells us we are God's children." Paul said that this feeling of "I'm sure" I am God's child comes from the Holy Spirit.

I know it can be hard to understand this. It is hard for big people, too. But just the way you knew for sure all those questions I asked you, God wants you to know for sure you are God's children. God loves you and cares for you and makes you feel sure through God's Holy Spirit in you.—Marcia Thompson

WORSHIP AIDS

Call to Worship: We are humbled as we come before God. In worship, we declare God's greatness and glory: "Know therefore that the Lord your God, he is God, the faithful God, who keeps covenant and mercy with those who love him and keep his commandments to a thousand generations" (Deut. 7:9).

Invocation: Dearest Lord, as we reach up to you, help us to know that you are just now reaching out to us. May our prayers and praise speak honestly of our need for and dependence on you. Mold us together as one people, united under Christ's reign, that we may be useful to the building of your Kingdom. Amen.

Offertory Sentence: "God, who supplies seed for the sower and bread to eat, will also supply you with all the seed you need and will make it grow and produce a rich harvest from your generosity" (2 Cor. 9:10).

Offertory Prayer: Father, our very sustenance depends on your gracious provisions. We thank you for our "daily bread." Apart from your giving, we would surely perish. Grant that our giving will reflect a loving spirit like your own. Your mercy overwhelms us. Help us to live mercifully. Amen.

Morning Prayer: O God, our help in ages past, beyond our knowing you have cradled us in the heart of your providence. You have surrounded us and sustained us with grace upon grace. Morning by morning, new mercies we see. On this Lord's day, we rise and gather to worship you. Great is your faithfulness.

We bring today to worship the spiritual victories of the past week—the moments when we have spoken openly the name of Jesus and have lived out in word and deed his claim on us. We bring today also our human frailty, the weaknesses of our spirits. We pray, "Lord we believe; help Thou our unbelief."

Pour out your Spirit on us that we may see visions and dream dreams. Anoint this people, this church, gathered in love and service in the Kingdom—the Kingdom for which Jesus died. Renew our spirits that we may faithfully proclaim and lovingly live out the gospel in the entire world, and in all the worlds of men and women, boys and girls, young and old. We pray in the Spirit of him in whom word and deed are one, who is present among us as Risen Lord, teaching us both to pray and live. Amen.—Lee McGlone

Benediction: Go with us, O Lord, whom we name as Father, Son, and Holy Spirit, as we step forth from worship into service. Make us strong in the days of this week, both that we shall bring honor to you and bold witness to the world. May your name be praised. Amen.

SUNDAY, JULY 27, 2008

LECTIONARY SERMON TOPIC: "What the Kingdom of Heaven Is All About"
TEXT: Matt. 13:31–33, 44–52
OTHER READINGS: Gen. 29:15–28; Ps. 105:1–11, 45b; Rom. 8:26–39

I'm sure that Jesus must have heard over and over, "Teacher, what is this kingdom of heaven all about? What is it like? We're having a hard time understanding." I guess if we were really honest with our thoughts, we too have some questions concerning the kingdom. This is true, even though we have the words of Jesus recorded for us in the Bible, and we have hundreds of years of theological history to help us understand. The truth is, the human language is so tied to our earthly existence that it is totally inadequate to describe the kingdom of heaven.

Jesus takes the challenge. "Well let's see," he might have said, "the kingdom of heaven is like a mustard seed. Or it's like yeast. Or it's like a treasure hidden in a field. Or it's like a pearl of great price. Or it's like a net thrown into the sea." I can almost hear his followers saying, "Well, which is it?" I think that in the dialogue that followed, Jesus must have explained that it was all of these and much more.

I. **The problem of language has plagued theologians for centuries.** How do you describe God? Is he a loving Father? Is he a Shepherd? Is he the Creator? Is he the Mountain One? Is he the Ground of our Being? And the answer is, yes—and much more. So Jesus turns to a series of parables, metaphors, or illustrations from everyday life to try to explain the kingdom of heaven.

A paraphrase of Matthew 13:31–32 might say, Let me try to explain. You see that tree over there. It sprouted forth from a tiny mustard seed, the very smallest of all the seeds. But look now, it furnishes a shelter for birds to build their nests. The kingdom of heaven is like that grain of mustard seed. It starts from the smallest beginnings, but no one knows where it will end. It will grow until it furnishes a safe haven for all the nations of the world.

I'm not sure they understood the full meaning of this. After all, they were a very small minority living in a remote province of the Empire. I don't think they could have, in their best moments, imagined what would happen in the near future. This movement—this kingdom introduced by Jesus—would spread like wildfire throughout the Roman Empire and eventually to the whole world.

II. **Jesus continued, "You know, there is another way I could explain the kingdom of heaven" (Matt. 13:33).** "When I was a boy, my mother baked a lot of bread. The main ingredient that gave it flavor was the leaven she put in it. Without it, the bread was hard, dry, and unappetizing. The kingdom of heaven is like that leaven. It has the transforming power to change people's lives. It will bring meaning, purpose, and a complete metamorphosis to individuals and societies."

Jesus said, "Look," he said, "I imagine all of you have experienced the toil of plowing a rocky field. Well, the kingdom of heaven is like a man who was hired to plow a stone-filled field. He had no sooner begun when his plow went 'plunk.' Hour after hour, it was the same sound: 'plunk,' plunk,' plunk.' One stone after the other blocked his plow. Then suddenly there was a different sound: 'clank.' What could this be? When he dug it up, it was a treasure box filled with gold coins and precious gems. He could hardly believe it. Immediately he reburied it, and with his heart pounding in his chest, he ran home, sold everything he had, borrowed the rest, and purchased the land. The law said if you found a treasure on your land it was yours. Folks, I hope you understand this. I want you to know that entering the kingdom of heaven is worth any sacrifice" (Matt. 13:44).

III. **Jesus continued to pile one illustration on another, hoping that in the end they would comprehend the nature and importance of the kingdom of heaven.** "The kingdom is like a merchant who had been searching for the rarest of pearls and finally finds the pearl of his dreams. It was so valuable, he sold all he had and bought it" (Matt. 13:46). This sounds like the preceding story of the man who was plowing the field. But there really is a difference. In the first story the man was not looking for the treasure; its discovery was a serendipitous event. The merchant had searched for the pearl for years. I think Jesus was saying that one can discover the kingdom of heaven in various ways. One can be a seeker, or one can discover it accidentally. Either way, it is such a valuable discovery that it is worth giving up everything in order to enter.

IV. **The final illustration must have brought some confusion to the crowd gathered there on the seashore.** "The kingdom of heaven is like a net which was thrown into the sea and gathered fish of every kind; when it was full men drew it ashore and sat down and sorted the good into vessels but threw away the bad. So it will be at the close of the age" (Matt. 13:47–48). Can't you hear the murmuring in the crowd? "What in the world is he talking about?"

My dad and I use to seine for fish bait. We couldn't determine beforehand what we would haul in. It became necessary to divide the catch at the end. Jesus is making it very clear that the kingdom can't be totally selective of those who say they want to enter, but in the end their commitment will be weighed, and those who weren't really serious about following Jesus will be cast aside. Jesus put it another way: "Not all those who call me Lord, Lord, will enter into the kingdom." A time of separation will come, as indicated in Matthew 25.

V. **I really like Jesus' closing words in verses 51 and 52: "Have you understood all this?"** They said to him, "Yes." And he said to them, "Therefore every scribe who has been trained for the kingdom of heaven is like a house-holder who brings out of his treasure what is new and what is old." I don't know about the people gathered there in the first century, but it took this twenty-first century man a long time to comprehend these words. But in the end it became very clear. Jesus was saying that when you enter into the kingdom, all you knew before is supplemented with the new knowledge imparted by the Holy Spirit. As they mix we become new persons. We are "born again."

So you want to know what the kingdom of heaven is all about. So did the crowd that gathered around Jesus that day by the seashore. Jesus, therefore, with the handicap of an earthly language, gave them all they could comprehend. He made it clear that the most wonderful event in people's lives is to discover the kingdom of heaven and to enter in with all their heart, and soul, and mind. Although not totally clear here, it is clear in other passages that entrance into the kingdom brought a renewed relationship with God and a new life here on this earth and in the life to come. What more could anyone want?—John Dever

---

ILLUSTRATIONS

Transformation. William Barclay points out that the gospel of Jesus Christ did—and does—transform lives of individuals. It brings about a conversion that turns people's lives around. The role of women was changed as news of the Kingdom spread. It transformed the lives of the weak and the ill. They were no longer outcasts, seen as burdens to the society. And it transformed the lives of children. Through the restoration of the family, the role of the child was elevated even to the point that in modern civilization life is almost centered on our children. In Barclay's own words: "There is nothing in history so unanswerably demonstrable as the transforming power of Christianity and of Christ on the individual life and on the life of society."[8]—John Dever

---

[8]William Barclay, *The Gospel of Matthew*, Vol. 2 (Philadelphia: Westminster, 1958), pp. 89–90.

Spiritual Gifts. For a long time, I have had a different understanding of the gifts of the Spirit from that of many of my colleagues. I have seen the gifts in two ways. First, it is entirely possible for God to give us new gifts at our conversion. There are many examples of this in the Scriptures. But I have also seen the gifts in a second way—a way that experience has validated. God gives us talents at our birth. Or we develop certain gifts during our maturation. I sincerely believe that God takes these gifts and talents and baptizes them at our conversion to be used for the Kingdom's glory. Isn't this what he is saying in verse 52? Every person comes to Jesus with some gifts, some abilities, and some knowledge. We don't have to totally abandon these. With the power of the Holy Spirit, they can be reconsecrated and joined with any new gifts to be totally dedicated to the work of the Kingdom.—John Dever

Musical Selections Appropriate to the Day

Hymn suggestions for lectionary texts:

Gen. 29:15–28	*Guide Me, O Thou Great Jehovah; God Moves in a Mysterious Way*
Ps. 105:1–11, 45b	*Healing Grace; This Is a Time to Remember*
Rom. 8:26–39	*O Love That Will Not Let Me Go; Christ Be My Leader*
Matt. 13:31–33, 44–52	*Jesus, Priceless Treasure*

❧ Children's Lectionary Sermon

TITLE: Sing Praises to God
SCRIPTURE: Ps. 105:1–11
KEY VERSE: *Sing to him, sing praise to him; tell of all his wonderful acts.* (Ps. 105:2, New International Version)
KEY CONCEPT: Worship through singing
MATERIALS: Bible, hymn books, rhythm-band instruments

PREPARATION: Place rhythm-band instruments nearby; ask an adult to help you distribute them to the children. Ask the children ahead of time to name some of their favorite hymns or choruses.

Hello, boys and girls. Today, I want us to do something a little different. I want us to sing some of your favorite songs you learned in Sunday school or children's choir. As we sing, I want you to choose a rhythm band instrument and keep time to the music. (*Pass out instruments. Depending on your comfort with singing spontaneously, you will need to decide whether you are going to choose the songs or let the children choose them. Some favorite songs written for children are, "Jesus Loves the Little Children of the World," "Jesus Loves Me," and "Away in a Manger."*) Can you name your favorite? (*Allow time for response. Ask the pianist to play through a verse of several familiar children's songs as they sing and follow with their instruments. Make sure to have a plan for the instruments when you are finished.*)

Singing can make us feel good. Singing can make us happy. I saw smiles on your faces as you sang. The psalmist, David, wrote many songs of praise as he watched over his father's sheep. The life of a shepherd was often lonely. David had no one but God to talk to. I can imagine him, alone with the sheep at night, looking up in the heavens and thanking God for his blessings. (*Open Bible.*) We read in Psalm 105:2, "Sing to him, sing praise to him; tell of all his wonderful acts."

When we sing together here at church, we are worshiping and praising God through our singing. God is happy when we worship through singing.—Carolyn Tomlin

❧ WORSHIP AIDS ❧

Call to Worship: Our world harbors much dishonesty and deceit. As we worship, we rejoice that the truth has come to us through Jesus Christ, the Lord: "You shall know the truth and the truth shall make you free" (John 8:32).

Invocation: Loving Father, come to us in our worship and make your presence known. Open our minds and hearts to hear the gospel story and the unique message it has for each of us. Let the light of your countenance shine upon us and give us peace. Amen.

Offertory Sentence: "The rendering of this service not only supplies the wants of the saints but also overflows in many thanksgivings to God" (2 Cor. 9:12).

Offertory Prayer: Gracious provider, Father of all humankind, and Lord of the earth, we return these gifts to you as expressions of our devotion and love. Bless these tithes and offerings so that no need goes unmet. Increase our ability to give, along with our desire to love. For the cause of Christ, we pray. Amen.

Morning Prayer: Father, we could not be here this morning worshipping you had you not first loved us and come to us and called us and redeemed us. Sometimes such great caring on your part seems almost too incredible to believe. Yet in our more reflective moments, we recognize the change that has come in us since Christ came into our hearts. Our spirits are changed: our caring for one another is greater; our longing to do right is stronger since we have discovered that you love us in spite of all our sins and failures and that by your Spirit you lead us onto a higher plane of life, guiding us, inspiring us, and keeping us after your fashion. How grateful we are that we can come into your presence as a congregation to be strengthened and renewed. The world about us so often frustrates us and pushes us down from the high place we have gained as we walk in your presence.

So this morning we come seeking to be cleansed from that which we cannot, of ourselves, wash away. We come seeking to be lifted by your grace from all that would bring us low. We come seeking to be made firm in our faith, even as we walk through a world where friction and doubt hold sway. Most of all, we come to abide in your presence for a while that love's chords may be strengthened and our heart's thanksgiving for your love and power may be expressed through our worship and praise. Amen.—Henry Fields

Benediction: Fill our hearts, O God, as we go forth today. Let your word be alive within us that we may so live and serve you that your holy name will be honored and praised. Lead us in the way of truth. And may the peace of God be with us all. Amen.

SUNDAY, AUGUST 3, 2008

LECTIONARY SERMON TOPIC: "Fighting God, God Fighting"
TEXT: Gen. 32:22–31
OTHER READINGS: Ps. 17:1–7, 15; Rom. 9:1–5; Matt. 14:13–21

Parts of the Bible urge us to be cautious and respectful toward God, who created all things and has power and knowledge beyond our imagining. Be careful how you talk to God, says Ecclesiastes; God is in heaven, and you are on earth, so let your words be few. Most humans who go toe-to-toe with God are overwhelmed. Jonah gets swallowed by the great fish and is forced to repent. Jeremiah says that when he tries to hold in the words he hates to speak, the marrow in his bones burns; God is too strong to resist, he says. Job, who roars his wish to argue his case with God, is silenced by the whirlwind and folds his hands in submission.

Other parts of the Bible, if they don't urge us to confront God, certainly set that example. The lament psalms, for example, ask: "God, how long are you going to hang back and do nothing?" Or think of Moses, complaining to God about his congregation one day and then trying to talk God out of burning them alive on another. But even seen as part of that biblical stream, this story in which Jacob wrestles God and wins, sort of, is a very unusual story, even for the Bible.

I. **Why is Jacob in the dark?** Jacob's the guy who usually outwits his opponents. He buys Esau's birthright with a bowl of soup and steals Esau's blessing by pulling the wool over his blind father's eyes. He was cheated once, on his first wedding night; Jacob then outsmarts his father-in-law constantly, until Laban is more than happy to see him and his clan leave. There's no grip he can't slip, no trap he can't spring, no law or parental directive he can't circumvent. God offers him a no-cut, no-conditions promise, and Jacob rewords it into a bargain: God, if you do this and this, then I will do that and that. Jacob is a fixer, not a fighter.

But now he's in the dark, wondering what to do. Ahead is his brother, who has vowed to kill him. Behind is his father-in-law, who has forbidden his return. All around him are his family and his possessions—things he has gained as an entrepreneur—but he stands to lose it all. And deep in the night, God (or God's messenger, which amounts to the same thing) comes to force him to do battle. No escape; this time he has to stand or perish.

II. **What does it mean to wrestle with God?** And why would anybody want to? It means to hold on until God blesses—to believe enough in God's goodness and in God's willingness to be involved with us that we do not let go. Jesus' parable of the widow and the unjust judge makes the same point: you have to pray always and never lose heart. This does not mean finding the silver lining in the tragedies of life. It means believing that our God means to do us good.

It means to hold on, even when we are wounded, even when it seems to us that the wound comes from God. The author of Genesis believed that God (or God's messenger) gave Jacob his permanent limp. I can't bring myself to attribute my own physical or spiritual injuries to God, but if I believe that God intervenes in our lives, then I am forced to believe that God at least permits these kinds of things. Again, like Jacob, I choose to believe that God's ultimate purpose is to bless the world, and so I hold on.

It means to hold on, even when we cannot get a straight answer. Jacob's opponent would not say his name and did not explain why the battle came that night. Even worse than the pain of loss sometimes is the unanswerable question that plagues us: Why me? Why now? Why this and not something else? When the morning came, Jacob had gotten no clear directive from God, but in reflecting on his experience, he understood that God had been with him.

It means to hold on, and to live, and to be changed thereby. Jacob, the deceiver, had his name changed to Israel, which one can read as "he fights God" or "God fights." It's perfect—paradoxical, reflecting the muddy truth of trying to discern God's will, and conflicted, since it is probably not in Jacob's nature to be named "he who sits quietly with God." Jacob hasn't been given a lobotomy; he has a plan to try to finesse Esau and protect himself and his family. But he has been changed: he lives, and now he knows that the God who knows him for who he truly is will never leave him.

III. Why fight God? Probably, none of us really ever wants to fight God. We would prefer for God to bless us and to light our way, and for God to fight for us. But sometimes life (or God) puts us with our backs to the river, and the choice is either to let go of faith or to fight to hold on to it. Like Jacob, let us hold on, confused, wounded, and afraid, until it becomes clear to us that we are wrestling with God.—Richard B. Vinson

---

ILLUSTRATIONS

Plow Work. Jesus said, "Any person who puts hand to the plow, and looks back, is not ready for duty in the Kingdom of God" (Luke 9:62). Here was a carefully chosen image that spoke to an immediate need. Plowing is the "heavy work" of the farmer's labor; sowing seed is comparatively easy. Gathering the harvest is attended with joyous celebration, but the early plowing is hard and laborious, demanding and dirty work. But yet it is foundational to the success of the intended crop. So it is with the Kingdom of God. The early followers of Jesus needed to know the demands of discipleship—that this would be no life of ease. Apart from strong convictions that went beyond the ecstasy of the moment, they were in danger of turning back. What they came to experience, even as we do, was the faithful presence of the Lord Jesus Christ as their steadying hand. This is no lonely furrow we plow. The Lord is with us.—Lee McGlone

    Grace. "Once they said to Onias the Circle-maker, 'Pray that rain may fall.' . . . He prayed, but the rain did not fall. What did he do? He drew a circle and stood within it and said before God, 'O Lord of the world, thy children have turned their faces to me, for that I am like a son of the house before thee. I swear by thy great name that I will not stir hence until thou have pity on thy children.' Rain began falling drop by drop. He said, 'Not for such rain have I prayed, but for rain that will fill the cisterns, pits, and caverns.' It began to rain with violence. He said, 'Not for such rain have I prayed, but for rain of goodwill, blessing, and graciousness.' Then it rained in moderation and continued until the Israelites went up from Jerusalem to the Temple Mount because of the rain."[1]—Richard Vinson

---

[1]Mishnah tractate Taanith 3.8—a story about a Galilean rabbi of the first century before Christ—in Herbert Danby, *The Mishnah* (London: Oxford University Press, 1954), p. 198.

Musical Selections Appropriate to the Day

Hymn suggestions for lectionary texts:

Gen. 32:22–31	*Be Still My Soul; Day by Day*
Ps. 17:1–7, 15	*Hear Our Prayer O Lord*
Rom. 9:1–5	*Faith of Our Fathers*
Matt. 14:13–21	*Let Us Talents and Tongues Employ*

✒ Children's Lectionary Sermon

TITLE: Jesus Feeds the Five Thousand

SCRIPTURE: Matt. 14:13–21

KEY VERSE: *When Jesus landed and saw a large crowd, he had compassion on them and healed their sick.* (Matt. 14:14, New International Version)

KEY CONCEPT: Miracles

MATERIALS: Bible

Hello boys and girls. Today, I want to share with you miracles of Jesus. After Jesus heard John the Baptist had been killed, he wanted to be alone. He was sad. He went away in a boat, trying to find a quiet place. But the crowds followed. They came from all the small towns and villages to hear and see Jesus. Sick people were brought so Jesus could heal them. (*Open Bible.*) Matthew 14:14 says, "When Jesus landed and saw a large crowd, he had compassion on them and healed their sick." Even though Jesus was sad, he loved the people so much he wanted to heal them.

Do you know what happened next? The disciples came and told Jesus it was almost night. He should send the people home. They would need to eat. They could buy food in the villages.

Jesus realized the people needed food, but the only food on hand consisted of five loaves of bread and two fish. Would this feed all the people? Jesus took the bread and fish. He blessed it, then broke the loaves and gave them to the disciples. The disciples handed the food out to the people. The people ate until they were not hungry. The disciples picked up twelve basketfuls of broken pieces. It was estimated that the food fed five thousand men, plus the women and children.

We must remember that Jesus did miracles then, and he still does them today. With the help of modern medicine and skilled doctors, Jesus heals our suffering and pain. The birth of a new baby is a miracle. We never know how Jesus will work miracles, but we always want to be his followers, loving and helping others. Maybe Jesus will make a miracle happen through you.—Carolyn Tomlin

WORSHIP AIDS

Call to Worship: Our greatest joy is the presence of God. To our God, we declare, along with the psalmist, "We will praise you with our whole hearts . . . we sing praise unto you . . . we praise your name for your loving-kindness and for your truth" (Ps. 138:1–2).

Invocation: Lord, you who neither slumber nor sleep, keeping a steadfast eye over all your creation, sustaining it—and us—by your power and might, grant that we may today enter into your presence and be strengthened for the work of grace you have begun in us. May today's worship prepare us for the opportunities for service we will face in the days ahead. Help us to worship you in spirit and in truth.

Offertory Sentence: "My God shall supply all your need according to his riches in glory by Christ Jesus" (Phil. 4:19).

Offertory Prayer: Loving Father, we bring before you now our tithes and offerings. They are given in response to your grace. You have loved us before we loved you and have forgiven our sin and opened to us fullness of life. Grant that our gifts will be given in cheerfulness and delight. And may they encourage your Kingdom here and around the world. Amen.

Morning Prayer: God, many of us are grieving. It is easy to lose our footing and tumble head over heels in dreams of endless, hopeless falling, when we are battered by death, disease, lost employment, separation, expectations unfulfilled, failing others, falling short, losing our sense of ourselves. Perhaps we must give ourselves over to this grieving, to give the event its due, to honor the loved one, mourn the dream, the future we have lost, to let grief have its way for awhile, until we can say, "Is that all you've got?" And then to stand again and find the earth beneath our feet.

Yet when we are unglued and free-falling, we may find there are gifts we receive when we are broken, presents that can only come to us when our usual routines and mind-sets are shattered. We, who seek our places in the infinite stretch of time, who travel amoebic strips of consciousness winding in and out of our daily lives, sometimes popping up in decades past, in memory, or past in present, intermixed, as we speak in family, with friend. There is treasure there. A new way. A loving word. Forgiveness and release. As we feel our way through these mists, let us remain open to the gifts drifting toward us, to the strong arms of family and community that will embrace us, if we let them. Let us lay down our paralyzing fears of judgment, exclusion, and hurtful gossip. For we all know too well the faults and weaknesses that have brought us low. And may we say, at day's end, "Still, We Believe." Amen.—Peter Pease

Benediction: People of God, go forth with joy into the opportunities set before us this week. Let us take with us the encouragement of this hour. And may we, in the days ahead, be faithful to our callings, in the name of the Father, the Son, and the Holy Spirit. Amen.

SUNDAY, AUGUST 10, 2008

LECTIONARY SERMON TOPIC: "The Price of a Dream"
TEXT: Gen. 37:1–4, 12–28
OTHER READINGS: Ps. 105:1–6, 16–22, 45b; Rom. 10:5–15; Matt. 14:22–33

Hold fast to your dreams, say the poets and the song writers. What coming-of-age movie has ever been filmed without a moment when the idealistic young person, confronted by the selfish, heartless nature of the world, is ready to give up. "I can't do it," he says, to which the wise, grizzled teacher replies, "Never give up on your dream." Or think of Kermit playing banjo in the swamp, singing of how he's sure that someday he'll find his "rainbow connection."

I. **Dreams are double-edged.** This story begins like that. Joseph is a bright young man, adored by his father, favored by God. He feels secure, it seems, or maybe it's just youthful naiveté that lets him tell his parents and older brothers that God has shown him that someday they will all bow down to him. How does Joseph imagine that they will feel about that? Does he feel so snug in his special robe that he believes that everyone sees the world as he does and that his elders will rejoice in his dreams?

Dreams come with a price, we find. The first is the jealousy, even hatred, of his brothers. The second is the suspicion and rebuke of his father: "What kind of dream is this?" Jacob asks. Ostracism, indignation, anger—we can only imagine how tense things became in the tents of Jacob, as the whole rest of the family reacted to Joseph's dreams. Isn't this the common experience for dreamers? If this dream of yours is real, how come God hasn't shown it to me? What about my dreams of becoming somebody—do they count for nothing? From Joseph's brothers' point of view, would it have seemed plausible or desirable to get behind the dream and to work toward their own servitude? Unlikely. And, short of seeing it all come true, what would have convinced them that the dream held the future for them?

Dreams like this are thus a very mixed blessing. Because they are so intensely personal, they fill the dreamer with a sense of purpose and wonder, but for the same reason, they tend to separate the dreamer from everyone else in his or her life. Think of Jesus saying, "Today this Scripture is fulfilled in your hearing," and his hometown synagogue's reply: "Wait a minute. We know you and your family, and we're not buying this." In your experience of church, what dreamers have announced what they felt was God's leadership, only to find varying degrees of indifference or hostility?

II. **It's hard to kill a dream.** When the brothers are plotting to kill him, they don't just say that they hate him and want him out of the way. They want to kill the dream: "Let us kill him . . . then we shall see what will become of his dreams." Eventually, he is sold into slavery—twenty pieces of silver the price of the dream and the dreamer. Their mistake (again, a pretty common one in religious communities) is to identify the dream with the dreamer. If we kill him, then the dream will die. If we censure him, then those troublesome ideas will go away; we won't have to listen to any more rubbish about becoming less materialistic, or being open and affirming to gays and lesbians, or facing up to racial prejudice.

You know how this story ends. Despite all that the brothers do to thwart the dream, it still happens, because it is God's dream, not Joseph's. How could they have known that in advance? I'm not sure. And what if they had believed their irritating younger sibling and had supported him in his dream? It's hard to imagine how the story would have gone. But we church people ought to take this story as a cautionary tale. It is completely likely that God is trying to tell us something and that there are dreamers who are providing us with insights we are ignoring or even trying to suppress. If these are God's dreams, then whacking the dreamer won't make the dream go away, and as Gamaliel says in Acts, we will find ourselves resisting God.

III. **What's the price of a dream?** What's it worth to us to stand behind a dream? Peter tries to walk on the water to get to Jesus; he sinks and must be rescued. Paul writes of all he has endured to bring the gospel to people who, as often as not, don't care to listen. Jesus says we must be willing to walk away from family, house, and job, and to carry our own crosses, prepared to die for him and for the gospel. Dreaming is risky, painful, discouraging work. But if the dreams are God's dreams, then it does no good to try to ignore or escape them.—Richard B. Vinson

---

ILLUSTRATIONS

"I Have a Dream." "Well, I don't know what will happen now. We've got some difficult days ahead. But it doesn't matter to me now. Because I've been to the mountaintop. And I don't mind. Like anybody, I would like to live a long life. Longevity has its place. But I'm not worried about that now. I just want to do God's will. And He's allowed me to go up to the mountain. And I've looked over. And I've seen the Promised Land. I may not get there with you. But I want you to know tonight, that we, as a people will get to the Promised Land. And I'm happy, tonight. I'm not worried about anything. I'm not fearing any man. Mine eyes have seen the glory of the coming of the Lord."[2]—Richard B. Vinson

Salvation. A story is told of a shipwrecked crew who had been drifting for days in a small boat off the coast of Brazil. They were suffering the horrors of thirst, but they dared not drink the seawater because the salt would have made it even worse. They saw a vessel coming toward them and called out, "Water, water!"

"Dip your bucket over the side," they were told. They thought they were being mocked. But no, the water was fresh. They had drifted into the flow of the mighty River Amazon, bearing fresh water far out to sea. God's salvation is that close, that available. It may not look like it; it may seem implausible, impractical, but you've got to dip your bucket in his water to find out.—Jackie Little

Musical Selections Appropriate to the Day

Hymn suggestions for lectionary texts:

Gen. 37:1–4, 12–28	*All the Way My Savior Leads Me*
Ps. 105:1–6, 16–22, 45b	*To God Be the Glory*
Rom. 10:5–15	*Jesus Saves*
Matt. 14:22–33	*Eternal Father, Strong to Save*

☙ Children's Lectionary Sermon

TITLE: God Dreams

SCRIPTURE: Ps. 105:1–6, 16–22

KEY VERSE: *Joseph was put in charge of all the king's household; he became ruler over all the king's possessions. He could instruct the king's aides as he pleased and teach the king's advisors.* (Ps 105:21–22, New Living Translation)

---

[2]Martin Luther King Jr., "I See the Promised Land," preached April 3, 1968, in Bishop Charles Mason Temple in Memphis; published in James M. Washington (ed.), *A Testament of Hope* (New York: HarperCollins, 1986), p. 286.

KEY CONCEPT: God's providence
MATERIALS: Bible, a pillow

I brought my pillow with me this morning. When you go to sleep, do you ever have dreams? (*Let the children respond.*) Sometimes when I am asleep, I have the strangest dreams—not really nightmares but unusual dreams. A long time ago God used dreams to help God's people.

God selected a young man by the name of Joseph to help his family and his people. God used dreams in Joseph's life. He dreamed about bundles of grain. His bundle stood up, but his brothers' bundles all bowed down. Joseph's dreams made his brothers mad, and they sold him into slavery. While in Egypt, Joseph was in jail. Joseph was stuck in jail until he interpreted a dream for one of Pharaoh's servants. Pharaoh had a dream, and Joseph was able to tell him what it meant. Joseph became a powerful helper for Pharaoh because he could interpret dreams. (*Open Bible.*) Listen to these verses from Psalm 105: "Joseph was put in charge of all the king's household; he became ruler over all the king's possessions. He could instruct the king's aides as he pleased and teach the king's advisors." He helped store food away because from the dream he knew there was going to be a time when food would not grow. Joseph provided food for many hungry people.

The Lord used dreams and many other unlikely things to bring about deliverance. The mostly unlikely thing that showed us the love of God is the cross. On the cross Jesus died for our sins. Jesus made it so that we can live with Jesus forever.—Ken Cox

❧ WORSHIP AIDS ❧

Call to Worship: We count it all joy to gather as God's people in this holy place. Along with those who have worshipped through the ages, we declare, "Lord, we love the habitation of your house, and the place where your honor dwells" (Ps. 26:8).

Invocation: Father of our Lord Jesus Christ, who said your house is to be a house of prayer, grant today that this will surely be so. When we call upon you, we do so confidently, knowing that you hear us. We now surrender to you our needs and longings, asking that your will and way be done among us, even as it is done in heaven. Amen.

Offertory Sentence: "Bear one another's burdens, and so fulfill the law of Christ" (Gal. 6:2).

Offertory Prayer: Gracious Father, we thank you for the gifts we have so lavishly received from your benevolent hand. Now we humbly and lovingly return a portion of your gifts as expression of our affection and devotion. Lord, accept these gifts as symbols of our faithful commitments, and may they provide the means necessary for the work of your Kingdom. Amen.

Morning Prayer: With joy and anticipation we come before you this morning, Father. We thank you for the days past, which have been challenges to us, as well as blessings for us. We thank you for the truths we have learned and the values we have found. As we come together in this sacred sanctuary this morning, visit us with the presence and power of your Holy Spirit. Create in us thoughtful minds, devoted hearts, and wills in tune with your justice and love. Turn our attention from every distracting care and interest that we may worship you in Spirit and truth.

In this holy hour, remind us of the wonder of your universe, even as we are reminded of the many revelations of your care for each of us. Recall how our every need has been met and most of our wants cared for. Remind us of the comforts we have received from you in times of stress and sorrow, as well as the joys that have invaded life with inspiration and cheer. And may we not forget the many times we have been recipients of help from loved ones and friends. How thankful we are for all these blessings, Father.

Because we have been so well blessed and because we are disciples of him who has called us from darkness to light and life, help us to take a more vigorous, active share in the tasks of the church and its ministry. Give us a new vision of what the church is all about. Deliver us from thinking it is designed for our comfort, and help us to see that it is designed to make us great in Christ's service. Grant us the strength to be the bridge builders of understanding for others as they struggle with life apart from the presence and power of Christ.—Henry Fields

Benediction: As we move from this sanctuary into the events of the week before us, let us go in the care of the gracious God who goes before us. May we know that the eternal God is our dwelling place, and underneath us are the everlasting arms. Amen.

SUNDAY, AUGUST 17, 2008

LECTIONARY SERMON TOPIC: "Learning Mercy"

TEXT: Matt. 15:10–20, 21–28

OTHER READINGS: Gen. 45:1–15; Ps. 133; Rom. 11:1–2a, 29–32

To appreciate the verbal skirmish between Jesus and the Canaanite woman, we need to understand a couple of things about each character. We'll take Jesus first (it is his gospel, after all). You've probably noticed that Jesus never loses an argument and always has the last word. The pattern goes like this: a hostile group confronts him with a complaint or a test question. Jesus has a great comeback, and the hecklers are amazed or silent. He does this at the beginning of Matthew, chapter 15. The Pharisees and scribes complain that Jesus' disciples do not wash their hands before meals, in accord with their traditions. Jesus zaps them for not obeying the Law of Moses as closely as they claim, and then says that nothing going into the body can defile, only what comes out. The Pharisees are offended, say the disciples; ignore them, says Jesus, and God will deal with them.

I. **Jesus and the Law.** So Matthew's Jesus is the snappy retort guy who always leaves his opponents in the dust. He's also the "more obedient than the Pharisees" guy. Notice that Matthew 15:19–20 does not go as far as Mark 7:18–23; in Mark's opinion, Jesus' parable is the end of the distinction between clean and unclean food. In Matthew's opinion, Jesus meant that eating with unwashed hands does not make one unclean, but the sins coming out of evil intentions do. Matthew's Jesus, true to his word in 5:17–20, is not setting aside any part of the Law of Moses, including the kosher requirements; instead, he is intensifying the reach of the Law, declaring wicked intentions to be defiling. We should worry about purifying our hearts, ridding ourselves of the nasty thoughts and intentions that are the precursors of sins. So Jesus enters the scene in 15:21 from the side of the Law. He has not come to abolish any of it or set any of it aside, and his mission, as he has made clear in 10:5–6, is to his own people, the Jews. He told his disciples to enter no Gentile town, but if he's in the area around Tyre and Sidon, that's where he is; maybe he needs a break from all the arguing with the Pharisees.

II. **An outsider asking for help.** The Canaanite woman enters the scene from the opposite end of the legal spectrum. Matthew deliberately changes Mark's "Syrophoenician" to "Canaanite" to emphasize the woman's Gentile status. Not only is she not Jewish, but calling her "Canaanite" links her to the nations about whom Moses warned Israel. You must have nothing to do with them, he said; don't marry them, don't let them live with you, and don't pick up any of their religious practices. She's about as far from "lost sheep of the house of Israel" as one can be. The other thing to observe about her is that she is one of a host of anonymous petitioners in this Gospel. We expect a request from her, but nothing else.

III. **A neat retort to Jesus.** She hollers for mercy, just like the two blind men in 9:27; Jesus' first response is to ignore her. The disciples report to him that this isn't working, and he answers (them or her?) that his mission is to the lost sheep of Israel. That should have ended the exchange. That's the sort of conversation-ending response that has shut the Pharisees up in the past. "I came to call not the righteous, but sinners," he says in 9:13. "Go and learn what this means, 'I desire mercy, not sacrifice,'" and they are silent. But instead of fading away, she comes and lies down in front of him, pleading, "Lord, help me!"

Then he calls her a dog. If he weren't Jesus, we'd have no trouble imagining how first-century prejudices over race and ethnicity could color thinking and speech. It isn't his first interaction with a Gentile. In 8:5–13, he seems willing to enter the centurion's house and then praises his faith and heals the sick servant without any question about his mission. Why is this woman's request more objectionable, and why does it provoke such an ugly response? We can't read the intentions of his heart; we can only hear his hurtful words that certainly sound like he does not want to defile himself by contact, even verbal contact, with her. He just wants her to go away.

Again, we'd expect that to be the end of the conversation, but it isn't. Her retort is classic: if I were a dog, then you would at least give me the scraps from your table. She has caught him as neatly as he caught the Pharisees: Do you really believe what you say? Yes, he does, and he heals her daughter.

IV. **Two examples of faith.** The woman shows us what great faith is really like. She will not let go until he blesses her. Like Jacob (Israel) wrestling with God, she will hold on, even as he wounds her, and she will prevail. How does she know that if she keeps pushing him, he will give her the help she needs? Who knows where she learned it, but this Canaanite knows how to live by a real faith in the living God. She knows that mercy will come, even if the agent of mercy at first seems reluctant.

And Jesus—well, Matthew considered Jesus the Son of God and the Messiah, but still he found room in his understanding of Jesus for this story. Jesus himself learns something about mercy, about the expanding scope of his mission, about being stretched through encounters with the Other. We all have our unexamined prejudices; let us hope that when those are exposed that we can surrender them as gracefully as Jesus does. May our Lord, who learned something about God's mercy from the Canaanite woman, mercifully grant us the chance to unlearn our racism and xenophobia.—Richard B. Vinson

---

ILLUSTRATIONS

God's Love. "Perhaps it makes it easier if we remember that this is how God loves us. Not for any nice, attractive qualities we think we have, but just because we are the things called selves. For really there is nothing else in us to love: creatures like us who actually find hatred such a pleasure that to give it up is like giving up beer or tobacco."[3]

Mercy. "The quality of mercy is not strained; it droppeth as the gentle rain from heaven upon the place beneath. It is twice blest; it blesseth him that gives and him that takes. . . . It is an attribute of God himself, and earthly power doth then show likest God's when mercy seasons justice. . . . We do pray for mercy, and that same prayer doth teach us all to render the deeds of mercy."[4]

---

[3]C. S. Lewis, "Christian Behavior." In *Five Best Books in One Volume* (Grand Rapids: Baker, 1977), p. 496.

[4]Shakespeare, "Merchant of Venice," Act 4, Scene 1, quoted from Alfred Harbage (ed.), *William Shakespeare: The Complete Works* (New York: Viking, 1969).

Musical Selections Appropriate to the Day

Hymn suggestions for lectionary texts:

Gen. 45:1–15	*Lead Me, Guide Me; O Master, Let Me Walk with Thee*
Ps. 133	*Sweet, Sweet Spirit*
Rom. 11:1–2a, 29–32	*Jesus Calls Us O'er the Tumult?*
Matt. 15:10–20, 21–28	*There's a Wideness in God's Mercy*

❧ Children's Lectionary Sermon

TITLE: Don't Fight, Seek Peace

SCRIPTURE: Ps. 133

KEY VERSE: *How wonderful it is, how pleasant when brothers live together in harmony.* (Ps. 133:1, New Living Translation)

KEY CONCEPT: God calls us to be peacemakers.

MATERIALS: Bible, boxing gloves

(*Show the boxing gloves.*) These are boxing gloves, boys and girls. Boxing is a sport like football and baseball. In the ring the boxers may be punching each other, but at the end of the match, the boxers hug each other. It's a sport. The boxers are not mad at each other; they are just trying to win a fight.

It is sad that some people fight other people, and they *are* mad at each other. It might be children at school in a fight on the playground, or it might be country against country, at war with each other—a war in which people die. It makes God sad when this happens.

God has called his people to peace. One biblical account of a family conflict has a happy ending. Jacob had twelve sons, but Joseph was his favorite. He gave him a special coat to wear. This caused his brothers to get angry. One day, the older brothers, who were angry, tied Joseph up and sold him into slavery to some merchants who lived in Egypt.

Years later the brothers and Joseph met again in Egypt. By then, Joseph had become an important person. He was second in command in Egypt. His brothers came to get food for the family. Joseph could have gotten angry and punished his brothers for what they did to him. Joseph chose to forgive them. Joseph's faith had produced a sense of peace and trust in God's ways. Joseph brought peace to his family.

When we forgive people, this pleases God. Because God has forgiven us in Jesus Christ, he wants us to be forgiving. (*Open Bible.*) Listen to this verse from Psalm 133: "How wonderful it is, how pleasant when brothers live together in harmony." Best of all, when God is pleased, we are happy, too.—Ken Cox

WORSHIP AIDS

Call to Worship: In gathering to worship, we rejoice that we are co-laborers with God. We are God's handiwork. He is the master builder. Let us take heed to know that "no other foundation can be laid than that which has already been laid, which is Jesus Christ" (1 Cor. 3:11).

Invocation: God our Father, we are laid bare before you as we worship. Your word cuts through like a two-edged sword. In the honesty that faith demands, may our words articulate authentic praise. We make our prayer in the name of Jesus, the Christ, whose will and way we seek. Amen.

Offertory Sentence: "As we have opportunity, let us do good unto all humankind, and especially to those who are of the household of faith" (Gal. 6:10).

Offertory Prayer: Lord, you have graciously given us all that we have and made us all that we are. We are grateful for the gifts of family and friendships, for churches that have nourished us, and for challenges that have kept us on our toes; especially are we grateful for the gift of salvation. Use us, we pray, and the offerings we bring, for spreading the gospel to the ends of the earth. Amen.

Morning Prayer: Spirit of life and love, we gather together again in this holy place. Be in our midst, we pray. We ask that you come into our hearts and open us up to deeper ways of knowing. We ask that you rekindle our sense of wonder and that you soothe our anxiety and our pain.

We pray today for those who are in the midst of change: for students going back to school and for their families; for those who are getting older, who can't do what they once could do; for all who need our prayers. May they know that they are not alone. Let us pray for those we love and for those we find it hard to love. We remember those in this community who died over the summer. Gracious God, be with all who grieve. May they feel that they are surrounded by love on every side. Let us pray also for the needs of the world, for those whose lives are forever changed by world conditions. Let us pray for our soldiers, for soldiers and civilians everywhere, for all who live with fear and danger.

And let us remember and give thanks for the blessings we have known: the love of family and friends, time for work and leisure, for the lives we have been given, for this sparkling day. We pray that you would show us how to bring your love into this world, so that one day, justice will roll down like waters, and peace will flow like a mighty stream. Amen.—Frank Clarkson

Benediction: Now may our God, whom we know as Father, Son, and Holy Spirit, fill us with all truth and peace that we may so live that others will experience the touch of grace. May the Holy One of Israel lead our way, for the sake of Jesus Christ and the world. Amen.

SUNDAY, AUGUST 24, 2008

LECTIONARY SERMON TOPIC: "Vigorous Women"
TEXT: Exod. 1:8–2:10
OTHER READINGS: Ps. 124; Rom. 12:1–8; Matt. 16:13–20

This passage begins the story of God's deliverance of Israel from slavery in Egypt. At the end of Exodus 2, the Israelites, "oppressed so hard they could not stand," cry to God, and God hears and looks and knows—intimately knows—

the depths of their pain. This passage is more of a prelude to the great salvation that God will bring through Moses, and it happens through the actions of many vigorous women.

The peril to Israel came from a man—the man Pharaoh, who created new, evil policies for his country. The Israelites were aliens in Egypt, something like Hispanics in our country today. At first their numbers were small, but they worked hard and their numbers increased until the local population grew worried about being displaced. Pharaoh's policies put the migrant workers in low-paying, dangerous jobs; the officers assigned to work with aliens were ruthless in applying penalties. But the Israelites kept growing as a percentage of the population, and this made the Egyptians very nervous.

I. **Two women resist.** So Pharaoh decided genocide was the only real solution, and he tried to enlist the Israelite midwives as collaborators. Often in antiquity, people exposed infant daughters, leaving them out to die or to become slaves or prostitutes. This policy would have killed all the males, leaving Israel (so Pharaoh thought) defenseless, as they would have no army. Exodus 1:15 imagines Pharaoh calling in two Israelite midwives to give them this order. Can you imagine this? It's like the president of the United States calling in two case workers from Tightsqueeze, Virginia, saying, "Let's really crack down on those illegal workers who are cutting tobacco for you." What are these two women going to do except bend to the will of the king?

But they don't bend. They fear God, and they do not murder the infants. And Pharaoh hauls them in to ask why they have disobeyed his order. "It's not our fault, O Great King," they say. "Israelite women just have their babies so much faster than Egyptian women, it's all done before we get there." They are the precursors, the patron saints, of anyone who has ever chosen to follow God rather than Caesar. They set the pattern for God's salvation of the Israelites through Moses, when Pharaoh will think he is calling the shots, when in reality Pharaoh is just a tool in God's hand.

II. **Three women cooperate.** Pharaoh now tries to turn his whole nation into murderers, ordering them to kill the baby boys. We are not told how many Egyptians were happy to cooperate. Instead, we are told about three more women who, acting in concert, make certain that God's deliverer is preserved alive. Moses' mother refuses to kill her own son, but she cannot safely keep him, so she builds a little basket and sets it on the bank of the Nile. Moses' sister also refuses to kill her brother. She cannot save him by herself, but she puts herself into position to do what she can.

Then Pharaoh's own daughter, who along with all the rest of her nation has been ordered to drown every baby boy in the Nile, finds the baby. She knows it is an Israelite child; she knows her father's will on this matter; but for no better reason than simple human compassion, she decides to save the baby. Then the sister steps up: "Shall I get an Israelite nurse?" And Moses' wet nurse is his own mother; Pharaoh's daughter pays her to do what she would have done for love had she been allowed to. And the man who will destroy Pharaoh's control of the Israelites is raised in Pharaoh's own house.

III. **We can do better.** This, too, is a picture of God's salvation. Pharaoh's daughter saves Moses from the Nile, just as Moses will lead Israel through the sea; the water is both a danger and a part of the salvation in both cases. But the Red Sea story is not as nuanced as this one, I think. Notice that in this story of women's salvation, nobody has to die so that the baby will live. Notice that the princess makes certain that the wet nurse gets a living wage. And notice that this story of salvation leads to a reconciliation of sorts between oppressor and oppressed, as all three women cooperate to circumvent a wicked government policy.

Surely, we can do better than we're doing in our treatment of the aliens among us. Surely we can stand with Shiphrah, Puah, Jochebed, and Miriam to say that unfair labor practices, oppressive immigration rules, and inhospitable treatment of aliens is ungodly. We should do as they did, crafting godly strategies that preserve life and that lead to true reconciliation within communities. Pharaoh's strategy (beat them down, fence them out, use them up) can yield to the ways of these vigorous women, who followed God and saved a whole people.—Richard B. Vinson

ILLUSTRATIONS

Mission Ministries. Ann and Adoniram Judson were Baptist missionaries in Burma (Myanmar). When there was war between England and Burma, the Burmese imprisoned Adoniram because they thought he was British. Unlike her husband, Ann had learned the language of their adopted country. Her repeated appeals to the government to spare his life and the lives of other missionaries also imprisoned eventually led to their release. In the meantime, she brought food and clothing daily and wisely hid her husband's papers in the pillow in his cell so that his work would not be destroyed.[5]—Richard B. Vinson

Conscience-Bound. In 1521, responding to the emperor's demand that he recant his teachings deemed heretical by the Church, Martin Luther replied:

Since then your Majesty and your lordships desire a simple reply, I will answer without horns and without teeth. Unless I am convicted by Scripture and by plain reason—I do not accept the authority of popes and councils, for they have contradicted each other—my conscience is captive to the word of God. I cannot and I will not recant anything, for to go against conscience is neither right nor safe. God help me.[6]

—Richard B. Vinson

Musical Selections Appropriate to the Day

Hymn suggestions for lectionary texts:

Exod. 1:8–2:10	*God of Our Life; God of the Ages, History's Maker*
Ps. 124	*I Greet Thee, Who My Sure Redeemer Art*
Rom. 12:1–8	*Come All Christians, Be Committed; Lord, Whose Love Through Humble Service*
Matt. 16:13–20	*The Solid Rock; Built on the Rock*

[5]See Phyllis Rodgerson Pleasants, *Freedom for the Journey* (Macon, GA: Center for Baptist Heritage and Studies, 2002), pp. 28–30.
[6]Cited in Roland Bainton, *Here I Stand: A Life of Martin Luther* (New York: Mentor, 1950), p. 144.

➷ Children's Lectionary Sermon

TITLE: Ordinary and Unexpected
SCRIPTURE: Exod. 1:8–2:10
KEY VERSE: *Then the baby's sister asked the king's daughter, "Would you like me to find a Hebrew woman to nurse the baby for you?"* (Exod. 2:7, International Children's Bible New Century Version)
KEY CONCEPT: God can use children.
MATERIALS: Bible

This season following Pentecost is called Ordinary Time—a time of living and growing in our faith in Jesus. There are no big celebrations, just a time of living out our faith being obedient to God. That is what happens in our story today.

(*Open Bible.*) Moses' mom was worried. She had heard about the Egyptians ordering the midwives to kill all the babies that were born. She knew her baby was in danger. I love the part where Moses' big sister Miriam was waiting for the princess to find Moses, just so she could offer to find someone to take care of the baby. It says this in Exodus 2:7: "Then the baby's sister asked the king's daughter, 'Would you like me to find a Hebrew woman to nurse the baby for you?'" And who did she go find? Why it was none other than her own and Moses' mommy!

This had to be a scary time for Moses' mother and Miriam to live through. But they let their faith in God help them decide what to do. Miriam didn't know what would happen, and she could have decided to hide or run away. Instead, she took a risk by playing a part and helping her brother live.

Moses grew up in Pharaoh's house and became the leader of the Hebrew people. But the day Miriam waited in the bushes, she had no idea who her baby brother would become. She never expected him to become the leader of God's people. She just wanted him to live because she loved him.

We do not know how our actions can change things. Miriam didn't know. She wasn't much older than you. But God can use us in unexpected ways if we try to follow God. God can help us change the ordinary to the unexpected.— Lizette Hunt

❧ WORSHIP AIDS ❧

Call to Worship: We are reminded that the plight of our human predicament is called sin. We are also reminded that God has provided a remedy for our plight. The prophetic word is clear: "All we like sheep have gone astray; we have turned every one to his own way; and the Lord has laid on him the iniquity of us all" (Isa. 53:6).

Invocation: Mighty God, Holy One, we approach you in worship because you have invited us here. Our sin, O Lord, is grievous, but your grace is greater than our sin. May this hour be such that your people will experience anew the power of forgiveness and the far reaches of your grace. Amen.

Offertory Sentence: "Let him who is taught the word share all good things with him who teaches" (Gal. 6:6).

Offertory Prayer: Lord, by our giving we seek to honor you and, in so doing, to honor and support the work of all those who serve in your name: pastors, missionaries, teachers, denominational workers, and all others worthily employed in your Kingdom. We offer thanksgiving for the joy of the ministry partnerships in which we share. Amen.

Morning Prayer: God, time passes quickly and quietly, like a train moving through the night. Days clip by like small droplets of rain, slowly filling the large bucket of our lives. God, I know that some days pass when I don't stop to fully appreciate a human exchange or a natural creation of yours. God, I also know that if these days turn into weeks, something in my core begins to erode, for the value of life on earth is not solely an accumulation of measurable accomplishments, but it is in the fleeting moments of beauty we bear witness to a flock of geese overhead, a year-old child who has conquered the feat of walking, and live mariachi music spilling into the streets from the restaurant down the block.

God, we know that these rich moments can be the fuel for the days, weeks, and years of our lives. These moments form the foundation from which we can then do the meaningful and routine work that needs to be done. By honoring the natural world and other human beings, through relishing the arts, and by being lifted up by family and lifelong friends offering unwavering love and support, we are allowing ourselves to be good humans.

God, help us to resolve this tension between doing and being, action and reflection; for it is in the balance where peace lies. God, help us to be spirited passengers on this lifelong train, watching the landscape pass with intent eyes, enjoying the company of others, and resting for the ride and destinations that lie ahead. Amen.—Stacey Keane

Benediction: We go forth today in the unshaken hand of the Mighty God, Father, Son, and Holy Spirit. We remember that God is God, and there is none other. With confidence, yea, boldness, we enter into the days ahead with assurance and joy. Amen.

SUNDAY, AUGUST 31, 2008

LECTIONARY SERMON TOPIC: "I Am, You Are"
TEXT: Exod. 3:1–15
OTHER READINGS: Ps. 105:1–6, 23–26, 45c; Rom. 12:9–21; Matt. 16:21–28

When you introduce yourself to someone, what do you say? Your name, of course, but then what else—occupation, where you live, something about your family, where you go to church, where you grew up? What you say may depend on context: Are you being interviewed for a job, or are you at a dinner party?

I. **What Moses knew about God.** Moses knew he was an Israelite and almost certainly knew about God before the burning-bush incident. Surely his mother, who served as his wet nurse, had told him about his people's history and about their God. But he did more than just know about God. Moses identified with God's people, because he had killed the Egyptian who was beating the Israelite (Exod. 2:11–12) and tried to mediate a conflict between two Israelites (Exod. 2:13–15). But when he realized his life was in danger, he fled to Midian, where he characterized himself as "a stranger in a strange land" (Exod. 2:22).

Had you met Moses then, how would he have introduced himself? Was he an Israelite living abroad? Was he a shepherd working for his father-in-law, or did he think of that as temporary employment until he found his true vocation? He does seem to have been a "stranger" (alien, foreigner), who indicated that he thought of himself as displaced.

II. **How God met Moses.** Then God met him at the bush on the backside of the mountain. God spoke first: "Moses!" God knew him, it turned out—knew all about him and his family, knew what he was capable of doing, knew how to get him to agree to the mission. But God introduced himself to Moses, recognizing that Moses, who may have known about God, needed to know God more intimately. God's first move was to link himself to Moses' ancestors: "I am your father's God, the God of Abraham, Isaac, and Jacob." Who were these people to Moses? Again, we can guess that his mother may have told him the stories of how God called Abraham out of his native country, how Isaac was born miraculously to fulfill the promise God made, and how God changed Jacob the trickster into Israel, the progenitor of this great people now held as slaves in Egypt. If this God appearing in the bush was that God, and if Moses knew something of how God had guided and preserved these three men along their way, then he'd have known that any promises God made him were trustworthy. What stories do you tell your children? What mighty acts of God in the history of your larger family serve to characterize and to introduce God to the next generations?

God's next self-description is about Moses' people—the Israelites with whom Moses identified, albeit somewhat inconclusively. Moses felt himself an alien estranged from his people, and God introduced himself as deeply knowledgeable and personally involved in their miseries. "I have closely watched . . . I have heard . . . I know . . . I have come down." The injustice of one Egyptian beating one Israelite was enough to drive Moses to murder? God has heard and seen countless acts and intends to protect all of them. God is the God of the suffering and the oppressed. If Moses knew that the Israelites were his people, he also needed to learn that they were God's people.

Moses wanted to know God's name; if he was to claim to be God's agent, then he must be able to name the Sender. Fair enough, says God: my name is "I am"—or something like that; the Hebrew is famously slippery. The four consonants of God's name (usually transliterated into English as YHWH) are a form of the verb "to be," but they can be understood as "he is" or "he causes to be" or "he will be." Verse 14 says, "I am who I am" or "I am what I am" or "I will be what I will be." Appearing in the form of a riddle, of sorts, God's declaration seems absolutely self-referential. God is the fixed point in the universe; everyone and everything else is defined by reference to God.

III. **Who Moses is; who we are.** So the question, Who are you? gets quickly turned back to Moses. God is who God is, and God has already said that God is the one who acted on behalf of Abraham, Isaac, and Jacob and who is now acting on behalf of the enslaved Israelites. Who will Moses be? According to God, Moses will be God's agent—God's servant sent back into the hotspot to deliver Israel. "Who am I that I should go to Pharaoh?" asks Moses. "I am with you," says God. Once you know who God is, then you also know that you are whoever God chooses you to be.

Have we known God as the God of the oppressed and the enslaved, or have we swallowed our national myth, believing falsely that God is the God of superpowers, blessing the rich and the strong with more and more? Do we believe that God is the God of the dispossessed and the aliens, and have we chosen, like Moses, to align ourselves with God's people? God is who God is; it may not be pleasant for us, but I believe we American Christians need to be reintroduced to the God who called Moses to set God's people free.—Richard B. Vinson

---

ILLUSTRATIONS

Consecration. "When I got the poor of London on my heart and caught a vision of what Jesus Christ, the reigning Lord, could do with those people, though I knew there were many with greater training, greater wisdom, greater intelligence, greater power than William Booth, I was determined that the Living Christ would have all of William Booth that there was."[7]—Richard B. Vinson

Stewardship. "Do not be one who reaches out your hands to receive but draws back from giving. If you acquire soothing with your hands, give it as a ransom for your sins. Do not doubt whether to give, nor grumble while giving. For you should recognize the good paymaster of the reward. Do not shun a person in need, but share all things with your brother and do not say that anything is your own. For if you are partners in what is immortal, how much more in what is mortal?"[8]—Richard B. Vinson

Musical Selections Appropriate to the Day

Hymn suggestions for lectionary texts:

Exod. 3:1–15	*Holy Ground; Christians, We Have Met to Worship*
Ps. 105:1–6, 23–26, 45c	*This Is a Time to Remember*
Rom. 12:9–21	*Make Me a Channel of Your Peace; Eternal Life*
Matt. 16:21–28	*Take Up Your Cross*

✦ Children's Lectionary Sermon

TITLE: Jesus' Way

SCRIPTURE: Rom. 12:9–21

KEY VERSE: *If someone does wrong to you, do not pay him back by doing wrong to him. Try to do what everyone thinks is right.* (Rom. 12:17, International Children's Bible New Century Version)

KEY CONCEPT: Doing what is right

MATERIALS: Bible

---

[7]Cited in C. Douglas Weaver, *A Cloud of Witnesses* (Macon, GA: Smyth and Helwys, 1993), p. 111.
[8]Didache 4.5–8; translation from Bart D. Ehrman (ed. and trans.), *The Apostolic Fathers* (Cambridge, MA: Harvard University Press, 2003).

Have you ever been treated badly by someone, and the first thing you wanted to do was to get back at that person? That is called revenge. You want to get back at someone who has done something bad to you.

Jesus teaches us something very different. (*Open Bible.*) This passage from the Bible is from the apostle Paul. He explains to the Roman Church that Jesus wants each one of them to treat everyone they met as Jesus would. Paul writes in Romans 12:17, "If someone does wrong to you, do not pay him back by doing wrong to him. Try to do what everyone thinks is right."

This is true for us, too. Paul is saying that my behavior and your behavior do not depend on anyone else's behavior. We are responsible for our own choices. This is hard to do, isn't it? Let's discuss what this would look like. I am going to ask you some questions, and I want you to answer them. Then we will act out together the choices we think Jesus would like.

If someone on the playground at school pushes you down, what are some things you could do? (*Let the children act it out, then answer each of the situations.*) If your brother or sister kicked you, what could you do? What if someone asked you to give answers for homework? What would you do?

Remember that you make choices and Jesus can help you. Jesus wants us to treat everyone with love and respect.—Lizette Hunt

❧ WORSHIP AIDS ❧

Call to Worship: God is our Father, and we are God's children—sons and daughters of the Eternal One. Our hearts are today called, in unity of faith, to lift high his Holy Name: "Worship the Lord in the beauty of holiness, tremble before him, all the earth" (Ps. 96:9).

Invocation: O God, our loving Father, teach us this day the far reaches of your goodness. While our world is filled with hatred and war, disease and hunger, may we see your goodness at work around us, and may we seek to be a part of that goodness. Lord, do not allow our needs to deny your unfailing grace. Amen.

Offertory Sentence: "Upon the first day of the week, let every one of you lay by him in store, as God has prospered him" (1 Cor. 16:2).

Offertory Prayer: Gracious God, we bring these gifts of tithes and offerings as expressions of our love and devotion. Grant that not only what is taught here today but also that which is given in this offering, will flow forth from a pure heart and sincere faith. Amen.

Morning Prayer: Come, Spirit, come. Come into our hearts and into this house. Help us to sense your mysterious presence. Living God, our prayer is always, "Be here with us; be with those we love. Be with those in need; be with those who suffer." Come, Spirit, come. Assure us that you are present, even when we are unaware of it, that you will never leave us, or this world, and that you are continually breaking into the world in new and surprising ways. Call us to pay attention, to expect a miracle, to be led where you would have us go. We thank you God for this new day and for this community, for the fact that we are here, together, right now. We give thanks for this blue-green planet earth—our home—for our brothers and sisters who inhabit it and for all your creatures. For all the good things we have been given, let us be grateful.

We also recall the ways we have fallen short. When we have taken life and love for granted, when we have loved ourselves more than our neighbors, when we have chosen fear over hope. Give us the grace to let go of the past and the courage to try again. Help us to forgive others and to forgive ourselves. Let us pray for those who are in need or in trouble, for the sick and the dying and those who care for them, for the impoverished and those most vulnerable—for refugees, prisoners, and exiles. Let us pray for peace in the world. God, you know the needs of the world are great. Show us how to be of use, we pray. Save us from despair; be with us on our journey, so that we might do what prophets have always called us to do: feed the hungry, bring sight to the blind, set the captives free. Source of life and love, whether we sense you in the starry sky or in human companions, in words or singing or blessed silence, we ask that you light a fire in our hearts and remain with us this day, and always. Amen.—Frank Clarkson

Benediction: Let us go forth, knowing the mercy and grace of God that goes with us. May our lives this week portray the deep commitments we have made and the affections that sustain us each day—all for the cause of Christ. Amen.

SUNDAY, SEPTEMBER 7, 2008

LECTIONARY SERMON TOPIC: "A Rejoicing"

TEXT: Exod. 12:1–14

OTHER READINGS: Ps. 149:1 or Ps. 148; Rom. 13:8–14; Matt. 18:15–20

Family celebrations bring out the rejoicing in us. Recall the times when you have joined with family on a holiday or anniversary, sat at table around a bountiful feast of good food, and shared in robust conversation mingled with memories, laughter, and perhaps tears. Reunions like that are rejoicing at its best. You share joy—and then do it again. You rejoice.

I. **Today's text goes back to a time when rejoicing seemed out of the question.** God's people had been in Egyptian slavery for four hundred years. They owned no land. They didn't even own themselves. What future they had was filled with images of continued gloom and desperation. They understood pain, misery, and oppression—the kind of ill treatment that comes with cruelty. Perhaps they had come to expect that nothing better would ever come their way.

Most of us have experienced similar circumstances. I recall a dear mother in a former church whose husband died abruptly two weeks prior to Thanksgiving Day. Then on the Sunday before Thanksgiving, her teenage son was killed in an automobile accident. You can imagine the severity of her pain. She cried out, "Pastor, this is the season of the year in which I am accustomed to thanking God for bountiful blessings. But right now the words of gratitude are having a hard time coming out." We have all been there—or someday we will be.

II. **As they cried out to God, God heard their cries.** The God we love and serve hears the deep longings of our souls. The sparrows may well fall from the heavens but not apart from the loving knowledge of God. Our greatest need is met, not so much in having our prayers answered by God, according to our intentions, but simply in knowing that God *hears* our pleas. We rejoice in the connectedness we feel with God. What matters to each human being matters to God.

The theologians speak of God's transcendence and imminence. Nothing can be more profound and confounding than to consider that the Creator

God who set the earth and the stars in motion—who created us in God's own image—is the same God who knows our names, who has numbered the hair of our head, and who hears our prayers. Our testimony in the initial years of the twenty-first century is the same as the preacher in the book of Hebrews: "We have a high priest who has been touched by the feelings of our infirmities, who has been tempted in the ways of our temptation, but has done so without sin" (Heb. 4:15). God hears our cries and knows our hearts.

III. **God provided the answer they most needed.** What they needed most was not a way of escape from their quandary but a revelation of God's own presence. And that is what they got. A bush burned but was not consumed. A voice was heard from beyond that called Moses to the task of deliverer. And in the process of the calling, God revealed himself as he gave his name: "Say to those who doubt your mission that 'I am' has sent you." With this word of divine revelation, Moses initiated perhaps the most significant and successful, albeit painful, exodus migration the world has ever known. To Pharaoh he declared, "Let my people go," and attended by miracle and signs, God prepared the people for their intended freedom.

IV. **On that night the Passover meal was born.** Its institution is recorded in our text. The Israelites were to gather in their homes on the night of the last of ten plagues—the night the death angel would arrive. They were to eat a special meal with a unique menu: roast lamb without spot or blemish, bread unleavened by yeast (there was no time for bread to rise), and bitter herbs that reminded them of the severity of their enslavement. When the slain lamb's blood was available, they were to splash the blood on the doors of their homes. When the hour of death came later that evening, the angel "passed over" their homes. Thus, it was the Passover meal, eaten that first time in anticipation of God's victory for his people. It was to be eaten in the years to come as a celebration of God's presence among his people. And so, year after year, even to this day, Passover is celebrated as the central feast of the Jewish community.

V. **Now turn the pages of the Old to the New Testament.** By that time, Passover had become a pilgrim festival. One hundred thousand Jews from most parts of the world descended on Jerusalem during the Passover celebration. Preparation for the event was elaborate. Early in the day, leaven was removed from the homes and burned in a ritual ceremony. Work ceased at noon. Around 3 o'clock in the afternoon, the slaughtering of the Passover sacrifices began. Temple Levites sounded the three-fold trumpet blast. Others sang the hallelujah psalms. Worshippers brought their lambs to be killed by the priests, and the animals' blood was caught in gold-and-silver trays. As the animals were being dressed, the priests tossed the blood against the great altar and burned it, along with fat portions of the animals. The dressed animals, with legs unbroken and with heads still attached, were then returned to the worshippers, who returned home and cooked the animal in a clay oven. The meal was served on low tables around which worshippers reclined on cushions. All were dressed in festive white garments. After the blessing, the meal was opened with the eating of the lamb with the bitter herbs, dipped in harosheth—a paste of mashed fruits and nuts. The designated "Son" of the family would then ask the ceremonial question, "Why is this night different from all other nights?" What followed was a recital in song and story of the exodus from Egypt. The long history of Israel was then recited, ending with a prayer for the redemption of the land from the occupying power of Rome.

VI. **The scene was surely similar that night in the upper room when Jesus ate the Passover meal with his disciples.** Although emotions of every sort filled the room, there is no mistaking the note of celebration. They celebrated the Passover meal and remembered their own holy history. At its end, Jesus took what we would call "the leftovers" and gave to both bread and wine new and elevated meanings. In the liturgy, Jesus took the bread and cup, gave thanks, and then gave it to the disciples and said, "Take, eat and drink. This bread, this cup, is given for you."

Each time we come to the Lord's table, we are reminded of God's grace so overwhelmingly poured out for us. This meal is a time of rejoicing. We sit at table together as the family of God, the Body of Christ. May each heart declare love and loyalty to our Lord, who has brought us here and has made us to sit forever in the heavenly places. Thanks be unto God.—Lee McGlone

ILLUSTRATIONS

Communion. "God lives not, I think, in bread and wine, but in the breaking of bread and the sharing of wine. Unbroken bread doesn't fortify the heart, but bread divided among us all who hunger will sustain the spirit."[1]

[1]Abbie Graham, *Ceremonials of Common Days* (Pleasantville, NY: Akadine Press, 2003), p. 61.

Vision of Love. There is a small book (not biblical) out of the second century named *The Acts of Peter.* It tells of Peter's life and gives otherwise unknown details. In the summer of 64 A.D., Peter was sneaking out of Rome for fear of Nero's persecution of the Christians there. Peter had been encouraged by a certain Marcellus to find a safe place and wait out the persecution, "for the good of the cause." Peter protested: "Shall we act like deserters, brothers?" "No," said Marcellus, "it's so you can go on serving the Lord." So Peter put on a disguise and tried to ease out of the city. At the city gate, a vision appeared to him. He saw the Risen Jesus going into Rome. Peter asked him, *"Quo vadis, Domine?"* That is, "Where are you going, Lord?" Jesus answered, "I must go to Rome to be crucified again!" Peter understood that his own desertion had caused it, so he returned to the city himself, where he was quickly captured and condemned to die. The vision of grace brought him back. To his friends around him, he boldly declared, "It is now time to surrender my body to those who are taking it." To his executioners, he said, "Take it, then, you whose duty this is. I request you, therefore, to crucify me head-downwards in this way and no other, for I am not worthy to be crucified in the same manner as was my Lord." A vision of love calls us to extraordinary measures of service and worship. God's grace changes everything.—Lee McGlone

Musical Selections Appropriate to the Day

Hymn suggestions for lectionary texts:

Exod. 12:1–14	*Grace Greater Than Our Sin; My Faith Looks Up to Thee*
Ps. 149:1	*Sing a New Song to the Lord* [or]
Ps. 148	*Praise the Lord! O Heavens, Adore Him; Let the Whole Creation Cry*
Rom. 13:8–14	*Sing Praise to the Father; O Word of God Incarnate*
Matt. 18:15–20	*God Is Here; Built on the Rock*

✺ Children's Lectionary Sermon

TITLE: Praise the Lord!

SCRIPTURE: Ps. 148

KEY VERSE: *Praise the Lord. He alone is great. He is greater than heaven and earth.* (Ps. 148:13, International Children's Bible, New Century Version)

KEY CONCEPT: Praising God

MATERIALS: Bible

(*Open Bible and read passage.*) What a great passage! Today I want you all to try something with me. I want you to repeat after me, "Praise the Lord!" (*Have the children repeat the phrase.*) Good job everybody. Now, I want you to say, "Praise the Lord," after I say a different phrase. OK, let's practice. I will say "God is good," and you say, "Praise the Lord!" (*Practice again with the children.*) Here we go:

> *God is good!*
>   (refrain) Praise the Lord!
> *He made the whole wide world.*
>   (refrain) Praise the Lord!
> *He made you and me.*
>   (refrain) Praise the Lord!

That was fantastic! Don't you feel good when you say, "Praise the Lord"? The person who wrote this psalm is telling you and me that God deserves all the praise we can give.

One way we live and grow in our faith is by being together with our church family and saying, "Praise the Lord!" Worship is a time when we sing together, pray together, and hear the Bible read out loud to us together, in a big group. Our time together worshipping God is important for our faith. The people who wrote the Psalms wrote a lot of poems and songs about God. The Church has always known that coming together as a church family to sing songs and worship God is a good thing. This is how we encourage each other. This is how we learn about God together. This is how we grow closer to the Lord and closer to each other. We learn together the songs of praise.

So when I say, "Sing praises to the Lord our God," what should you say? How about, "Praise the Lord!" (*Encourage the children to repeat. You might even repeat the last phrase again so the children will respond.*)—Lizette Hunt

❧ WORSHIP AIDS ❧

Call to Worship: We enter worship with hearts open to receive the fullness of God's grace. Here is our hope and our strength: "The one who dwells in the secret places of the most High shall abide under the shadow of the Almighty. I will say of the Lord, he is my refuge and my fortress: my God, in him will I trust" (Ps. 91:1–2).

Invocation: Lord, we who have labored much and worked steadily have returned to partake of the rest promised to the faithful and rejoice in the promises of God in the life of believers, through Christ our Lord. Amen.—E. Lee Phillips

Offertory Sentence: "Will a man rob God? Yet you have robbed me. But you say, How have we robbed you? In tithes and offerings" (Mal. 3:8).

Offertory Prayer: We thank you, loving Father, for the abundance of your gifts to us, for the pain and suffering you bore for us, and for the joy at work within us. Receive these offerings we bring as expressions of our devotion. And lead us in the way of faith that we may learn more clearly of you and follow you more closely. Amen.

Morning Prayer: God of might and mercy, we come into this sacred place this morning and on this weekend, focused on labor to worship you in spirit and in truth, even as we seek your guidance. We thank you for work to do and the energies to perform the tasks demanded of our work. We thank you for the gift of skills that enable us to work efficiently. We are thankful this morning for the earning power that comes through our work so that we can meet the needs of those for whom we are responsible and be a part of the larger work of Christ through our gifts to his Church. Pray, Father, grant us contentment in our labors. Deliver us from always looking for what is wrong in our work setting and lead us to focus on what is right about what we do. Keep us from complaints that magnify the trifles until they become major obstacles to doing our best. Call us from petty criticism of the system wherein we must function on our jobs and enable us to be examples of harmonious effort.

Bless us with a continuing sense of humor in our relationships with fellow workers, even as you deliver us from the sin of feeling overly important. Keep us humble enough to learn new ways of doing things better, wise enough to be open to the suggestions of others, and willing enough to change when change is called for. In all situations that we confront, guide us to be strong examples of Christian commitment without being so pious that we lose the winsomeness that Christ imparts. So through us make our workplace a better place for everyone around us, that in our labors your will might truly be done. Amen.—Henry Fields

Benediction: People of God, as we leave the sanctuary and move into the events of the week before us, go in the grace and peace of our Lord Jesus Christ. May we live this week in the power of God's love and share God's love to the ends of the earth. Amen.

SUNDAY, SEPTEMBER 14, 2008

LECTIONARY SERMON TOPIC: "Seeing the Lord's Deliverance"
TEXT: Exod. 14:19–31
OTHER READINGS: Exod. 15:1b–11, 20–21; Rom. 14:1–12; Matt. 18:21–35

This is a fascinating story. God's people were in slavery in Egypt for four hundred years and lived under the hand of cruel taskmasters. Then God called a deliverer named Moses. Recall the story of the baby's rescue by his sister Miriam from the bulrushes of the Nile. Remember a bush burning but not being consumed. There were ten plagues, the passing of the death angel through the Egyptian families, the hurried escape in the night—and then, freedom! But soon they heard the thunder of many hooves. The armies of Pharaoh approached, and the people cried out in despair, "Moses why did you bring us here—between Migdol and the sea? To die in this desolate place? Coming fast are the armies of Pharaoh and before us lie the waters of the Red Sea. What are we to do?" And Moses responded with this fascinating word: "Don't fear, but stand firm and see the deliverance of the Lord." And as he held his rod, the rod of God, over the waters, the waters parted and the people walked through the sea on dry land. "Stand firm and see the Lord's deliverance!" It's a fascinating declaration—one needed in our day.

Soon the image changes. Once across the river, the armies of Pharaoh continue to follow. "What do we do . . . what do we do?" Moses stretches out his hand again over the sea, and at dawn the waters give way and cover the surprised armies. Then a gruesome word appears: "The Lord saved Israel but they saw the Egyptians dead on the seashore." Sounds like an after-battle report. You can almost see the news camera making a slow, sweeping wide-angle shot of the beach covered in water and death.

I. **What's this about? It's about deliverance.** It's about the deliverance that comes when we face struggles for which there appears to be no way out. Let's not miss the place: Israel is camped between Migdol and the sea. The people of God are trapped. The sea is on one side, and Migdol is on the other, and the army of Egypt is closing in. They have no place to go. As we might say, "They are between a rock and a hard place." It was either death by the Egyptians or drowning in the Red Sea. Not good options. Have you ever been between Migdol and the sea? Maybe you are there today.

This is about the Lord's deliverance. The God of Scripture, the Father of our Lord Jesus Christ, is our deliverer. We are not left alone to fend for ourselves; God is forever working alongside us to encourage and strengthen our resolves.

II. **We see the Lord's deliverance as we face our enemies.** The Christian, and the Christian Church, will do well not to deny the reality of our enemies. We know, because we are fully human, that very real and hurtful circumstances arise with which we must deal. The enemies may be intensely personal and deeply spiritual. They may be matters of family life that seem to have no clear answer. At some point, and in every person, we will deal with the last enemy: death. But whatever the circumstance may be, in order to move beyond the anxiety and uncertainty, we must face it.

In facing the enemies, we take the first step toward resolution. The faithful "rising up" in the face of calamity unleashes within us resources for strength often unknown. The circumstance for Moses and Israel was not good; the prospects were intimidating, yet Moses refused to be overwhelmed by the odds. Had he shied away from the moment, we can suspect that the grand history of Israel may never have happened. The masses would probably have followed his fearful lead, and the power of God would have been ignored. We must face our enemies.

III. **And then as we overcome them.** Often good Christians who suffer the loss of loved ones to death or to a difficult and disquieted life raise the question, "How can I overcome this?" My response is often, "The goal here is not so much to overcome as it as to learn to cope with the changes that have come to you." But even the having ability to cope is a way of overcoming.

In some matters, however, overcoming is not only the goal but the very real possibility. Let's not lose the idealism that drives our faith: we believe in a God who takes the dark days of our Good Fridays and turns them into Easter mornings. The Exodus event, with its declaration of liberation, becomes the focus for Old Testament faith, even as in the New Testament the Resurrection of Jesus is the centerpiece of its proclamation.

Israel did overcome the enemy. They passed through the sea on dry land and looked back and saw the dead bodies of Egyptian soldiers washed up on the seashore.

IV. **And we move on to face other enemies.** Creation was full and complete just as God intended, but very soon the chaotic waters of a great worldwide flood would enter and almost spoil what God had made. The Egyptians were defeated, but there were still ahead the Moabites, Hittites, Jebusites, and the Midianites. Other battles were yet to be fought—and won.

The Lord Jesus Christ is our model. Nailed to the cross, there was no way out. The enemy was all around him, and it seemed that nothing but death loomed ahead of him. Until the third day. Then God parted the waters once more, and Jesus—alive—got up and walked out. It was God's way of saying that "nothing in the entire world, not even death, can separate us from the love of God seen in Christ Jesus, our Lord." There is a way out, even in death.

Whenever we find ourselves in a tight spot, between our own Migdol and the sea, our help doesn't come from clever insights, sophisticated imaginations, and the power of positive thinking. Our help, just as the psalmist said, "comes from the Lord who made heaven and earth."—Lee McGlone

---

ILLUSTRATIONS

Starting Over. Walter Brueggemann, the insightful scholar at Columbia Seminary, suggests in the Exodus commentary from *The New Interpreter's Bible* that the crossing of the Red Sea replicates the Creation story. Remember how in the Creation story that God separated the waters from the dry land so the land could be usable for people. Through the Exodus liberation, God did something as powerful, original, and life-giving as the newness of Creation. It was like starting over again.—Lee McGlone

Newness of Life. When we think of Israel's exodus, we can't help but think about the American slaves. They were caught in a servitude that they could not change (between their Migdol and the sea), but in their creative imagination they knew that the Ohio River stood between them and freedom. And so they sang from the fields, "Deep river, deep river, my home is just over Jordan." No wonder they called Abraham Lincoln their Moses. And, too, we ought not forget that the act of baptism is a ritual that re-enacts the exodus. It is a passing through the waters. To enter the waters of baptism is a fitting and intended symbol of God rescuing us from the waters of chaos. Just as the children of Israel came up on the far shore prepared for a new life, we are raised in newness of life.—Lee McGlone

---

Musical Selections Appropriate to the Day

Hymn suggestions for lectionary texts:

Exod. 14:19–31	*Guide Me O Thou Great Jehovah*
Exod. 15:1b–11, 20–21	*He Is Exalted; What a Mighty God*
Rom. 14:1–12	*Not for Tongues of Heaven's Angels*
Matt. 18:21–35	*Help Us Accept Each Other*

✺ Children's Lectionary Sermon

TITLE: Have Mercy on Me
SCRIPTURE: Matt. 18:21–35
KEY VERSE: *I had mercy on you. You should have had the same mercy on that other servant.* (Matt. 18:33, International Children's Bible, New Century Version)
KEY CONCEPT: Forgiveness
MATERIALS: Bible, crown, raggedy-looking shirts for servants (optional)

(Open Bible and have it turned to Matthew 18. When the children come to the front, pick three people to help act out the story. One is to be king, the other two servants. Tell the children to say the words you tell them.) One day Jesus told Peter this story about a king and two servants. One day the king wanted to get all the money his servants owed him. There was one servant, *(say the name)*, who owed the king *(say the name)* thousands of dollars. The king said, "I want all my money back." *(Let the child speak this.)* The servant got on his knees and begged the king to give him more time, saying, "I don't have that much money. Please give me more time." Because the king felt forgiving, he said to the servant, "You don't have to pay all the money back."

The first servant went on his way relieved. As servant *(say the name)* was on his (or her) way home, he saw servant *(say the name)*. The first servant went up to the second servant and grabbed his collar. "You owe me money. I want it back now." The second slave begged on his knees but got nowhere. *(Say the name)* was taken to prison.

The king heard the story of what happened. He was very disappointed. He said, "I had mercy on you. You should have had the same mercy on that other servant." The servant wasn't forgiving.

Jesus knew that people would always make mistakes and they would always need forgiveness from each other. Jesus knew we need mercy. One way we show mercy to each other is by forgiving. Jesus is telling us because we have been forgiven we can forgive. Jesus is telling us we have his forgiving power inside of us.

Sometimes we are just like the servant who could not forgive his friend, even after he had been forgiven himself. Jesus is telling us, we must keep practicing using his power of forgiveness so when our friends ask for forgiveness from us, we are able to forgive them.—Lizette Hunt

WORSHIP AIDS

Call to Worship: God's Word says, "Since we have a great high priest who has passed through the heavens, Jesus, the Son of God, let us hold fast our confession" (Heb. 4:14). This we do—and so we live. "Then let us with confidence draw near to the throne of grace, that we may receive mercy and find grace to help in time of need" (Heb. 4:16).

Invocation: Creator God, we come to you boldly but not arrogantly. We come thankful that you have invited us to this holy place and that here mercy is available and our needs are met in you. Give us a fresh vision of the Savior, the great high priest, who knows us, loves us, sympathizes with us, and empowers us at the very place of our need. Amen.

Offertory Sentence: "Every good and perfect gift is from above, and comes down from the Father of lights, with whom there is no variableness, neither shadow nor turning" (James 1:17).

Offertory Prayer: Gracious Father, week by week we are reminded of your caring and tender ways. Like a good shepherd, you lead us. You provide all our needs—and beyond! These gifts of tithes and offerings we bring as cheerful reflections of the trust we have in you. Use them for the building of the Kingdom here and around the world. Amen.

Morning Prayer: Our Father, we gather this day to worship you, to rededicate ourselves to Jesus Christ, and to rediscover ourselves in relation to you. Because we live in a world filled with many sights and sounds, often consumed with struggles and confusion and busyness, we need an hour dedicated to spiritual concentration. For this moment, enable us to relax in your presence. Allow the worried to drop their burdens and to kneel before the cross. Grant that we may set aside side momentarily the decisions about life that will be required of us this week and give clarity to our thinking that we may choose rightly. Help good and godly parents to experience a resurgence of hope and love. Let the confused find clarity; the sad, comfort; the weak, strength; the unsuccessful, courage; the successful, humility; give faith for those who doubt.

Father, you have more than abundantly provided for our every need. Grant that we may recognize the needs around us, the inequities in the world. And then bend our energies and our fortunes to setting them right. Bless your church with perseverance and power and love and loyalty to Jesus Christ. Keep us pure in heart—pure in our intentions, open to the leadership of the Holy Spirit, and compassionate in dealings with others. When our souls are tired and tested, give us the will to remain faithful to our Savior.

May our stewardship constrain us to put more into your church than we take out. Encourage us that we may grasp the opportunities around us to be a part of Christian service. Help us to be thankful for our place in your eternal plan for all things. Now may the living presence of Jesus be with us, keep us, and sustain us to the end that your Kingdom may come, your will be done, on earth as it is in Heaven. Through Jesus we pray. Amen.—Lee McGlone

Benediction: In God's strength we go forth to live and serve. May our homes, businesses, schools, and communities become the places where faith becomes real. Lead us, O God, whom we know as Father, Son, and Holy Spirit, to be your witnesses. Amen.

SUNDAY, SEPTEMBER 21, 2008

LECTIONARY SERMON TOPIC: "Christian Triumph"
TEXT: Phil. 1:21–30
OTHER READINGS: Exod. 16:2–15; Ps. 105:1–6, 37–45 or Ps. 78; Matt. 20:1–16

A recent letter to the editor of the local newspaper raised a question concerning the well-known social issues of our day: the demise of family life, lack of trust in government, depression, hopelessness, and so on. The writer asked, "What kind of a world do we live in?" I wanted to answer the inquiry. We live in a world like we've always lived in. It's not perfect and won't be until the day God renews his creation. And between now and then, we are called to live as faith allows and not as fear demands. We are people of triumph.

This positive approach to living in triumph is modeled for us in the life experience of Paul. When Paul wrote the Philippian letter, he was in jail. He wasn't in control of his own destiny. He knew not whether he would live or die, or whether he would ever visit the beloved Philippians again, or see them only in eternity. But he wasn't overwhelmed by his condition. Instead, he declared, "Whatever happens (what a sense of determined mind), conduct yourselves in a manner worthy of the gospel of Christ." What did he mean? Already, in earlier verses, he had made it clear that he wanted never to be ashamed of the gospel, nor that he ever wanted the Father to be ashamed of him. Now he asks us to live "worthily." In the next two verses, he would rejoice that they were *standing firm* (v. 27), *not intimidated* (v. 28), and *convinced of God's sure hand of grace* (v. 28). In short, the pastor wanted for his people to face life as victors and not as victims.

I. **Triumph is the tone that settles around this text.** It's not about pie-in-the-sky-by-and-by—a Pollyanna approach to life that says all is always well. Triumph is, instead, about the real experience of faith in the here and now—a state of mind and of spirit that declares, as Jesus said, "We know who we are and where we are going."

Did you ever have schoolbooks that had the answers in the back? What I liked best about them was that they took some of the tension away and allowed us to work a problem with greater confidence. At least you knew from the beginning that there was an answer. That's the confidence we Christians live with: we know there is an answer. We may not yet know what the answer is, and so we ask the questions: "Why, gracious Father, why?" In fact, we Christians are the only ones who have the right to ask the "why" question. The atheist has no right to ask why. To whom would he address the question? But we Christians have the right because we know there is an answer. And someday we'll know what it is.

Are we living triumphantly? Yes or no? How would we know? On the athletic field, triumph is determined by the number of points on the scoreboard. Financial triumph is measured by the size of a bank account. Politicians are measured by the number of votes and how many times they can be elected to office. But what about life? How is it measured?

II. **Triumph isn't determined by the world around us.** The world's grading instruments too quickly write us off. I'm not sure that Paul would be considered a success. Sure, he wrote most of the New Testament, but the world of that day wasn't as convinced as we are today. I came across this not long ago in a preacher's résumé, where he tells of his background, activity in the ministry, and some of his accomplishments, in hopes of being called to a new position. This one read, "I'm a preacher of the gospel, but those who hear me say I'm not much with words. I'm also not much to look at. I'm bald, stooped over, and almost blind. I was called to preach later in life and was not able to attend a theological seminary. I've had some experience with local churches, but have never stayed at one more than a year and a half. I travel around a lot and haven't baptized anyone, except one man and his family. I'm prone to giving long sermons, so much so that one young man fell asleep in a third story window and fell to the ground. We thanked God that he didn't die. During the course of my ministry, I've instigated any number of riots and have been thrown out of town more times than I can count. I hope you're not offended that I have been in jail several times. It's given me the chance to write a lot. And, by the way, I take a little wine for the stomach's sake." Signed—the apostle Paul. And Jesus, you know, didn't make much of an impression of many people either. So where are we to discover the life of triumph?

III. **Triumph is found in the larger picture.** When Moses came to the Red Sea, he could have dwelt on the little picture: the water that stood before them. But with an eye to the larger picture of the Promised Land, victory was theirs. David, in a moment of fear, cried out: "One of these days, I'll be destroyed by the hand of Saul" (1 Sam. 27:1). Only when he looked beyond the immediate moment could he become the greatest king in Israelite history. The Emmaus disciples, on the very day of Jesus' Resurrection, almost missed it all. They walked with him, talked with him, and didn't know who he was. Only later as they sat at table as he broke the bread did they experience the power of his presence: "Remember how our hearts burned within us."

The experience of the "larger picture" is encouraged by what we are doing right now. Our weekly corporate worship, daily private worship, study of the Bible, prayer, friendship, witness—all these are helping us see the larger picture. I think some of the saddest people in the world may well be those who have no background of belief, no reservoir of faith.

IV. **Triumph relates not to how things seem but to how things are.** We will not be frightened or intimidated by anything, for we are sure the hand of God is with us all along the way. The people said to Moses, "These waters will come crashing down on us." Moses said, "Stand back, and see the triumph of the Lord." The psalmist cried in despair when taken into captivity: "Oh, can we sing the songs of Zion in a strange and foreign land?" Then later, the full truth emerged: "God is our refuge and our strength, an ever present help in trouble. Therefore, we will not fear, though the earth give way and the mountains fall into the heart of the sea" (Ps. 46:1–3).

Our triumph is in Christ. That doesn't mean that following Jesus is easy or that along the way we will understand all the dilemmas. It does mean, though, that we never face life alone. The enemies of our Lord thought they were rid of him when they saw him die on the cross. The believers weren't sure what it all meant until Jesus declared this ennobling word of faith: "Behold, I am with you always—even till the end of the world." The living presence of Jesus means everything. He is our triumph.

Nikolai Ivanovich Bukharin was a Russian communist propagandist and leader of the Bolshevik Revolution in 1917. In the spring of 1920 he was summoned to Kiev to speak at a large pro-state, anti-God rally that was attended by thousands. For an hour Bukharin used the most violent rhetoric to ridicule religion. When he stepped down, the audience was asked if there were any questions. An old priest with the Russian Orthodox Church rose and asked to speak. Standing beside Bukharin and facing the crowd, he spoke quietly the liturgical Easter greeting, "Christ is risen." Instantly, the assembly rose and in unison thundered out, "He is risen indeed." When the world falls in around us, when hearts ache until they almost break, the fact remains, Jesus is alive, and we stand with him. He is our triumph.—Lee McGlone

ILLUSTRATIONS

Success. Often the opinions of others serve as the gauge by which we determine our sense of worth and success. Charlie Brown, the lovable and lamentable character in Charles Schultz's comic strip, "Peanuts," on one occasion bemoans the nature of his existence: "When I first set foot on the stage of human history, they took one look at me and said, 'Not right for the part.'" I suspect that most of us have felt that common anxiety. But God says, "You are right for the part. You are perfect for the person I created you to be."—Lee McGlone

Church. Albert Camus surmised that whenever a contest is held between the world and the Church, he would bet on the world every time. That surmise may be true of an alarming number of people. But that wager has merit only in the short term. The Church doesn't do well when compared to the gods of this world. But when the stakes are spread out over eternity, the Church wins every time.—Lee McGlone

Musical Selections Appropriate to the Day

Hymn suggestions for lectionary texts:

Exod. 16:2–15	*Glorious Things of Thee Are Spoken; O God Your Constant Care and Love*
Ps. 105:1–6, 37–45	*This Is a Time to Remember* [or]
Ps. 78	*Give to Our God Immortal Praise*
Phil. 1:21–30	*Lord for the Years; Steal Away*
Matt. 20:1–16	*For the Fruits of All Creation*

❧ Children's Lectionary Sermon

TITLE: Bread of Heaven

SCRIPTURE: Exod. 16:2–15

KEY VERSE: *The Israelites were puzzled when they saw it. "What is it?" they asked. And Moses told them, "It is food the Lord has given you."* (Exod. 16:15, New Living Translation)

KEY CONCEPT: God provides for our needs.
MATERIALS: Bible, various types of bread

A slice of bread may not be your favorite food, but properly baked it can taste very good. In many countries folks rely on bread as the main thing they eat. Bread comes in various shapes and flavors, too. (*Show the children the different types of bread.*) They may have consumed some meat and vegetables, but bread is the nourishing staple of their daily diets.

When God delivered Israel from slavery in Egypt, they had to travel through the desert. To provide meals for his people in the desert God created "manna." (*Open Bible.*) Listen to this verse: "The Israelites were puzzled when they saw it. 'What is it?' they asked. And Moses told them, 'It is food the Lord has given you.'" Manna was a type of bread that appeared like the morning dew. Dew is the wetness on the ground.

Each morning the people would leave their tents and gather manna for that day and every day for a long time. God gave manna to show God cared for his people. They even had complained to Moses about not having anything to eat. Yet God took care of them because he loved them.

The Lord takes care of us, too. At each meal we should say a prayer to thank God for the food we enjoy. The Lord helps us another way, too. God can give us what we need to get through the day. It might be to make right choices. It might be to tell someone about Jesus. God gives us strength inside to help with what we do each day. We need to ask God for help instead of complaining the way his people did. We need to thank God for our food and for the help he gives us to live each day the way he wants us to live.

The next time you eat a delicious roll or biscuit, remember the lesson of the manna. God provides for us every day.—Ken Cox

ᐳ WORSHIP AIDS ᐳ

Call to Worship: Worship is the most natural act of the human heart. Our thoughts, lovingly and sincerely, are raised to God. With the psalmist we declare, "Oh that men would praise the Lord for his goodness, and for his wonderful works to the children of men! For he satisfies the longing soul, and fills the hungry soul with goodness" (Ps. 107:8–9).

Invocation: Kind, divine, Heavenly Father, give us today a fresh experience of your grace. May we see, deeply in our souls, your love that knows no end. Then, Father, help us to express to you appropriate praise in psalms and hymns and spiritual songs, in the reading and preaching of your Word, and in the commitments of ourselves we make to you. Amen.

Offertory Sentence: "Offer the right sacrifices to the Lord, and put your trust in him" (Ps. 4:5).

Offertory Prayer: Dearest Lord, teach us to serve you as you deserve. May we give cheerfully and without murmur. May our actions and attitudes reflect your grace alive with us. May we serve and give sacrificially and not expect reward, except in knowing that we are doing your will. Amen.

Morning Prayer: Our Father, we come before you again this day, grateful for your openness that welcomes us here. We need you, loving God, more than we need any other thing—more than the next breath of air, more than the next meal, more than rest, more than labor. Grant that as we come to you now, seeking you, that we shall find you.

Receive our words of praise. May they be authentic expressions of our hearts. As the words from hymn and anthem, Scripture and prayer, and private meditation rise to you, hear them as the devout expressions of our faith. Grant that we may not only speak but that we will pause to hear. Speak to our hearts, Lord Jesus; calm every doubt and fear.

Grant to each of your children the grace gifts you have planned for us today. You who own the cattle of a thousand hills and the hills on which they stand, shower us with your care. Let your forgiveness wash over us and cleanse us of every sin. Where we are blinded by the care of this world, open our eyes that we may see. Where there is a troubled soul, give your gentle, encouraging touch. If by chance there are some at the point of exhaustion, on the verge of despair, Lord place your strong hand upon their souls and help them through another day—and tomorrow—through another—and then through another, forever.

We love you, Lord, and we seek to do your will. Our love is neither perfect nor complete. We pray as did our Lord's disciples long ago: "Lord, increase our faith." May your hand of loving mercy guide us to seek you and your way for us. May your name be honored and your people be strengthened. In Jesus' name. Amen.—Lee McGlone

Benediction: We are called, by the power and grace of God, to go out with joy and with a decided intention to do God's will. May we allow his favor to rest upon us and to be faithful in every opportunity for service that rises before us. Amen.

SUNDAY, SEPTEMBER 28, 2008

LECTIONARY SERMON TOPIC: "Clear Thinking About Christianity"
TEXT: Phil. 2:1–13
OTHER READINGS: Exod. 17:1–7; Ps. 78:1–4, 12–16; Matt. 21:23–32

I think there is no place in Scripture that so clearly defines our faith as this text. Paul had already thanked God for the Philippian Christians; he had prayed for them, that their love would abound in knowledge and discernment; he had called on them to live worthy of the gospel, standing firm, without fear, knowing of God's presence with them. That's a good definition of Christianity, but it doesn't stop there. We shouldn't stop there either. Is it an intellectual inquiry, a moral code, a particular style of worship? You can have all of those and have a pretty good religion. But that's not all that God intended for us and not all we need when we face the dilemmas of life. "Have this mind among yourselves, which is yours in Christ Jesus." That's the Scripture's instruction of hope and help. It gives us a clear word about Christianity.

I. **We begin with this simple word.** We are by definition Christ-minded people. "Have this mind, or mind-set, perhaps attitude, or motivation in you— the one that you see in Jesus." Defining, summarizing, describing the mind of Jesus is an awesome task—truly an impossible one. Martin Luther said we walk on thin ice when we dare to express the meaning of Jesus, for as he said, "we are like little children, learning how to speak, speaking with only half words, or quarter words." That is, our most eloquent speech about Jesus is but mere baby talk. Ralph Waldo Emerson finished his volume *Representative Men* and was asked why he didn't include Jesus in his study. He replied, "It would take too much strength of constitution." In other words, he felt inadequate to the task. We sense that same inadequacy. All we know of Christ, have experienced of his presence, is only a scratching of the surface of the depth that is God's Eternal Son. It's enough to say that, by definition, we are Christ-minded people. That's who we are. That's clear mindedness.

II. **Something else enters here.** To help our definition be more focused, Paul suggests that we remember the event that made us who we are. He then breaks into song that tells a story: "Christ Jesus who was in the form of God did not count equality with God a thing to be grasped, but emptied himself taking the form of a servant; being born in the likeness of men. And being found in human form he humbled himself and became obedient unto death, even death on a Cross" (vv. 6–8).

The essential word here is *form*. Three times it is used. The word means "essence," the very nature of a thing, not just how it looks on the outside. Here Jesus is called the essence of God—God's very nature. But unlike the two created in God's image in the garden, he refused to take advantage of that position for his own self-interest. Instead, he took on our form, our essence. Jesus became one of us—fully human. What that meant for Jesus, Paul then declared, "And being found in human form he humbled himself and became obedient unto death, even death on a Cross" (v. 8).

He became obedient. What does that mean? It means that the defining event that makes us who we are is the obedient nature of Christ. That is important for us, for there are other ways to go at life. The ancient Greeks would say, "Know yourself." The Romans would say, "Discipline yourself." But Christ would say, "Give yourself." Materialism says, "Take care of yourself." Christ says, "Give yourself." Egocentricity says, "Live for yourself alone, make up the rules as you go along." Christ says, "To live for yourself only is far too small a life; give yourself to others." Education says, "Train yourself and prepare yourself well." That's good, but Christ would say, "When you are trained and prepared, give yourself to something worthwhile."

How very sad to come to the end of our days and an obituary is written that says, "He (she) took care of himself (herself)." There is a better way. Remember Jesus, the dying life-giver, who saves us and never gives up changing us. He gave us life. He brought us together as a church. Let's not forget.

III. **Now beyond remembering what Christ has done, there's another thing at work here.** We are called to follow his example. Have in you the mind of Christ. It's not that we could possibly imitate the life of Christ. His life was unique. He was God's Messiah. His finished work of redemption doesn't need to be duplicated. So what does it mean to have the mind of Christ? It means to live out the same love and servanthood that Jesus lived and to do so in daily living.

That's why Paul wrote this letter—because the Philippian Christians weren't living this way. He confronted them and forced them to face up to their sin. Factions in the church, centering around two prominent women, needed to cease. Some thought of themselves as "super Christians." Their sense of spiritual superiority needed to end. To answer their dilemmas, Paul said, "Have in you the mind of Christ—and live like it!" Treat others as Christ has treated you.

Christ is the model. We are to follow him. I've marveled over the years at Mother Teresa, who with such love and tenderness worked among the poorest of the poor in Calcutta. She spoke of herself as "God's pencil, writing love letters to the world." Senator Mark Hatfield, from Oregon, some years ago wrote of an encounter with her. He asked her, "Don't you ever tire, grow discouraged, when you look around and see this abject poverty and be able to change so little of it?" "Oh, no," she said, "for you see, the Lord hasn't called me to be successful, only faithful." Her model for life was Christ.

IV. **I would add this final word.** Remembering the event of Christ, his outpouring of love and life for us is an inspiring thing. Committing ourselves to following his model is equally inspiring. But it occurs to me that there are times when we need far more than a model to remember and to follow. When you are in the water deep over your head, arms weary, going down for the third time, what you don't need is an Olympic swimmer to come by and model for you how to swim the backstroke. No, what you need is a life preserver. What you need is a Savior. There are times we need saving. Jesus said, "I have come to seek and to save the lost."—Lee McGlone

ILLUSTRATIONS

Faith. I recall reading with great appreciation an interview with Dayna Curry and Heather Mercer—the two Baylor University students who were held captive for three months by the Afghanistan Taliban. At one point in the interview they were asked, "As you prepared to go to that difficult land, did you think about what might go wrong?" One of the young women answered, "You deal with it, yes. You say, 'well it's worth taking a risk for those who are hungry and in need.'" That's a clear and simple explanation about how faith was lived out for these two. In a world overwhelmed by complicated speech and confused thinking, it is refreshing to see young people translating their faith into a vital Christian witness. Such clear thinking about our faith is perhaps more significant than ever before.—Lee McGlone

Christ and Family Life. Think how having the mind of Christ can be lived out each day. Ephesians 5:21 is a strong statement, a thesis statement that defines and summarizes Christ-mindedness in three avenues of our daily walk. The thesis statement is this: "Be subject one to another out of reverence for Christ." This theme of mutual submission, or mutual respect and love, is defined first in the marriage relationship: "Wives be subject to your husbands." That's the one most men know. But it follows, "Men, love your wives and give yourself for them as Christ gave himself for the church." That's mutual submission. He then moved to the relation of parents and children. "Children, obey your parents, for this is good." But parents, he said, "do not provoke your children to exasperation but bring them up in the nurture of the Lord." That's mutual submission. It extends even to the workplace: "Slaves, obey your master." But likewise, "Masters, treat your slaves in the same way." That's mutual submission. Having the mind of Christ will force some changes.—Lee McGlone

Musical Selections Appropriate to the Day

Hymn suggestions for lectionary texts:

Exod. 17:1–7	*Rock of Ages*
Ps. 78:1–4, 12–16	*Great Is the Lord*
Phil. 2:1–13	*All Hail the Power of Jesus' Name; He Is Lord*
Matt. 21:23–32	*Trust and Obey*

🐚 Children's Lectionary Sermon

TITLE: God Quenches Thirst

SCRIPTURE: Exod. 17:1–7

KEY VERSE: *"I will meet you by the rock at Mount Sinai. Strike the rock, and water will come pouring out. Then the people will be able to drink." Moses did just as he was told; and as the leaders looked on, water gushed out.* (Exod. 17:6, New Living Translation)

KEY CONCEPT: Trusting God

MATERIALS: Bible, bottle of water

It's football season, and besides the football, there's another necessity for the game. After the players get all hot, they need water. (*Show the water bottle.*) A key person on the team is the water boy. During time-outs, the water boy will hurry onto the field carrying water to give to the players. Over half of the weight of our bodies is water. To live, we all need water. If we are outside in the heat of summer, we need more water than usual.

When God freed his people from slavery in Egypt, they lived in the desert. In the heat of the desert wilderness, God's people got really thirsty. They were so thirsty they were complaining. To provide water for thousands of God's people, the Lord told Moses to strike a rock. (*Open Bible.*) Listen to this verse from Exodus: " 'I will meet you by the rock at Mount Sinai. Strike the rock, and water will come pouring out. Then the people will be able to drink.' Moses did just as he was told; and as the leaders looked on, water gushed out." From the rock flowed a pure stream of water to help God's people not be thirsty. God showed his people they needed to trust God to meet their needs. God gave them water. God wanted his people to trust God.

God wants us to trust, too. Instead of complaining the way God's people did long ago in the desert, God wants us to talk to him through prayer. God wants us to read his Word. Just as we need water to keep our bodies healthy and alive, God gives us the help we need each day if we just ask through prayer and read his word.—Ken Cox

🐚 WORSHIP AIDS 🐚

Call to Worship: God has moved—and is moving—in and through us. He has lifted us out of troubled places and set before us a new direction. With thanksgiving, we declare: "Out of my distress I called on the Lord; the Lord answered me and set me free" (Ps. 118:5).

Invocation: Dear Lord, teach us today that perfect peace is found in your will. Come to us in this hour that we may experience your presence again. Speak tenderly, yet clearly and powerfully, your Word to us. Having heard your Word, may we be not only attentive but also obedient. Amen.

Offertory Sentence: "Lay not up for yourselves treasures on earth, where moth and rust corrupts, and where thieves break forth and steal: but lay up for yourselves treasures in heaven, where neither moth or rust corrupts, and where thieves do not break through and steal: for where your treasure is there will your heart be also" (Matt. 6:19–21).

Offertory Prayer: Merciful Father, giver of all things good and proper, source of peace and love, bless these tithes and offerings given in your name for the work of the gospel. Strengthen our resolves to more accurately reflect Jesus' love, to the end that our witness, by word and deed, will draw many into the family of faith. Amen.

Morning Prayer: Again, we come together in prayer, knowing that the Spirit of Holiness is present in our midst. We bring into the silence of this place those who are absent from us, those who are ill or in pain, those who are low in spirit. Raise them up, renew their energy, and restore their faith. In the clarity and crispness of the morning, lift our eyes to the hills from whence comes our help and give thanks to God the Creator for the beauty of the season, a magnificent gift of color—red, orange, brown, and yellow. May we respond to the gift so freely and expansively given to us all.

Help us to subdue our fears, to be steady and strong in faith, constantly aware of your reassuring presence. May we be faithful in seeing the needs of others; may we minister to those in poor health, ease the burdens of those who struggle, console those who are grieving, lighten their despair, and help in any way we can, always remembering that underneath are the everlasting arms, ready to give us rest, to renew our energy, to clear our vision, and restore our patience as we wait for light in the darkness.

As we go forth into a new week, watch over our families, our children, and their teachers. Protect those who must travel in the pursuit of their business and keep them safe. And include in our care and concern those victims of bombings here and abroad. For all your love and gifts of life, we offer thanks.—Martha DeNormandie

Benediction: Now go forth in the power and the purpose of the Lord, and may God, whom we know as Father, Son, and Holy Spirit, guide and guard and keep you through the days of this week and bring you back again to worship next Lord's Day. Amen.

SUNDAY, OCTOBER 5, 2008

LECTIONARY SERMON TOPIC: "The Meaning of the Christian Life"
TEXT: Phil. 3:4b–14
OTHER READINGS: Exod. 20:1–4, 7–9, 12–20; Ps. 19; Matt. 21:33–46

How would you answer the question, What is the meaning of the Christian life? No doubt, we have all been taught that it means various things as we have grown up. I think Paul gets to the heart of it here in these words to the Philippians.

He begins with a word of joy and warning: "Brothers and sisters, rejoice in the Lord." The Christian life is meant to be a life of joy. There are seasons in our lives when our joy seems to fade. And though at times the feeling of joy weakens, there is a certain indestructibility in Christian joy, and that is because Christian joy is not based on a feeling but on a person—Jesus Christ. Paul writes, "Rejoice in the Lord." And though at times it seems God is absent, the reality is that God is present in the person of Christ, though our circumstances may be so hard that the presence is hidden. We are promised the presence of Christ. And in that presence we find our center. And from that center we find the meaning of our lives.

I. In his writing and teaching, Paul understood the value of repetition. He says, "To write the same things to you is no trouble to me, and it is a safeguard for you." Obviously, Paul had written other letters to the Philippians. He wrote for roughly sixteen years, yet we only have thirteen of his letters. Like any good teacher, Paul was not afraid of repetition. School teachers know the value of repetition. Perhaps the reason we often lose sight of the meaning of the Christian life is that we do not hear about it often enough. We get distracted with those things that are not primary, and the meaning of the Christian life gets hidden. That is one of the purposes for Sunday school—to continue to revisit the central elements of the biblical story.

What does Paul feel the need to repeat here? It is first a warning about those who would place the meaning of the Christian faith somewhere other than where it should be. He says, "Beware of the evil workers; beware of the false circumcision"—or, as one commentator put it, "Beware of the party of mutilation." Paul was talking about those who still believed and taught that a male must be circumcised to belong to the people of God. Paul says, "True circumcision is not of the flesh, but of the heart."

By that he meant two things: First, true circumcision belongs to those worshipping in the Spirit of God (those who worship God in the Spirit, as opposed to the worship in the flesh through circumcision). Christian worship is not adherence to the details of a law; it is a thing of the heart—the heart completely devoted to God. Rituals, observances, and symbols can help us in worship, but the heart of Christian worship is the love of God and service to others. Circumcision of the heart, therefore, means, worship in the Spirit.

Second, it also means that our only boast is in Christ, not in any act of the flesh, like circumcision. We boast not in what we have done for Christ but what Christ has done for us. That is the glory we share. We cannot boast in human achievement; that is not the heart of our relationship to God. "We put no confidence in the flesh," Paul says, "but if we did, I have a right, more than anyone, to boast about my human achievement."

II. **Then he states his credentials**. He was circumcised like any other Jew and was part of the chosen people of God—the nation of Israel. By calling himself an Israelite, Paul stressed the absolute purity of his descent. But he was not only an Israelite; he belonged to the tribe of Benjamin—the elite of Israel, the highest aristocracy of Israel. He was not only a religious Jew but a member of their strictest and most self-disciplined sect—the Pharisees.

Paul claims that from his birth he was a God-fearing, Law-observing Jew. And he had the zeal to match. In persecuting the Church, he had possessed in his heart a burning zeal for what he had thought was the work of God. And he had a record in Judaism that was blameless.

All these things Paul could have set down on the credit side of the balance sheet. That is what we do many times. We hold up our morality, our church attendance, our knowledge of the Scriptures, our offerings. Many times it is these things that are held up as marks of the true circumcision—the true Christian. And Paul could have done the same with his achievements in Judaism. He could have written them down on the credit side of his religious balance sheet, but he did not. When he met Christ, he wrote them off as nothing more than bad debts (3:7–11).

All the things Paul had believed were reasons to boast were, in fact, useless—or, at best, secondary. It is important that we be moral and that we worship God, that we know the Scriptures and that we give our offerings. But if we are to get the meaning of the Christian life, all human achievement, all our works of righteousness, must become secondary; we must realize that the meaning of life comes in knowing Christ, having a relationship with Christ. And out of that relationship springs the fruit of Christ's Spirit.

Paul knew that the only way to find peace was to abandon the way of human achievement and accept the way of grace. Paul realized that knowing Christ was what really mattered. And he spoke from experience. Because he had lost his prestige in the Jewish religion, he suffered the loss of all things, for the sake of Christ. It was because of Christ he had lost all things. And he said it was worth it.

Do you think that maybe our difficulty with wanting to cling to our achievements comes from the fact that many of us have not lost much at all for the sake of Christ? This is not true of everyone. There are those who have lost things or given up things because of Christ. But for most of us, it is hard to relinquish our own achievements, our own possessions, for the sake of Christ because they have such a hold on us. If we could only get to the bottom of things. If we could only come to the realization that joy and peace is not to be found in our achievements or our possessions but that what gives meaning to our existence is knowing Christ in an intimate relationship. When Paul lost it all, he didn't grieve over the losses, as I expect you and I would, depending on what we had lost. Paul lost his very identity; he lost his prestige and respect in the Jewish world when he chose to follow Christ. But he said, "I count those losses as rubbish—literally, garbage—compared to gaining Christ."

Paul says, in effect, "I want to be found in Christ. I do not want to be found in a life based on my own achievements, my own merit, and my own righteousness. I do not want to live a life based on a legalistic list of dos and don'ts." Instead, he says, "I want a life based on knowing Christ, a righteousness that comes from God on the basis of faith. I want to live life with grace, not based upon what I can do. I want to know Christ!" What does it mean to know Christ? Paul is speaking of an intimate knowledge of another person. The Old Testament uses "to know" when speaking of the intimate knowledge shared between a husband and wife. It is not Paul's aim to know *about* Christ but to know him personally.

III. **How have you viewed the Christian life?** Has it been to learn things about Christ? Or has it been to know Christ, to know him as a friend? That is the meaning of the Christian life—to know Christ as a friend and to walk in his steps. For Paul that means certain things. It means to know *the power of Christ's Resurrection*. For the dark times of our lives, the times of suffering and grief, it is this power that we hope for—the power of new life springing forth out of the dark night. To know Christ in the power of his Resurrection did not mean, for Paul, life in heaven when he died. That is a part of what it means to know Christ. But Paul is talking about life down here on earth. We cannot live life just waiting for pie-in-the-sky-by-and-by. God has granted importance to life here on this earth, and what Paul is wanting is the power of new life that Resurrection brings to give him the energy and power he needs to live life day by day.

It also means to know Christ in *the fellowship of his sufferings*. In several places in Paul's letters, he talks about how Christians who are suffering are sharing in the work of Christ. Jesus said, "The world hates you because it hated me first." To find meaning in the Christian life may involve suffering in certain places of the world. It may involve a loss of prestige. One thing we can be sure it involves is the self-giving that Paul talked about throughout chapter 2 of this letter. Paul writes about being conformed to the death of Christ. Christ gave of himself, even to the point of death. And Paul wants to give of himself as Christ gave of himself, because meaning is found when we give of ourselves.

IV. **And then the end of the road for the earthly Christian life is the resurrection from the dead, "the prize of the heavenly call of God in Christ Jesus."** That is where, Paul says, it will all be worth it. We will have run the race, and life everlasting will be ours. The meaning of the Christian life is found in knowing Christ as intimately as you know your best friend. This knowing is a lifelong journey, a goal toward which we press onward. We put behind those things from the past that would hinder our journey of knowing Christ and press forward to what lies ahead.—W. Gregory Pope

---

ILLUSTRATIONS

Christian Life. George Will writes in *Men at Work* of baseball umpires "carved from granite" and "stuffed with microchips." Once when Babe Pinelli called Babe Ruth out on strikes, Ruth made a populist argument. Ruth reasoned that Pinelli was the only one out of the forty thousand people at the game who couldn't see that "the last one was a ball, tomato head." Pinelli replied as a statesman, "Maybe so, but mine is the only opinion that counts." The same is true for us. There is only one opinion that counts, so to speak. It belongs to the Designer of the universe, for we are designed to live according to the moral law of God.—Lawrence Vowan

Martyrdom. According to the ancient historian Eusebius,[1] the old man stepped forward and was asked by the Roman proconsul if he really was Polycarp. When he said yes, the proconsul urged him to deny the charge that he was a Christian. "Respect your years!" he exclaimed, adding similar appeals regularly made on such occasions: "Swear by Caesar's fortune; change your attitude; say: Away with the godless!" (Christians were considered atheists.) But Polycarp, with his face set, looked at all the crowd in the stadium and waved his hand toward them, sighed, looked up to heaven, and cried: "Away with the

---

[1]Johannes Quasten and Joseph Plumpe (ed.), "The Martyrdom of Polycarp," in *Ancient Christian Writings* (Mahwah, NJ: The Newman Press, 1948), p. 90.

godless!" The governor pressed him further: "Swear, and I will set you free: curse Christ."

"For eighty-six years," replied Polycarp, "I have been his servant, and he has never done me wrong. How can I blaspheme my king who saved me?"

The proconsul was amazed and sent the crier to stand in the middle of the arena and announce three times: "Polycarp has confessed that he is a Christian." Then a shout went up from every throat that Polycarp must be burnt alive. As the crowd piled logs and kindling around him, Polycarp prayed: "O Father of your beloved and blessed Son, Jesus Christ, through whom we have come to know you, the God of angels and powers and all creation, and of the whole family of the righteous who live in your presence; I bless you for counting me worthy of this day and hour, that as one of the martyrs I may partake of Christ's cup." When he had offered up the Amen and completed his prayer, the men in charge lit the fire, and a great flame shot up.—Lee McGlone

Musical Selections Appropriate to the Day

Hymn suggestions for lectionary texts:

Exod. 20:1–4, 7–9, 12–20	*Jesus Calls Us O'er the Tumult*
Ps. 19	*This Is My Father's World; Let the Whole Creation Cry*
Phil. 3:4b–14	*And Can It Be?*
Matt. 21:33–46	*Christ Is Our Cornerstone*

❧ Children's Lectionary Sermon

TITLE: The Sound from the Stars

SCRIPTURE: Ps. 19

KEY VERSE: *The heavens tell of the glory of God. . . . They speak without a sound or a word; their voice is silent in the skies; yet their message has gone out to all the earth and their words to the entire world.* (Ps. 19:1a, 3–4, New Living Translation)

KEY CONCEPT: Creation

MATERIALS: Bible, a cut-out star

I brought a star I made out of construction paper. Have you ever heard a star speak with a voice? (*Let the children respond.*) I haven't either. If a star could speak, what do you think it would say? (*Let the children respond.*) But have you thought about how a star could speak to us?

The writer of Psalm 19 (*open the Bible*) tells us that stars and other heavenly bodies *do* speak. Listen to these verses: "The heavens tell of the glory of God. . . . They speak without a sound or a word; their voice is silent in the skies; yet their message has gone out to all the earth and their words to the entire world." The psalmist tells us the beauty of the clouds, sun, stars, and planets tell us of the beauty of God's creation. The stars don't talk like you and me, but because they are so beautiful to look at, the psalmist praised God.

One night when your parents can take you away from the lights of (*name your city or town*), go out and look at the beauty of the moon and the stars. You might see for yourself what the psalmist saw long ago—God's beautiful creation in the stars that are so far away from us. It can be awesome.

On a night when you get to listen to the stars with your eyes, think about God. From God's creation, we know God is infinite and powerful. God is everywhere. If stars did talk, they would sing praise to the awesome power and love of God.—Ken Cox

❧ WORSHIP AIDS ❧

Call to Worship: We gather, not as victims in a difficult world but as victors in the world for which Jesus Christ died: "Thanks be unto God who gives us the victory through our Lord Jesus Christ" (1 Cor. 15:57).

Invocation: Lord, in this hour of worship, let the broken body and shed blood of our Savior bring us to renewed commitment and greater appreciation of that grace that knows no bounds and saves, to the uttermost, those who believe. Amen.—E. Lee Phillips

Offertory Sentence: "Whatsoever you do in word or deed, do all in the name of the Lord Jesus, giving thanks to God and the Father by him" (Col. 3:17).

Offertory Prayer: Father, accept these gifts as tokens of our loyalty and love. We are ever mindful of your presence in our lives. Grant that we may, even today, discover the joy of selfless giving. Give us the desire to live as good stewards in word and deed. Amen.

Morning Prayer: O God, who is in us and all around us, grant us the grace and the humility to turn to you in prayer so that we may stand in the presence of our Creator and give voice to our confessions, our gratitude, and our hopes.

We ask that you hear first our prayers of confession for the kind word left unspoken and for the hurtful word we wish we could have back; for the times when we avert our eyes from injustice, saying nothing; for whatever we may have done, or left undone, that we now regret and could repair. When we don't see the obvious task you have set before us, open our eyes and hearts. And when we fall short, which we will, forgive us.

Hear also this day our prayers of thanksgiving for the reassuring sounds of small children on a playground, for birds on the wing in the October sky, for country lanes lined with a canopy of colors, for the pleasures of a well-played game, for a friend who is always there for us, for the gift of life itself, for all the blessings that lift our souls, renew our hope. And remind us of what we love about this life. Our voices become one in thanks and praise.

As we consider our prayers of intercession during these difficult days, we ask for grace and guidance. Guide our leaders, we pray, and the leaders of other nations. Help us learn to work together on the difficult tasks before us. May the combined strength and resolve of a united family of nations bring us again to a place of peace and then charge us to continue working together to mend and restore this fragile, wounded, beautiful world you have entrusted to our care. On this day, grant us grace we pray, sufficient both to the size of our hope and to the size of our despair, neither more nor less than we need.—Roger Paine

Benediction: People of God, let us go forth today, strengthened in our resolve to be faithful followers of Jesus Christ. In the days of this new week, may we speak his name often and lovingly, and may our spiritual gifts be used in work of the Kingdom. Amen.

SUNDAY, OCTOBER 12, 2008

LECTIONARY SERMON TOPIC: "The Twenty-Third Psalm"

TEXT: Ps. 23

OTHER READINGS: Exod. 32:1–14; Ps. 106:1–6, 19–23; Phil. 4:1–19; Matt. 22:1–14

The words of the Twenty-Third Psalm are, I think, the most well-known biblical words in the entire world. They have perhaps been used to bring more peace and comfort to wounded, grieving, dying hearts than any other work of literature. We reserve these words for our most tender times and places: in hospital rooms, at gravesides, at the bedsides of the elderly and of children. People who have never set foot in a synagogue or church request to hear these words when their lives have entered the darkness and shadows. How many times have you heard these words spoken or uttered them yourself, especially in those moments when you needed all the faith you could muster? They are not words of magic; rather, they are words that touch the deep places within us with the gifts we want more than anything.

I. **"The Lord is my shepherd, I shall not want." Is that really true?** Can you honestly say those words about yourself? Or are you among the many who, no matter how great their faith, still want things? Most of us want good health, happiness for our children, relief from pain, and some measure of inner peace, love, and understanding. But many of us, believers and unbelievers alike, go on wanting our whole lives through. We long for what never seems to come. We pray for what never seems to be clearly given.

So could it be that when the psalmist says, "I shall not want," he is speaking of a deeper contentment met by The One Who Made Us. Perhaps this poet is saying that we will never lack the one thing we want more than anything else, that whatever else is withheld, the Shepherd never withholds himself. And whether we know it or not, the Shepherd is what we want more than anything else—a Sacred Presence that quenches our deepest thirst. This is, I think, a most appropriate word in a culture that teaches us to want everything. Driven by greed rather than need, we can hardly imagine having only the necessities of life. However, when we learn the contentment of having only our daily necessities, we realize that in our Shepherd's arms we have all we truly need. God feeds our souls. God feeds that part of us which is most hungry and most in need of feeding.

II. **This song calls us to a time of respite and retreat from tall metal buildings, cluttered offices, busy lives, stormy waters, crowded traffic.** These words offer us a place to rest, a place to be restored—places of green pastures and quiet waters. Our souls need such a place of restoration. Our Shepherd is here to hold us through the stormiest of seas until they subside and the waters are quiet again, and we find ourselves planted in the softest, greenest grass we've ever seen or touched. And we find the peace we long for most of all.

Peter writes, "For you were going astray like sheep, but now you have returned to the shepherd and guardian of your souls" (1 Pet. 2:25). Are you in need of returning? You can, you know. The Shepherd is calling your name. You're in the Shepherd's hand, whether you know it or not. You always have been. And nothing and no one can snatch you away. Return and let your Shepherd guard you from the dangers of a wrong turn and lead you in the right path.

III. **And yet, even in paths of righteousness the way sometimes grows dark: "Yea, though I walk through the valley of darkest shadow."** Original Scripture doesn't use the word *death* here; it says, "valley of darkest shadow." We add the word *death* because death is the darkest shadow we know, and any dark time can feel like a death. But the psalmist refrains from naming the shadow, and I, for one, am grateful. It means these words can be claimed by anyone in any difficult place. It may be the valley of the shadow of death; it may be just some deep, impenetrable darkness. Some days we are in green pastures beside still waters; other days we go down, in Shakespeare's words, "to the bottom of the worst." Have you been there?

Our Shepherd God takes rod and staff in hand to comfort and mend us when the world has broken us into pieces. Our love has been spurned by another. Our best efforts at reconciliation have left us still estranged. Someone has been taken from us. The whirlwind of depression, the agony of rejection, the grief of a dream turned nightmare. This darkness, this pain, God enters with healing in his wings. God is present and at work to bring an end to debilitating desire, fear, and grief. And out of debilitation, God comes to bring quiet restoration, guidance, peace, Presence. Anybody here without need of these things? They are the needs that make us human. They are the gifts that save our souls from the fear that terrorizes us.

In our world where the powerless often act out of desperation and the powerful use their power dangerously, we have much that makes us afraid. And we come to this psalm, not as a psalm of protection. God does not promise to shield us from all evil. The psalmist lets go of her fear, not because there is nothing to fear. The psalmist lets go of her fear because, in her words, *thou art with me.* Here is the heart of the psalm. It beats with Holy Presence. It pumps life eternal through our veins. We are safe from our enemies, the psalmist says—enemies who may seek to destroy us and may kill our bodies. But eternally we are safe in the arms of God. For "in life, in death, and in life beyond death, God is with us. We are not alone."[2]

IV. **The image of God as Shepherd shifts to God as Extravagant Host, feeding us from God's table, healing us, and filling our cup to overflowing, even with enemies all around us.** And yet, says this psalmist, it is not our enemies that will follow us most closely; it is Goodness and Mercy. God's goodness and mercy will pursue us, will hunt us down, wherever we are, all the days of our life, and bring us home to God's house. And God will open the gate wide, and we will go in and out and find pasture—the green pastures of God's goodness and the quiet waters of God's mercy. And there we will find life abundantly.

The shadows of lostness and fear and grief will not last forever. In the presence of God, there is the promise of light coming out of the darkness. Here and there, now and then, as we approach the light, we can see God's greeting arms and shining face. God is glad to see us. "Welcome to my home," God says, and leads us into a room that has our name on it. We are home safe and sound. There are enemies and danger still outside, but here we are safe. We're safe to be who we are without fear. We are in a place where we are utterly loved, fully understood, fully known, fully received. And nothing can change that.

---

[2]From the Affirmation of Faith, United Church of Canada.

And in that great house, we enter the dining hall with a table piled high for a feast, a cup filled to the brim with God's goodness and mercy. And we hear an invitation to take our place at God's own table and to be at home in God's own house, "a house that is older than Eden and dearer than home." And just outside the window, spring is blooming and the birds are singing to us, "Welcome home! Welcome home! Home Forever!" Amen.—W. Gregory Pope

ILLUSTRATIONS

Peace. Do you remember that old commercial in which a housewife holds a crying baby in her arms and there's another child in the kitchen pretending to be a cook but instead is creating a disaster? Then somebody knocks at the door, and the phone rings, and in desperation she cries out, "Oh, Calgon, take me away!" And the next time you see her, she's lying in the bathtub, covered in Calgon soap, in the dreamland of green pastures and quiet waters. Peace. Sometimes, the need for peace streams from the confusion of our lives. We're lost and we can't find our way. We've made a wrong turn. We've done something that's brought damage to ourselves or to someone we love. We've fallen off the path into the ditch of guilt and shame. And we're in need of cleansing. And our Shepherd comes and lifts us out of the ditch and cleans us up and leads us into the beauty of righteousness.—W. Gregory Pope

God's Presence. Wendell Berry begins his novel, *Remembering*, with these words: "It is dark. He does not know where he is. And then he sees pale light from the street soaking in above the drawn drapes. It is not a light to see by, but only makes the darkness visible."[3] At times God's presence may only provide enough light to make the darkness visible. Fear has wrapped itself around our hearts and minds, and there's only enough light to see the darkness. The light of God's presence is with us, even through the blackest of nights. And God walks with us until the morning light breaks and leads us to a place where no one is afraid or anxious. Because whether we feel it or not, everywhere and all around us are the everlasting arms of a shepherding God.—W. Gregory Pope

---

[3]Wendell Berry, *Remembering* (New York: North Point Press, 1988), p. 1.

Musical Selections Appropriate to the Day

Hymn suggestions for lectionary texts:

Exod. 32:1–14	*This Is My Father's World*
Ps. 106:1–6, 19–23	*Rejoice the Lord Is King*
Phil. 4:19	*Rejoice ye Pure in Heart*
Matt. 22:1–14	*Where Cross the Crowded Ways of Life*

⁀ Children's Lectionary Sermon

TITLE: Remember God's Blessings

SCRIPTURE: Exod. 32:1–14; Ps. 106:19–23

KEY VERSE: *They forgot God, their savior, who had done such great things in Egypt.* (Ps. 106:21, New Living Translation)

KEY CONCEPT: Remembering God

MATERIALS: Bible, sticky notes

(*Show the children the sticky notes. Ask them what you could use them for.*) I put yellow sticky notes on the phone, the computer screen, or coffee cups to help me remember things I need to do. This one reads, "Call home and get shopping list." This one says, "Visit hospital this afternoon." People use these notes to remember what they need to do.

When Moses was leading God's people, they needed a reminder to help them remember what God had done for them. Right after God's people got away from Egypt, Pharaoh changed his mind and went after them. God's people were trapped by the Red Sea. God told Moses to hold his staff out over the Red Sea. The water parted so God's people could walk between two walls of water on dry land. God's people got away, and Pharaoh's army was destroyed when the water came flooding back on them.

Sadly, just a short time later God's people forgot this miracle of the parting of the Red Sea. They made a golden calf to worship instead of God. (*Open Bible.*) Listen to this verse from Psalm 106:21: "They forgot God, their savior, who had done such great things in Egypt."

Sometimes we forget God. We think about the things we want or what we want to do. We need reminders, too. We can read our Bibles every day. We can go to church and worship. Being with other Christian friends can help us remember God. Another way to remember is by singing songs about Jesus. When we sing our favorite Christian songs or hymns, we can remind ourselves of God's love and care for us.

We can use sticky notes to help us remember things we need to do. We can use God's Word, Christian friends, and music to help us remember that we belong to God.—Ken Cox

WORSHIP AIDS

Call to Worship: Worship, the work of the people, rises from hearts fully trusting in God. We join the prophet from days of old and declare: "Blessed is the man that trusts in the Lord, and whose hope the Lord is" (Jer. 17:7).

Invocation: Lord, you have called us to be your people, and we gladly are! We exist in order to bring honor and glory to your holy name. We are your witnesses in this world. Strengthen us today with your Spirit's power that we may be all that you intend us to be. Open our hearts to receive the fullness of your grace. Amen.

Offertory Sentence: "I will freely sacrifice unto you, O Lord. I will praise you name, for it is good" (Ps. 54:6).

Offertory Prayer: Gracious Father, we too often stray from you, but you have lovingly brought us back. You have delivered us from our troubles and shown us the path of light in a dark world. You have given to us material gifts that meet our needs—and far beyond our needs. We praise your goodness, not in words alone but also in the giving of tithes and offerings. Multiply these gifts that your presence shall be brought to many others. Amen.

Morning Prayer: Our Father, you are the source of life and the light of seeing. We acknowledge with joy and steadfast faith that the earth is your creation, that we are your handiwork, that life is your gift. Lift up our thoughts from the littleness of our own works to the greatness of your majesty, wonder, power, and unending love.

Grant, our Father, that we may so think of your loveliness that we may grow into your likeness. Teach us the meaning of grace—that it is to love in the presence of hatred, to forgive in the face of slander, to celebrate life even in death, to be bearers of light in a world often filled with darkness. We pray this morning for the fulfillment of your purposes in our lives. Encourage us never to yield to lesser goals. Keep our minds on the prize of the high calling of Christ among us. For our youth, encourage them in their high aspirations to make the world a better place. For our parents, grant increased faith and much wisdom that we may lovingly guide our sons and daughters. May in all things your will and way have the place of highest supremacy among us.

Before you now, we have bowed our heads and hearts. We give thanks for every good gift and commit to walk in your way. In all things, may we discover that the greatest joy in life is to do your will and that in your service there is perfect freedom. Through Christ we pray. Amen.—Lee McGlone

Benediction: The world stands before us as an open door. Let us go out into it and into all the opportunities that await us this week, energized by the presence of our God, Father, Son, and Holy Spirit. And may God's peace be with you. Amen.

SUNDAY, OCTOBER 19, 2008

LECTIONARY SERMON TOPIC: "The Hidden Face of God"
TEXT: Exod. 33:12–23
OTHER READINGS: Ps. 99; 1 Thess. 1:1–10; Matt. 22:15–22

An emphasis on the hidden presence of God is not exactly what we expect to hear in Scripture and sermon. Sometimes when we talk about faith and God, we are tempted to iron out all the wrinkles of life. Sometimes we give the impression that faith in God is the most obvious thing in the world. We speak as if everyone should believe in God. We sanitize the world of its darkness. As one writer put it, "We cross out its tragedy and terror, and offer a comic-book version of the gospel that sooner or later proves as useless as an umbrella in a hurricane."[4]

I. **Authentic conversation about God in a world like ours must express God's hiddenness as much as God's revelation.** For whatever else God is, in a world like ours God is not obvious. God is deeply hidden by our human limitations, hidden by our sin. God is no show-off. The God revealed to us in the pages of Scripture is a hidden God. The prophet Isaiah exclaims, "Truly you are a God who hides yourself" (Isa. 45:15).

Time and time again, I am struck by how intensely realistic the Bible is about the hiddenness of God. The religious propaganda we sometimes hear and read might lead you to expect God to be as obvious as a billboard on a highway. There are those who can package and deliver absolute truths who find receptive audiences and produce best-selling books. Tune in religious broadcasting for a few hours, and you will hear those who speak with absolute certainty that he (or occasionally she) has all the answers to life's most troubling questions. And that can be dangerous. The need for certainty in a dangerous world like ours is real and understandable. But as Andrew Greeley said, "If one wishes to eliminate uncertainty, tension, confusion and disorder from one's life, there is no point in getting mixed up either with Yahweh or with Jesus of Nazareth."[5]

II. **In our story for today, Moses is learning that lesson.** The children of Israel have just completed dancing a jig (or something like that) around a golden calf. Moses had been up on the mountain talking with God, and the people had lost patience with him. They doubted whether he would ever come back down. So Aaron, the minister of music, shaped a calf made of gold and the people danced around it, offering their worship to this god made of hands, this god they could see.

---

[4]Allen C. McSween Jr., "The Darkness of Faith," in James Cox (ed.), *Best Sermons* 7 (San Francisco: HarperSanFrancisco, 1994), p. 96.
[5]As quoted in Philip Yancey, *Reaching for the Invisible God* (Grand Rapids: Zondervan, 2000), p. 92 (quoting a *New York Times* Book Review).

Well, God had about had it with these people. God told Moses to lead them out but that God was not going with them because God was so angry he might consume them. God tells Moses an angel will go with them. But Moses the mediator is not willing to permit God to withdraw his presence from the people. Moses says, "Lord, you know them by name. After all, they are your children." And then he says, "If your presence does not go with us, don't take me any further." So God relents and changes his mind, and says, "OK, I will go with you." Then Moses makes one final request: "Lord, show me your glory." Glory is another mode of God's presence. It speaks of God's awesome, shrouded, magisterial presence, something like an overpowering light. And this request for glory is a plea to draw even closer, more dangerously, more intimately into the very core of God's own self.

Moses always wants more from God; what he has of God's presence is never enough. And who among us has not been there? And you know, there's something admirable about that, always wanting more of God, more of God's presence, more of God's nearness. Moses doesn't want to be touched by an angel; he wants to come face-to-face with the very person and presence of God. Moses wants a clear guarantee of God's presence. "Lord, if you say you're with us and that I'm the one to lead, then show me your whole glory, show me your face right here, right now."

And God says, "I will make all my goodness pass before you. I will bestow grace and mercy. I will proclaim my name before you. But Moses, I can only give you a glimpse of my glory, for if you were to see my face in all its transcendent majesty, you couldn't handle that much light. You'd die." So the ever-gracious God counters with a deal. "Moses, you cannot see my face, but I will stand you upon a rock and while my glory passes by I will hide you with my hand in the cleft of the rock. And then when I have passed by I will take my hand away and you shall see my back; but my face shall not be seen." Moses asks to glimpse God in all of God's transcendent splendor. But God draws a protective cover around the inscrutable mystery of God, because such seeing is too dangerous. There is mystery and danger here.

III. **This is one of those texts that remind us we do not approach the Other as we would our own kind.** Thomas Merton suggests that if you find God with great ease, perhaps it is not God that you have found. And that is why friendship is not the primary model used in the Bible to describe our relationship with God. Worship is. For in the presence of God there is always mystery and splendor. And human language reaches its limits when it attempts to describe God or even to capture the experience of the encounter with the One who is both radically other and immediately present. There is in this story a striking anthropomorphic language in reference to God—God has a face, a hand, and a back—all of it symbolic language, as is all language about God. There is an encounter with God that feels both intimate and distant. Even Moses, who communicated more directly with God than any other Old Testament figure, could only catch a fleeting glimpse of God's back.

One of the things I love most about Scripture is that it never shuts its eyes to the darkness that makes faith the most challenging of adventures. The Bible never pretends for a moment that God is easily known in a world like ours. Job flings his cry into the darkness: "Oh, that I knew where I might find God. . . . Behold, I go forward, but God is not there; and backward, but I cannot perceive God; on the left hand I seek God, but I cannot behold God; I turn to the right hand, but I cannot see God . . . for I am hemmed in by darkness, and thick darkness covers my face" (Job 23:3, 8–9, 17). Scripture itself demands that we acknowledge the darkness that often hides God from us. Whatever else life is, it is not an open book in which we read clearly the ways and works of God.

And we must never forget that it is a journey of faith, not certainty, learning step by step as we follow. Merton wrote: "We receive enlightenment only in proportion as we give ourselves more and more completely to God by humble submission and love. We do not first see, then act: we act, then see. . . . And that is why the man who waits to see clearly, before he will believe, never starts on the journey."[6]

IV. **Moses, like us sometimes, has had about all the ambiguity he can take.** So he finally comes right out and demands of God, "Show me your glory." No more hints and clues. No more mystery. Show me your glory, face-to-face. But his demand is not granted, not as he asks it, only partially. For in marvelous poetic imagery, God hides Moses in the cleft of a rock and covers him with his hand as God's glory passes by. What Moses sees is not the blinding glory of God but the "back of God." We are not given to see the full glory

---

[6]Martha Greene, *Christian Century,* Sept. 25–Oct. 8, 2002, p. 19.

of God. In this life we always see "through a glass darkly." What we see are glimpses of God.

And what we hear is the name that is the promise: I AM with you always. I wonder if this scene was in the mind of Paul when he wrote the words: "For now we see in a glass dimly, but then we will see face to face. Now we know only in part; then we will know fully, even as we have been fully known" (1 Cor. 13:12). Moses could not know God fully. Neither can we. And though we cannot fully know God, we are fully known by God. God knows our name. Though hidden, God accompanies our every step. And the promise of faith is that someday we shall "no longer see through a glass darkly, but face to face." Then we shall know in full, even as we are fully known and fully loved. Until that time, we live the life of faith in a hidden God.

V. **And in honesty, we have seen traces of God in each other's faces and in the mystery and splendor of the Creation perhaps.** Or maybe in the face of Christ. As John Claypool put it, "To the mystery of God-ness the man Jesus gives a face, and on that face is the smile of grace." To say that God is a mystery, writes Buechner, is to say that you can never nail him down. Even on Christ the nails proved ultimately ineffective.[7] To see and to know the living God is a dangerous, mysterious, life-giving adventure of faith and grace. The "seeing" is dim; the "knowing" is in part. But "dimly" and "in part" are enough.—W. Gregory Pope

---

ILLUSTRATIONS

God's Hiddenness. In the *Front Line* television documentary titled "Faith and Doubt at Ground Zero," an angry man who had lost many friends expressed his rage toward God, saying, "I don't have problems with the Son, but I have real problems with the Father." For many, many people, there is and always has been this seemingly unbridgeable abyss between God and humanity. Even though God has been revealed in Jesus Christ and through Holy Scripture, there is the sense in which God always remains hidden.[8]

---

[7]Frederick Buechner, *Wishful Thinking* (San Francisco: HarperSanFrancisco, 1982), p. 64.
[8]Greene, *Christian Century,* p. 19.

Richard Friedman has addressed this question in his fascinating book *The Hidden Face of God*. He points out how as the biblical story progresses, God's presence appears more hidden. God does not cease to exist, to care, or to affect the world, but God's action becomes less and less publicly visible than it appeared at the beginning of the biblical story. But why the ambiguity? By all appearances that is how God intends it. We might wish that it were otherwise. We might wish that God would light up the night sky with the words *I AM* written in letters a thousand light-years high. But God will not. God will not take away the ambiguity of faith. Always the mystery remains, and with it the risk of faith.[9]—W. Gregory Pope

Religion. Wake Forest religion professor, Charles Kimball, has written a book I think every person should read. The title of the book is *When Religion Becomes Evil*.[10] Having spent much of his life observing many religious perspectives, Kimball says that topping the list of what makes religion turn evil are claims of absolute truth, believing you have the truth, the whole truth, and nothing but the truth about God, and all others are heretics. History teaches us that attitudes of absolute certainty about God lead to rigid doctrine and increase the likelihood of religious violence. However, says Kimball, to realize, with Paul, that when it comes to understanding God we can only see through a glass dimly and only know in part, we can significantly decrease the possibility of religion becoming evil.—W. Gregory Pope

Musical Selections Appropriate to the Day

Hymn suggestions for lectionary texts:

Exod. 33:12–23	*Find Us Faithful; Our Father We Have Wandered*
Ps. 99	*How Great Thou Art; Holy, Holy, Holy*
1 Thess. 1:1–10	*Will You Let Me Be Your Servant?*
Matt. 22:15–22	*I Would Be True; Great Is Thy Faithfulness*

[9]Allen C. McSween Jr., "The Darkness of Faith," in James Cox (ed.), *Best Sermons* 7 (San Francisco: HarperSanFrancisco, 1994), pp. 99–100.
[10]Charles Kimball, *When Religion Becomes Evil* (San Francisco: HarperSanFrancisco, 2003).

☙ Children's Lectionary Sermon

TITLE: Did You Get the Message?

SCRIPTURE: 1 Thess. 1:1–10

KEY VERSES: *For when we brought you the Good News it was not only with words but also with power, for the Holy Spirit gave you full assurance that what we said was true. And you know that the way we lived among you was further proof of the truth of our message.* (1 Thess. 1:5, New Living Translation)

KEY CONCEPT: Actions speak God's message.

MATERIALS: Bible, printout of an answered e-mail

What happens when we call out to a friend? (*Let the children respond.*) When we call out to friends down the street, we know they hear us when they look at us. It is nice to get a letter or a postcard in the mail. I write a lot of e-mails. Raise your hand if you or your family writes to others on the computer. (*Show them a printout of an e-mail.*) This is an e-mail I got after I wrote someone. They sent it back with a note to me. I wonder though if people get my e-mails when I don't get an answer. Did I have the wrong address, or did it get lost? I like to just know people got my message.

The apostle Paul knew that the members of the church at Thessalonica had gotten the message about Jesus. He could tell because their lives were changed. (*Open Bible.*) Listen to this verse from 1 Thessalonians 1:5: "For when we brought you the Good News it was not only with words but also with power, for the Holy Spirit gave you full assurance that what we said was true. And you know that the way we lived among you was further proof of the truth of our message."

Paul knew that the church members had become followers of Christ because their actions showed it. When Paul had been there before, he showed them how to live as Jesus would want them to. Now, the church was doing it so well that they were spreading the story of Jesus everywhere.

We can show in our actions how much we love Jesus. When we believe in Jesus, we want our actions to show all those around us how much we love and obey God. We want to even share the story of Jesus with people who have not heard it. This is the important message we want to share.—Ken Cox

❧ WORSHIP AIDS ❧

Call to Worship: Worship is an expression of profound hope. We stand not alone but with God who empowers us. "They that wait upon the Lord shall renew their strength, they shall mount up with wings as eagles; they shall run, and not be weary; and they shall walk, and not faint" (Isa. 40:31).

Invocation: O Lord God, we gather today expecting an encounter with you. We desire it more than we desire our next breath. Grant that we may know you, hear you, feel you—all to that great end that we will be strengthened to win in this world. Let our hymns, prayers, the sermon, and the fellowship we share give us power to live as victors. Amen.

Offertory Sentence: "As you abound in everything, in faith, and utterance, and knowledge, and in all diligence, and in your love to us, see that you also abound in this grace also" (2 Cor. 8:7).

Offertory Prayer: Gracious Lord, we admit that often our giving is the last thought of our busy and hectic weeks. Many other concerns crowd out this grace. Grant, O Lord, that every arena of Christian discipleship will come to bear on our lives. Make us faithful, cheerful, sacrificial givers, for the Kingdom's sake. Amen.

Morning Prayer: Because of the cross of Christ, we are called again to witness your love exemplified, and we cannot remain immune to such a mighty display of sacrifice for us. Thus we lift our voices in praise and adoration in the presence of your holiness, knowing that there is something in us that cries for the expression of awe and wonder and thanksgiving. In all about us, we see the handiwork of your caring and grace. Only callousness on our part would refuse worship of the one who ever abides with us and creates for us and dies to express eternal love to us.

As we bow here in prayer, help us try to pray. Please, Kind Sir, be responsive to the deep needs of our lives, even as you are responsive to the cravings of our souls that we cannot find words to express. Meet the restlessness in our lives that cannot be stilled until it finds resolution in you. Search deeply our struggling questions, and bring them to resolution through your truth. Hear our deepest weeping, stirred by life's losses and pains and problems, and soothe our aching hearts, even as you turn weeping to joy, loss to gain, and problems to possibilities. In the quiet of these sacred moments, grant us the balm of your peace in our hearts, even as you call us to come to the restoring fountain of your gracious salvation for our very lives and soul. Amen.— Henry Fields

Benediction: We go now under the power and influence of our Lord Jesus to live as worthy followers. We are not perfect, far from it, but we are God's people. Let us go, rejoicing in the good news of our salvation, and may we share it wherever we go. Amen.

SUNDAY, OCTOBER 26, 2008

LECTIONARY SERMON TOPIC: "Anatomy of a Christian"

TEXT: Matt. 22:34–46

OTHER READINGS: Deut. 34:1–12; Ps. 90:1–6, 13–17; 1 Thess. 2:1–8

One day when Jesus was teaching, a man stepped forth and said, "Jesus, what is it you're trying to say? I don't want a sermon on the mount or any stories. Just tell me what your message is. In one or two brief and concise sentences, tell me, what does God really want from us?" (Matt. 22:36).

On one of the rare occasions when Jesus spoke with clarity, he obliged the man with two sentences so concise that they can almost be united as one. Jewish scholars have counted all the commandments in the Law of Moses and discovered 613. Rabbinic tradition says its 365 negative ones numbered for the days of the year and 248 positive ones for the number of bones in a man's body. There were so many that neither saint nor CPA could keep count. However, if you were to hang all of these laws on one nail (actually, Jesus uses two nails), it would be these: love God and love neighbor. "You shall love the Lord your God with all your heart, and with all your soul, and with all your mind, and with all your strength; and love your neighbor as yourself. On these two commandments hang all the law and the prophets."

I. **The Judaism of Jesus' day, much the way Christians sometimes do in our day, had become so focused on the letter of the Law that they had forgotten the essence of what it meant to be God's people.** There is a tendency in every religious tradition to focus on one aspect of the tradition and forget that at the heart of all true religion is the love of God and neighbor. The heart of all true religion—the calling of every Christian, the very purpose of the Church—is to love God and love neighbor. St. Augustine, the fourth-century Church father, said that here lies the guiding principle for all true biblical interpretation: Does your interpretation increase the love of God and neighbor? If it does not, Augustine says it's wrong.

With these two commandments, Jesus summarized the entirety of Scripture. On these two commandments, he said, hang all the law and the prophets. Everything in the Bible must find its way under this command to love God and neighbor. To answer the question of what it means to be a Christian, one can do no better than to respond with these words of Jesus: "to love the Lord our God with all of our heart, soul, mind and strength, and to love our neighbor as ourselves." It's that simple. It's that difficult. One is tempted after hearing these words to sing with Beatles: "All You Need Is Love."

II. **But to say that love is "all you need" is perhaps to underestimate love's demanding cost.** If we were to think of these commands to love God and neighbor as words that shape the anatomy of a Christian, we might realize how truly demanding is the call to become Christian. John Wesley, the great founder of Methodism, once summarized the great commandments by saying that Christians are those who love and serve God with their "head, their heart, and their hands." Loving God with all of our *head* points to the cognitive aspect of the Christian life. It requires that we have a solid understanding of what we believe and why. It requires reading the Bible informationally, knowing what it says. It requires growing in one's understanding of theology, Scripture, and worship, so that we are better able to think about our faith and view the world in light of our faith. It's about loving God with our intellect. Christians should be informed, thinking people.

Christians, we must be able to talk about public issues and allow our Christian faith to inform our decisions and our actions. We are called to love God with all of our minds in ways that shape the living of our faith. An Episcopalian church ran some newspaper advertisements to attract baby boomers. One of them depicted the face of Christ with the slogan: "He Died to Take Away Your Sins, Not Your Mind." Christians love and serve God with all their minds.

III. **We also seek to love and serve God with all of our *heart*, to cultivate a personal relationship with Jesus Christ that transforms our lives.** This is done through daily prayer, worship, and reading the Bible in ways that shape us spiritually; it involves an openness to and desire for the Holy Spirit's work in our lives. Wesley called this "holiness of heart."

We are commanded to love God with all our mind and heart and *hands*. Loving God with our hands always translates into loving our neighbors, which is the second part of Jesus' command. It is about putting our faith into acts of ministry and compassion. It's about using our time and gifts in service to God and neighbor. This includes being involved with the needs of people who hurt, giving away a sacrificial portion of our resources to share with others, and ministering both within and outside of the church to demonstrate the love of Christ to others. Wesley called this "social holiness." It is a call to do something about our faith by serving our neighbors and serving the world.

Being Christian is not all a matter of the heart. It is also a matter of the mind and soul and strength and hands. It's about loving God with all that we are unconditionally. Can we do that? No conditions, no matter what, always? It was Satan's question to God about Job's faithfulness in the midst of God's great blessing: "Will he serve you for nothing?" It's easy to love and serve God when things are going well. But will we love and serve God when tragedy strikes, when things turn unbearably difficult? Will we love God not for what God can do for us, but when God seems as silent as the night sky?

To love God is to give yourself fully and completely to God. It involves, among other things, a desire to be near God, to nurture a relationship with God, wanting at least to do things for God.

IV. **To love God is to also love our neighbor.** Some would equate loving God with loving neighbor. And surely loving our neighbor is a part of what it means to love God. But it's not the same. Loving a neighbor may, at times, be easier than loving God. Neighbors might make fewer demands on us. And as we said last week, God is a mystery and sometimes hidden from us. How do you love a hidden God?

Besides, we have to love God *before* we can love our neighbor. Because eventually, like when our neighbor is our enemy seeking to do us harm, the question will arise as to *why* we should love our neighbor. And the reason is that God loves our neighbor. And as lovers of God, we are called to love what God loves. In fact, Scripture tells us that if we say we love God but do not love our neighbor, we are nothing short of liars. Being a good moral person is not enough. And while loving God and neighbor are not the same, Scripture says you can't do one without the other and call yourself a Christian. And to truly love our neighbor, we have to love God first.

V. **We have to love God before we can truly love ourselves.** The purest, truest, most healing love of all is when we can say to God or to another: "I will love you no matter what, no strings attached, without condition. I will love you for who you are, not for who I want you to be, or for what you can do for me. I will love you with all of my heart. And I give to you my life." It is how God has loved us in Jesus Christ, from the moment we came into this world. It is how we are called to love God and neighbor. And it all begins with God's love for us. We love, Scripture says, because God first loved us. And what follows is the most life-sustaining experience in the entire world. We need more than anything to love God with all that we are and all that we have. For in loving our Creator, our Savior, our Divine Friend utterly and without condition, we find our deepest healing, our truest freedom, our greatest joy. Loving God with the whole self is the balm of Gilead that makes the wounded whole—no longer divided, but whole. All loves and loyalties are brought under the One Great Love—the love of God.

Healing comes to the deepest part of our lives when our entire being— head, heart, and hands—is engulfed in love for God. And then, having received God's healing love, we offer ourselves to be broken for the world as ministers of God's healing love in the world, loving our neighbor as we love ourselves.—W. Gregory Pope

ILLUSTRATIONS

Neighbor Love. Charles Kimball says: "At the heart of all authentic, healthy, life-sustaining religions, one always finds this clear requirement. Whatever religious people may say about their love of God or the mandates of their religion, when their behavior toward others is violent and destructive, when it causes suffering among their neighbors, you can be sure the religion has been corrupted and reform is desperately needed."[11] To love God and neighbor as Jesus calls us to love demands all of us, everything we have, and everything we are. Ask Jesus, who has nail prints in his hands. Ask the prophets, most of whom died for speaking God's truth. Ask Moses, who tried to teach a bunch of wandering Israelites how to love God and neighbor. Ask Jeremiah, who spent his ministry in depression and solitude, often crying out in anger to God. Loving God and neighbor—it's that simple; it's that difficult.—W. Gregory Pope

God's Love. We must hear God say to us in the waters of baptism, "You are my beloved child in whom I am well pleased." We must hear our story of Creation, born into original blessing, created in God's own image. We have to hear and know and experience this truth about ourselves before we can truly love ourselves. And we are called to love ourselves, to take care of God's gift of life to us. And because of God's great love for us, because of God's gift of life to us, we return those gifts of life and love by offering everything we are and all that we have to God in worship and thanksgiving.—W. Gregory Pope

Musical Selections Appropriate to the Day

Hymn suggestions for lectionary texts:

Deut. 34:1–12	*Sweet Hour of Prayer*
Ps. 90:1–6, 13–17	*O God Our Help in Ages Past; God of Our Life*
1 Thess. 2:1–8	*Loving Spirit*
Matt. 22:34–46	*Jesus Calls Us, O'er the Tumult; We Praise You with Our Minds, O Lord*

---

[11]Kimball, *When Religion Becomes Evil*, p. 39.

∾ Children's Lectionary Sermon

TITLE: Pleasing God

SCRIPTURE: 1 Thess. 2:1–8

KEY VERSE: *Our purpose is to please God, not people. He is the one who examines the motives of our hearts.* (1 Thess. 2:4b)

KEY CONCEPT: Pleasing God

MATERIALS: Bible

Have you ever tried to do something so someone would notice you? (*Let the children answer if there are any volunteers.*) A friend of mine said when he was little, there was a girl at church he really liked. She was also in his class at school. He tried to do something to get her attention and fell out of his chair and almost broke his nose.

Sometimes we do things to show our parents or others so they will be pleased with us. We want to be wanted. We want to be special. (*Open Bible.*) A long time ago, Paul wrote a letter to the church in Thessalonica to encourage them. In this letter he wrote, "Our purpose is to please God, not people. He is the one who examines the motives of our hearts." Paul wanted to let the people know that to be God's followers he had learned to please God, not people. He told how they showed them love because they were God's people. They were caring when they were there with them because God was the one who helped them love. When he wrote, "God knew the motives of our hearts," Paul was saying that God knew why Paul loved the way he loved. God knew everything about Paul. Paul could not hide his feelings or thoughts from God.

Sometimes it can be hard to be God's followers. We want to please others to get attention instead of trying to please others by helping them. When we say we love God, God wants us to be his helpers and to please him with all we do and say. God knows our thoughts and how we feel. We can pray to God to help us have good thoughts and to please God with what we choose to do and say.—Marcia Thompson

☙ WORSHIP AIDS ☙

Call to Worship: We are a liberated people, made so through the work of grace that has come in Jesus Christ. Here we stand—and celebrate! "Stand fast, therefore, in the liberty wherewith Christ has made us free" (Gal. 5:1).

Invocation: Mighty God, who holds the earth and all the world in your hands, to you we come in worship. Stir up, teach us, inform us, and mold us in the image of your dear son, Jesus, and may our lives reflect the high priorities that faith demands. Amen.

Offertory Sentence: "He who has a bountiful eye shall be blessed; for he gives of his bread to the poor" (Prov. 22:9).

Offertory Prayer: Gracious and loving Father, we offer these gifts, the fruit of our labor, to you out of the abundance of your gifts to us. Accept and perfect these gifts that they may inspire within us a deeper love for you and a greater desire to build your Kingdom—here and all places in the world. Amen.

Morning Prayer: Eternal God, our heavenly Father, on this day of worship we see again that every single day is a precious gift; every minute is fragile; every hour is valuable, and life goes quickly by. O Lord, we know that to be conscious of time is a mark of our humanity and our mortality. All our awareness depends on it—remembering the past, looking forward to the future. Comparing moment with moment, we experience hope and fear, satisfaction and regret, pain and happiness. And we give thee thanks for the capacity to learn, to grow, and to forgive. Now we ask forgiveness, O God, for the times we have deceived a loved one or a dear friend. And we ask forgiveness for all the times we have thought of ourselves and our own needs, and less of the needs of another who is close to us. So just now we pray for one whose life would be lifted if we just made a phone call. And just now, we visualize and pray for one who we know needs healing. We name and pray for one who needs to be comforted. We've been unwilling to forgive others and yet have the audacity to ask you, O Lord, to forgive us. And so just now, we pray for that person against whom we carry a grudge, either a little slight or a deep resentment.

It is on this day of worship that we stop to take hold and to take stock of our lives, praying that we will see you in our moments and in our days, that we will see you in our work and in our leisure, in our sorrow and in our joy, in our hopes and in our despairs, that we will see you in our families and loved ones and our friends and in this fellowship. So bless us, O God, as we come together to catch a vision of your glory and a vision of the persons we want to be in the Spirit of Christ. Amen.—George L. Davis

Benediction: We go today in the power of the Living One. His presence—one that disturbs and comforts us—goes before us. May we in these days walk with our God, Father, Son, and Holy Spirit, and be encouraged for the faithful living of our days. Amen.

SUNDAY, NOVEMBER 2, 2008
All Saints' Sunday

LECTIONARY SERMON TOPIC: "Accepting God's Challenge"

TEXT: Josh. 3:7–17

OTHER READINGS: Ps. 107:1–7, 33–37; 1 Thess. 2:9–13; Matt. 23:1–12

Wes Seeliger, in *Western Theology,*[1] a satire of sorts, confronts Christianity with a great many of our weaknesses. The Church, he says, has fallen out of favor with a great many people. Seeliger suggests that we have the wrong mental images attached to faith. He gives two contrasting images to clarify the issue: the *settler spirit* and the *pioneer spirit*. The settler spirit was satisfied with the surrounding conditions. He liked where he was and would fight to protect his territory. The pioneer spirit, on the other hand, was never settled. Adventure was his middle name. For him, life was forever a new and exciting pilgrimage.

---

[1]Wes Seeliger, *Western Theology* (Atlanta: Forum House, 1973).

I. **It's not hard to see where the thrust of the Biblical witness is.** The book of Joshua is clear. God's people are a people on the move. God has been called "the great deity of the road." Look at it broadly. God called Moses to lead his people out of Egypt. They came to a mountain—Sinai—and were reminded of the covenant. The harsh wilderness disciplined and prepared them for their destination. It seems to be that way with God's people. We begin in liberation and proceed to covenant formation. Then there is our wilderness training. But only then are we able to think about settling down—and that only beyond the river.

Their deepest desire was to enter the Promised Land. It began as a glimmer of hope in Egypt. But after forty years of wandering, their desire reached fever pitch. They stood on Jordan's stormy banks and cast a wishful eye into Canaan's fair and happy land. But standing between them and their desire was this river—one more time. They had fought the good fight but had not yet finished the course. There was this river. By this time, the spring of the year, the snow caps of Mt. Hermon had melted and caused the river to be at its highest. There were no bridges to cross, no ferries to ride, no shallow shoals to wade—only the deep and fear-laden waters of the Jordan. Perhaps they feared they would never make it all the way home.

We have all been to that river, many times. The river is there whenever we risk a new adventure: a marriage, a birth, a child's first day at school, a graduation, a career, a move, buying a home, aging, even death. Wherever fear is, there is that river.

II. **What then to do? The Bible helps us here.** Here is the word to God's pilgrim people: "When you see the ark of the covenant of the Lord your God, and the priests, the Levites, bearing it, then you shall set out from our place and go after it. Yet there shall be a space between you of about two thousand cubits. Do not come near it, that you may know the way by which you must go, for you have not passed this way before" (vv. 3–4). The Ark of the Covenant was only a simple wooden box, forty-five inches by twenty-seven inches. It got its significance for what it represented. Inside were relics from Israel's holy history: Moses' rod, some manna, and the tablets of the Ten Commandments. The ark represented the presence of God. "When you see the ark being carried before you, set out and follow it."

And in the end, beyond our reading, we learn how it ended. Verse 17 declares: "Then the priests who bore the ark of the covenant of the Lord stood firm on dry ground in the midst of the Jordan; and all Israel crossed over on dry ground, until all the people had crossed completely over the Jordan." Do you hear what it says? When God moves out ahead of us, we are to get up and go with God. That's how we face and cross the swollen rivers of life.

III. **The Ark was the symbol of God's presence.** It was built with rings along its sides into which poles were inserted for carrying. There was no static legalism here. The God of the Covenant was on the move. It's a funny thing about the Ark of the Covenant. With so much significance put on it, you never hear about it after the Temple is built. Somehow the symbol of the times changed. Maybe that's why they were told to walk behind it two thousand cubits (almost a thousand yards). It was a way of saying, "don't get too attached to this thing." It's only going to be here for a while. When you enter the new land, a new faith will be required. The God you have known in the wilderness has something new and vital in store for you. Be ready for it.

Where is God moving among us? All around us—in the renewed sense of commitment that so many of our people feel, in the vitality of our children, in the warmth of our fellowship, in the sense of "being" the family of faith. If ever we can stop long enough to listen, we'll find that God is near. Having a God who cares is a thrilling thing.

IV. **Notice the movement of God's people.** God's people go where God goes. God is at work in our world and in us. God is on the move, and we go with him. That sounds simple enough. Yet the journey is not simple. Crossing the river, reaching the land of promise, begins with deep belief on the part of every believer.

For us, the journey extends in two directions. There is a journey inward. It is intensely spiritual. The inward journey provides depth of faith, strength of character, an inner resolve to be everything that God intends. There is also the journey outward. It is the life of service and ministry that flows out of the inward experience of grace. Much like an artesian well, it flows freely out of the depths, bubbling and effervescent. The journey inward provides depth; the journey outward provides fruitfulness. The first—the inward journey—

defines who we are. The second, the journey outward, describes the work we accomplish. One without the other is a counterfeit Christianity. We may be theologically correct and yet irrelevant to the world. Our future is still open, available for God to develop and to bless. Tomorrow is not yet determined. *"You've not passed this way before!"*

A passion-driven faith is required to claim the land beyond the river. Someone wrote, "A wolf never attacks a painted sheep." A wolf is not fooled by fakery, even if it is good fakery. Counterfeit Christianity fools no one. Either we choose to be resolved in our work of mercy and redemption, service and ministry, journey inward, journey outward, or we don't.

There is one other word in our text: Joshua said, "Sanctify yourselves, because tomorrow the Lord will do wonders among you" (v. 5). "Sanctify yourselves." What does that mean? For Israel, it may have meant ceremonial washing and sacrifices to be made on an altar. But outward expressions can have little to do with inward realities. And so we come today confessing our sin, accepting forgiveness, deepening commitments, and deciding within our hearts: "I have decided to follow Jesus, no turning back, no turning back." I wonder this morning, are we ready to move across the river? I think I hear the washing of many waves and the shuffling of many feet. God, let it be so!—Lee McGlone

ILLUSTRATIONS

Seeking, Finding. In C. S. Lewis's *The Last Battle*,[2] one of the enemy soldiers who had fought Aslan's forces all his life discovered in a vision that Aslan was the true Lord of Narnia. The soldier expected to be killed and then was confused when Aslan welcomed him warmly. The Lion told him that because he had searched long and hard for the true God, he had found what he was looking for.—Richard Vinson

Fair-weather Christians. John Bunyan, in his classic work, *The Pilgrim's Progress*, depicts those whose small faith is insufficient to see them through the

---

[2]C. S. Lewis, *The Last Battle* (New York: HarperCollins, 1956), pp. 154–155.

hard days. In the allegory, Christian and Hopeful confront Mr. By-ends, who describes the people who live in the town called Fair-speech: "We differ in religion from the stricter sort. We never strive against the wind and love to walk with Him when the sun shines and when people applaud him." Christian replies, "If you will go with us you must go against the wind . . . and you must stand by Him when bound in irons as well as when he walks the streets with applause." Then By-ends makes his decision: "I will never depart my old principles. They seem harmless and profitable." So Christian and Hopeful left Mr. By-ends with others who shared his goals, Mr. Hold-the-World, Mr. Money-Love, and Mr. Save-All.—Lee McGlone

Musical Selections Appropriate to the Day

All Saints' Sunday hymn suggestion: *For All the Saints*
Hymn suggestions for lectionary texts:

Josh. 3:7–17	*Guide Me, O Thou Great Jehovah*
Ps. 107:1–7, 33–37	*Now Thank We All Our God*
1 Thess. 2:9–13	*Day by Day*
Matt. 23:1–12	*Will You Let Me Be Your Servant?*

∾ Children's Lectionary Sermon

TITLE: Look at Me!

SCRIPTURE: Matt. 23:1–12

KEY VERSE: *But those who exalt themselves will be humbled, and those who humble themselves will be exalted.* (Matt. 23:12)

KEY CONCEPT: Being humble

MATERIALS: Bible

(*Share a personal story, or use the one presented here.*) I remember when I was little, I wanted my dad or my mom to notice what I was doing. I was really excited when I learned how to swim and jump in the water. I yelled to my mom and dad, "Watch me—look what I can do!" I would jump and swim. Then I would look to them and they would say, "That's great!"

Have you ever wanted to get your parents' attention to show them something you could do? (*Let some children share their experiences.*) We want to share the new things we learn. Did you know that in the Bible there were some grown-ups who wanted people to see them for the wrong reasons?

(*Open Bible to Matthew 23.*) One day, Jesus was teaching his disciples. He explained to them that the Pharisees were the teachers of God's Word, but they didn't do what they taught about God's Word. Jesus called them show-offs. They did things so other people could look at them to see how good they were.

Jesus said in Matthew 23:12, "But those who exalt themselves will be humbled, and those who humble themselves will be exalted. Jesus was teaching the people about being humble. Humble people live life simply without being show-offs about what they do to follow God's ways. Humble people will be exalted in God's eyes. This means they will have a place of honor before God.

This doesn't mean we can't show those new things we learn to the people we care about. Jesus is teaching us that being humble in our actions with others as we follow God's way means we will serve and help others to know God's love without ever having to say "look at me."—Marcia Thompson

☙ WORSHIP AIDS ☙

Call to Worship: God is both creator and sustainer of life. We stand amazed in God's presence and at his glorious work. With others through the ages we declare, "The Lord by wisdom has founded the earth; by understanding he has established the heavens. By his knowledge the depths are broken up, and the clouds drop down the dew" (Prov. 3:19–20).

Invocation: Creator God, you have formed the world in beauty and majesty. Open our eyes to behold your handiwork. May we see clearly your imprint on all that exists. Especially, may we see in the life and work of our Savior, Jesus Christ, your intent for all of creation. Help us to serve with gladness the One for whom all things were created. Amen.

Offertory Sentence: "I have showed you all things, how that in your labor you ought to support the weak, and to remember the words of the Lord Jesus, how he said, 'It is more blessed to give than to receive'" (Acts 20:35).

Offertory Prayer: Lord, yours is the greatness and the power and the glory. All that is made is yours, the cattle of a thousand hills—and also the hills. Our daily needs, and more than our needs, are met by your bounty. Give to us the grace necessary to give generously, cheerfully, and sacrificially that the needs of your church in the world will be fully met. Amen.

Morning Prayer: Father, across the centuries we hear your ancient call to your people that they would come to you and receive your grace, forgiveness, comfort, and peace. Let that same call register with us this morning as we gather in this sacred place to worship you. Stir our hearts and convince us of the need to open our lives to the sweeping power of your Spirit, who longs to fill us and guide us as we journey across life's terrain. From this hour may we rise up as God-stirred people to do your will and bring to our world the blessings wrought for us by Jesus Christ, even as have the saints through the ages.—Henry Fields

Benediction: We depart this place in peace and go out prepared to live peacefully. As we go, be assured of God's presence to lead the way. May we be found faithful to the callings of God upon us and be brought back safely to this place again next Lord's Day. Amen.

SUNDAY, NOVEMBER 9, 2008

LECTIONARY SERMON TOPIC: "We Believe in the Blessed Hope"
TEXT: 1 Thess. 4:13–18
OTHER READINGS: Josh. 24:1–3a, 14–25; Ps. 78:1–7; Matt. 25:1–13

The question of life's destiny is the heart of the Christian gospel. Philosophers have raised the question since the beginning of human thought, though today there is severe skepticism abroad as to whether *any* answer can be given. It has been said that a philosopher is one who lives in a dark cellar looking for a black cat that isn't there and the theologian as one who claims to have found it. Do we dare raise the issue for our world today? Indeed, we do. Indeed, we must.

I. **The blessed hope signals God's direction for the world.** It declares that history will be brought to its rightful conclusion in God's own time. Some talk about the doctrine of the "end times" and may well miss the meaning of it unless we define "end" as a goal to be reached. What God began in Creation, God completes. Paul understood that some in Thessalonica were concerned that Christ had not yet appeared. Years had passed, and some in their membership had died. Had the return of Christ already occurred? Was there no longer hope that they would see their loved ones again? How were they to think of life, death, and eternity? They wanted to know, "What is the purpose of life? Where is it going?"

Paul wrote to alleviate their worries: "Brothers, we do not want you to be ignorant about those who fall asleep, or to grieve like the rest of men, who have no hope" (v. 13). Pay attention to these three words: *ignorant, grieve,* and *hope*. These are the three major problems that people have who don't understand the blessed hope. Paul was saying, "I don't want you to go through the rest of your life in sadness or dejection and with nothing to live for. Unbelievers speak that message. Unbelievers have no clue about the afterlife. But we do! We know that there is life after death. We know that there is hope beyond the grave." Paul remembered the words of Jesus: "I've come from the Father, and I return to the Father" (John 14:12).

II. **The blessed hope is assurance of the Savior's return.** When you hear the phrase, "the second coming of Christ," what comes to your mind? Perhaps fear that accompanies judgment? Or the mindless dating of the end of the world by unscrupulous, self-appointed prophets? Or the image of tanks lumbering across the valley of Megido? Or perhaps a sigh? After all, how is all this important? Let me add another. What about the certainty of God's ownership of the earth and God's supremacy in time and eternity!

There is a great deal of fascination with the second coming of Christ. Thousands of books have been written on the subject. A number of authors have attracted attention with their "predictions" of an imminent return. Dating back to the first century, even to Paul himself, there was the sense of a hurried return of Christ. The Thessalonian Christians were no different. Some quit their jobs and waited in idleness. Paul suggested that if such people refused to work, neither should they eat. He believed we should make the most of life between now and then.

We have a somewhat contradictory belief about the presence of Christ among us. We believe that Christ is already here. He said so: "And, lo, I am with you always." But in another way, Christ is not here. That is, he is not here as he will be here in some future day. How that day will come, and when, we don't and can't know. All human efforts to qualify that event fall short of their goal and often come close to blasphemy. Sufficient for us is the mystery with which the Scriptures clothe these themes. Faithful unknowing may well represent our stance. But the word of assurance is absolutely clear. There is a direction toward which our world is moving. God's well-designed universe isn't haphazard. We are going somewhere. We have a hope that the world cannot understand, because we know for a certainty that Christ is coming again.

III. **The blessed hope affirms the resurrection of the dead.** Death is not the end. The grave is not the final resting place! Paul states that when Christ returns, it will be these "dead" individuals who will rise first. The Greeks of old believed in a natural immortality of the soul. Christian faith never has. We believe in resurrection of the dead: "This mortal must put on immortality." And it comes with the territory of faith.

Verse 17 is a joy for the believer. Paul discusses the death and Resurrection of Christ, then the death and future resurrection of the dead in Christ. But praise God, Jesus doesn't leave out those who are still alive. When Jesus returns in the clouds, he not only raises the bodies of the believing dead; those living are caught up with him to forever be with the Lord. Aren't you glad that God didn't leave anyone out? Those who by faith have continually believed in the finished work of redemption, whether already deceased or alive at his coming, will be taken up in the clouds to be with Jesus throughout all eternity. Although currently living in a body corrupted by the disease of sin, the believer will receive a new body, translated in a twinkling of an eye. It will be a body of purity and holiness. It will be like Jesus.

IV. **The blessed hope is our source of eternal comfort.** Verse 18 says, "Therefore, let us encourage one another with these words." Some here today know what it's like to lose a loved one, grandparent, parent, wife, husband, child, or friend. Some have worked through the grief. But for others the pain is still real. You can't imagine trying to get through the rest of your life alone. And you may wonder, "Do I really want to go on living? I miss my loved ones so much. Life isn't the same without them."

If you have ever known these feelings, then this word of God is for you. It declares a light at the end of the tunnel. Life doesn't end. As we trust the Lord, we discover strength for each new day and, in the end, a glorious celebration of new life that never ends. This is the blessed hope, and on it we stand.—Lee McGlone

ILLUSTRATIONS

Hope. I recall sitting in a chapel service at the United Theological Seminary in Monroe, Louisiana, and experiencing for the first time the "lining" of a hymn. The worship leader would sing the "line" of a hymn called, "I Don't Get No Ways Tired," and the congregation would respond. It went like this: "I'm working on a building . . . it has a sure foundation . . . because I'm holding up the blood stained banner of my Lord . . . I never get tired working on the building . . . a sure foundation . . . holding up the blood stained banner of my Lord . . . Just as soon as I'm through working on the building . . . I'm going on to heaven—to get my reward." Then the leader declared in a thunderous voice, "That will be a glad reunion day. With all the holy angels and loved ones to stay, that will be a glad reunion day." And in my heart, I rejoiced. What a blessed hope!—Lee McGlone

Victory. Two men heard a sermon about the end times. The first man said, "I just can't understand this stuff. It's way over my head." The second replied, "I think I have the gist of it. And I can sum up the end times in two words." The first asked, "Well, which two words are those?" The second declared, "We win!"

"Are you sure," someone may ask, "of the blessed hope?" The believing community says, "Yes, we are sure!" Either God's purpose for the world will be fulfilled and God will take us to himself, perhaps today or in another thousand years or more—or very soon, within the limits of a human lifetime, a death, we will go to be with him. Either way, we are sure. Our Savior keeps his promises.—Lee McGlone

Musical Selections Appropriate to the Day

Hymn suggestions for lectionary texts:

Josh. 24:1–3a, 14–25	*The Family Prayer Song; I Have Decided to Follow Jesus*
Ps. 78:1–7	*Faith of Our Fathers*
1 Thess. 4:13–18	*How Great Thou Art; It Is Well with My Soul*
Matt. 25:1–13	*Wake, Awake, for Night Is Flying*

⁓⁓ Children's Lectionary Sermon

TITLE: God's Stories for Us

SCRIPTURE: Ps. 78:1–7

KEY VERSE: *We will not hide these truths from our children but will tell the next generation about the glorious deeds of the Lord. We will tell of his power and the mighty miracles he did.* (Ps. 78:4, New International Version)

KEY CONCEPT: God's Word

MATERIALS: Bible, words to Bible songs familiar to the children or to you

PREPARATION: Enlist someone to lead Bible songs that tell various stories from Scripture, such as *Joshua Fought the Battle at Jericho, Zacchaeus Was a Wee Little Man, Jesus Loves Me, Father Abraham,* or others familiar to you or the leader. You may even want to choose a hymn to sing that emphasizes the narrative of Scripture.

There are many different songs we can sing together that tell stories from the Bible. (*If you are brave, you can ask the children to share some of their favorites, or if you have someone else to help lead songs, use this time to do a few. Include the congregation in the singing.*)

We have sung some songs that tell about different people of the Bible. What are some of your favorite Bible stories? (*Let the children answer and tell about the key message of the story they share.*)

Every Sunday we come together to study and hear God's Word. We hear stories of how people learned to trust God and how God helped them. God sent them leaders to help them learn God's ways. God did miracles to help God's people. In Psalm 78, the writer of this song also tells us how important it is to tell the stories of what God has done. (*Open Bible.*) In Psalm 78:4 it says, "We will not hide these truths from our children but will tell the next generation about the glorious deeds of the Lord. We will tell of his power and the mighty miracles he did."

This is why we think it is important to come together each Sunday and read Scripture. We are able to share with you the stories of God's love so that you can tell them to your children when you grow up and have families. We also share with each other ways that God helps us today when we have people tell about what God has done for them. We want you to know the stories of God because God loves you, and we love you, too. God's Word is important to us because we can learn how God wants us to live.—Marcia Thompson

☙ WORSHIP AIDS ☙

Call to Worship: The presence of Jesus Christ brings new life to his people. We rejoice and honor his name. "If you then are risen with Christ, seek those things which are above, where Christ sits on the right hand of God" (Col. 3:1).

Invocation: Father, you who brought from the dead our Lord Jesus Christ, enable us by your presence to live as people of the Resurrection. Help us to walk in newness of life. Lift our thoughts and intentions high above the intrusions of life that would steal away our delight. Let your purpose be fulfilled in us. Amen.

Offertory Sentence: "Whatever you do, do it heartily as unto the Lord, and not unto men; knowing that of the Lord you shall receive the reward of inheritance; for you serve the Lord Christ" (Col. 3:23).

Offertory Prayer: Gracious Lord, you have perfectly modeled the high virtue of giving. Teach us to give gladly and cheerfully from the fruits of our labor for the cause of your Kingdom. Bless these offerings that they may meet the immediate and long-term needs of your church, both here and around the world. And, Father, give us joy in the doing of it. Amen.

Morning Prayer: Our Father, we come to you with thanksgiving and praise, but not with words only. We come with deep commitments, surrendered wills, and humble hearts. Grant today the experience of your presence. Let this hour be a time of honest appraisal, of introspection and searching, and a time for renewing and deepening of faith.

Lord, we need you. We need you more than anything. We need you in the rising of the sun and in its setting, in the dusk and in the dawn. We need you in this place. We need you in our homes and in our offices, in our schools, in our communities—and within our hearts. We need you in the depths of our souls where personhood lies, in the moods through which we wander, in the highs and lows, the ups and downs, in the quiet and the noise, in the hope and in the dread. Lord, we need you every hour.

We rejoice that you are with us, just as you promised, and will be until the end of the age, when you will then come and receive us unto yourself, that where you are we shall be also, or else you would have told us. In Christ we pray, Amen.—Lee McGlone

Benediction: Go with God in the days of this week. Walk in his steps and in his strength. Listen to his Word and obey his voice. Rejoice in the opportunities that rise before us and find great joy along the way. Amen.

SUNDAY, NOVEMBER 16, 2008

LECTIONARY SERMON TOPIC: "Courageous Faith"
TEXT: Judg. 4:1–7; Matt. 25:14–30
OTHER READINGS: Ps. 123 or 76; 1 Thess. 5:1–11

The Scriptures today speak about watchfulness. It is a timely theme. Terrorism, war, hatred, suspicion, unsettledness—these are the emotions of our day. Ours is a day to keep our guard up. We are well monitored and electronically tracked: "Every step you take, every move you make, I'll be watching you," says a popular song. But are we, really, a vigilant society? Not really. Because security measures, despite their high technology, cannot offer anything like what is offered in the Scripture.

I. **In Judges 4, more is told of the seemingly endless cycle of Israelite covenant-breaking, consequence, and deliverance in the Promised Land.** "The Israelites cried out to the Lord for help; for [Sisera] had nine hundred chariots of iron, and had oppressed the Israelites cruelly twenty years." Who were the watchers? There was no general, but there was a prophet named Deborah who led the army into battle for liberation. In the end, Israel prevailed and then thanked God for their deliverance in what is called "The Song of Deborah" (located in chapter 5), which is still repeated today. Who arose in the hour of need? Deborah arose as one who watched over her children.

What is this all about? Simply this: watchfulness is not the possession of powerful egos—the kings and princes and mighty men. It is first the work of the prophet who sees the way and will of God and who seeks justice for all. Deborah was a leader but not from a throne room. She sat under a palm tree up in the hills of Ephraim, between north and south Israel, where she could "see" the nation. From that vantage point, she discerned God's voice. Such watchfulness is the requirement of our day. Spiritual watchfulness is alert to the moral dilemmas of the day, as was Martin Luther in pre-Reformation days and as Martin Luther King Jr. was during the civil rights movement of the 1960s. Such watchfulness was careful and attentive long before the first steps were made to initiate change and long after change had begun. This is what Paul commended to the Thessalonians. Watchfulness, vigilance, is required, as danger arises like a "thief in the night" and as suddenly as labor pains. In such times, we must not fall asleep or be drunk with vain glory. Our destination is eternal salvation and, therefore, we are to "encourage one another and build one another up." The watchman is not a doomsayer, not a pessimist. Instead, the vigilant watchman is one who sees the moving hand of God in the events of human life, even in the most tragic.

II. **Look at the parable in Matthew 25 where vigilance is demanded of those who will follow Jesus Christ.** It is the parable about the servants who invested their master's money and about one who didn't. It has an awful lot to do with vigilance. The parable begins as do others: "the kingdom of heaven is like . . ." This is the way the kingdom of heaven works. There is some mystery here. I have always felt sorry for the servant given only one talent, instead of two or five like the others. Why did he receive less? Was he less deserving? And his master's treatment seemed so harsh. After all, he gave back what he had been given to take care of. That made him trustworthy, didn't it?

Let's stop a moment and talk about this money. In fact, each of the men was given a lot of money. The Greek "talent" was worth fifteen years' wages for a laborer, perhaps about $300,000. So while the last of the three servants got the least, he still got a lot. Why he was given one-half or one-fifth the others' amounts we cannot know. What we can know is that he sensed no responsibility to do anything with it, except to place it safely where no one could find it. The parable hinges on what the other two servants did with their money. They hadn't earned it either. But they took what they received and invested it vigorously in order to make more money. They put into action that with which they had been entrusted. This is how God's gifts work. We are graced by God's goodness and then called to invest that goodness in making change for the better—to invest it in the lives of the neighbor. God's good news can't be kept to ourselves. We cannot sit on it. We cannot neglect it. God's gifts are living gifts.

But the gift didn't seem real to the third servant. It was a burden he feared. It demanded too much. The consequences of receiving it were too great. He would rather have remained "ungifted." It is a curious thing that the unit of money described here is translated from the Greek as "talent." Our English word *talent*, however, doesn't refer to money but to the special abilities that gifted people possess that enable them to perform in unique ways. As such, these human abilities—musical, administrative, intellectual, and so on—are to be used for the common good and not for selfish ends. But the broader and deeper application declares the glorious gospel of Jesus as the "gift" we have received. It is the gospel in word and deed, on our lips and beneath our feet and in our pockets. Truly, we have been given much, whether we consider ourselves a one-talent, or a two-talent, or a five-talent person. Today, we hear this parable as if for the first time.

III. **We have often read this parable as a commendation of risk taking.** The risk takers, the courageous ones, took what they had and doubled it. But, truthfully, their courage is only superficial. Nothing really changed for them. They did what was expected. When the master returned, he said to them: "Well done, good and trustworthy slave—enter into the joy of your master." But they were still slaves. Their only joy was the property of the master's. They were more captive than ever.

If we substitute "God" for "the master" and "ourselves" for "the servants," then the "joy of the master" is granted only to those who perform well. Do we believe we can earn God's favor by performing well, or lose it by performing poorly? Of course, God invites us to risk. Love demands risks: marriage, parenting, church, culture. Our call is to live in the adventure of the grace of God, as did Deborah, who left her relatively safe position, who stepped out into the dominant patriarchal culture as a woman of insight—a watchman who saw clearly the moving hand of God, who risked her life in battle.

But most of all, may we live like our Savior, who clearly saw the mounting tragedy all around him. "Father, if there is any other way, let this cup pass from me—but nevertheless, not my will but thine be done." Father, we pray, give us courage both to see your hand at work in our lives and in our world and so to speak and live the noble gospel truth. Let it be.—Lee McGlone

---

ILLUSTRATIONS

Persistent Courage. Sojourner Truth, a former slave who preached against slavery in the 1840s, would go from city to city, trying to get people to see that God wanted slavery ended. Once a heckler said, "Old woman, do you think your talk about slavery does any good? Do you suppose people care what you say? Why, I don't care any more for your talk than I do for the bite of a flea." "Perhaps not," she replied, "but the Lord willing, I'll keep you scratching."[3]—Richard Vinson

---

[3]Cited in C. Douglas Weaver, *A Cloud of Witnesses* (Macon, GA: Smyth and Helwys, 1993), p. 134.

Unfailing Faith. A legend tells us that when Jesus returned to heaven he was asked by an angel: "What have you left behind to carry out the work?" Jesus answered, "A little band of men and women who love me." "But what if they fail when the trial comes? Will all you have done be defeated?" "Yes," said Jesus, "if they fail, all I have done will be defeated." "Is there nothing more?" "No," Jesus said, "there is nothing more." "What then?" "They will not fail," said Jesus. Nor will we.—George W. Hill

Musical Selections Appropriate to the Day

Hymn suggestions for lectionary texts:

Judg. 4:1–7	*Let All Things Now Living*
Ps. 123 or Ps. 76	*Mine Eyes Have Seen the Glory*
1 Thess. 5:1–11	*Soon and Very Soon; My Lord! What a Morning*
Matt. 25:14–30	*Come All Christians, Be Committed; God Whose Giving Knows No Ending*

Children's Lectionary Sermon

TITLE: Blocks of Encouragement

SCRIPTURE: 1 Thess. 5:1–11

KEY VERSE: *So encourage each other and build each other up, just as you are already doing.* (1 Thess. 5:11)

KEY CONCEPT: Encouragement

MATERIALS: Bible, thirty small wooden blocks

Today we are going to split up into two groups. (*Divide into two groups and choose a "builder" for each group. The others on the team are the builder's cheer-*

leaders.) I want the builder to come to the front, because you have a job to do. When I say, "go," I want you to build a tower as fast as you can. The rest of you will cheer for your builder. On your mark, get set, go! (*Let the children build for thirty seconds or so and then "accidentally" knock over the tower of the one who is ahead. Depending on the nature of the children, there will probably be a protest. Have the children come together to talk about what happened.*)

We had a race between (*child's name*) and (*child's name*). Each of you cheered and encouraged your builder. I have to confess, I knocked over your tower on purpose. How did you feel when you saw it fall? (*Let the builder respond.*) I did this because I wanted to help you understand something Paul asked the church members in Thessalonica to do for each other. He wrote (*open Bible*) in Thessalonians 5:11, "So encourage each other and build each other up, just as you are already doing."

We had our race and encouraged our team. We didn't want the blocks to fall down, and when they did, it caused us to have bad feelings toward each other. Paul was encouraging this church to continue living their lives as Christ had taught and to help each other do this. This is also true for us today. We don't want to cause bad feelings. We want to encourage and help each other to live as Jesus would want us to live. Think of some ways you can encourage someone this week and build him or her up.—Marcia Thompson

❧ WORSHIP AIDS ❧

Call to Worship: God draws us to himself that we may become all that God intends. We praise God for the mighty acts of his grace: "Praise the Lord. I will praise the Lord with my whole heart, in the assembly of the upright, and in the congregation" (Ps. 111:1).

Invocation: Father, we gather in your house as your people to express our love and devotion. Come and be with us. Make your presence known among us. In sermon, song, prayer, and fellowship, we would speak boldly your saving message. For the cause of your Kingdom, we pray. Amen.

Offertory Sentence: "Walk in love, as Christ has also loved us, and has given himself for us as an offering and a sacrifice to God for a sweet smelling savor" (Eph. 5:2).

Offertory Prayer: Generous God, accept our tithes of your rich bounty that at this time of harvest we may ever be thankful and faithful stewards of our many blessings. Amen.—E. Lee Phillips

Morning Prayer: Our God, though you have told us in your Word that your throne is always open to us and that you take delight in our prayers, still we find it hard to pray. And though we believe the promise that where our prayers are inadequate, your Spirit prays for us with language beyond language, still it's hard to pray. But you are our only hope and salvation. We have nowhere else to go. So we lift our voices again in the hope that the words we choose will truly reflect the reality and the needs of our hearts.

See us, we pray, as we really are, as we truly are. We are people with both hopes and fears, so grant your blessed assurance and your comfort as we offer in a moment of silence those hopes and fears to your tender mercy. See us as we really are: people with friends and loved ones who are sick in body or sick in spirit and who need your healing touch. Grant us the assurance that touch is forthcoming, as we offer them by name to you. See us as we are: people who are part of the great society and partly responsible for both the good and the evil in it. So grant us both the wisdom and the power to make this world a more lovely and loving place, as we bring to you our strong desires for a peaceful world.

Now we thank you, our Father, that having prayed, it wasn't so hard after all. May your Spirit remind us to open our hearts to your gracious love more often. You are the source of our being and the ground of our confidence in the future. So help us to pray without ceasing and to celebrate the gift of this life without compromise. We pray this through him who came that we might have life. Amen.—Bob Morley

Benediction: People of God, depart today in the joy of the Risen and living Lord Jesus Christ. Go forth bearing in word and deed the message of Christ's salvation. And may the peace of God, which passes all understanding, be your hope and shield. Amen.

SUNDAY, NOVEMBER 23, 2008
Christd the King Sunday

LECTIONARY SERMON TOPIC: "The Power Within"
TEXT: Eph. 1:15–23
OTHER READINGS: Ezek. 34:11–16, 20–24; Ps. 100; Matt. 25:31–46

The Thanksgiving season motivates us to consider reverently and gratefully the gifts of life. Hopefully, in these days we will pause to say, "God, thank you." But gratitude is no certainty. Today, we look at a text that declares within us the power to live gratefully. By faith we have the creativity and encouragement to move through life unafraid and victorious. As Paul wrote to the Ephesians, he gave thanks to God for the power that was at work within them. Their faith in the Lord and love for the saints had not gone unnoticed. His words of gratitude offer insight into how we, in our day, may, like those in days of old, live and express a vital thanksgiving through the power at work in us.

I. **We possess the power of patience.** Paul said he had heard, and continued to hear, of the Ephesians' faith. Paul prayed for them and continued to pray for them, giving thanks. He patiently listened and patiently spoke. Here is one of the difficulties our culture faces. We have learned that we need not wait for anything. Instant gratification is the value we honor. Instead of a fine meal, prepared meticulously, we choose fast food. We want our Web sites and our churches to be more user-friendly. If prayer doesn't "work," according to our definition and calendar, then we are quick to quit praying. If the Bible offers complexities not readily resolved, we move on to the latest fad. Patient waiting seems to be a left-over relic from our more primitive past. A patient person can become a thankful person.

II. **We are armed with the power to bless.** Notice Paul's words: "I ask that your minds may be opened to see God's light, so that you will know what is the hope to which he has called you, how rich are the wonderful blessings he promises his people, and how very great is his power at work in those of us who understand. This power working in us is the same as the mighty strength which God used when he raised Christ from death. . . ."

What God has brought to us, he works through us for the world. The French priest and philosopher, Teilhard de Chardin, wrote of a coming day when after we had mastered the elements of the physical world that we would move to harness the energy of love. Then, armed with God's gift of love in our hands, mankind would, for the second time, discover fire. Such blessing renders gratitude.

III. **We submit to the power greater than ourselves.** Paul says that we can bring into every circumstance of life the same power as "the mighty strength that raised Christ." Jesus walked confidently among those who found authority in a legal code to which they gave homage. Such laws enabled them to judge one another and to believe that salvation rested only in their system and in the performance of it. But Jesus saw and declared a better way: "Don't you know that I must be about my father's business?"; "Get behind me, Satan, for you seek the things of man and not the things of God"; "Father, let this cup pass from me, but nevertheless, not my will but thine be done." Perhaps the best we can do is to get our personal interests out of the way and conform to the moving Spirit of God within us. "We are to put all things under his feet."

IV. **We gladly participate alongside God for the redemption of the world.** "He gave Jesus Christ to be the head over all things to the church, which is the fullness of him that fills all in all." The work of the church is to be Christ's body in the world. As God's power and love are at work in us, God's intention is fulfilled through us. When the power of God's love flows through us, mountains move, hatreds cease, suspicion yields to trust, forgiveness is freely received and given, generosity increases, peacefulness persists, and thanksgiving abounds. These are the results of the power within.

I have read of a church in London that has above its entry into the sanctuary a sign with only three words: think and thank. The meaning is obvious. If we truly stop to think more, surely we would stop to thank more.—Lee McGlone

ILLUSTRATIONS

Word Studies: The apostle Paul's desire for the Ephesians is that they understand God's power. He uses four different Greek words to emphasize the greatness of God's power. From the word *dunamis,* we draw the words *dynamite* and *dynamo.* It is the "surpassing greatness of His power to us who believe." It is all we need for faithful living. The word *energea* is the word from which we derive "working." It is the force of the Spirit that gives energy to live effectually for the Lord. Paul uses the word *kratos* as "strength." It is the power of his might (1 Tim. 6:16), not human strength. Paul uses *ischus* to define "might," that is, the abilities we have that we could never achieve on our own. Paul did not pray for power to be given to these believers but that they would become aware of the power they already had. In further chapters, Paul encouraged them to use that power in fruitful living for the Lord Jesus Christ.—Lee McGlone

Thanksgiving. Certainly, one of the things I am most grateful for this Thanksgiving Day weekend is the fact that I am learning, little by little, to live in the realm of God's mysterious and abiding love and that in the process I have found more of my real self. It was in the back of this very sanctuary that I took my first steps in deeply trusting God's existence in my life. It took place nearly eight years ago as I struggled with the direction of my career. I was working in the corporate sector at the time. I felt pulled to put my faith and relationship with God at the center of my work and lifestyle instead of on the side, away from the heart of my daily routine and choices.—Lael P. Murphy

Musical Selections Appropriate to the Day

Christ the King Sunday hymn suggestion: *Crown Him with Many Crowns*
Hymn suggestions for lectionary texts:

Ezek. 34:11–16, 20–24	*Rain Down*
Ps. 100	*All People That on Earth Do Dwell*
Eph. 1:15–23	*Rejoice the Lord Is King; Open Our Eyes, Lord*
Matt. 25:31–46	*Take My Life and Let It Be; God Whose Giving Knows No Ending*

☙ Children's Lectionary Sermon

TITLE: In Everything Everywhere

SCRIPTURE: Eph. 1:15–23

KEY VERSES: *Now he is far above any ruler or authority or power or leader or anything else in this world or in the world to come . . . and the church is his body; it is filled by Christ, who fills everything everywhere with his presence.* (Eph. 1:21, 23, New International Version)

KEY CONCEPT: Christ the King

MATERIALS: Bible, crown, pictures of real kings and queens from various countries (can be found on the Internet)

(*Have the crown in your hands or at a central place for the children to see.*) What do I have here? (*Let the children answer and reflect back their answers.*) Who wears a crown? (*Let the children answer. They may say king, ruler, queen, or something similar.*) I brought some pictures of real kings and queens. (*Show the children the pictures, and tell them what country they are from.*) These are real people whose job is to be king or queen.

Did you know today is a special day in the church year? We all look forward to Advent, which leads to Christmas, and sometimes miss this important Sunday. Today is Christ the King Sunday. We celebrate Christ's presence in everything everywhere. We celebrate Christ as the ruler over all of earth and heaven. This means Christ is present with us everywhere.

(*Open Bible.*) In Paul's letter to the Ephesians, he wrote, "Now he is far above any ruler or authority or power or leader or anything else in this world or in the world to come . . . and the church is his body; it is filled by Christ, who fills everything everywhere with his presence." We can be glad Christ is with us and can help us everywhere we go.—Marcia Thompson

☙ WORSHIP AIDS ☙

Call to Worship: Thanksgiving rises from our hearts as we celebrate Christ's rule over us and over all things. We echo the thoughts of the seer of Revelation: "Then the seventh angel blew his trumpet, and there were loud voices in heaven, saying, 'The power to rule over the world belongs now to our Lord and his Messiah, and he will rule forever and ever!'" (Rev. 11:15).

Invocation: Lord, in our bounty we have much for which to be grateful. We know neither hunger nor deprivation. Hear our thankfulness for blessings too numerous to count and our praise overflowing for all we have been given through Christ our Lord. Amen.—E. Lee Phillips

Offertory Sentence: "Offer unto God thanksgiving and pay our vows unto the Lord Most High" (Ps. 50:14).

Offertory Prayer: We come with not just the gift of the hand, O Lord, but of the heart, for we give as stewards with gratitude and praise to Christ our King. Amen.—E. Lee Phillips

Morning Prayer: Lord God, in these important moments we look for you. We seek the vital sense of your presence with us as we pray. We ask that you will make this time special as we try to open our hearts and lift our souls to you. We come first of all in thanksgiving, and we pray that our living may somehow reflect a humble gratitude for the abundance of our wealth, that we might truly live as thankful people.

We pray that you will give us the gift of simplicity, that you will spare us from greed, that you will teach us compassion, that you will restore to us some of our youthful idealism and our commitment to justice for all your children. We pray that you will tune our heart to the message of Jesus, which speaks grace and relief to all who suffer. We realize this morning, O God, that when we pray to be like him, we surely ask more than we know. And yet, this is our prayer, our tentative quest for a more excellent way. Hear our prayers, O God, as we ask them in the name of Christ. Amen.—Charles F. Hoffman

Benediction: Now may the eternal presence of the Lord Jesus Christ walk with you and keep you company in the days of this week. May his Word and way become your very own. And may his peace be with you, now and forevermore. Amen.

SUNDAY, NOVEMBER 30, 2008
First Sunday in Advent

LECTIONARY SERMON TOPIC: "A Cry from the Depths of Human Darkness"
TEXT: Isa. 64:1–9
OTHER READINGS: Ps. 80:1–7, 17–19; Mark 13:24–37; 1 Cor. 1:3–9

How can we ever forget the destruction and devastation left in the wake of Hurricane Katrina. Months, even years of repair and restoration will not wipe away the disaster visited upon the Gulf Coast of the United States. Many serious questions have been asked about that destructive natural event. One that is often heard by God-fearing folks is this: "Why would God let a thing like that happen to his people?" There is no easy answer to that question, even though some have tried to equate the disaster with the sins of the nation. Such answers are not new.

Long ago, Israel—the darling of God's heart—had met monumental disaster. It came in two stages. Exile had claimed the elite of the land, who had been marched off the Babylon as captives, there to spend seventy years amid pagan people who knew unprecedented luxury and power. Once the leaders had been moved from the Promised Land, the less fortunate and less skilled in managing national affairs were visited with poverty and corruption, as well as cruel management by those left in power positions. Prophets and insightful people of Israel viewed these disastrous happenings as a result of Israel's sin and turning from following the leadership of the Lord God. Surely, these thinkers and proclaimers thought, the resulting circumstances of exile and shame that had befallen the people would turn them back to following the ways of God. Yet such did not take place with most of those involved. Look for a moment at the consequences of each group's reaction to their imposed circumstances when conquering Babylon invaded their sacred land.

I. **Follow those carted away to the land of the Tigris and Euphrates rivers, a land boasting vast wealth and unprecedented beauty carved out of the desert dunes.** Nineveh, with her hanging gardens and multitudes of temples, awaited these exiles in what is today's Iraq. Commerce flowed through Babylon's borders. Armies scattered across the then-known world to claim more territory for the empire.

Coming to a place of such power, wealth, and wonder would have its effect on any group. The exiled Israelites reacted no differently from the way we would today if we were in their place. Long dominated by their religious heritage of God's supreme leadership in their lives, the exiles were suddenly confronted by other gods who were given credit for making such power and prosperity possible. The natural consequence was that many continued to give lip service to the God of Israel while dallying in the pagan religions of Babylon. Others, such as Ezekiel and Daniel, remained firm in their loyalty to Israel's God. However, distance from the Promised Land and the structures of Hebrew worship seemed to give license for many to taste the offerings of their home in exile. Such abandonment spelled sin against God in the minds and eyes of the devout followers. Many of the exiles lost their souls and, like prodigals, needed a savior lest full darkness enveloped them.

II. **Meanwhile, those left in the Promised Land amid the ashes of poverty and need turned away from sacred practices also.** Other uprooted people moved into their beloved homeland. Soon marriage practices were abandoned, and Israelites married non-Israelites, thus corrupting the purity of Israel. Surrounding cultures and tribes intermingled with those left behind, bringing with them their pagan gods that so corrupted their faith that only a bare semblance remained of what once was.

Still the devout in both camps—the exiles and their kinsmen in the Promised Land—prayed for deliverance from God. Out of the darkness of disaster they prayed, knowing that every person is a created child of God, whom he loves with an enduring love. He is the Father who, like a potter, had molded the clay of his people into a nation he loved, and he would not abandon them forever. So they prayed, "Be not exceedingly angry, O Lord, and remember not iniquity forever. Behold, consider that we are all thy people." There came a day when the exile was over, a day when the Promised Land was reclaimed and when God was again seen as the true leader-father of his people.

III. **What does all this ancient history have to do with us in prosperous, powerful, lush America of today?** Are we any different from our ancient forebears? A cursory look will tell us that we, like long-ago exiles, have become fascinated to the point of spiritual captivity with luxury, wealth, and self-satisfaction. While many practice the ritual of faith, they are not overly involved in letting Christian faith direct life day by day. At the cafeteria of religions, all are seen to be valid, and none is needed to make life meaningful and spiritually strong. Yet such attitudes and practices soon lead to disaster, and life grows dull or caves in.

At the same time, poverty works from its end to create circumstances that cause followers to question God, doubt the validity of Christ, and turn to lesser faiths that fail to satisfy spiritual hungers. Still, even in such circumstances, strong voices call for repentance from sin and a reliance on the presence and leadership of the Lord who will lead from darkness to light.

Perhaps we need to pray in our day the prayer of the exiles and poverty-stricken of long ago: "Be not exceedingly angry, O Lord, and remember not iniquity forever." Like those in the ancient days, we cry from the depths of human darkness for the Savior and God, in his infinite love and mercy, to hear our prayer and to answer it in Christ Jesus, who brings light and life to our self-chosen darkness. He does that for every exile from his grace and love.—Henry Fields

---

ILLUSTRATIONS

Community. A mule named Jim was being driven by his owner. When everyone got on the wagon, the driver yelled "Giddy up, Jim. Giddy up, Sue. Giddy up, Sam. Giddy up, John. Giddy up, Joe." As the wagon started to move, one of the passengers said: "When Jim is the only one there, why did you call all those other names?" The owner replied: "If Jim knew he was the only one pulling this wagon, he'd never budge an inch."—Lawrence Vowan

Abba. T. W. Manson, the great English New Testament scholar, said that Jesus rarely spoke in public of God as Father but considered the fatherhood of God so sacred that it was reserved for his disciples, who would understand. "Father" was not an image he used broadly about God, because people could not always understand it. But Jesus pushed this image even further and used an expression about God that, to many Jewish minds, may have appeared disrespectful. In a prayer in Mark 14:36, he used a radically new and different word to describe God: Aramaic word, *Abba.* This Aramaic word was so untranslatable that the early Church preserved the original. The closest translation would probably be "Daddy." Jesus' sense of the fatherhood of God was intimate and personal.—William P. Tuck

Musical Selections Appropriate to the Day

Hymn suggestions for lectionary texts:

Isa. 64:1–9	*O Come, O Come Emmanuel; Have Thine Own Way, Lord*
Ps. 80:1–7, 17–19	*Savior Like a Shepherd Lead Us*
1 Cor. 1:3–9	*Great Is Thy Faithfulness*
Mark 13:24–37	*Come, Thou Long Expected Jesus*

❧ Children's Lectionary Sermon

TITLE: Make Us Yours

SCRIPTURE: Isa. 64:1–9

KEY VERSES: *And yet, Lord, you are our Father. We are the clay, and you are the potter. We are all formed by your hand. Oh, don't be so angry with us, Lord. Please don't remember our sins forever. Look at us, we pray, and see that we are all your people.* (Isa. 64:8–9, New International Version)

KEY CONCEPT: Prayer, forgiveness

MATERIALS: Bible, clay pieces for each child

Here is a piece of clay for each of you. I want you to take the clay and make it into any shape you would like. (*Give the children some time to make their creations. While the children are working, notice those who "start over." Talk about their creations as they are making them.*)

You are doing a great job making things with the clay. (*Let them share what they made.*) I noticed some of you started over. You didn't like how it looked, so you squished the clay and started again. You were able to start over again.

A long time ago, God's people prayed for a chance to start over. They prayed this, which is found in Isaiah (*open Bible*): "And yet, Lord, you are our Father. We are the clay, and you are the potter. We are all formed by your hand. Oh, don't be so angry with us, Lord. Please don't remember our sins forever. Look at us, we pray, and see that we are all your people."

This can be our prayer, too. Today is the beginning of Advent. We are getting ready to celebrate God coming to us in the baby, Jesus. We want God to reshape us into the people God wants us to be and to forgive us when we aren't living God's way. We can pray to God to forgive us. God will forgive us and give us another chance. What a wonderful gift of love from God. We know we are getting ready to celebrate the birth of Jesus who is our Savior, and this makes us glad. Let's pray together, asking God to help us get ready for Jesus' birth, to make us God's people so others will know the happiness we know in Jesus.—Marcia Thompson

❧ WORSHIP AIDS ❧

Call to Worship: Advent is a time of waiting and preparing. God is at work among us calling us to renewed lives. Here it begins: "Repent for the kingdom of heaven is at hand" (Matt. 3:2).

Invocation: Lord, we begin today our pilgrimage toward Christmas. As in years past, we rejoice in the good news of Jesus Christ, born in Bethlehem as the Savior of the world. Purify our hearts, O Lord, that we may welcome his coming with heart, mind, soul, and strength. We praise you for the gift of Christ, born in winter's darkness to be the Light of the world. Amen.

Offertory Sentence: "Greater love has no man than this, that a man lay down his life for his friends" (John 15:13).

Offertory Prayer: Gracious Father, we offer ourselves and our means as expressions of gratitude for your love and forgiveness. You showed us the way to love. You loved us first, even while we were still in our sins. We ask that you bless these gifts for the Kingdom's purpose—for the purpose of reconciling all people everywhere to you. Amen.

Morning Prayer: Holy God, in this season of waiting and anticipation, we lift to you the dreams and yearnings of our hearts. This is a season of hope and new beginnings. Fill us, we pray, with a passion for justice, a renewed commitment to mercy, and the love to work for reconciliation among those whose lives we are able to touch. As we think of giving gifts to others, we ask you, O God, for gifts that only you can give. To those who are sick and facing an uncertain future, give the gift of a vision of healing and wholeness that is your desire for all creation.

In your mercy, Lord, hear our prayers. To those who are mourning and who face the holidays with mixed emotions, give the gift of a deepened awareness of your presence with them, as well as with the loved ones they miss so much. In your mercy, Lord, hear our prayers. To those who are lonely, sorrowing, or anxious, give the gift of your power, peace, and patient endurance for these difficult times. In your mercy Lord, hear our prayers. To those who are out of work, those without a home to go to this Christmas, and all who struggle with the reality of living day to day, give the gift of hope that doors will be opened in their future. In your mercy, Lord, hear our prayers. May each of us welcome your Son—the Son before whom even the desert blooms and rejoices—with an open heart and a receptive spirit. For you send your gifts, not with ribbons or fancy wrappings but with simplicity and humility. We give thanks for all your gifts of life. Amen.—Susan Gregg-Schroeder

Benediction: Go out today with hearts filled with joy. The days of Advent require us to think deeply and lovingly of God's great work of grace among us. This same God, who we name as Father, Son, and Holy Spirit, walks with us along the way. Amen.

SUNDAY, DECEMBER 7, 2008
Second Sunday in Advent

LECTIONARY SERMON TOPIC: "God's Answer to a Cry for Deliverance"

TEXT: Mark 1:1–8

OTHER READINGS: Isa. 40:1–11; Ps. 85:1–2, 8–13; 2 Pet. 3:8–15a

President Franklin Roosevelt called December 7, 1941—the day of the bombing of Pearl Harbor by the Japanese—"a day that will live in infamy." It was a day that ushered in a world struggle that brought war more vast and deadly than any before fought in human history. During those dark days of struggle, people everywhere were looking for a sign of hope that World War II would soon end, with freedom and peace assured for all people. As allied victories mounted, so did the hopes of millions of war-weary citizens the world over. When the atomic bomb was dropped on Japan, creating such devastation and horror, the cessation of war came and with it a new and frightening world.

One of the great and positive results of the war was a return to faith in God. As servicemen and servicewomen came home from the battlefields, the Western world experienced a major surge of church attendance and membership. It signified a return to the Giver of all hope—a return to the Creator God and Father of us all.

I. **Many years prior to World War II, in the nation of Israel, God gave an eternal call to hope for people peering into the darkness of their time, searching for a gleam of guiding, saving light.** In his Gospel, Mark begins his story of the good news by telling of the coming of God's answer for deliverance from human sins. It was a welcomed answer to an ancient, often-sounded cry of God's chosen people and to all people who find themselves walking in the darkness of their sins. The first person Mark mentions in the fulfillment of hope is John, the baptizer. Living a desert lifestyle and possessing the qualities of a prophet, John's message was brand new for the Jews to whom he spoke. He called for them to repent and be baptized. To a people who considered themselves the chosen of God already within the bounds of God's Kingdom, a call to baptismal repentance was something they had never heard from religious leaders. Such baptism was reserved for Gentiles who converted to Judaism. It was part of the cleansing ritual, along with offering a blood sacrifice that would "clean up" the Gentile and get him or her ready for entry into Judaism. No Jew needed this pathway to God, or so they thought.

But John saw things differently. He understood the truth that no person can be saved from sin's darkness unless and until that person repents of sin and turns away from it in order to follow the higher calling of God's righteousness. So powerful was this strange messenger's conviction that folks from all quarters of Israel responded to his call for repentance and Gentile baptism to symbolize their readiness to follow God's chosen path of righteousness.

Any person or any people who would find the hope they seek fulfilled must begin at the door of personal and corporate forgiveness. Like the people of John's day who recognized, claimed, and confessed their sins and washed them away in symbolic baptism, so must we. Those repentant sinners, like people of every age, were joining the movement back to God that led them away from past and present sins and failures. John's purpose was to prepare the people for what was to come, to give hope a positive direction, and to offer light in the darkness of human bondage to sin and separation from God. How we need to hear and heed John's call to repentance in preparation for what is yet to come!

II. **John knew that all he could do was call the people to repent and then point them in a new direction.** In essence, he knew that another would have to enter the picture and lead them further. So he told the people to whom he spoke, as well as people of the ages, of another who was on the way, one who would take the repentant people and give them a new kind of baptism—a baptism of the Holy Spirit of God. John humbly declared the greatness of this newcomer, going so far as to say that he was not fit to be the slave who removes the sandals from the feet of the coming One. He even declared that the coming One must increase in recognition and power among the people while he, John, must decrease. Thus John yields to Jesus, the embodiment of God dwelling for a season among men.

Repentance—acknowledging and turning away from sins—is essential before God's life—God's holy or different kind of Spirit—can live in us and make us into new creations. Does it work in our religion-saturated, satisfied world? Roy was a housepainter. He scoffed at God, lived a life that deprived his family of the very necessities of life, and seemed not to care. Had it not been for the little community church feeding his family and providing shoes and clothing for his children, no one knows what would have happened to them. Numbers of people tried to help Roy get his life straightened out, but they were met with hostility and rejection.

Then, as Roy tells the story:

One day I woke up at the bottom of what seemed like a deep pit. I knew I couldn't get out by myself and didn't know anyone who would help me. I had run everybody who cared about me out of my life. For the first time since I was a little boy, I prayed to God for help. That day I knew that I would have to leave my old sinful life behind (repent) if anything good was ever going to happen. I asked God to give me the strength to do it and started the hardest climb I have ever taken.

In church the next Sunday, I met Christ and asked him to give me a new life, and he did. Some folks don't think it will last or will make a difference, but they are wrong. Since that day I have paid the rent and provided a roof for my family. Money I once spent on booze and gambling and all that goes along with that kind of life is now spent on food for my family, shoes for their feet, and other necessary things they need.

Now I am home every night with the people who loved me, even when I wasn't fit to be loved. I am blessed. I once had no hope, but God heard my cry in my darkest moments and answered me with hope and Christ who showed me how to live a new life.

Does God's hope in Christ make a difference? Does life lived in God's way, in his Spirit, change things from darkness to light? Roy and multitudes of others respond with a resounding *yes!* So it will be for all who, in the darkness of their sins, hear John's call to repentance and follow his pointing to Jesus, who gives God's gifts of salvation and grace, and a baptism of God's life through the indwelling of his Holy Spirit.—Henry Fields

ILLUSTRATIONS

Power of God. Most of us know the story of the tortoise and the hare. More than likely our attention is focused on the high energy of the rabbit. So too in our living, we are caught by the frenzy of a hurried life, thinking that our rushing to and fro is a most productive pursuit. It is said that Alexander the Great, having so hurriedly conquered the known world, sat down and wept, for he had no more worlds to conquer. Such displays of human energy at work (power) are but a flash in the pan in light of God's power that works slowly, meticulously, in unperturbed pace, making the rough places smooth and the crooked places straight.—Lee McGlone

Journeying. I came across an interesting book recently. It was not new. It was printed in 1961, but it was new to me. It's Daniel Boorstein's *The Image: A Guide to Pseudo-Events in America*[1] and is a critique of American life. The third chapter is titled "From Traveler to Tourist: The Lost Art of Travel." He suggests that taking a journey has changed in the last hundred years.

I had never realized that our word *travel* comes from the same root word as *travail*. It indicates hardship, trouble, work. Before the middle of the nineteenth century, travel was not a pleasant experience. It was a kind of torture— a difficult thing and full of troubles. Ocean voyages took several weeks. There were no Hiltons or even Holiday Inns. Comforts were left behind. There were risks out there: highway robbery, strange diseases, strange food. But the traveler who risked the pain was rewarded with a great adventure. The traveler then truly experienced the people and ways of a different culture. The traveler's horizons were expanded.

All that has changed over the years, as travel has become easier. Air flight gets us where we want to go quickly and in comfort. Once there, we can reside in nice hotels, with all the conveniences of home. Most risks have been removed. But with the advent of such ease in travel, one thing is lacking: the true *experience* of travel. The traveler of an earlier day encountered the world

---

[1]Daniel Boorstein, *The Image: A Guide to Pseudo-Events in America* (New York: Random House, 1961).

and was broadened in the process. Today's tourist simply has our stereotypes confirmed. It's what Boorstein calls a *pseudo adventure*.

It's not too much to suggest that the Christian life is like travel—a great adventure. There is a beginning point, the weariness of travel, even travail, and in the end a blessed destination. We're changed by it. Jesus' whole life can be seen as a journey. And we're on the journey with him. Our challenge is to follow him wherever he goes. His journey becomes ours.—Lee McGlone

Musical Selections Appropriate to the Day

Hymn suggestions for lectionary texts:

Isa. 40:1–11	*Comfort, Comfort Now My People; Prepare the Way, O Zion*
Ps. 85:1–2, 8–13	*Make Me a Channel of Your Peace*
2 Pet. 3:8–15a	*Praise, My Soul, the King of Heaven; Songs of Thankfulness and Praise*
Mark 1:1–8	*On Jordan's Bank the Baptist's Cry; When John Baptized by Jordan's River*

Children's Lectionary Sermon

TITLE: Preparing the Way

SCRIPTURE: Mark 1:1–8

KEY VERSE: *There is a voice of a man who calls out in the desert: "Prepare the way for the Lord. Make the road straight for him."* (Mark 1:3, International Children's Bible New Century Version)

KEY CONCEPT: John the Baptist, proclamation

MATERIALS: Bible, a gong with a striker (or something to bang on that is loud and not too obnoxious)

Today, the passage we read is about John the Baptist, but it is also about a herald. Do any of you know what a herald is? (*Let the children give a response.*) I do not mean a person named Harold; I am talking about the position or title, "herald." The word *herald* means someone who goes ahead of someone special to announce that the person is coming. A herald might carry a trumpet or a gong to make a big noise so he can get people's attention.

Let me give you some examples. When the president of the United States travels, he sends a group of people ahead of his arrival to prepare the people he will visit for his coming. Rulers of all countries usually send their people before them to prepare the way.

Today, we are continuing to wait in this season of Advent. This is a season of expectation and preparation. We are expecting a visit from our King, Jesus. We read and remember how God's people were waiting for a savior. God's people were waiting for the promised King, Jesus, just as we do now.

In Mark's Gospel we read (*open Bible*): "There is a voice of a man who calls out in the desert: 'Prepare the way for the Lord. Make the road straight for him.'" This herald was John the Baptist. God told John the Baptist to herald the arrival of the King. John the Baptist told the people: "Prepare the way of the Lord." Today, we are going to herald the arrival of our King. Each one of us is going to hit this gong with the striker, and we will all say, "Prepare the way of the Lord." (*Show the children what to do, and help them say the words, either before or after the gong is struck.*)—Lizette Hunt

❧ WORSHIP AIDS ❧

Call to Worship: In Advent, God works to prepare our hearts to receive the fullness of his grace. That work may come in unexpected places: "The voice of one crying in the wilderness, 'Prepare the way of the Lord. Make straight in the desert a highway for our God'" (Isa. 40:3).

Invocation: Dear Lord, prepare us for the great things you intend to do in and through us today. May our journey through the Advent season awaken our slumbering souls and quicken us to a fresh and vital walk of faith. What we seek we cannot do alone—so we await your help. Amen.

Offertory Sentence: "Every one of us shall give account of himself to God" (Rom. 14:12).

Offertory Prayer: Father of mercy, you do indeed open springs in the desert and provide good things when we least expect it. Your grace is truly marvelous. Your compassion knows no end. Give to us now the gift of cheerful giving, even in times when stewardship is difficult. Amen.

Morning Prayer: We are blessed again with this season of Christmas. Open our hearts to its mysteries and miracles. Fill the coming days with starlight from clear December skies and candlelight reflected in clear windows. Let us be reminded of the beauty of light from all its sources, and remind us to hold each other in the light. Fill the coming days with fragrances of evergreen, spices, and curling smoke from wood carried in. Remind us to open our senses to what is natural.

Fill the coming days with sweet carols of angels and kings, of shepherds and a baby born. Let us be reminded that music has a way of lightening and lifting worries we may carry. Fill the coming days with family and friends gathered round. Let us be reminded to be grateful for those we can hold close in our folds and those whose memory we hold close in our hearts. Fill the coming days with gifts more given than received. Let us be reminded that gifts bring wonder and surprise. Fill us with love, Lord. Help us to love even the stranger in places our lives will never take us but whose stories we have heard. Fill us with hope, Lord. Help us to believe that those who are lonely, hungry, or broken will find you by whatever name they call you. Fill us with peace, Lord. Help us to dream dreams of trust, tolerance, and understanding for all living on this fragile earth. These are the true gifts of Christmas—love, hope, and peace. Open our hearts and minds to receive them.—Sarah Bishop

Benediction: People of God, go forth today, energized to serve faithfully and lovingly in the days of this week. May we live in the light of God's redemptive love and share that love with others. May we speak the name of Jesus often—and lovingly! Amen.

SUNDAY, DECEMBER 14, 2008
Third Sunday in Advent

LECTIONARY SERMON TOPIC: "The Promise of the Coming Light: A Dramatic Improvisation"
TEXT: John 1:6–8; 19–28
OTHER READINGS: Ps. 126; Isa. 61:1–4, 8–11; 1 Thess. 5:16–24

It is the year 101 of the Christian era. I am a Greek living in a world dominated by Rome. My name is Artimus. This is my story of a journey that led me to discover the Christ of God. Much of my life, like that of many through the ages, has been spent trying to solve the riddles and mysteries of life. I live in a world of multiple gods. Pantheons of government-sanctioned gods with magnificent temples exist everywhere. Through the years I have tried to find hope, light, and meaning for life at the various altars of these many gods. None has brought sensibility out of senselessness, hope to hopelessness, and light in the darkness, nor has any given purpose to my life. That has been the story of multitudes prior to me and will be the story of any future seekers of hope, light, and life along the avenues I have followed. There is and always will be a feeling of failure that haunts anyone following the ways of limited gods, be they materialistic, man-made, or government-ordained. For me there seemed to be no solution to my search.

I. **Then one first day of the week, in the year 101 in the city of Ephesus, I stumbled on an extraordinary new sect—a group with no massive temple, no god statues, none of the usual religious trappings.** They were a vibrant, hopeful, joyful group, singing praise to their God and listening to the reading of what was, for me, a document of profound revelation. It was written by a man named John—a promoter of this sect called Christians and a disciple of the founder. John used terms that Greek thinkers would readily grasp.

He used the term *logos*, which in the Greek language means "the word, the reason." It is defined as "making things happen"; it creates, it guides, it directs. John saw this concept as being descriptive of God. It was this *Logos*—this Word—that made everything that exists happen; it existed before Creation. It was with God and was none other than God. To my Greek mind, God the Creator was at last identified and explained! He was not a dumb statue or an idea conjured up by the human mind, or a governmental decree. He was eternal creator and sustainer of the universe (John 1:1).

Still, while who and what God is was clarified for me, there remained remoteness from God. There was no personal association with this newly revealed God. The basic mystery of how everything got here was explained, but where was the hope, the light, the assurance that people mattered—that I mattered in the vast reaches of creation?

John, in his writing and wisdom, does not leave me or anyone only partially answered. He said that the creative Word, the maker of all that exists, is the source of life that is the light of man (John 1:4). John has grasped and expressed what we Greek thinkers understand: life is the opposite of destruction, condemnation, and death. The *Logos*—the Word—is altogether life devoid of death. His is the life that never perishes, and he gives security in this life, as well as in the life that continues when this one on earth is done.

II. **Then again, John declares that the life of the eternal Word is the light of man; it shines in our darkness and cannot be put out (John 1:4–5).** That one statement was like great music to my ears! God sent light to scatter the darkness of my life and world. No matter how dark I had made life, God could and would chase away the darkness with glorious, cleansing, guiding light! Could it be that, at last, a source had been revealed that would illuminate willful ignorance that enslaves the mind and allow truth and knowledge to emerge? Could this light from God's source sweep the shadows of skulking evil, causing evil to wither in the light of eternal goodness? Could this light focus on the dark, sinful places of my personal sins and wrongs and chase them away with the light of forgiveness? Such cleansing light would be a welcome presence in my dark and hopeless world of fear and lostness. But where would I find the embodiment of that life-giving light that cannot be put out by my darkness or the darkness of the world?

John does not leave me dangling on that question. He tells of a forerunner, John the baptizer, who would declare the news of the coming One who would bring life and light to our darkness. Then he writes, "the Word, the Logos became human and lived among us, and we have seen the glory of the one and only Son of God who came from the Father, full of grace and truth" (John 1:14). What a needed revelation! God was and is among us. The Word, identified by John as Jesus the Christ, lived like one of us, taught, healed, forgave, and revealed God to the world.

III. **Then came my greatest question.** How could I find this light that Christ had brought to us with his life? How could I enter into that life? I discovered from John's writing that the only way is to believe in Jesus Christ. That means three things. First, it means that I must be convinced that Jesus Christ is really and truly the Son of God. I must make up my mind about him so that I have no reason to not give my complete obedience to his demands. That means I have to look at him, study him, think about him until I am absolutely sure that he is none other than the Son of God. Second, it means I must take Jesus Christ at his word, accept his commandments as binding, believe that what he says is true, and then base my actions on his truth. Third, I then seek his guidance as I learn what he said, listen for the leadership of his Spirit, and allow him to live in and through me. This is how I found hope and light in my darkness and life with a capital "L." That is the way you can find hope, light, and life also. In fact, there is no other way, except through accepting that Jesus is the Word—the *Logos*—made flesh, dwelling among us, seeking us in our darkness that he may bring us eternal light and life.

It is my prayer that you may find his light to dispel your darkness and give you life worth living now and for all eternity.—Henry Fields

ILLUSTRATIONS

The Road Not Taken.
I shall be telling this with a sigh
Somewhere ages and ages hence:
Two roads diverged in a wood, and I—
I took the one less traveled by,
And that has made all the difference.—*Robert Frost*

Transformation. A lady who had a small house on the seashore of Ireland at the turn of the century was quite wealthy but also quite frugal. The people were surprised, then, when she decided to be among the first to have electricity in her home. Several weeks after the installation, a meter reader appeared at her door. He asked if her electricity was working well, and she assured him it was. "I'm wondering if you can explain something to me," he said. "Your meter shows scarcely any usage. Are you using your power?" "Certainly," she answered. "Each evening when the sun sets, I turn on my lights just long enough to light my candles; then I turn them off."

She tapped into power but did not use it. Let's not be satisfied to live in the shadows.—Max Lucado

Musical Selections Appropriate to the Day

Hymn suggestions for lectionary texts:

Isa. 61:1–4, 8–11	*Praise the One Who Breaks the Darkness; Rise, Shine, You People!*
Ps. 126	*Bless His Holy Name; As Water to the Thirsty*
1 Thess. 5:16–24	*What a Friend We Have in Jesus*
John 1:6–8, 19–28	*Christ Is the World's Light; Of the Father's Love Begotten*

Children's Lectionary Sermon

TITLE: Jesus Can Show Us the Way

SCRIPTURE: John 1:6–8, 19–28

KEY VERSE: *He came to tell people about the Light. Through him all people could hear about the Light and believe.* (John 1:7, International Children's Bible New Century Version)

KEY CONCEPT: How Jesus is called "the Light"

MATERIALS: Bible, string of Christmas lights

PREPARATION: Let the sound-and-light technician know ahead of time to dim or turn off the sanctuary lights when you ask.

Have you noticed all the Christmas lights as you drive through town? I think it is so pretty to drive around in the evening, when it is dark outside, and look at all the lights on people's houses. It creates a glow, even when it's very dark. People have all different shapes and colors of lights to show Christmas is near. I brought some Christmas lights for us to turn on. (*Have the lights dimmed or shut off; turn the flashlight on and shine it into as many dark areas as possible.*)

In our Scripture passage today, we hear about a special Light. It wasn't a light bulb a lamp or even a flashlight. "The Light" was another name for Jesus. (*Open Bible.*) John came to tell people about the Light. Through him all people could hear about the Light and believe. We can change this verse: John came to tell people about "the Jesus." Through him all people could hear about the Jesus and believe.

Let's think about this a minute. What does light do for us? (*Let the children answer, but if they seem stumped, suggest "help us see in the dark," "find our way," or something similar.*) Jesus does this for us, too. Jesus helps us know how to be his followers. Jesus teaches us by the way he lived how we should treat people. Jesus helps us find our way. Light is another name for Jesus.—Lizette Hunt

❧ WORSHIP AIDS ❧

Call to Worship: Advent declares that God has come to live among us and did so in the human flesh of Jesus Christ. Just so, God dwells with us for eternity: "I heard a great voice out of heaven saying, 'Behold, the tabernacle of God is with men, and he will dwell with them, and they shall be his people, and God himself shall be with them, and be their God'" (Rev. 21:3).

Invocation: Dearest Lord, we rejoice that you are with us, that you have always been with us and will be with us forever, and that we will rejoice forever. Through your presence we are strengthened for the life of faith and duty. Grant that in this Advent season, we will be further strengthened to live in fullness all our days. Amen.

Offertory Sentence: "As every man has received the gift, even so minister the same one to another, as good stewards of the manifold grace of God" (1 Pet. 4:10).

Offertory Prayer: Lord, let Jesus coming into the time of earth affect our giving this day so others may know the Incarnation that heaven and earth cannot forget. Amen.—E. Lee Phillips

Morning Prayer: Creator God, we seek your cresting wave of hope. Our days grow darker, shorter, more of night. Loved ones founder; yes, we're weary. Still, we're here, together, afloat.

This life we share—our time alive in your mind's eye—can take so many shapes and forms. We grow and change, drift and surge, fall and rise, in your rhythmic daily waves of challenge. Thank you for each day. Our shells get thicker, year by year, crusted o'er with layers of knowledge, collected wisdom, wounds, and scars. Yet at this time, there is a window clear.

May we look back now upon innocence and feel its pure glow inside us—one child's soft, clear voice singing, "Do you hear what I hear?"—an entry point to the possibility of transcendence, to the blessing of receiving the gifts that really matter. Can we dare to dream, to open our heart's eye to see a star, and follow? "Do you see what I see?" Some kinds of truth are best perceived by hearts, not minds.

And so we listen, once again, to the story we know so well. Hear the child who calls our spirits: "Do you know what I know?" Dear God, we will make our way through the night, guided by your light, and open ourselves to your loving message. May it be so. Amen.— Peter Pease

Benediction: We go forth today, assured of God's presence. As truly as God dwelt with his people in Christ long ago, he dwells with us today. May God, whom we know as Father, Son, and Holy Spirit, bring life and light to this holy season. Amen.

SUNDAY, DECEMBER 21, 2008
Fourth Sunday in Advent

LECTIONARY SERMON TOPIC: "Light Comes to a Dark World"

TEXT: Luke 1:26–38, 47–55

OTHER READINGS: 2 Sam. 7:1–11, 16; Rom. 16:25–27

The angel had told her she was highly favored by God. That must have been a frightening encounter for a young girl in her teens. I wonder if, in that moment of revelation, the maid from Nazareth thought this heavenly messenger had come to the wrong address. Here he was telling her that she would "bring forth a son and you shall call him Jesus" (Luke 1:31). Mary knew enough of the history of her people to understand that this was not just any child that the messenger was talking about. This child was the long-awaited Messiah—the deliverer of God's people from their bondage in every area of life. Maybe she thought something like this: "Why me? I am not even married. Joseph and I are engaged, but I am still a virgin and will remain such until my wedding day. Surely this messenger is wrong. Should I tell him to check his assignment book because he has the wrong house?"

But the messenger went on to tell Mary that this coming child would be great; he would be called the Son of the Highest and would occupy the throne of his father, David. He would reign over the house of Jacob forever, and there would be no end to his Kingdom (Luke 1:32–33).

Confessing to the angel that she was a virgin, Mary asked one question: "How can this be since I have no husband?" In answer the angel tells her that this child will be of the Holy Spirit, that the power of the Most High will overshadow her. Thus the child will be called "holy, the Son of God" (Luke 1:34). This child was not to be conceived in the normal, human manner but would be the creative work of that Spirit that brought all things into being. Working through the human system of birth, he would be a new creation of God's creative Spirit. Pondering this encounter causes several thoughts to emerge that need expression.

I. **First is the fact that Mary did not volunteer for this awesome responsibility; she was drafted.** Her name did not even appear on a list of the most eligible of the land to be the mother of Jesus. She really had no say in the matter. It was God's choice. Sure, she could have refused. She could have said no. God does not force his will on anyone. He chooses, but we must accept his choosing. To Mary's eternal credit she did not argue; she did not question the wisdom of God. Instead, this devout young Jewish girl from the small village of Nazareth, nestled in the quiet hills of the north country, humbly accepted the choice of God.

What a difference life would be for most of us if we, like Mary, in simple trust and humility, would accept God's choice for us. Instead, we too often turn from accepting what we know is his will and plot our own course on life's road map. Then when all our planning fails, and we have nowhere to turn, we turn to God. How different life would be for us if we could answer God's choice when it is first made known, at the beginning gate of the journey with Christ.

II. **Second, Mary certainly did not know all that the "favor of the Lord" entailed.** How could she know that the favor of the Lord would bring shame upon her, Joseph, and her family when she became pregnant prior to marriage? How could she know that the favor of the Lord would send her on a long trek down to Bethlehem where the only available shelter was a stable in a cave? How could she know that the favor of the Lord would find her suffering from labor pains in the late night hours in that cave in Bethlehem—pains that would usher her child into the world with no human help but that of a clumsy husband? How could she know that her baby's first cradle would be no more than an animal's rough feed trough? How could she know that the Lord's favor would mean running away to Egypt to protect her child and later slipping back to her hometown like a thief to escape the wrath of the tyrant, Herod, king of Judea? How could she know that the favor of the Lord meant year after weary year would pass in the routine life of Nazareth—so many years that the promises of that long ago day seemed but a dream? How could she know that the Lord's favor would one day send her beloved firstborn through rejection by those he came to deliver—first, a mock trial; then a death on a cross where they hung him out like some wild animal to die? How could she know that the favor of the Lord accepted with joy in the morning of her life would one day create circumstances that would break her heart?

God's favor does not guarantee peace, prosperity, pleasure, and unending happiness. Some of these may, on occasion, come from God's hand, but there are other kinds of blessings that he bestows. God's favor many times is discovered by us at the end of great difficulty or heartache or seeming failure. It is discovered by confronting the hard circumstance, working through it, and discovering that it has enriched life beyond anything that can be imagined. Facing the hard moments and dark events of life are not only frightening but many times cause us to doubt the reality of our faith in the power of God. Yet, if we remain faithful to the highest values and convictions Christ has taught us, we will discover the strength to continue, even in the darkness. Then one day we will emerge from the struggle, knowing that because of the favor of the Lord, we were called to live with and through the dark difficulty. God's blessing still comes through the horror of crucifixion. God's favor does not allow us to escape life's hard places and difficult times. His favor does enable us to grow in grace and truth and trust because we deal with those hard places and difficult times. Beyond them, we discover their meaning and power in life.

III. **Third, Mary heard the promise that her child would be royal like the great king David and that his Kingdom would never end (Luke 1:33).** She certainly could not have grasped the full significance of this immense promise. Likely in her mind, she envisioned a dynasty linked to David that would be perpetual throughout future history, that Israel would establish itself under Jesus and forever grow in power, territory, and world influence. It was only after all the events of experiencing the favor of the Lord, after the Crucifixion and the Resurrection, that she grasped, in part, the truth that his Kingdom was a spiritual realm—a new creation that would grow and last forever.

I wonder if Mary or any of Jesus' early followers would recognize his Kingdom's boundaries today. After all, theirs was a world of limited geographical knowledge. Yet today his Kingdom knows no end, neither geographical nor in terms of time. The centuries have rolled, and he has and still does rule the hearts and lives of faithful followers in every land on this fragile planet. His Kingdom has outlasted any earthly kingdom and will never come to an end. If Mary could see the wonder and power of her child's

Kingdom today—how it has grown from meager beginnings to embrace multi-millions, how he has changed governments, councils, and individuals—what would she think?

Perhaps she would find new meaning in the words of her song, the praise she sang when told she had been chosen to be the earthly mother of God's Son. I think, even after all that she experienced she would still sing, "My soul magnifies the Lord, and my spirit rejoices in God my Savior!" (Luke 1:46–47). She would see that her child,

The Christ who was born on Christmas day
Laid on the earth his two small hands
Lifting it worlds and worlds away
Up to the level of love's demands.—*Author unknown*

In him light and hope had forever shattered the darkness!—Henry Fields

---

ILLUSTRATIONS

Joy. A UCLA researcher defined *joy* as the ability to adjust to things beyond our control. This is not surrender or fatalism; it is faith. *Joy is adjusting to Jesus.* Adjusting to Jesus' salvation—believing in him to save us from our sins. Adjusting to Jesus' teaching—believing what he says. Adjusting to Jesus' leadership—doing what he says.—Leith Anderson

A Courageous Response. Having heard the call of God upon her life, Mary replied, "I am your servant. Let it be unto me according to your word." These are dangerous words but absolutely necessary words for the searching disciple. When God speaks our names—Mary, Moses, Samuel, Paul—the situation is getting intensely personal. God surely knows who we are, far better than we know ourselves, and knows where we are. But the courageous response to God is always our choice to make. Mary declared, "Let it be to me according to your word." Moses said, "Here am I." Samuel spoke, "Your servant hears." Paul cried out, "Lord, what will you have me do?" They made themselves available to God and took the risk of faith. When we respond to God's voice, we are taking a chance.—Lee McGlone

Musical Selections Appropriate to the Day

Hymn suggestions for lectionary texts:

2 Sam. 7:1–11, 16	*Long Ago, Prophets Knew; Blessed Be the God of Israel*
Luke 1:47–55	*For Ages Women Hoped and Prayed; Savior of the Nations, Come*
Rom. 16:25–27	*My Tribute*
Luke 1:26–38	*Tell Out, My Soul; To a Maid Whose Name Was Mary*

❧ Children's Lectionary Sermon

TITLE: The Promise

SCRIPTURE: Luke 1:47–55

KEY VERSE: *God has done what he promised to our ancestors, to Abraham and to his children forever.* (Luke 1:55, International Children's Bible New Century Version)

KEY CONCEPT: Promise

MATERIALS: Bible

PREPARATION: Ask the children to fold their arms across their chests and tap their toes very time you say the word *wait*. Every time you say the word *promise*, have the children raise their hands and say (with excitement), "Hallelujah!"

(*Open Bible.*) "God has done what he promised to our ancestors, to Abraham and to his children forever." This is part of a song Mary sang in praise to God. It started way back, with God's promise to Abraham. For a long time, God's people had been *waiting*. They *waited* while they farmed. They *waited* while they watched the sheep. They *waited* year after year. They *waited* through the good times and bad times. Sometimes while they were *waiting*, other people came and captured them, and they had to be slaves while they *waited*. A few times they had good kings and the people prospered, but they still *waited*.

While God's people were *waiting*, God sent messengers to tell them how to live while they *waited*. Sometimes they didn't like the people God sent to them, and they got rid of them. The message they didn't like was, "Stop, you are not following God's law."

God kept sending his messengers called prophets, and they kept telling the people when the time was right God *promised* God would send a savior. And in the meanwhile, keep living the way God said to live and keep *waiting*. When they remembered God's *promise,* the people had hope. Sometimes they forgot about the *promise,* and they were grumpy. God wanted them to remember God's *promise*, so God would always send another messenger.

Finally, the *wait* was over; the time was right. God sent a messenger to Mary to tell her about her part in God's *promise*. The angel told Mary she was to be the mother of a baby and to name the baby Jesus. The angel said the baby was God's *promise* to God's people—a king to rule forever. Mary was so overcome with emotion she sang a praise song to God. She thanked God for keeping God's *promise*.—Lizette Hunt

WORSHIP AIDS

Call to Worship: On the Sunday prior to Christmas Day, we rejoice in the angel's message to the world: "Fear not, for behold, I bring you good tidings of great joy, which shall be to all people. For unto you is born this day in the city of David a Savior, who is Christ the Lord" (Luke 2:10–11).

Invocation: God of Incarnation, make known your will this Christmas that as children of the new birth in Christ Jesus, we may reflect the nativity light of Bethlehem, even the Light of the World, Christ Jesus, that never dims. Amen.—E. Lee Phillips

Offertory Sentence: "When they were come into the house, they saw the young child with Mary his mother, and fell down, and worshipped him: and when they had opened their treasures, they presented unto him gifts: gold, and frankincense, and myrrh" (Matt. 2:11).

Offertory Prayer: Gracious Lord, receive our gifts this day as expressions of our devotion to you. May the thoughts of Bethlehem and Calvary capture our minds today and throughout the year. Bless these gifts for the work of ministry in Jesus' name here in our city and in the whole world. Amen.

Morning Prayer: Almighty God, our Heavenly Father, we come again in our spiritual pilgrimage to the manger of Bethlehem, following the shepherds, following the Wise Men, opening the doors of our minds, remembering the feelings and events of Christmases past: childhood hopes and fantasies, the gifts and the candy, dinners with parents and grandparents, celebrations of Christmas carols and lights, the exchange of greetings.

Indeed, music fills the air, lights sparkle, candles glow. And yet with all the tapestry of customs and culture, we pray so deeply and sincerely that the good news of the loving kindness of Christmas will come into our hearts and lives. Help us to sift through our feelings and our faith, that through the music and the carols we will experience the good news of great joy, that through the Scripture we will read, we will hear your divine word through the Word, that through the meditation of our minds and the reflection of the sermon, we will be led to a deeper awareness, a greater peace, a more profound understanding. Come to us in some unexpected insight—a surge of power that we haven't looked for. O God, surprise us with a transforming miracle in our hearts, so the joy and the spirit of Christmas may stay with us, now and forever. In the name of Jesus of Bethlehem, the Light of the World. Amen.—George L. Davis

Benediction: As we go, we celebrate the joy of this season. While the lights on our trees and in our streets may well dazzle us, may our faith be lived brightly that the warmth and joy of Christ will be revealed to our world. God, let it be so. Amen.

SUNDAY, DECEMBER 28, 2008

LECTIONARY SERMON TOPIC: "The Joy of God's Salvation"
TEXT: Luke 2:22–40
OTHER READINGS: Isa. 61:10–62:3; Ps. 148; Gal. 4:4–7

The caravan of adoration was over. Shepherds representing the humble of the earth and the Wise Men denoting the royalty found in the land had come and gone. Life for the holy family seemed to have settled into normal routine. Now it was time to go to the Temple and observe the ancient rituals of the Jewish people. Thus on the eighth day after Jesus' birth, Mary and Joseph present their child in the most sacred place on earth to the Jews—the magnificent and beautiful Temple in Jerusalem. Here Jesus will go through the required ritual of circumcision, the identifying mark required of God of the Jews for all males of his chosen people. At that time the baby would be named.

I. **Then would come the ceremony of the Redemption of the First Born.** Jewish law, as given in Exodus 3:2, stated that every firstborn male, human or animal, was sacred to God. However, the parents, for the sum of five shekels paid to the priest, could buy back their son from God (Num. 18:16). The eighth day was also the time of purification for the mother, who until this sacrifice was made could not participate in family, religious, nor social activities. She had to bring a lamb to the Temple for a burnt offering and a pigeon for a sin offering, but if she could not afford a lamb, she might bring another pigeon. The two pigeons were called the "offering of the poor." It was the offering of the poor that Mary brought. The ancient ceremonies had back of them the conviction that a child is a gift of God, not given but lent by God. It is the one gift for which we shall have to answer above all others.

II. **While at the Temple on this important day, Mary and Joseph encounter Simeon, who verifies the truth that Jesus is the hope of the world, the light that ever shines in the surrounding darkness, a light that penetrates, heals, and changes life forever.** Simeon is a pious, saintly old man, filled with the

Holy Spirit waiting the comforting of Israel. He knew he would not see death until he had seen the Lord's Anointed one. Simeon joins the holy family at the altar, takes the child in his arms, and, looking heavenward, speaks those words that comprise what is known as the *Nunc Dimittis* [now dismiss] (Luke 2:29–32). His words have a major sweep: "Lord now let your servant depart in peace for my eyes have seen your salvation." Holding the child, he further proclaims: "This child shall be for the rise and falling of many in Israel. Here indeed is a child who is the watershed of human history. He gives a new eternal dimension to the human soul and splits time in two. All the past will be numbered as coming before him, and all future happenings will be dated from the time of his birth. He will either be received as Savior or rejected—at man's peril. No one can ultimately be indifferent to him.

III. **Look at a few of the ramifications of this Christmas fact.** Christmas is an event, a happening within history. It is the actual advent of the life and love and light and hope of God into our world of darkness, sin, lostness, pain, hopelessness, and death. At Christmas when Christ was born "Emmanuel, God with us" became visible reality. In a sublime, unique way the heavenly became human and God made his entry into earthly life. He wrapped his glory up in the tenderness of a child and offered himself to humanity that needed him so much. Little wonder Simeon cried, "My eyes have seen your salvation!"

The second Christmas fact is that this child is a measuring rod, a moral barometer, a spiritual yardstick for all of civilization. He is more than the universal child. He is the cosmic child! Using him as a measuring rod, humanity will rise and fall. Truth and falsehood, good and evil, right and wrong will forever be gauged by this child of Bethlehem's manger. Because of this God-given child of Christmas, our task is shaping our world so that all God's children of every age, race, culture, and condition, from the oldest to the youngest, may experience safety and grow joyfully into usefulness in God's Kingdom. Jesus, the Christmas child, is our best hope for this broken, battered, weary world. If we are going to rebuild a world worthy of approaching the Kingdom of God on earth, we must rebuild around the teachings and spirit of the one whom God laid in a manger crib.

The other Christmas fact is that Bethlehem's child is pointing us to the road that leads to abundant and eternal life. This realization thrilled Simeon's heart. For many years he had been on the alert, had stood on tiptoe, peering into the face of every boy child brought into the temple, waiting, watching for the "consolation of Israel." Now, holding Mary's and Joseph's eight-day-old child, he opens his aged heart to him who is salvation and eternal life and joyfully declares, "Mine eyes have seen your salvation!" As always, personal quest ends in personal discovery. May this be the experience of the multitudes of our day, beginning with each of us![2]—Henry Fields

ILLUSTRATIONS

Immediate Goals. Charlie Brown is at bat. *Strike Three!* He has struck out again and slumps over to the bench. "Rats! I'll never be a big-league player. I just don't have it! All my life I've dreamed of playing in the big leagues, but I know I'll never make it." Lucy turns to console him. "Charlie Brown, you're thinking too far ahead. What you need to do is set yourself more immediate goals." He looks up. "Immediate goals?" Lucy says, "Yes. Start with this next inning when you go out to pitch. See if you can walk out on the mound without falling down!"

Take one thing at a time and work on that.—William Powell Tuck

Courage. There is one thing about the courageous. They never give up. I'm sure the temptation comes to give up. But they don't, even in face of the gruesome torture. Never giving up carries its own reward. I suspect that one of the most quoted lines out of World War II was Winston Churchill's radio address after the bombing began in London: "We shall go to the end, we shall fight in France, we shall fight on the seas and oceans, we shall fight in the air, we shall defend our Island, whatever the cost may be, we shall fight on the beaches, we shall fight on the landing grounds, we shall fight in the fields and in the streets, we shall fight in the hills, we shall never surrender."

And neither shall we!—Lee McGlone

---

[2]Points 1–3 are based on a 1965 Advent sermon by Aaron N. Meckel.

Musical Selections Appropriate to the Day

Hymn suggestions for lectionary texts:

Isa. 61:10–62:3	*Joy to the World*
Ps. 148	*Praise the Lord, O Heavens Adore Him;*
	Angels We Have Heard on High
Gal. 4:4–7	*Hark! The Herald Angels Sing; God of*
	All Time
Luke 2:22–40	*Good Christian Friends Rejoice; Once*
	in Royal David's City

 ## Children's Lectionary Sermon

TITLE: Simeon's Story

SCRIPTURE: Luke 2:22–40

KEY VERSE: *This child will be rejected by many in Israel, and it will be their undoing. But he will be the greatest joy to many others.* (Luke 2:34b, New Living Translation)

KEY CONCEPT: Jesus is Savior.

MATERIALS: Bible

PREPARATION: Get an older man to do the monologue that follows, or tell it as a story. If you choose to do this as a monologue, make sure it is very dramatic and seems spontaneous.

(*Before Simeon enters, open your Bible and tell the children they are going to have a Bible visitor. Tell them his story comes from Luke 2. The person portraying Simeon walks down the aisle waving to the children, acting out of breath.*) Have you been to the Temple? Have you been to the Temple? I saw him. I saw him with my own eyes. You don't know who I am talking about, do you? Let me begin at the beginning. My name is Simeon and I live right here in Jerusalem. I love God so much, and I knew through Scripture read in the Temple that God would send a Messiah to rescue God's people. In a vision I had, the Holy Spirit of God told me I would see the Savior.

Well today was the day. I went to the Temple because God's Spirit told me to go. While I was there, Mary and Joseph came into the Temple with their new baby. Yes, it was him. It was Jesus. I asked if I could hold him. She gave him to me, and I shouted praises to God. "I have seen the Savior," I shouted. I blessed Mary and Joseph. They were still amazed at all that was happening.

I told them, "This child will be rejected by many in Israel, and it will be their undoing. But he will be the greatest joy to many others." He is the greatest joy to me. I lived to see the Savior. I hope Jesus' birth is a joy to you! (*Have Simeon talk with the children individually, saying things like "Jesus is here; the Savior is here."*)—Marcia Thompson

❧ WORSHIP AIDS ❧

Call to Worship: At year's end, we celebrate the remarkable faith that has sustained us all the days and that will lead us onward. "The Spirit and the bride say, 'Come.' And let him that is athirst come. And whoever will, let him take the water of life freely" (Rev. 22:17).

Invocation: Almighty God, we gather in your name to worship you in spirit and in truth. Encourage us just now that we may so clearly experience you that we will be transformed for the faithful living of our days. Give us strength, Father, greater than our own. Let you might be lived out in us. Amen.

Offertory Sentence: "Verily, verily, I say unto you, He who believes on me, the works that I do he shall do also; and greater works than these he shall do" (John 14:12).

Offertory Prayer: Father, we can never understand the nature of your unlimited grace. Your mercies know no end. Yet with limited insight, we bring to you these gifts as imperfect expressions of our thanksgiving. Bless and multiply them for the cause of your Kingdom. May your name forever be praised. Amen.

Morning Prayer: Our Father, through countless ages you have guided your people. With sure hand you have brought them through many a troubled day.

As with our fathers of old, you have given steadiness in our often unsteady world, solid footing in a world so often shaken. Once again we come to express gratitude for your love and care, borne out in the practical ways of our lives. You have given your all to us and continue to give to us. You are our greatest joy.

Because of your grace to us, we know saving faith, the forgiveness of sin, assurance of eternal life, and the glory of the world to come. Because of your grace, we have come to know meaningful life where productive pursuits and eternal challenges give us increased motivation for faithful living. Because of your grace, we have healthy bodies and sound minds; families that love us and friends that encourage us; churches that nurture our souls. Father, because of your grace, we are who we are and are thankful for it.

Now we ask that your grace be sensed acutely among us and that we will open ourselves to a more perfect love and devotion. Encourage us to accept the new challenges of life with openness and determination. Strengthen our resolves to serve you faithfully. We praise you now and forever, world without end. Through Christ the Lord. Amen.—Lee McGlone

Benediction: With gratitude in our hearts for the victories of the year and with eagerness to face the challenges of the next, we go forth boldly in Jesus' name, both to speak and to live for him and the world for which he died. Guide us, O Thou great Jehovah. Amen.

SECTION III

RESOURCES FOR
PREACHING

CHAPTER ONE

Preaching Biblical Sermons:
God's Word for God's World

Dr. Terry G. Carter, Vaught Professor of Christian Ministries,
Ouachita Baptist University, Arkadelphia, Arkansas

By definition, a resource is something that can be used or drawn upon to aid a person in the performance of a task. The title of this chapter suggests the offering of some aids for preaching biblical sermons. Part of that task includes providing definitions. Often when the phrase *biblical sermon* is used, people (including preachers) hold differing opinions as to what it means.

WHAT IS A BIBLICAL SERMON?

Defining *biblical sermon* is not as straightforward as one might expect. Misconceptions abound, both in practice and description. Back in the 1960s, H. C. Brown believed preaching was in crisis due to "inadequate and inferior concepts about the ministry in general and preaching in particular."[1] Those inadequate and inferior concepts still exist. Some count a sermon as biblical if a Scripture text is merely attached. Others put sermons into the biblical sermon category, even when they depart from the intended meaning of the text, as long as the Bible is referred to occasionally.[2]

Perhaps some guidelines and parameters for biblical sermons would help. One way to define the term is to connect the sermon to the concept of biblical

---

[1]H. C. Brown, *A Quest for Reformation in Preaching* (Nashville: Broadman, 1968), p. 16.
[2]Much of the material in this section comes from Terry G. Carter, J. Scott Duvall, and J. Daniel Hays, *Preaching God's Word: A Hands-On Approach to Preparing, Developing, and Delivering the Sermon* (Grand Rapids, MI: Zondervan, 2005).

authority. A biblical sermon is one that carries with it high biblical authority. In such a sermon the biblical text serves as the basis of the sermon, and the message communicated through the sermon follows closely the intended meaning of the biblical text, thus drawing its authority from that text. If our goal is to preach with the authority of "thus says the Lord," then it is critical that we ground our sermons firmly and directly in the Bible.

GROUNDING OUR SERMONS IN THE BIBLE
A biblical sermon first requires a text. That sounds trite and obvious. However, confusion reigns concerning what constitutes a sermon text. The Latin term for text (*textus*) comes from a root word connected to the concept of weaving a fabric. As the original, inspired human authors of the Scriptures wove together the words of God to declare his message, so do we strive to declare this same message. In biblical preaching, the text becomes the material or fabric to be woven into the sermon. When we declare a text from the pulpit, the sermon to follow should reflect that biblical passage in points, theme, and message. It should be clear to the audience that the scriptural passage is the foundation and material of the sermon.

A sermon is not a biblical sermon if a passage is merely read and then ignored while the preacher tells humorous stories or deals with other, unrelated topics. Some time ago I sat through two sermons. In each sermon the preacher set up a text and stated clearly to the audience that he intended to use that text as the basis for the sermon. After reading it, he rambled through a series of subjects ranging from morality to ethics to the church. He never referred to the text, made a point from it, explained it, or even gave us cause to look at the Bible again. We could have closed our Bibles; several of us did. He missed the idea of a sermon text.

How does a text become the basis of a biblical sermon? It begins with an exegesis of the text. *Exegete* means to work through the text (commentaries, original language, historical, cultural, and literary context, theological background, and so on) sufficiently to "bring out" the meaning. The fruit of a good exegesis provides more than enough fascinating and relevant material to fill any sermon with principles originating from God. Exegesis seeks to determine the meaning of the text for the original audience, the differences and similarities between the original audience and our congregation, universal spiritual principles or truths that apply to the original audience, as well as to our congregation, and applications for our audience.

THE MAIN IDEA OF A BIBLICAL SERMON

For a sermon to be biblical, the main theme of the sermon should derive from the main theme (or at least one theme) of the sermon text. A proper exegesis provides the main idea of the text for the preacher. It never hurts to write out a *text thesis statement*—a statement in the past tense that explains what the text is about, as directed to the original audience. For instance, the text thesis statement for Luke 15:11–32 (Parable of the Prodigal Son) might read: *Jesus told the Pharisees and teachers of the law that God loves sinners so much that even though he allows them freedom to reject him, his love and mercy toward them never ceases, he always values them, and he rejoices over them whenever they return to him.*

A biblical sermon's main idea reflects the text thesis statement, showing the close connection between text and sermon. It is also good to write out the sermon thesis statement, which should be in present tense and addressed to the congregation. A sermon thesis sentence for the Luke 15 passage might read: *God loves and values us so much that while he allows us to reject him, his love and mercy toward us will never cease, and he will rejoice over us when we return to him.* The entire sermon would then flesh out that sermon thesis, which grows out of the text thesis. No one in the audience would doubt this sermon comes from—and is, in fact, based on—the text designated as the sermon text. We are preaching the Bible, and it is important to indicate that in the sermon.

THE POINTS IN A BIBLICAL SERMON

A biblical sermon includes spiritual truths that come directly (or sometimes indirectly) from the biblical text. The main points of a sermon, whether openly stated in the sermon or not, must grow out of and support the sermon thesis statement. As already indicated, that statement comes directly out of the text thesis statement, which means that the points, spiritual truths, or principles presented in the sermon arise out of the text as well.

Let's use another passage to illustrate this process. A text thesis statement for Luke 5:36–39 might be this: *Jesus informed the Pharisees that he represents the new, true, unique, and better way to God and that even though it will be difficult for them to grasp, the truth Jesus represents cannot be put into their old system but must replace the old way.* Out of that, we develop a sermon thesis statement that might read: *What Jesus offers us cannot be added onto our previous beliefs about spiritual reality because his truth is unique and better, and even though it will not be easy for us, it must replace our old ways to God.*

Now the sermon points from Luke 5:36–39 must explain the sermon thesis statement. The important role of the sermon points is to build and support the main idea. At least three points might be derived from the passage: (1) Christianity is not an add-on religion; (2) it may be difficult for people to give up old beliefs for Christ, and (3) people must replace their old ways to God with his new wine—Jesus. You can see each of these points in the text and sermon thesis statement.

To make sure you are staying true to the text and therefore developing and preaching a biblical sermon, ask the following questions concerning your sermon thesis statement and points:

- Does my statement really reflect what this passage is all about?
- Do my sermon thesis statement and my sermon points truly capture the intent of the biblical author?
- Do they fit the context of the passage?

How many points or spiritual principles should the sermon have? Once again, the points in a biblical sermon are determined by the text itself and not by what the preacher wants to say. The text guides the sermon content—a characteristic of a biblical sermon. Remember, whether stated openly in the sermon or not, all spiritual truths shared in a sermon must derive from the text itself. This guideline ensures that the preacher will not chase rabbits that are not addressed in the passage. These rabbits cause confusion in the minds of the listeners and take them away from the main message of the text.

INCLUDING EXEGETICAL FINDINGS IN THE SERMON

Every sermon contains several communicative elements designed to make it flow well and communicate clearly. For instance, introductions grab attention and establish relevance; conclusions wrap up and call the audience to response; transitions connect all the concepts together, and illustrations make the sermon points more understandable. But to be biblical, the sermon must contain an explanation of the text and its spiritual truths. Whether a sermon has defined, stated points (deductive) or allows the listener to discover them in the process (inductive), it must include a clear explanation of the text, its meaning, and the spiritual truth it contains. This is where biblical authority becomes evident.

After completing a thorough exegesis, it is time to decide how much of this mass of exegetical material should appear in the sermon. Although each passage and sermon is unique, some direction may help.

How much of the information discovered in the exegesis does the audience need to know to truly understand the passage's meaning? In the explanation segments, the biblical sermon includes historical context and background for the text, theological and literary contextual issues, and clarification of biblical language. For example, a sermon for Luke 5:12–26 might include background information on leprosy and paralysis in biblical times. A sermon from Jeremiah 29 needs explanation of the historical context informing the listeners how the Hebrews got into captivity and why. What was happening in Jerusalem and Babylon? The connections and setting for the three stories found in Luke 15 (literary context) help make the point of the stories in a sermon. In all sermons the meaning of words or the significance of grammatical constructs helps the audience understand. Including such material in the sermon enhances the biblical authority of the sermon and ensures the listener that the preacher has made an honest attempt to wrestle with the truth found in the text. Of course, not all exegetical data are fit for the sermon. Include only that necessary for audience comprehension of the text.

SAMPLE SERMONS

The following sermons are examples of biblical preaching that reflect the insights described above.

TITLE: A New Way
TEXT: Mark 2:18–3:6

One issue that Christianity has always struggled with is the issue of legalism. By *legalism,* we mean reducing Christianity to a set of rules that are inflexible and that become more important than people. In the process, the personal relationship aspect of Christianity becomes less important or even nonexistent.

Jesus spent time trying to show those he encountered what real spirituality and Christianity is about. Sometimes he faced hard cases—people so set in their own ideas of what religion is to be that they couldn't be convinced; they just killed him. We need to see the Christian religion as Jesus intended it. Some of us, if we would admit it, are closet legalists and may need to pay attention. Some of us are seekers who have rejected Christianity because of the legalistic forms we have seen. Let's see the faith as Jesus explains it in the passage we have selected.

Mark 2:18–3:6 is a very interesting passage for several reasons. It consists of several encounters of Jesus with a group of people called Pharisees. They were Jews to the core and equated good religion with keeping the law. Not all Pharisees were bad guys who always played the hypocrite role; most were serious followers of Yahweh who simply interpreted that task as keeping the Jewish law faithfully and pleasing God through doing so. Their driving passion was to fulfill God's commands. For them, people, things, times, and actions served as opportunities for holiness or unholiness—indications of how good they were "doing" religion and how spiritual they were.

Their world was rocked when Jesus came in with new ideas and ways of doing things. In our passage we see that Mark has grouped together several stories, starting as far back as verse 13, that correspond well. These events probably didn't all happen on the same day or even in sequence (look at the introductory phrases). But Mark puts them together because, as a unit, they teach us some very important lessons about the Christianity that Jesus came to inaugurate.

Clearly, the Pharisees are not Christians and didn't want to be, but they do represent a way of being religious that is based on rules. Jesus uses these encounters to teach us a different way—a new way.

The three encounters (we could have included a fourth by going all the way back to the eating-with-the-sinners encounter) are between Jesus and the Pharisees. In the first encounter, some people (disciples of the Pharisees) complain to Jesus that the Pharisees fasted, as did John's disciples, but the disciples of Jesus did not. In the second, the complaint is that the disciples of Jesus picked grain on the Sabbath, which was to be kept holy and without work. In the third encounter, Jesus gets a little upset because the complaint is over whether or not it is OK to heal someone on the Sabbath. The work of healing was considered too much work for the Sabbath. The logic may have been that the man had suffered this long, so what difference would another day make. Jesus' response to these challenges outlines "religion according to Jesus." In these responses we get the elements of the new way Jesus is inaugurating.

I. **The New Way.** *Focus on the bridegroom—Jesus the Messiah—not rules.* There were many reasons to fast. Some fasted for sadness; maybe the disciples of John fasted for this reason, as John was in prison. Some fasted for repentance, as an expression of piety. The Pharisees fasted two days a week as a spiritual act, which in their minds proved their spirituality and fulfilled the law. Although the law did not require that many fasts, they went beyond the requirement. But the question being asked was, Why did Jesus' disciples not fast? Answer: because their focus was on the Messiah.

The picture is of a wedding feast. We all know that guests eat at weddings; they do not fast. The idea of the bridegroom is part of a picture of the Kingdom and the messianic wedding feast, with believers as guests. Jesus is the bridegroom, and we are his bride. To be with him is like being at a wedding feast. Who in the world would fast at a wedding feast? It is the time for joy, happiness, and soaking up all you can in relationship with the bridegroom. The new way is focused in the person of Jesus and knowing him and being in relationship with him, not in rules determined to keep one in good stead with God. Jesus does mention that there will be a brief sadness at his death. That will pass when he is raised and ascended. The Christian faith consists of Christ with us and in us.

In addition, Jesus used two parables to teach his disciples and the Pharisees that you can't add that old "rule" method of religion to the new way. It just doesn't fit. It's like a piece of new cloth sewn into an old shirt. When it is washed the new piece will shrink and ruin the shirt. Or it's like new wine stored in old, cracked wine skins. When the new wine ferments, the old skins will burst. There is a bit of irony here because Jesus is explaining inappropriate behavior, which is the very thing the Pharisees sought to avoid. Jesus did not come to patch up the old system. He transformed it and moved it from external focus to internal.

The new way—the way that Jesus introduces by his very presence—is the real Christianity that focuses on the person of Jesus. Salvation is in him alone. He is the way. He is our righteousness. The Christian life consists of following him. This is Mark's favorite phrase for discipleship: follow me. But still we get caught up in doing specified things, avoiding other things, following rules, and we think that makes us a good Christian. All the while, we forget the focus; it's all about Jesus and our relationship to him. It is a grace relationship, not works salvation.

II. **What other elements belong in this new religion?** *Worship the Lord of the Sabbath, not rules.* In the second encounter, Jesus' disciples eat grain they picked in the field. The law allowed picking ears of corn by hand as you walked through a field, as long as you didn't get the tractor out. The Pharisees had thirty-nine categories of rules concerning work on the Sabbath, and reaping was number 3. But it was the Sabbath, and the law, as interpreted by the Pharisees, regarded such action as work. It was not allowed. Mark uses the phrase, "the Pharisees said," but Jesus' response indicates it really doesn't matter what they said. Jesus used David as an example. He and his men ate the showbread in the tent of worship, even though that was not allowed. David was not condemned.

The real kicker argument comes with Jesus' statements concerning the Sabbath. It is for man's benefit (which certainly would include eating) and, more important, Jesus himself claims to be Lord of the Sabbath. He transforms the rules about Sabbath to center on him and the good of the worshipper. When we think about the Sabbath, we should think about Jesus and the benefit we receive spiritually by worshipping him. Remember, it's all about Jesus. Jesus has sovereign authority over the Sabbath and everything else. So we must worship Jesus and concern ourselves with his desires. Don't worship a set of rules set up to equal Christianity.

III. **The last story tells us one more thing about Christianity, according to Jesus.** *Value the people Jesus loves, not rules.* The last encounter is perhaps the saddest, and Jesus uses it to prove his lordship over the Sabbath. Here is a man with a withered hand who comes into contact with the only person around who can do anything about his hand. But the Pharisees who value keeping the law above everything else step in to see if Jesus will heal on the Sabbath. Jesus takes the initiative here. He is a little irritated with the Pharisees. Their legalistic adherence to the rules without regard to the needs of people angered Christ. They missed the point of true religion. Micah 6:8 says, *"And what does the Lord require of you? To act justly and to love mercy and to walk humbly with your God."*

Jesus tells the man to stand and then questions the Pharisees about what is the proper action on the Sabbath. Then Jesus commands the needy man to stretch out his hand, and Jesus heals him. It was more than the Pharisees could take. They were furious. Surely, this man could wait another day to be healed. But Jesus has another idea in mind: do good on the Sabbath, heal, and consider a human's need more important than concern for the law. The Pharisees decided to kill Jesus. He was dangerous to their way of religion. This encounter reminds us that somehow our faith should have an impact on the world. What kind of impact did the faith of the Pharisees have— ignoring a hurting man and killing Jesus? Priority of human need always trumps the need to conform to ritual.

What is Jesus trying to say to them and to us? He says you can't reduce Christianity to things you do or don't do or to rules meant to keep one always coloring inside the lines. It is about a person—Jesus—and the people who need him. It is the greatest commandment: Love the Lord your God with all your heart and your neighbor as yourself. There is no commandment greater than these.

So does this mean God has no expectations, no standards to live by? Of course he does. Christians are created for good works, but those works grow out of a grace relationship with Christ. We love him, know him, and follow him, and we love and do good for those around us, including those who have withered hands on the Sabbath. God's expectations and standards are reached in Jesus, and when we know him personally, focus on him, and live in him, all the rest takes care of itself. Real believers *act* like real believers. It's about grace and relationship. You can't do enough to please God, so you just love him, worship him, and then walk in his ways the best you can.

IV. **So now the real question.** *Are you a legalist?* How can you tell? I can offer you at least three tests. In the tradition of Jeff Foxworthy:

1. If you evaluate your spirituality purely by how well you follow "shoulds" and "should nots," then you might be a legalist.
2. If you worry more about the things you should have done or not done than you do about your relationship with Jesus and feel guilty all the time, then you might be a legalist.

3. If you are constantly critical and judgmental toward others because they are doing things you think they shouldn't or not doing things you think they should, then you might be a legalist.

Christians who say yes to the questions have some issues to consider. Why? None of us can even keep all of our own rules. We can do all the Christian things and not do the un-Christian things, but we will make mistakes, and if our legalistic theology is correct, then God will be mad. But God loves us, and he knows we will blow it from time to time. To be spiritual is not to follow all the religious rules but rather to know Christ personally, to walk with and worship him and live for him to the best of our ability. In addition, because legalism is so stressful, it brings misery and anxiety, not joy and fulfillment. Legalists are usually very unhappy people. They are constantly upset with themselves and struggling with guilt because they can't keep all the rules, and they are critical of others for the same reason. I think that is why some church members rebel. They can't take that spirit-killing kind of Christianity they have been burdened with anymore. Do you ever feel your faith is like that—weighty, no fun, just stress in trying to be good? Christianity focuses on Jesus and values the people he wants to influence, and therein lies the key to real joy and pleasure. Jesus' goal for his people is that they might experience the "full measure of his joy" (John 17:13).

How about you? Are you a closet legalist? Or are you a blatant legalist? Does your faith mostly consist of doing certain things and avoiding others? That may result in a clean life, but it won't result in fulfillment.

Have you ever watched ballroom dancers? The recent movie *Shall We Dance?* has made it popular again. Now there are television programs highlighting ballroom dance, with stars as competitors. Dancers who are just learning are stressed and filled with concern over the steps. They can't even enjoy the dance because they are too focused on the details and rules. Is my foot in the right place? Is it two steps or three? Where should I turn? Don't step on the partner's toe. It's no fun. But after a while they take what they've learned, listen to the music, and just dance. If they make a mistake, they recover and then dance some more. They enjoy it. Isn't that what a Christian should do—enjoy Christianity?

But some Christians only worry about the steps and making sure they don't step on God's toes. The stress of their faith makes it no fun. Jesus makes the music, but they don't hear it. They just walk through the steps. But Jesus—the Bridegroom, the Lord—intended another way. He wants you to focus on him and the music he makes and just dance the best you can. If you miss a step, then ask forgiveness and keep on dancing.

Jesus played a new tune that the Pharisees refused to hear or dance to. The tune had a new focus—the Bridegroom, Jesus, the Messiah—as well as a new object of worship and a new value: people who are loved by God. That is the Christian life. If we learn to dance to that tune of grace instead of to legalism, then we will be able to enjoy the dance.

TITLE: A Compassionate Heart
TEXT: Matt. 9:35–38

When we see compassion in action, we are always impressed. It affects our opinion of people. It affects the world's impression of the Church when they see Christians exercise compassion.

In 1979 Mother Teresa won a Nobel Peace Prize. Why? From the window of St. Mary's High School in Calcutta, Mother Teresa could see the poverty and suffering of the people, and it broke her heart. She asked for permission to go outside the convent walls to work with the poorest of the poor. She spent her life in the slums. Her compassion for lepers and the abject poor gained the attention of the world. Her Nobel Peace Prize was for exemplary compassion.

It was the compassion of Jesus that drew so many people to him. Compassion motivated God, the Father, to send Jesus, his Son, to earth. The Scripture records a long history of compassionate action by God. When God spoke to Moses from the burning bush to commission him to lead the people out of Egypt, it was because God had seen the Hebrews in their misery and had compassion on them.

If the church is going to really make an impact in the world and in communities, we must have hearts of compassion. We must care for and about people—truly care. What can we learn from Jesus about compassion? God sent his Son to demonstrate it, and the passage we have read exemplifies it. When we love like Jesus, we will minister more like Jesus, and our world will be drawn to God.

What does real Christian compassion do? How are people driven to serve the needs of others?

I. **True compassion is moved when it sees people in need.** Failing to see need usually means we are self-absorbed or even church-absorbed. That problem always hinders us from ministering as we should. Jesus exemplifies the opposite. The four verses we read are found in the midst of a larger passage reflecting compassion in action. In the previous verses we find a trail of miracles. Jesus has just healed a paralytic (vv. 1–8) and a woman with a bleeding problem; he raised a dead girl (vv. 18–29), gave sight to two blind men, and freed a demon-possessed man who was mute (vv. 27–34). The passage is followed by the account of Jesus sending out the twelve disciples for the purpose of driving out evil spirits, healing, and proclaiming the Kingdom. These stories are bunched together in Matthew's Gospel for a reason. The text is trying to make a powerful spiritual point. Why does Jesus do all this?

Matthew 9:35–38 provides the clue. Jesus does all this because he sees the people in their great need and has compassion on them. This Greek word for compassion (*splagchnon*) is powerful. It carries the idea of deep love and concern. The word includes the idea of "entrails" or "bowels." It means to love from the very depth of your gut or being. Jesus cared deeply that they were hurting. He was moved with love down deep in his gut. When Jesus saw the needy people, he hurt inside for them.

The people were impressed. The text indicates that some were amazed because nothing like this had happened before. The Pharisees were convinced that Jesus was a demon receiving his power from Satan. The text indicates that Jesus was going around to all the cities and villages. We merely get a sampling of what Jesus was doing for people. "All" may be hyperbole or an exaggeration, indicating that Jesus was going a lot of places and meeting a lot of needs. He was looking for people in need, and when he saw them he had great compassion.

Compassion sees people as they are—physically and spiritually. Some were sick and hurting, and Jesus healed many of them. But these people had deeper problems—spiritual needs. They were harassed and helpless. The phrase means they were bothered like sheep, continually harassed by predators. They were beaten down and helpless. Ultimately, they were like sheep without a shepherd. They had no guide, master, or direction. Their lives were aimless and futile. They were going nowhere and knew not where to go. Jesus is the shepherd who sees how desperately they need him. The question is, Do we see? Are we aware of the great needs of those around us?

True compassion, if we have it, looks for those in need and sees. That compassion moves us to action. In other words, we see and we care.

In *Les Miserables* Hugo tells the story of Jean Valjean, whose life hits bottom after he steals a loaf of bread. He serves nineteen years for the crime before being turned out penniless into the streets. He ends up in the home of a merciful old bishop. The bishop feeds Jean supper and offers a bed for the night. He serves Jean with his best silver. Yielding to temptation Jean steals the silver plates and runs. The police catch him and take Jean to the bishop, informing him of the theft of the silver plates. To Jean's surprise the bishop claims he gave the plates to his guest; then he adds that Jean forgot the candlesticks. The bishop gives them to Jean.

Here was a man who saw Jean Valjean's need and had compassion—deep enough compassion to take a personal, financial loss to meet Jean's need. It changed Jean's life and brought about true repentance. For Jesus the ultimate compassion was to give his life to meet our greatest need. What about us?

Many Christians excel in seeing needs and having compassion. They see and care. But what about you? Are you looking, noticing, and caring actively? Even if you can remember a moment of compassion, remember that this kind of love should characterize your entire life. It must be daily and renewable constantly. Many people all around us have needs. We must see and have compassion—the kind Jesus exemplified. See the people who are poor or lost spiritually, like sheep without a shepherd, and people who are sick or in need. If we see and care, we will be motivated. The world needs to be amazed again and again by our compassionate heart. But compassion goes further than seeing and caring.

II. **Compassion always acts**. James proclaimed that those who claim to have faith and love must show it by action. John agreed, saying that claiming love and refusing to act on it makes you a liar. Jesus hurt in his very core for those in need, and he acted. The text makes it clear that he went about doing things for people out of compassion.

Three participles tell the story. Jesus went about all the villages *teaching* in the synagogues because these people were lost without the light. He went about *preaching* the gospel of good news and the Kingdom. He went about *healing* every kind of disease and infirmity. The stories in previous verses are specific examples of this action. Jesus physically and emotionally healed the woman with the issue of blood. He gave her life and salvation. The little girl received physical life, literally. Jesus gave sight to two blind men. The demon-possessed men gained freedom and a voice to proclaim it. Jesus didn't just *say* he loved them. He acted forcefully and broadly and specifically. Are we acting on our love as well?

In an article titled "From Wall Street to the Street," Randy Bishop tells the story of Kevin Bradley, a big-time Baltimore stockbroker who was caught up in big money. Every day as he walked to the office, Kevin passed by the homeless on the street. Often he took them to breakfast and just listened to their stories. He wanted to know who they were and how they had ended up on the street. He wasn't looking for a mission, but God wouldn't let him go. In 1991 after prayer and Bible study, Kevin quit his job and started the Community Outreach Center to meet the needs of the homeless. He lived off his savings until the money was gone. At times he and his family had less food than those he was helping. His perseverance paid off, and finally others caught the vision and backed the ministry financially. What moved Kevin Bradley to action? Compassion!

Now think. When was the last time you noticed need, were hurt to the core over it, and then acted to remedy the problem? Christians should be able to answer that question quickly. Our call is to be like Jesus—the one who saw and loved and acted to help, even to the point of death on the cross to meet our spiritual need. If we are not doing something to alleviate the suffering around us, then we must evaluate our love. Sometimes the need is so great we need others to help. Then what?

III. **Compassion prays for needs.** Jesus encountered many in need and many more to come. He met the needs of many, but the great numbers and the future generations demanded a plan. Therefore, Jesus' compassion compelled him to do one more thing. He noted that the fields are "white unto harvest"—a poetic way of speaking, possibly a metaphor for the mission of sowing and reaping spiritually in the world. The day is short and the task is great. The idea of harvest may be connected to eschatological ideas or the end time. As such, taking the gospel to the world and meeting needs is the

Kingdom work until the end. But here is the tragedy. There were not enough workers to get the job done. Jesus called twelve to be with him in the task of meeting spiritual, physical, and emotional needs. The field demands more. What should his followers do?

The command is simple. Pray! Beseech! Ask! Entreat God to send workers into the fields to the people in need. Why? Because God has compassion on them, and we should, too. It is an imperative command. We must pray to God for help. In crisis, faith responds by turning to God in trust through prayer. If we really love and care, we will beseech God to send helpers.

However, take care. Expect two things from God when we pray this prayer: (1) God will raise up workers to heal and teach and preach the good news, and (2) God will send us personally into the field. This is what happens with the disciples. Jesus sends them out (Matt. 10). Some of us need a push. The phrase *send out* is strong in tone. It can mean to thrust or throw us into the ministry. This prayer is an urgent request for God to thrust people into the work. Some of us need that kind of push.

This kind of prayer is working right now all over the world. An intercessory prayer movement right now in Brazil has grown to include more than 188,000 women in the last ten years and is changing the city of Goiania, which was steeped in Spiritism. More than 370 fellowships were started in one month, after one group of believers prayed and fasted forty days. It is believed that the number of evangelicals has multiplied by five in the last six years.

In Argentina, pastors have seen the task as too great and have turned to God in prayer twice monthly in vigils and retreats—times of intense prayer. Others conduct all-night prayer meetings. They believe that prayer will help meet the tremendous need. Why shouldn't they? That is exactly what Jesus commanded.

Pray about it. That could be a problem. We pray often, but most of the time we pray for ourselves and about ourselves. Jesus' command concerns prayer for the work of the Kingdom, prayer for people to be mobilized to meet the great physical and spiritual needs of people around the world. How often are we praying to that end? Compassion turns to God and lifts up the need in prayer. God, in turn, empowers the ministry to meet the need.

CONCLUSION

People respond to love. When they see Christians express it genuinely, they are touched and changed by it. They are drawn to the faith.

In 1834 Johann Gerhardt Oncken established the first Baptist church on the continent of Europe in the city of Hamburg, Germany. The German Constitution forbade any church other than Lutheran or Catholic. The Hamburg police chief told Oncken that as long as his little finger could move, Oncken and his Baptists would feel its pressure. Oncken replied that he could see a greater arm. It was the arm of God, and as long as it moved, the police chief would not silence the Baptists. The people of Hamburg considered the Baptists as cult members and avoided them. Then something happened. A great fire destroyed a large portion of Hamburg in 1842. The Baptists looked around at all the people who were homeless, without food or clothing. They had compassion and opened up the church building as a shelter. They fed, clothed, loved, and provided for the people. It changed everything. Compassion does. The Hamburgers (the people of Hamburg) opened up to hear the gospel when they saw the love of the Baptists.

That still works. Christians must be people of compassion who see need, care, and act. They pray that God will meet the needs through his people. We must express God's love. How are we doing?

TITLE: Public Faith
TEXT: Luke 12:1–3, 8–10

I grew up in West Texas as an avid Arkansas Razorback fan. Surprisingly, I survived. Being so far away from Arkansas, I seldom got a chance to see the Razorbacks play in person. However, during my seminary days, Arkansas came to Ft. Worth to play TCU. I decided to go to the game, and being the only Razorback fan I knew, I went alone. When I arrived at the game, I didn't really know which side of the field would be filled with Razorback fans. I just bought a ticket and went in. Soon I discovered my mistake. I was the lone Razorback fan in the middle of a sea of purple and white. On the opposite side of the field, hog hats and red filled the stands. I was in a pickle.

I faced a dilemma: reveal my true loyalty by my action and cheers or keep it a secret for safety's sake. I chose to live. I cheered inside but made sure that on the outside I looked like a Horned Frog devotee, even though somewhat subdued.

The same issue faces us in a world where often the pressure is to conceal our true identity. Many of us are afraid to really be ourselves in the presence of those we encounter, some of whom we know well but still hesitate being honest with. That dilemma becomes more difficult when we throw religion or faith into the mix. And this problem is two-sided. Some want people to think they are people of faith when that is far from true. Others try to conceal their faith. The way we act all depends on the circumstance and who we are trying to impress.

Jesus encountered all kinds of public displays concerning faith and relationships to God during his ministry. The issue became a theme of his teaching. In this passage Jesus addresses his disciples in order to warn them and inform them of what he expects of them. When we think of faith, many of us want to paint a simple picture: there are those who are believers and those who aren't, and it is easy to see the difference. To a point that is correct. But when we consider the expressions of faith or the way people portray their faith, it becomes more complicated than that. In this passage Jesus addresses three different portrayals of faith or lack of faith. As disciples, we need to learn from this study and make sure we do what pleases Christ. How do people portray faith?

I. **Some will say they are believers in God but really aren't.** Jesus brings up the subject of Pharisees. In that discussion he says the Pharisees have yeast that disciples of Jesus should beware of. That yeast is hypocrisy. *Hypocrisy* means to play a part, pretend to give the impression that you are something you're not. The Pharisees were devotedly religious. They received honor from the common people for all their ritual and religious activity. The sinner on the street considered the Pharisees to be the best of all believers. Yet Jesus accuses some of them of playing the hypocrite role. They were not as spiritual as they portrayed themselves to be. They were involved in ritual piety, a veneer covering a sinful, contaminated soul.

Jesus knew it. Beware of this type of faith. Be on your guard. It has a spoiling effect. Why would Jesus warn the disciples? Because this type of surface faith is a possibility for all of us. We get so busy playing the game that we forget about the real inner relationship of trust in God. As a result we can develop a thin veneer of religion with nothing of substance underneath. We portray sanctity while we are truly far from God on the inside.

The disciples had to beware. They were believers, but often Christians act like they are close to God while on the inside the opposite is true. They give the pretense of being the most spiritual, when in reality they are unspiritual. All of us possess a little of this quality within us, but the goal is to minimize it as much as possible. We strive to be as real and genuine as possible and stay as close to God as possible.

Bill Hybels, in his book *Honest to God,*[3] told about attending a personal growth conference for Christians. Midway through the meeting a question over a delicate decision led to debate and then to ugly division. For forty-five minutes heated argument followed. Things were probably said that would have been better unsaid. Before it was resolved the session ended, and they moved to worship time. The leader of the last session, who had been in the heat of battle, stepped to microphone and, smiling ear-to-ear, announced, "Scripture tells us the mark of a true Christian is love, so let's all join hands and sing 'They Will Know We Are Christians by Our Love.'"

Jesus adds teeth to the warning. Our true self will eventually be made quite clear. The person you are behind closed doors when you are whispering to those like you or just by yourself will be revealed. God penetrates to every corner of the house. He knows all, and all will be known. In other words the game is up. God already knows. We may fool all those around us, but we are not fooling the One that matters. Hypocrisy gets us nowhere permanently or eternally.

Sir Arthur Conan Doyle knew of this human tendency to pretend and to live a lie. It was said that he played a dirty trick on twelve of his friends. He sent a telegram to all twelve men, who were known as men of virtue, reputation, and honor in London society. The anonymous telegram simply said, "Fly at once, all is discovered." A good American translation might be, "Get out of town at once, your secret has been discovered." It was reported that within twenty-four hours all twelve had left the country. They were hiding something but covering it up with an apparently reputable life.

---

[3]Bill Hybels, *Honest to God* (Grand Rapids, MI: Zondervan, 1992).

Are we spiritually genuine or are we playing the game of religion and Christianity? On the outside do we put on Christianity while being something quite different on the inside? In the church there are always those who say they are but in reality aren't. They know it. We may not see it when we look at them, but it is no secret to God. Some day it will be revealed. All will be laid bare before God.

But here is some good news. If you are playing the hypocrite, you don't have to continue the charade. It takes courage to give up the act and truly become a believer. It may be an embarrassment at first to admit the hypocrisy. We fear others will laugh or ridicule us for admitting it. But the church has a tendency to be very happy when someone finally gets authentic with God and his people. They love it. Why? Because we all have struggles with the same hypocrisy and fight it daily. When someone finally says, "I won't live that way anymore," then we rejoice. There is another public expression of faith that Jesus touches on.

II. **There are those who say they are not believers, and they aren't.** Some will deny publicly that they are believers, and, indeed, they tell the truth. They have no part of the faith and often don't want it. They don't believe in Jesus. If you ask them whether they have a relationship with Christ, the answer is a straight-up no.

These people are lost unbelievers, not children of God. They publicly deny they are believers, and according to the text that is repeated in heaven. God does not claim them as his children either. They do not have a part in God's Kingdom, and they accept that reality.

Verse 10 is one of the most difficult verses in the New Testament. We could pass over it without comment, but it is important. It refers to those who deny the faith completely. They are the ones who blaspheme the Holy Spirit. They are not forgiven. What does this mean? Commentators struggle as we do with this statement. Some say it means to count Jesus as part of Satan's realm—Beelzebub. But I believe a better interpretation exists. They reject the Holy Spirit and therefore the main task of the Holy Spirit, which is to present the message of Jesus to you. As a result they are not believers. To reject the truth that Jesus is the Son of God, the Messiah, and Savior is to miss being part of God's family. It means to live a life rejecting Jesus.

To speak a word against the Son is forgivable. We can use Peter as the example. He denied Jesus three times but was forgiven. But had he rejected completely that Jesus is God and Messiah, he would have missed eternal life. The one who blasphemes the Holy Spirit lives a life of denial concerning Jesus.

While I was a campus minister in Texas, we went out on campus with students to witness. This was a difficult task. We approached one guy and asked him if we could talk to him. He recognized us and immediately went into a violent tirade. He used every word imaginable to say that he was not a believer and not interested in it. Guess what? I believed him. We never bothered him again. Many students we encountered did allow us to share but not this man. He was in this category Jesus described: he publicly denied Jesus.

What should we think about such people? Just forget about them? No! They are the mission field. We pray for them and share the truth with them when given any chance. We live a life so publicly Christian in front of them that they will want what we have.

C. S. Lewis, in *Man or Rabbit,* made this observation:

> Honest rejection of Christ, however mistaken, will be forgiven and healed—"whoever shall speak a word against the Son of Man, it shall be forgiven him." But to *evade* the Son of Man; to look the other way; to pretend you haven't noticed; to become suddenly absorbed in something on the other side of the street; to leave the receiver off the telephone because it might be He who was ringing up; to leave unopened certain letters in a strange handwriting because they might be from Him—this is a different matter. You may not be certain yet whether you ought to be a Christian; but you do know you ought to be a man, not an ostrich hiding his head in the sands.[4]

To continually avoid and reject God and decide not to allow him room in your life is the idea here. These people claim to be unbelievers, and they are. Yet they can change as long as they physically live. We continue to pray and look for opportunities to share. Jesus noted one more type of public faith.

[4]Clyde S. Kilby (ed.), *An Anthology of C. S. Lewis: A Mind Awake* (New York: Harcourt Brace Jovanovich, 1968), pp. 119–120.

III. **Those who say they are believers and truly are.** Jesus' desire for all disciples is that they reach a stage in life where they publicly, boldly, even at the risk of ridicule or worse, confess him before men. Confess in public. Verbal confession is a part of authentic faith. Romans 10:9–10 says to confess with your mouth that Jesus is Lord. It means to publicly acknowledge that you believe in the Jesus described in the Bible. *Confess* means to agree with God that Jesus is Lord, Messiah, Savior, and true God.

Let me be clear here. We are not saying that we should reduce becoming a Christian to some ritual words spoken in public. I think the idea is that real, authentic Christians are those who publicly proclaim that truth, regardless of the consequence or circumstance. They stand as Peter and John stood before the Sanhedrin. When threatened they respond: We must witness, we cannot stay silent. This does not mean we must witness or stand on street corners screaming out our faith. It does mean real, authentic Christians are not ashamed to let people know who they are. It is not a secret. It is something to be proud of and to let others know about.

From a study of history we know that many have verified their Christian witness by their life and death. In the year 112, Pliny served as the governor in Bithynia under Trajan, the Roman emperor. Pliny persecuted Christians, as he deemed his duty. He described his plan in a letter to Trajan for the purpose of gaining some reassurance of his actions.

> Meanwhile, this is the course that I have adopted in the case of those brought before me as Christians. I ask them if they are Christians. If they admit it I repeat the question a second and third time, threatening capital punishment; if they persist I sentence them to death. For I do not doubt that, whatever kind of crime it may be to which they have confessed, their pertinacity and inflexible obstinacy should certainly be punished. There were others who displayed a like madness and whom I reserved to be sent to Rome, since they were Roman citizens.[5]

---

[5]Henry Bettenson and Chris Maunder (ed.), *Documents of the Christian Church* (Oxford: Oxford University Press, 1999), p. 3.

Why were they killed? Because they publicly admitted, confessed, even under pain of death that they, indeed, were believers in Jesus. Authentic Christianity is open. It amazes me how often we as believers attempt to hide that fact. We are never threatened with death or imprisonment. Yet we do not openly, publicly make it clear to those around us that we are believers. Why? Is it embarrassment, a desire to fit in, to get something we want? Who knows? But most of us are guilty of it to some degree.

What is God's desire? "I tell you, whoever acknowledges me before men, the Son of Man will acknowledge him before the angels of God" (v. 11). God will be with you in this public expression of faith.

How transparent are you concerning your faith in Christ? Is it clear or is it hidden? Christianity—real, authentic Christianity is public—always has been—always will be. That is the nature of the faith. Not secret but open, visible, available. How about you?

CONCLUSION

Jesus made it clear that hiding who you really are will not work in the long run. There will come a day, a time, when all that we are will be laid bare. God knows it—all the parts and areas of our life. When will the revelation be? Who knows? Certainly, we should be aware that there is no guarantee of time. Today, openly confess and take care of hypocrisy.

When the world looks around, it sees those who claim to be Christians but may not be, those who are not Christians and admit it, and true, authentic believers. The important fact for us to remember is this: only true, public, authentic Christians are acknowledged by God and belong to his family. They are claimed by God.

What are you? Are you pretending to be Christian but know inside that is untrue? Are you willing to openly confess your Christianity? Today is the day to confess God publicly.

CHAPTER TWO

Preaching the Sermon on the Mount:
The Upside-Down Kingdom

Dr. Danny M. West, Associate Professor of Preaching and Pastoral Studies,
M. Christopher White School of Divinity,
Gardner-Webb University, Boiling Springs, North Carolina

The Sermon on the Mount (Matt. 5–7) signals the dawn of the reign of God in the life of the follower of Jesus Christ. These words of Jesus are like a peephole into another dimension of reality. They offer us an opportunity to see the real-life implications of living in the Kingdom of God, for in the reading of these words, the hearer is introduced to the consequences of discipleship.

The sermon is about living under the authority and influence of Jesus through choosing the lordship of Christ. As a result of that lifestyle, there are ethical and lifestyle consequences. These consequences confront the follower with gut-wrenching choices, and these choices are fleshed out in human circumstance. There is an expectation that living under Kingdom rule will look different than the surrounding culture. Thus at the heart of the Sermon on the Mount is the principle of the opposites. Those things that naturally fit within the structure of the secular world are foreign to that of the Kingdom; likewise, those areas of life that resonate with the Kingdom are at odds in the culture.

It has been espoused that these words constitute Jesus' "inaugural address"[1] in establishing his new and coming Kingdom. If that is indeed the case, then these words offer us clues into that special world. Not only is there practical advice that is offered, but there are sobering reminders that this life is no easy one. It is not a coincidence, then, that these words were uttered on a mountain.

---

[1]Douglas A. Hart, *Interpretation: A Bible Commentary for Teaching and Preaching, Matthew* (Louisville: John Knox, 1993), p. 33.

Not only is there the connection to the legacy of Moses, but a careful reading of the words is a haunting reminder that to follow Jesus Christ is to climb steep mountains and to face daunting challenges all of our days.[2]

TOPIC: The Upside-Down Kingdom
TEXT: Matt. 5:1–12

I recently learned an important Kingdom lesson from the most unlikely of places! The awakening occurred to me during a rerun of *The Jerry Seinfeld* show on television. This particular episode featured the hapless character, George Costanza. George is a classic loser. There is no politically correct way to describe him otherwise. In the storyline George attests to his own inadequacies and ineptness. Bemoaning the fact that all of his decisions in life have turned out wrong, George vows to choose the opposite of what he would normally select. His reasoning is sound: if his instincts are always wrong, he must try the opposite. The culmination of this thinking comes when he sees a lovely young lady in a restaurant. Whereas the "old" George would try to impress her with tall tales of success and prosperity, the "new" George strolls up to her and says, "Hi, my name is George. I am single, unemployed, and I live with my parents." To his amazement, the opposite response won the heart of the young lady.

I. **The Sermon on the Mount in general and the Beatitudes in particular exemplify this opposite motif.** A simple look at the great reversal motifs exemplified in the statements of the Beatitudes reinforces this concept. Those who are "poor in spirit" will inherit the kingdom of heaven (Matt. 5:3). Those who "mourn shall be comforted" (Matt. 5:4). The things of this world will be turned upside down in the new world being established by Jesus. Hence, when Jesus unveiled his Kingdom instinct, at every juncture there is an unavoidable conflict with the way "we" respond to life matters and the way a follower of Christ responds. The responses that are de-

---

[2]The following resources were helpful in the development of these sermon ideas: (1) Donald A. Hagner, *Matthew 1–13, Word Biblical Commentary* (Dallas: Word Books, 1994); the introductory remarks to the Sermon on the Mount are outstanding and provide a valuable framework for understanding the context of the passages; (2) Scott Nash (ed.), *The Sermon on the Mount: Studies and Sermons* (Greenville, SC: Smyth & Helwys, 1992).

manded of the followers of Christ are in utter conflict with the way, as humans, we are wired. Thus a Kingdom instinct is the opposite of our human instinct. It beckons courage and a response that can only come from a deep and passionate devotion to Christ.

II. **Inherent in this Kingdom rule is a great reversal of fortune and spirit.** This does not mean that serving God is a panacea for all ills and that pain will escape those who love and serve God. To be sure, the follower of Christ will face hardship and difficulty. The vindication comes when God rewards those trampled under by the values of this world with the blessings of his Kingdom. God turns the things of this world upside down. Clearly, there is a reminder toward patience and trust in God that the things that burden us now will be addressed by our God.

III. **Endurance is rewarded in eternity.** There is, however, a strong hint of realized eschatology in the Beatitudes. This great reversal will come in its own good time, but in the coming of Christ, the wheels are already in motion. In the lives of his followers, the values of this world are already examined in a different light. Old loyalties are now weighed very carefully. Former allegiances fall into their rightful place now that Christ is Lord. The world that is to be *is already* because of the coming of Christ.

Everything is different. It is looking at the world through a different lens. It is allowing the world to turn upside down so that the secular is spilled out among us and the sacred takes its rightful place.

With the coming of Christ the old ways begin to fade into obscurity. He changes everything and everyone who comes into his path. It is as if we become the opposite. And that, I suspect, is exactly what he had in mind— the opposite! The opposite where this world and its values are turned upside down and in the process are finally turned right side up for the very first time. We are back to George Costanza, it appears. Choose the opposite of what we would naturally desire. For in so doing, we finally get it right after all.

TOPIC: High Stakes

TEXT: Matt. 5:13–16

Jesus never coddled his followers. I suspect had he done so he would have rendered those first disciples a great disservice. Had they been seduced by fancy promises of smooth sailing, they would have been in for a rude awakening when they were jolted back into reality by the fangs of the real world in which they lived and served. Having set forth the basic premise of what Kingdom living entailed in the Beatitudes, Jesus then proceeds to unpack the bottom-line expectations he held for his followers. Ever mindful that the Christian witness is borne in the trenches of life, Jesus ups the ante.

Discipleship in this Kingdom is not addendum material; it is at the core of the lifestyle to which believers are called. There is no cozy existence, and the demands are brutal at best. The cost of being a follower of Jesus Christ is one that requires everything, even, potentially, life itself. Jesus employs very common metaphors that are applicable in both his era and ours. He speaks of the disciple being salt and light.

I. **Jesus declared, "You are the salt of the world; but if salt has lost its taste, how shall its saltiness be restored?" (Matt. 5:13).** Inherent in these words is the expectation that the Christian life will be lived out, not in hiding but by merging itself into the everyday traffic pattern of life. Increasingly, the Christian community is in cultural retreat. With a weak understanding of both ecclesiology and eschatology, the church mistakenly believes that its best work is done within the shadow of the steeple.

These words of Jesus confront that misperception. He fully expects his followers to be persons of influence. That influence is to be one that invades and penetrates the surrounding powers. The Christian witness is to be like that of the crock-pot. Through a slow and steady method, the blandness of life is to be seasoned by the presence of Christ, poured out through a life of discipleship. The "salt-like" influence is to invade the world and even soak into the world so that the world itself is changed by that presence.

II. **Furthermore, Jesus continues the discussion of faith in the public eye by insisting, "You are the light of the world. A city set on a hill cannot be hid" (Matt. 5:14).** The image is a bold one. The mind's eye immediately conjures personal images of tall cities and bright lights that even miles away can be seen and almost magically invites a closer look.

The matter at stake in these words is the notion that to not bear light betrays the very definition of light. Light illuminates. It reveals. To *not* do so is not light. Thus Jesus calls his followers to a deep and sobering level of commitment.

Ordinarily, these verses are preached in generic, plain-vanilla terms: "Be salt and light." But there is nothing ordinary about these high-stakes words of Jesus. The challenge is not benign. Discipleship demands that a life of following offers a penetrating influence like that of salt and a beaming example of loyalty like that of light. These demands are non-negotiable. No excuse for noncompliance is admissible; ransom and threat are not tolerated. To be a follower of Jesus Christ means that accommodation to culture is not acceptable. A wink and a nod to the "powers that be" are not consistent with one who professes Jesus as Lord.

Jesus raises the bar of expectation. Recognizing the dangers that lurk off in the distance for his followers, Jesus presses his disciples into a full awareness and accountability of what is expected. The stakes are high. The demands are great. That leaves only one question: Is our loyalty to Christ equal to the task?

TOPIC: Not Only Hard . . . Impossible!
TEXT: Matt. 5:21–48

It does not take a rocket scientist to sense a setup! Having clearly prepared his listeners and followers for discipleship through reminders about blessed reversals (Matt. 5:1–12) and a life that leaves its imprint upon the world and not vice versa (Matt. 5:13–16), Jesus proceeds to unpack one of the most difficult issues that he encountered in his earthly ministry, namely the relationship between the Kingdom he was building and the Law of Moses.

The message that he offers up is sharp-edged and harsh. It continues the theme of discipleship and deep commitment to Christ, but the message detours through the relationship of the follower to the Law of Moses. The expectations for observance of the Law are now ratcheted up to not merely a doable, manageable level but to a virtually impossible one. For Jesus it is not enough to merely observe the external, social components of the Law. Now it is mandatory to do it, both externally and internally. It is discipleship at the most strenuous level—commitment of both body and mind.

I. **Discipleship—true discipleship—takes the Law of Moses seriously.** But in this new Kingdom that Jesus establishes, this discipleship begins not with external observance but with internal resolve. In the entirety of this passage Jesus sets up a litany of scenarios in which his followers are called to the stratosphere of commitment. He calls several crucial issues to the forefront of his teaching to highlight the complexity of discipleship. He speaks of killing (vv. 21–26), adultery (vv. 27–30), divorce (vv. 31–32), swearing falsely (vv. 33–37), retaliation (vv. 38–42), and the love of an enemy (vv. 43–47). In each of these examples Jesus challenges the traditional understanding of what constitutes faithful compliance to the Law. Traditionally, it is believed that to refrain from killing, committing adultery, and so on, constitutes Kingdom compliance with God's Law. On the surface that is certainly true. But it must always be remembered that the Kingdom of God is not one-dimensional. In this Kingdom there are always layers and subtexts to be found. In Jesus' interpretation of the Law, there is no Kingdom compliance if only the body is obedient to the Law but the mind and spirit is an active participant in sin. The mind must be restrained, as well as the body.

II. **These words show the uphill climb of discipleship.** It is easy for many to observe the external expectations of the Law. In other words, many can restrain the body and thus give the appearance of being a dutiful follower of Christ. But what lurks beneath the surface is a far more troubling portrait of the true nature of life. It is in the shadow-world of our internal being that Jesus expects the most challenging work to be done.

To be a perfunctory Christian is not enough. To be able to discipline the body while an all-out conflict rages within does not constitute the kind of consistency that is demanded of a follower of Christ. Thus we quickly realize that life in this new Kingdom is not only hard—it is impossible! It is difficult enough to keep the body in check but the mind? Who among us can reign in his or her mind? Who can master the monsters that lurk just beneath the surface of all our lives? That is the struggle to which, as followers of Christ, we are invited to share.

III. **Ultimately, this struggle is with consistency.** These pressing words about discipleship in concert with the Law are about living lives that are consistent on the outside (where others can observe) and the inside (where only the person and God know the true picture). The words are reminiscent of the message of Psalm 24:3–4, where it is asked, "Who shall ascend to the hill of the Lord? Who may stand in his holy place? He who has clean hands and a pure heart."

To have clean hands, while important in service to God, is not enough under the new demands placed upon the follower of Christ. The imperative is to accompany those clean hands with pure hearts.

This is no easy matter. It is a journey filled with steep inclines of challenge and dark, lonesome valleys of inner struggle. To follow Jesus in the manner that he demands is not only difficult—it is impossible. It is impossible to attain this level of commitment. But to merely relent without struggle is not acceptable. God expects serious-minded followers to wrestle with these uphill challenges. If we were serious about discipleship, we would have it no other way.

Oh, there is one more "slight" challenge offered by Jesus in these words. As if he has not already raised the bar of expectation to an unbelievable level, for good measure he throws out one more barb: "You, therefore, must be perfect, as your father in heaven is perfect" (v. 48). So once more be warned. This life is not just hard—this is impossible. But as followers of Christ we have no choice. We are to follow this impossible path, and we are to die trying.

TOPIC: Bumper-Sticker Theology
TEXT: Matt. 6:1–7

Several years ago while traveling on an interstate in Tennessee, I followed a car with a "Honk if you love Jesus" bumper sticker attached to the bumper. I am ordinarily not one to respond to this kind of invitation, but for some crazy reason I decided to take my Christian brother up on the offer. As he slowed to begin his departure onto an exit ramp, I pulled around him and honked my horn. To my astonishment what I received in return was not a smile and a blessing but rather an extended middle finger and words that I gather were not altogether holy.

What is it about the need to display our faith in a public manner that is so troublesome? Why are we so ready to display our faith on a fender? Jesus, in the earlier challenges of the Sermon on the Mount, clearly admonishes us to be "Salt and Light" (vv. 13–14). We are to be people who offer public affirmation of our internal commitment to God. But what happens when we become so enamored with developing a public image that we neglect the real person?

I. **Jesus once again calls his listeners to ponder long and hard about loyalty to him.** Again, remember the words about "not hiding the light beneath a bushel" (v. 15). Apparently, though, many of us struggle with appropriate expressions of that light. In many instances we are so concerned about others seeing "our" light that we fail to allow them a glimpse at "God's light in us."

The words of the text are sobering and ego-deflating. Be careful that you do not parade your faith in public with motives that are not altogether pure. Impure motivation of faith expression is one that demands to be seen by others and affirmed in the public sector. It is, one might say, a bumper-sticker faith. It displays one thing, but it demonstrates another.

II. **Perhaps the greatest difficulty in processing these words is that most of us desire accolades and public affirmation.** We want to be seen and heard. And that is no more evident than in the manner in which our spiritual insecurities are masked by external masks of piety. For Jesus the heart of the matter is this notion of motivation. What truly motivates us? Is it a desire to please and serve God? Or, coupled with that desire, is there a more insidious ingredient that includes a thirst for the spotlight, too?

III. **The warning of Jesus is a precarious one.** While it is necessary to be disciples in the public realm, we must be careful that we do not become seduced by the applause that our actions often generate. Once again the message comes full circle, back to the level of commitment we have to the Kingdom of God. If our sole motivation is to "display" our faith, then the object of our loyalty is not God but self. That is all that Jesus argues.

For in the end, public displays of faith result in a short shelf life. The spotlight always dims, and the applause always ceases. On the empty stage of life we are forced to drop the mask and look at the real person hiding there. And this one, Jesus Christ, will not allow us to linger there for long without asking hard questions of ourselves. Why do we do the things we do? And more important is the question, "For whom do we do it?" Once that is settled, the most difficult struggle of discipleship has been answered.

TOPIC: Gavels and Robes

TEXT: Matt. 7:1–5

One of the most seductive dangers of right living is a wrong attitude. How often have we been guilty of attaining a modicum of spiritual maturity and success, only to discover that the predominant attitude that follows is one of self-sufficiency, smugness, and spiritual arrogance? The issue typically revolves around a lack of true self-awareness. We lose our focus. Again, we find ourselves confronted with the true self.

In ministry I hold my breath when persons find themselves in emotionally charged "mountaintop" experiences. What often follows is a holier-than-thou attitude to those around. Accusatory fingers are pointed in judgment. Snide remarks are whispered about a lack of commitment to the things of God. In the midst of a spiritually intense moment, many of us lose our focus. The words of Jesus could not be more confrontational: "Judge not, that you be not judged. With the judgment you pronounce you will be judged and with the measure you give will be the measure you get" (vv. 1–2).

I. **Jesus is careful to note that his followers are to never allow themselves to become ensnared in the trap of spiritual superiority.** When that occurs, we become narrow in spirit and more judgmental of others. Nothing is more harmful to the Christian cause than those who presume the right to don black robes and to hammer gavels of judgment upon others. To do so is utterly ridiculous, but we all struggle with this, don't we? We all believe that *we* see things clearly and that our opinion is the correct one. To deny that of ourselves is to lie to ourselves.

Furthermore, this self-awareness demands that we exercise great caution in the measure we employ in judging others, for in essence Jesus says, "The yardstick by which you measure others will be the same yardstick by which God measures you!" As a friend wisely said to me, "I must be careful. I want only justice for my enemies and only grace for myself!"

II. **This is all about perspective.** Jesus employs a wonderful image of the eye in helping us to "see" what is at stake here. At stake is this matter of sight. To be clear, this is not an ophthalmologic condition but rather one of the heart and spirit. Jesus engages with compelling hyperbole the absurdity of seeing "specks" in the eyes of others while our own eyes are clogged with "logs." A rightful perspective recognizes that before judgment is pronounced on one with a minor problem in life, the log wedged in our spirit must be first addressed.

None of us is morally equipped to pronounce sentence upon others. None of us possesses the spiritual credentials to become the judge of others. There are enough logs in our lives to keep us busy. Before we don the robes and polish the gavels, we must attend to the more pressing matters at hand. And those matters do not start outside, with others. They start on the inside, with us.

TOPIC: Saying Our Prayers
TEXT: Matt. 7:7–11

Whew! The longer I follow Christ and the more closely I listen to his words, the more winded I become in my spirit. This is not easy stuff. Jesus is calling me to flip-flop my human instincts in order to be in tune with his Kingdom. He calls me to a stringent life of discipleship and commitment that is not only difficult but, given my own capacity, it is downright impossible. And yet, in spite of the severity of his claims in my life, he still expects me to continue to follow.

In this passage the Sermon on the Mount shifts to a highly personal and uniquely practical level. No doubt those first hearers of Jesus were scratching their heads and wondering, "How can we find the strength to do the impossible? Where will we gain spiritual stamina that will help to follow and not fall?" They had to be asking those questions. I know that I ask them. Earlier in the sermon, Jesus gave us a real-life example of prayer that we call the Lord's Prayer or the Model Prayer (Matt. 6:9–13). It is the nuts-and-bolts of prayer. But now Jesus steps back to offer a beautiful glimpse into his theology of prayer. This is not the "what" of prayer; this is the "why" of prayer.

I. **Jesus identifies the larger matters of prayer by once again forcing contrasts to be considered within the arena of human instinct.** Whereas in previous comments in the sermon, human instinct is called into question, here Jesus offers a different glimpse into the matter. Here he exemplifies the great potential that human instinct possesses and holds it up as a way in which the heart of God is seen. There is a tender dimension to the nature of prayer as it relates to God's desire to offer good things to his children. The response is predicated upon the imploring, as it were, of a child to a parent. "Ask, seek, knock, find," is the reminder.

II. **Perhaps this glimpse into Jesus' theology of prayer is his way of saying to his sons and daughters, "You wonder where you will find the strength to do the impossible things that I ask of you?"** You will find them in prayer. God will give you what you need when you need it. Say your prayers. And in the saying of our prayers, God's good Kingdom gifts are found.

The provision for the things that are needed will be supplied. God does respond to the prayers of his children. For all the tasks of living, both the great and the small, the things that daunt us are truly nothing to our God. Therein lies the difference, and therein lies the command to say our prayers again and again in order to find the strength to live and serve in this uphill Kingdom that Jesus builds.

TOPIC: Proof Positive
TEXT: Matt. 7:13–28

So, what do we do now? We've heard the words of Jesus. Some of us have heard them again and again. But what do we do now?

The proof is in the pudding, they say. The ultimate objective of absorbing the words of Jesus is that there is a resultant change in behavior. Thus Jesus provides a summary for all that his listeners have encountered. That summary centers upon appropriate foundations. Having been taught what this upside-down Kingdom looks like and what expectations are to follow, the onus is now upon the listener. The responsibility now shifts from the lips of the proclaimer—Jesus—to ears of the listeners. It is in this crucial shift of responsibility that true discipleship is born.

I. **Jesus offers a very a simple and yet telling contrast of lifestyle.** To those who listen to him and heed his counsel, the result will be a life of stability. He speaks of one who has built his life upon a firm foundation. The implication is not a subtle one. The words that make up the Sermon on the Mount are rock-like. They offer stability in the midst of turmoil. They provide a glimpse into the Kingdom realm, into which Jesus invites his followers. The appropriate foundation, however, is the key. For even when the foundation is solid, there will inevitably be storms that assault us. The storms cannot be predicted or controlled, but preparation for the storm is essential. Built upon a solid foundation and when the storms do blow in, the life that is appropriately grounded will survive the onslaught.

II. **On the contrary, a life built upon the sands of carelessness will likewise encounter the winds of the storm, but the results can be catastrophic.** The same winds that assault firm foundations blow upon the sandy ones, but that is where similarities end. To the one that fails to heed the wisdom of Jesus, the fate will be a harsh one. The difference is in the building of the foundation. But the warnings come to all: to those who build appropriately and to those who choose not to build.

III. **In the end it is only those who both listen and obey the teachings of Jesus that enjoy the blessings of the Kingdom of God.** The proof is found in this dual relationship of taking the words of Jesus so seriously that they find their way into everyday living—the kind of living that builds upon the solid foundation of Jesus Christ.

Thus Jesus concludes the Sermon on the Mount with a very simple and straightforward reminder that life is about choices. And in the end the choices we make determine everything about us.

CHAPTER THREE

Advent and Christmas Preaching: Personalities and Perspectives

Dr. Ronald D. Sisk, Academic Vice President and Dean; Professor of Homiletics and Christian Ministry, North American Baptist Seminary, Sioux Falls, South Dakota

Preaching in Advent year after year requires all a preacher's creativity to remain fresh. Lectionary preachers must develop a new slant on the familiar cycle with each three-year repetition. Those from other traditions face a similar dilemma. More and more churches across the denominational spectrum are lighting Advent candles and building services using the familiar themes of hope, peace, joy, and love. Even those whose tradition suggests no thematic approach at all will find that the constraints of retelling the familiar story yearly impose a challenge. One way to deal with this is to tell the story from the perspective of key participants. For 2008, we focus on four key personalities ("Christmas people"): Isaiah, John the Baptist, Mary, and Jesus.

FIRST SUNDAY OF ADVENT

TITLE: Christmas People: Isaiah

TEXT: Isa. 63:16b–64:9

It is well before dawn. No hint of light yet softens the darkness of the eastern sky. In the tiny room the old man sits hunched over a parchment, his fingers black with ink, the smoky lamp flickering in the winter draft. Outside his window the shabby, tumbledown Jerusalem of the exile sleeps its fitful, discontented dreams of better days. But these are not better days in Judah. The children of Israel have always seen themselves as God's own, God's special people. But for more years than anyone can remember, they have lived under the heel of foreign conquest. The leaders have been taken away. The Temple has been destroyed. Grass grows in the streets of the city. Goats graze over what was once the holy of holies.

In the little room, Isaiah leans back for a minute, sighing. He's been writing and praying all night. Now in the bottom of his despondency, he comes to the moment we all reach sooner or later—the moment when what you and I say we believe gets personal. Will I give in to despair? Will I conclude that my life and the lives of the people I love have no meaning? Or will I believe God will yet answer?

Advent begins, my friends, at the very instant you feel farthest away from God's answer. Christmas is coming; Jesus is on his way to our world. But redemption is a long way off yet when we start the season of Advent. With Isaiah, who lived more than half a millennium before Jesus, you and I must start by asking ourselves whether we're willing to believe what we cannot yet see.

The truth, you see, is that most of us have been where Isaiah was one time or another. Some of us are in that place right now. Church folks aren't exempt from life. You're living with grief, and the truth right now is that you don't know whether life will ever feel good again or not. It feels like you work all the time, and you wonder how long you'll be able to go to school and meet your family's needs. There are health problems that will not go away and money problems that sap the joy out of Christmas, turning it to a time of resentment and despair.

Relationships seem to get worse at the holidays instead of better. And surrounding it is the saccharine suggestion that we (especially we Christians) have to be happy at the holidays, whether we can actually, legitimately feel happy or not. Spiritual saccharine causes spiritual cancer.

But Isaiah is too brave to take refuge in false hope. So he writes, "You, O Lord, are our father. Our Redeemer from of old is your name. . . . But now our adversaries have trampled down your sanctuary. We have long been like those whom you do not rule, like those not called by your name." The first rule of Advent is to be honest about the hurt. There is truth here that you and I need to grab hold of. We've gotten the idea somehow in modern Christianity that if you and I just wear a little smiley face and believe hard enough and pump up our feelings high enough, everything will be OK. That's part of why so many churches have gone to worship services that are not much more than glorified pep rallies. Hear me carefully. I am all for feeling positive and thinking positively. But the religion of the Bible is not Pollyanna and ice cream sundaes.

Back in the little room, the prophet rises from his chair. He stretches his aching muscles, glances down at what he has written, then moves over to the window to look out over the sleeping city. Even in the predawn dark, the silhouettes of desolation break his heart. Almost without realizing it, he dissolves into prayer once again. Isaiah isn't afraid to look God in the eye and say, "I know you're supposed to be our redeemer, Lord, but it's been a long time now. It's been too long now since you acted like it—since we felt like it, since we experienced this redemption you promise." God is a God who can handle your discontent and mine, your anger and mine. And you and I, with Isaiah, ought never be afraid to tell God the truth about how we feel, as long as we are willing to hear the truth from God in return.

The proverb goes, "Life is too short for anything but the truth." The truth is, we do hurt this Advent season, my friends. We live in a hurting world. Way too many Americans and countless Iraqis died in that catastrophic war. The Gulf Coast struggles back toward normalcy after Katrina. Congress responds by cutting welfare payments and Medicaid. As always, the real victims seem to be those who can least defend themselves—the very old and the very young. We live in a hurting world this Advent.

We also live in a hurting community. The more we grow as a community, the more problems we have. Immigration means we have cultural and racial issues we don't know how to handle. Not too far from here, neighbors have grown suspicious of one another because of a new homeless shelter. Children go hungry, violence is real, and parents are afraid to let their kids out of their sight anymore. It's time we Americans learned the difference between our American culture of violence and the prophet, Isaiah, who says, "Woe to those who trust in chariots because they are many and in horsemen because they are strong and do not look to the holy one of Israel." The truth is you and I live in a hurting community.

The truth is we are hurting ourselves. Isaiah wants to say it's because God has turned away from us—that we sinned because God turned away first. But you and I know that's a matter of perspective. The real truth is, like Israel of old, you and I have been stubborn and indifferent and self-satisfied, so we have paid the price individually and as a people. If you and I don't become who God calls us to be, it will not be because God has turned away from us. Again and again, you and I earn God's absence, God's silence. So what do we do?

Back in the little room, the prophet raises his hands in prayer: "Oh that you would tear open the heavens and come down, so that the mountains would quake at your presence . . . no one has heard, no ear has perceived, no eye has seen any God besides you who works for those who wait for him, you meet those who gladly do right, those who remember you in your ways." What do we do? We wait upon God. We turn back to the Lord. The word *wait* in the Hebrew doesn't just mean "do nothing for right now." It ties together the one who is waiting and the One we are waiting for. It means to wait, expecting something good to happen.

Let's be honest. Advent is a wonderful time in the church. We all enjoy the music and the decorations and the anticipation. But the truth is for most of us, much of that anticipation has to do as much with the time off from work and the presents under the tree as it does with God's coming into our world through Jesus.

Relatively few of us really expect or want anything deeply spiritual to happen in this season, especially if it requires us to change. So I want to issue a challenge. I'm going to pray every day this Advent for a renewal of God's Spirit among us. My experience tells me that we are too busy for much authentic growth to happen during December. But I'm going to pray that God will move you and me this Advent. I'm going to pray that God will take these Advent services, the music, the celebration, the people we know, and those who come to our church for the first time this season and touch us all with the wonder of grace through the Holy Spirit. I'm going to do my very best to clear from my life anything that may be getting in the way of experiencing a new birth of God's power. And I challenge you to do the same. And I believe with all my heart if you and I do that, if we genuinely, faithfully wait upon the Lord this Advent, then the Lord will come.

In Jerusalem's darkness the first songbirds—harbingers of the day—stir themselves, stretch their wings, and start their sleepy chorus. The stars begin to pale in the east. The first feeble light of the dawn breaks down the stronghold of the night. The old man settles back into his chair to write down his soul's struggle. He has been through doubt to near-despair, and yet he ends his lament where he began, with words of faith: "Yet, O Lord, you are our Father." He will die and his children will die and his grandchildren will be dust before the thing that he hopes for comes to pass. But he was right, that night so long ago.

Once on the old TV series *Murphy Brown,* Murphy was trying to decide what to tell her son when he asked her what happens to people when they die. She had no faith of her own, so she asked her colleagues—a Catholic, a Jew, and two Protestants—and after she had heard their answers she said to a friend, "I just don't get it. I'm a journalist and we require evidence for everything. How can I believe something I cannot see?" The answer: that's the difference between people of faith and people of this world. We, as people of faith, believe things we can't see all the time. We believe the brothers and sisters of our families and our church who have passed away this year are alive right now. We believe they are with the Lord, and we believe we will see them again.

We believe God put into Isaiah's heart the idea that God would one day rescue Israel, whether Isaiah ever lived to see it or not. We believe that hundreds of years after Isaiah wrote his lament, God sent Jesus as a newborn baby to Isaiah's descendants as a direct answer to Isaiah's prayer and the prayers of people of faith through the ages. We believe Jesus lived to teach us how to live and died to pay the price for your failure and mine to live the way he taught us, and was raised from the dead to prove that you and I can live with him. We believe that because he lives, you and I can help make our own lives and the lives of those around us better than they have been. And we believe that, no matter how bleak things may sometimes look for you or for me, Jesus will one day come again and make everything new.

You and I have one advantage over Isaiah, you see. You and I have seen the difference Jesus makes. I wonder, as we begin this Advent season, is there a special need in your life? Do you need to see again the light of morning? Do you need to feel again the Spirit's soft caress? Do you long for a new sense of purpose in your work, in your ministry? If so, will you take your place by Isaiah? Will you turn to Jesus once again? Will you wait in faith for the Spirit? "O that you, O Lord, would tear open the heavens and come down!"

SECOND SUNDAY OF ADVENT
TITLE: Christmas People: John the Baptist
TEXT: Mark 1:1–8

We know a lot about John the Baptist. First, he went to University of Sioux Falls, then North American Baptist Seminary, then he got in trouble over the dress code! Well, we don't really know that, but we do know he was the beloved only son of the priest Zechariah and Mary's cousin Elizabeth. John's birth was predicted by no less than the angel Gabriel, his career planned by heaven before he was even conceived. "He will turn many of the people of Israel to the Lord, their God," the angel said. "With the spirit and power of Elijah he will go before him to turn the hearts of the parents to their children and the disobedient to the wisdom of the righteous, to make ready a people prepared for the Lord."

We know a lot about John the Baptist, but that doesn't mean you and I are at all comfortable with him. He has the air of a fanatic, after all, not quite nice for Christmas. Even today, the wilderness of Judea is a harsh place, searing hot in summer, frigid in winter, with the settled country around Jerusalem huddled to the west and sheer cliffs plunging to the Dead Sea and the valley of the Jordan on the east. Like the South Dakota badlands, no one goes there unless they want to be alone with the wind and the sky and the eternal. It's not a place city dwellers like me would understand. I get mad when the thermostat's not set right. You and I like our regular programs and our favorite chair. But it is just that kind of comfortable self-satisfaction in Israel that drove John to the wilderness in the first place.

You can almost see him in your mind's eye, dressed in the poorest of cloth, eating the food of the homeless, shouting his great, ranting fire-and-brimstone sermons, a preacher's son gone extremist. He's not like sweet Mary, whom we'll talk about next, or the innocent babe in the manger, or even visionary old grandpa Isaiah. John's the kind of preacher who makes you and me wish church would hurry up and be over before we get asked to do something uncomfortable, something out of the ordinary. But then that's precisely the point.

These are not ordinary times. At long last the Messiah is coming. God is stepping into history to set things right. "See, I am sending my messenger ahead of you," Mark quotes him as saying. "The voice of one crying in the wilderness, prepare the way of the Lord." More than any other human being who has ever walked the earth, John lives with a sense of urgency, a fire in his belly that he can no more damp down or hold in than he can stop the erupting of a volcano or keep the wind from blowing where it wills. So what difference does John make to you and me? As we come to this Advent communion, he reminds us that our old, comfortable ways are not enough. If you expect this Christmas to be just like last Christmas and next Christmas to be just like this one and your life to stay as it has been, then John's message is to you, my friend. You just can't stay the same when Jesus is coming.

You prepare the way of the Lord. It's time to get ready. Mark actually quotes two Old Testament passages. The first is from Malachi, and it talks about purifying a lazy and corrupt priesthood. You get the feeling that, like many a preacher's child, John knows too much about what goes on behind the scenes. Some commentators say that's the reason for his simple dress and his simple food. John, they say, was bringing a message about the self-indulgence of the priesthood in his day. He said plenty, but in addition, his poverty, his simple lifestyle was his message. People flocked to hear him because they longed for a faith they could trust, just as you and I do today. As he nears the end of his career, Billy Graham is becoming more and more a hero of American Christianity. Not that he's always been right or that everybody's always loved his preaching but that he's always been honest with us. And he's not gotten rich off the people he was supposed to be trying to help. All the big churches and flashy TV shows in the world don't prepare the way of the Lord as well as simple, honest faith does.

You prepare the way of the Lord, John said. Make straight in the wilderness a highway for our God. John's second quote is from Isaiah. It's about the exiles coming home from captivity. When John speaks, the prophecy in one sense has already been fulfilled. The exiles are home physically, and they have been for four hundred years. But John's not talking about building the interstate from Babylon to Palestine. He's talking about the highway of the heart.

John's Israel is a world of hypocrisy and hatred—a religion proud of its theological correctness but with little real spirituality. Sound familiar? Here's a people chafing under Roman occupation then, just the way the Palestinians chafe under Israeli occupation and the Iraqis chafe under American occupation today; here are priests getting rich by collaborating with the Romans on the one hand and abusing the poor on the other; here are people sacrificing animals to atone for their sins but not bothering to change their own lives.

John's world was in desperate need of change. But then so is this one. I've challenged you to pray every day during Advent for real spiritual renewal in your church. Let me take it one more step. I'm going to pray this Advent for real spiritual renewal in my own life, renewal that makes me more willing to act for good. Will you pray for your life? Change begins with you and me. You and you and you prepare the way of the Lord, John says.

What we need is a baptism of repentance. We're so used to those words that it's hard for us to hear what they meant. The only way to get inside them is to walk down the dusty road out of Jerusalem to the spot by the river on the edge of the wilderness where John is preaching. The Jews know what baptism is, all right. When a pagan turned from his sins to Judaism, he would be immersed completely in water to wash away his Gentile life. But baptism was only for pagans, never for a good Jew. Now John—a Jew's Jew, a hereditary priest from the tribe of Levi—is saying to the whole nation, "Being a Jew isn't enough. We need a revolution. We need to change our ways so completely it's like the change from being a pagan to being a Jew."

The crowd asks for examples, and John gives them. "If you have two coats, give to somebody who has none. If you have more food than you need, share with the hungry. Tell the truth. Give an honest day's work for an honest day's pay." Today, in the twenty-first century, John would say pretty much the same things to you and me: "Prepare the way of the Lord." If you're not giving to others at the same time you're spending on yourself and your family this Christmas, then you're really not doing very much to prepare the way of the Lord. People are cold in our country this morning. How many of us have only two coats? *Prepare the way of the Lord.* "Turn the disobedient to the wisdom of the righteous." The video games we play and the TV we watch and let our children watch get more and more violent. Could that possibly be wise? *Prepare the way of the Lord.* "Turn the hearts of the parents to their children." Before you give your child or your grandchild a video game this Christmas, play it yourself and ask yourself what kind of values this is teaching. Is it teaching respect for others and ways of solving problems without violence? And if it isn't, why in the world do you want your child to have it?

The baptism of repentance isn't easy, you see. John never intended it to be. It's a whole new way of thinking and acting. Just as baptism is washing away the old life and taking on a new one, so repentance means changing from the inside out, turning around and going in a whole new direction. It's always specific. You and I may not think we have anything to repent. But if you're still fighting with that family member this holiday, Christ says you are obligated to try and make it right. And if you haven't yet given Christ control of your business life or your social life, John is preaching repentance to you. When John tells you and me to repent, you see, he doesn't just shake hands at the door of the church. He gets in the car and listens to our conversation on the drive home; he watches how we spend our time when we get there; he goes along with us to the office in the morning to see how we act at work. It's tough. Things have to change to prepare the way of the Lord. But there's a reason to do it. The Lord is coming.

The Lord will baptize us with the Holy Spirit. John knew he was only the messenger. He knew there was another who would come with power. In Luke, when the angel Gabriel visits Zechariah to tell him John will be born, he says John will be filled with the Holy Spirit from his mother's womb. But John couldn't pass that Spirit along to someone else. He could call people to change their ways, but he couldn't give them the power to change the world. But the first time John saw Jesus, he knew that Jesus could. And when John's disciples came to him one day to complain that people were beginning to go to Jesus to be baptized, John answered with the word that tells us what Christmas people are all about. His disciples complained, and John answered. "That's the way it's supposed to be. He must increase, but I must decrease."

Maybe when it boils right down to it, that's what John is asking of you and me. I can't tell you what you need to change about your life this Advent. I'm busy looking at my own. But chances are you already know. You've been thinking about it the whole time I've been talking. And that very thought is the Spirit calling you to do what you need to do to prepare the way of the Lord. Will you? Christ is coming! Are you ready?

THIRD SUNDAY IN ADVENT
TITLE: Christmas People: Mary
TEXT: Luke 1:26–38

Imagine her as a ninth-grader, fourteen or perhaps fifteen at the most, on the brink of young womanhood but not yet fully mature. Marriages were arranged early in those days. Adolescence as a concept didn't exist, and the teen years did not constitute a separate, relatively carefree time of life. A girl went straight from her father's house to her husband's. At fourteen Mary would already know all she needed to know to become the carpenter's wife, to be the mother of his children. Life was hard in Nazareth town. Girls learned the facts of life early on. So when I think of Mary, I don't visualize her as idealized innocence the way the Renaissance painters did, as though the gritty details of motherhood never touched her, even after the baby came. Instead I see intelligence, character, a sense of humor, and a lively imagination. The truth, of course, is that she was going to need it.

The text tells us little about the scene. I like to think of her there in her father's house in the gathering shadows of late afternoon, quietly working on the wedding robe she would never get to wear, daydreaming perhaps of that glorious feast when Joseph would come to take her home, wondering, as any girl would, what kind of husband, what kind of man the carpenter would prove to be. She would be virtually his property, after all—property of this rough man who made his living with his hands. You find yourself wondering if the prospect was enough for her or if somehow, in ways we're never told, Mary prayed for more.

Suddenly, the air in the little room changes, becomes almost electric. Specks appear in the air, floating in the sunlight that beams in through the tiny window. No one walks through the door, but a moment before, Mary had been alone with her thoughts. Now a form stands before her, like no man she's ever seen—gentle, powerful, urgent. "Hail, Mary, full of grace" (Greetings girl, whom God has graced). The word we translate as *favor* here is the same word we usually translate as *grace*, and in Gabriel's greeting it is filled with irony. It's as though the angel is saying, "Be glad, Mary! God has chosen you to do the most difficult thing in the world."

Why Mary? Why is Bernard Ratzinger pope? Why was Billy Graham America's greatest evangelist? Why did Teresa of Calcutta become the twentieth century's most famous Christian woman? Why do you and I have the lives we have, with their challenges and their opportunities? The theologian Beverly Gaventa says, "God chooses because God chooses." Every year when I was a pastor, the church would choose new deacons. And then it was my job to call them up. So I would put on my Gabriel suit, dial the phone, and begin with something very close to, "Greetings, favored one, the Lord is with you!"

The reactions I got usually weren't puzzlement as much as they were consternation: "Who, me? What are you talking about, preacher? I couldn't possibly do that." The preacher Barbara Brown Taylor says of Mary that she responds, "How can this be?" But there were several other questions I believe I would have asked: "Will Joseph stick around? Will my parents still love me?

Will my friends stand by me or will I get dragged into town and stoned for sleeping around? Will the pregnancy go all right? You say the child will be king of Israel, but what about me?" With Mary, God's grace takes you and me out of our simple, selfish plans for our lives and flings us out into God's great, grand unknown future.

So, of course, Mary "pondered what sort of greeting this might be." There was a folk legend in those days that is preserved for us in the apocryphal book of Tobit. It tells of an angel who kept killing a girl's fiancés to keep her from marrying. At first Mary wouldn't have known for sure whether this angel meant her well or ill. There in her room, with Gabriel waiting for her answer, Mary asks that entirely natural question: "How can this be? Joseph and I haven't been together yet." As she does, she sets off two thousand years of debate. Was Jesus born of a virgin?

Let me say this carefully. Some doctrines are central to the faith. You can't be a Christian if you don't believe them. The Resurrection of Jesus from the dead is the central doctrine of the Christian faith. Christmas just wouldn't matter if there were no Easter. So if you find it hard to take this part of the story literally, I think you can still be a Christian. For myself, though, I think the God who could raise Jesus from the dead and seek me out until he found me could easily pull off a little thing like a virgin birth. I don't blame Mary for asking the question. She was the main one involved, after all. But God can do what God can do.

"The angel said to her, 'The Holy Spirit will come upon you and the power of the most High will overshadow you; therefore the child to be born will be holy; he will be called the Son of God.'" Gabriel tells her about Elizabeth's heavenly fertility treatment to illustrate his point: "For nothing will be impossible with God." And Mary, practical young woman that she is, leaves all further debate to the theologians.

The real issue for us, of course, isn't what happened to Mary as much as it is what can happen to you and me. The Christian promise has always been that the same Spirit who changed Mary's life forever that quiet afternoon in Nazareth can change your life and mine as well. I find myself wondering again how she was chosen. Could it be that a peasant girl in that utterly ordinary village, listening to the reading of Scripture in the synagogue, growing up with the prophecies of the Messiah to come, could somehow have focused her attention on God's promise to David to establish his throne forever? Did she dream beyond her station? Did she pray for God to use her? And what will God do through you and me, if we will but ask? One thing I have observed to be absolutely consistent in my years in ministry is that God's Spirit works when you and I invite God in. God is, indeed, the lover of our souls. Through sending us Jesus, God seeks to win your trust and mine so that we will invite God's Spirit to work new wonders in us. Taylor says Mary could have decided to say no, dropped her eyes to her work in the time-honored gesture of a woman protecting herself, refused to look up again until she was alone, and then given her head a shake as though she'd been daydreaming, and gone back to her own plan for her life.

We don't know how long it took her to answer. I doubt very much somehow that it was as cut-and-dried as the words of the story seem to suggest. More likely, the silence grows as the angel's words die away. Mary catches her breath as she realizes nothing in her life will ever be the same again. And then, with a young person's courage, with an almost reckless bravado, she raises her eyes to the messenger.

"Here am I, the servant of the Lord. Let it be with me according to your word." In that moment Mary becomes what the Eastern church calls *Theotokos*, the God-bearer. All God's promises to the Jews come alive again. Inside Mary's body a cell begins to grow in the usual way—zygote to fetus to child. The important thing for you and me to remember is that this is not a passive process. Mary wasn't just a convenient test tube in which the child could grow. Think of her instead as telling him stories as any mother does, maybe some of the very stories he himself would tell later on. They say you can tell how a man's mother taught him by the way he treats women later in life. When Mary sings the song we now call the Magnificat during her visit to Elizabeth, she signs on to a vision of Jesus as the champion of the poor and the oppressed. If that's the way she raised him, if that's the human side of his heritage, it's no wonder he turned out as he did.

The question that Mary's surrender raises, of course, is the question of your surrender and mine. Because of what she did, because of the risks she took, because of her leap of faith, you and I have the opportunity to take a leap of our own. For each and every one of us, there is something surprising, something unexpected, something new that God will do through you and through me, if we are willing to be the servants of the Lord with Mary. And the truth, my sisters and brothers, is that this is what Christmas is all about. It isn't about what happened to that peasant girl in Palestine so long ago. It's about what hasn't happened yet, or has just begun to happen, or may yet still happen in you and me, if only we will respond as Mary did. If you and I, here in the city, in this Advent season will say today and every day, "Here am I, the servant of the Lord!" If we do that, then you and I will become risk takers with Mary. Our lives will take on meaning and direction. This church will find new ways to change this community for the better, to liberate the captives, to fill the hungry with good things, to teach ourselves and one another how to live lives of integrity and compassion.

The medieval mystic Meister Eckhardt said it this way:

> We are all meant to be mothers of God. What good is it to me if this eternal birth of the divine son takes place unceasingly but does not take place within myself? And what good is it to me if Mary is full of grace, if I am not also full of grace? What good is it to me for the Creator to give birth to his Son if I do not also give birth to him in my time and my culture? This is the fullness of time: when the Son of God is begotten in us.

Our joy this season, my brothers and sisters, will be if Mary's boy becomes your boy and my boy—if Mary's boy comes alive in you and me. "Greetings, favored one. The Lord is with you. Do not be afraid. For nothing will be impossible with God."

FOURTH SUNDAY IN ADVENT
TITLE: Christmas People: Jesus
TEXT: Isa. 9:1–7

What will you name the baby? Some parents choose old family names. Others simply pick things they like, combinations that sound good together. My mother tells me she lifted my own first name out of a mystery novel. When I was born, the hero of the book she was reading happened to be named Ronald. I'm just glad she wasn't reading Sherlock Holmes! Names don't mean as much in Anglo culture, of course, as they do in some others. Native American names often attempt to describe the essence of a person's character. Nobody ever accused Sitting Bull of being a wimp! The Hebrews believed your name told the world something about your nature.

That's why Christ is given so many names. There are so many things about him that you and I need to know. *Messiah* means "the anointed one." *Jesus* means "God saves." *Emmanuel* means "God with us." I like the names the prophet gives Jesus here in Isaiah, though. They focus on what Jesus means to people like you and me. We feel a lot of the time as though we walk in darkness, don't we? So let's listen in a new way this morning as Isaiah names the baby.

His name will be called Wonderful Counselor. Handel's "Messiah" and the King James Version of the Bible notwithstanding, there's no comma between these words. They're one term. Jesus is a wonderful counselor. He knows just what to do, and he knows when and how to do it.

The truth is that many of us spend much of our lives wishing for a wonderful counselor. When you or I have a problem and seek help from a friend or a minister or a psychologist, what we really want is someone who can understand our situation and accept us, warts and all, and care about us as we decide what we need to do. The Christian counselor Scott Peck says that's exactly what a good counselor does. Good counselors accept their clients with all their problems just as they are; they build a trust relationship that clients experience as grace and that allows them to face the truth about themselves and their world and begin to get well. So does a good pastor. So does a good friend.

The good news here, though, is that even if you and I don't have anybody else in our lives we can count on, we can count on Jesus. If you walk in darkness this morning, he will be your wonderful counselor. He knows you and me so well that he always tells us the truth. He loves us so well that he never stops listening, never gives up caring and hoping and calling you and me to a better life. He is always available. And yet he respects us so well that he always leaves the choices strictly up to us. His name is Wonderful Counselor. Even beyond that, though, if you and I will work with him, he will accomplish whatever you or I need done.

His name is Mighty God. In all the Old Testament, this is the only clear reference to any human being as a God. Not only does the Messiah know what to do and how to do it, Isaiah tells us, he has the power to get it done. Several years ago Mary Tyler Moore and Donald Sutherland starred in a movie called *Ordi-*

nary People. They played a suburban Chicago couple trying to cope with the death of a teenage son. Mary's character just couldn't go on. It was too tragic.

She didn't have the strength. Ultimately, none of us ordinary people have the strength. Oh, you and I like to think we can succeed on our own. Our American success ethic and our culture of rugged individualism teach us that we ought to be able to manage life without any help. But the fact is that the more we try to do that—the more we rely on ourselves alone—the more isolated and friendless and powerless we become, the less able we are to get what we want out of life, the more we walk in darkness. The only way to break out of that cycle is to realize that the One whose very name was power itself didn't try to make it on his own either. He relied utterly on God. He was obedient, even when it cost him his life, because only in perfect obedience is there strength.

Is there perfect strength? "My strength is made perfect in weakness," Christ told the Apostle Paul. What that means to you and me is that plenty of power to cope with life is available to us, ordinary people though we are. But you and I can't get what we want from Jesus the way we'd handle a business deal. We can't wait until we're able to bargain with him from a position of strength, precisely because that day will never come. Jesus has the power. Only Jesus can give you or me ultimate success. His name is Mighty God.

Fortunately for you and me, his name is also Everlasting Father, and that keeps his power from crushing us altogether. The Bible speaks in pictures, of course, so it's not really a contradiction that the Messiah is both Son of God and Everlasting Father. Most sons become fathers at some point in their lives. And we're not talking about "macho male" in the earthly sense but about "heavenly parent," with all the best qualities of both mother and father. One of the greatest tragedies in our world is so many children growing up without proper fathers. Childbearing outside marriage means many children never live in the same house with their fathers at all. Broken homes mean many fathers are weekend parents at best. Some fathers who live with their children are so busy or so blind or so demanding that they never take time to be proper fathers either. In fact, some people have a hard time relating to God because they don't know from their own experience what a good father is.

But Jesus is Everlasting Father. You see, even if you or I do know our natural father, even if our earthly father is a loving, kind, nurturing man, even then he is certain to disappoint us sooner or later. Part of growing up is realizing your dad isn't perfect. If nothing else, sooner or later our fathers disappoint us by turning out to be mortal.

But Jesus is our Everlasting Father, and he is perfect. He never had a natural child, precisely so that all of us could be his children. So you and I can know for ourselves his tender mercy, his constant love, his willingness to believe in you and me, even if we've given up believing in ourselves. So he could teach us by his own example just how far a real parent's love is willing to go. So he could be to us like the father in his own story of the prodigal son. Waiting always, waiting even now for us to come back, pacing at the window, searching the horizon, spotting us as soon as ever we have the good sense to turn toward home, running out to greet us, folding us in his loving arms, rejoicing over us, as though we were the only children he had. Love that never gives up. His name shall be called Everlasting Father.

His name is Prince of Peace. On the one hand, you and I know what peace is because our world doesn't have it. Jews still live on Arab land. Arabs still dream of pushing the Israelis into the sea. Death still lurks beside the highway in Iraq, reaching out to grab soldiers and civilians alike. We long for the day when the government will be on his shoulders, when peace in our world will be a reality and not a dream. Carl Sandburg once wrote, sarcastically, "the peace we now see will last until the next war begins, whereupon peace will be ushered in at the end of the next war." He realized that ultimate peace can never be enforced from the outside while this world lasts. The most all our troops and firepower will ever succeed in enforcing in Iraq is the absence of war. And that is something. In our world it is a great deal. But it is not Christ's peace.

Because on the other hand, the One whose name is Prince of Peace offers you and me something else entirely. He offers us his personal government, peace not as the world gives but citizenship in the peaceable Kingdom of God. In his care you discover peace conceived in the innermost corner of your being, built from the inside out to precise individual specifications, constructed human heart by human heart until it fills the world with its health. What is this peace?

One of the commentators suggests we really ought to translate Isaiah's word for peace as "success"—the enjoyment of all of the good things of life. That's the gift Christ offers if you and I will have it. He offers us success—the only kind of success worth having: success that isn't based on money or power or family or appearances or health but success that is your life and my life lived in harmony with the purposes of God. Because that's what Jesus' peace is. Jesus wants to be your peace and mine. Living today and every day in God's will, surrendered to God's purposes, in companionship with the Holy Spirit: life at peace with God; life at peace with others; life at peace with yourself. That's what Jesus offers you and me, because that's who Jesus is. We know because of his name.

His name shall be called Wonderful Counselor, Mighty God, Everlasting Father, Prince of Peace. Like banners across the sky of eternity, these are his names. For every person who has ever followed Jesus, this is who he has been. The people who walked in darkness have seen a great light. But the real question this Christmas is still, What will you and I do with this Jesus? Will you call him Savior? Will you call him Friend? Will you let him be for you all that he came to be? What will you name the Baby?

CHAPTER FOUR

Messages for Lent and Easter

Lent has historic ties to the preparation of candidates for baptism. By the fourth century, the forty days prior to baptism were given over to fasting and to instruction in the catechetical lectures of Cyril of Jerusalem. The forty days are reminiscent of Jesus' fast at the beginning of his ministry, Moses' fast on Sinai, the forty years of wandering in the wilderness, and Elijah's fast on his way to the mountain of God. When Christianity was legalized in 313 A.D., the forty-day preparation for baptism became a general period of preparation for Easter—for all Christians. The fast lasted thirty-six days (six weeks), not counting Sundays, which are always feasts celebrating the Resurrection.

SERMON STARTERS FOR PREACHING IN LENT

These brief devotions are intended to encourage creative thinking about Lenten themes as well as personal meditative moments.

TOPIC: The World's Most Decisive Question
TEXT: Matt. 16:13–25

Matthew wrote his Gospel some fifty years after Jesus' death. As he wrote, his world was collapsing. The beloved Temple in Jerusalem was destroyed, and he and his fellow Jewish Christians were expelled from the synagogue. In these dire circumstances, he needed to know whether or not faith in Jesus Christ could be maintained when everything seemed to be going down the drain. His concern is crystallized in the probing question Jesus raised in the Scripture: "Who do people say I am?"

Is Jesus only, as someone said, a fascinating religious genius? Or is he more? Is he not surely, as Peter declared, the Christ of God? He is the One who bears the future for us all, who breaks in upon us and melts cultural barriers and bridges hostile civilizations. He brings to our world a whole new look, so that the first is last and the last is first, and concern for the dignity and respect for all persons is borne out in the victory of justice and human solidarity.

If we can envision an answer like that, as Lent of 2008 begins, then our confession surely must rise from a place beyond ourselves ("not from flesh and blood"). It comes as nothing less than God's gift to us.

How can we remain loyal to such a confession? There's one way: "Take up your cross and follow me," Jesus said. We must take upon ourselves the risks that love assumes. We must surrender our present loyalties and move in a different direction. We lay our lives, time, money, vocations, families, hearts, minds, and souls on the line for the sake of the Crucified One. Instead of following the ways of our cynical and malicious world, we choose to follow the courageous and transforming Christ.—Lee McGlone

TOPIC: An Unfulfilled Dream
TEXT: Gen. 11:31–32

Here is the story of a man who had a dream. The man is Terah, the father of Abraham. It's a part of the Abraham story often missed. "Terah took Abram his son and Lot his grandson and Sarai, his daughter in law, and they set out from Ur of the Chaldeans to go into the land of Canaan." But the sad truth is that Terah never got there. What happened isn't exactly clear, but one word in the text helps us understand. "He came to Haran and he *settled* there." He settled there. He found something he liked and decided to stay there. There is nothing wrong with that, except that in doing so he lost his dream.

"Settling," in terms of religious faith, is not seen in the Scripture as a good thing. Believers are more pioneers than settlers. "Settling" brings sorrow. Not only did Terah settle there. He died there. But God's dreams never die. Let's take our eyes off Terah and look at God. Jesus lived for a dream he called the Kingdom of God. He saw it as a hidden treasure, a lost sheep, a lost coin, and a lost son. He spoke of the tiny seed, the little leaven, and the coming of the Kingdom that is already in you. Think of how it happens for us. What of those strange imperatives that rise up within and propel us onward? Where did they come from? What of the strange twist in our situations, the unexpected maneuver in our souls? What of the sorrow and the hurt? Can it be that God is moving among us and toward a dream that perhaps we can't even now recognize?

God comes to us in strange angles. We may not be sure of where God is going, but we can be absolutely sure of God's guiding hand. And so we're to live by faith and not by sight. In doing so, we are to live together honorably, to serve faithfully, to love unconditionally, to yield before Christ unapologetically, and in the end, we allow God to do the rest! And that's how God's dream is fulfilled in us.—Lee McGlone

TOPIC: A Second Chance
TEXT: Luke 13:1–9

Luke points to a barren fig tree. It is planted in a lush garden spot. The gardener treats it carefully. But after three years, nothing! The owner gives up. "Get rid of it!" But do you recall the gardener's reply? "Not so fast. Let's give it another year. Maybe I've failed to do everything necessary to nourish it. Give it another chance. If next year it continues to fail, then maybe we'll get rid of it."

The point is clear. He compares us to the barren fig tree. Though we are placed here by the creative love of God and set here on this earth as a part of the glorious human family, we often reflect anything but God's redemptive power in the world. Our perfectly located fig tree can be barren. Let's give thanks for the Gardener who, out of compassion and patience, provides for us hope in this story. Because of such tender unending love, the future is open and available.

The end of the story is its true beginning. With God's grace abounding always, there is before us the open door of opportunity. Perhaps failure has raised its ugly head and we have hurt, our families have hurt, and we sense no clear direction for the future. As the Lenten season continues, we become increasingly aware of God's intervention into the affairs of human life, making us ready for life eternal.

We can rejoice that we serve the One who is forever the God of the second chance. Thanks be unto God!—Lee McGlone

TOPIC: Peace with God
TEXT: Rom. 5:1–11

No way out. No way out. That's how Paul begins his description of the grim and depressing bondage he calls human sin. There's no way out, that is, until

God comes and makes a new way. In a new and radical act of God's love—in the person and life of Jesus Christ—God has given the gift that permits us, prisoners of despair, to become children of eternal hope. "Therefore, seeing we are justified by faith, let us have peace with God through our Lord Jesus Christ."

During Lent, one emphasis is the sure conviction that we can let go of our pain, grief, loss, and sin. Ours is a forgiving God who wants to carry our burdens and lighten our sorrows. God has appointed a place where the heavy-laden pilgrim is invited to lay down the burden and discover rest and peace. That place is always the same: it is where we meet God, cast our burdens upon him, and trust him for all our strength. There is no peace until we come to that place.

The peace we seek is more than simply the absence of turmoil and conflict. It is more than getting our way. This peace, that which passes all understanding, comes with the territory of faith. It rises up within a life that has yielded itself to God, who we know in Jesus Christ. Here is our hope, joy, and ultimate peacefulness. That's why the Christian story is the old, old story. It continually tells of God's redeeming love and the power of grace to restore broken lives. Each day is given to the Crucified One.—Lee McGlone

TOPIC: Hitting Rock Bottom
TEXT: Deut. 2:1–15

Most of us have hit rock bottom before. When it happens, the real issue is not how you got there but how you will get out. This age-old text helps us. We must make good choices in order to move forward. Perhaps your rock-bottom experience is an illness, a marriage or family crisis, a financial or vocation crisis, or some other. For ancient Israel it was the fearfulness they felt as they came upon an uncertain future.

Regardless of the nature of the hurt, our most significant need is to remember that the God who has always loved us loves us still (v. 7). That is an incredible truth. We are never, never out of the loving embrace of the Heavenly Father. This is really the heart of the gospel. There is nothing we can do to make God love us more—or less! God knows who we are and where we are, and his affectionate eye is never blind to our rock-bottom experiences.

The last word from this old story suggests that life can be, and must be, picked up so we can move along to the next experience that lies before us.

Whatever the hurt, it's time to be moving again. There is more of life yet to be lived than yet has come and gone. It was necessary for God's people in the days of old to suffer so that they could learn that obedience is the way to live. They learned that lesson and moved on. They never got to the Promised Land, but future generations did.

During Lent, we are challenged to the deep belief in a good and gracious God who calls out to us from the darkest of our moments, speaks our names, lays his hands upon our lives, and walks beside us along the way—all the way from rock bottom to the Rock of Ages.—Lee McGlone

TOPIC: The Rending of Our Hearts
TEXT: Joel 2:12–13

The book of Joel was written after the exile. The people had worked very hard after they returned home. Slowly, it had all come together again. All that had been destroyed during those hard years of exile and domination—schools, government, farm land—was behind them. Even the Temple had been rebuilt. Ordered life returned. And then it happened. A plague of locusts came and stripped the land bare. Nothing was left untouched. And if that were not enough, just as they were getting over this natural disaster and new growth was beginning again, a drought settled on the land. The rain just stopped. They would get up morning after morning and look up at the sky. Surely, they would say, it will rain today. And the rain did not come. And the little green shoots of promise dried up.

I. **So Joel spoke: "Rend your hearts and not your garments."** The tearing of the garments was an expression of deep emotion and great grief. But Joel says, "The rending of garments is not enough." This is really a matter of the heart, not church attendance, not outward displays of piety. What we have here is an inner command: "Rend your hearts."

But it was more than that. Joel then said it is also an outward thing. Return. Repent. Turn. It is an about-face. Change your ways. We might interpret this as "review your checkbook, look at your church attendance." We might ask, What is your attitude? What does God think of your attitude? And if that is not enough: What are you doing to serve God in the world?

II. **Ash Wednesday is the beginning of the Lenten season.** This is the first of forty days—forty days of looking at the damage the locusts have done in your life. And the locusts have come. Like a plague they have stripped everything and left vulnerable everything they have touched. It is all laid bare: marriage, church, commitment, faith, hope, love, relationships. So this forty days is a time for recommitment. It is a time of beginning again.

We are a vulnerable people. The locusts come and take it all. There is nothing we can do except pray that the chemo will work, that the grief will fade, that the pain will stop, that we can put aside the anger and the grudges and the power of some addiction that cripples us. And so the ashes we touch our forehead with are a symbol of fragility, our humanness, the flawed nature of the Church.

And this is what Lent and Ash Wednesday are all about. We rend our hearts, for it is a matter of the heart. We touch our foreheads with the ashes, for we know, deep in our hearts, that the locusts have come to us, too. They have touched it all. They have left their damage. And we have all lost. And every heart has been touched by some brokenness. And it is a scary and unsure time.

III. **And then Joel says, "Return to the Lord."** For, you see, the ashes are a sign that we can begin again. Why? Listen to Joel: "Return to the Lord your God, for he is gracious and merciful slow to anger and abounding in steadfast love, and relents from punishing" (2:13). I am told that in countries where the locusts come, they leave their dead carcasses everywhere. Sometimes the shells of the carcasses are ankle deep in the land. And the strange thing is that the dead insects provide fertilizer for the days ahead. And the next year's crop will be the finest it has been in years and years. This is an old mystery. God takes the devastation and pain and sorrow of your life and mine and makes next year's crop better than it has ever been before.

And Lent comes once again, and we touch our foreheads with ashes. We read the old words once more. We are to rend our hearts and not simply our garments. We repent of our sins. We remember the devastation and the miracle of the locusts: God takes the devastation of our yesterdays and makes next year's crop the best that ever was. And so Lent is the claiming of a promise. "I will pour out my spirit on all flesh; your sons and your daughters shall prophesy, your old men shall dream dreams and your young men shall see visions. Even on the male and female slaves, in those days, I will pour out my spirit" (Joel 3:28–29).—Roger Lovette

TOPIC: Barrier Breaker
TEXT: John 20:1–20

A darkened garden, an empty tomb, abandoned grave clothes. We begin there. But John offers more: a grief-stricken woman, a footrace between rival disciples, a mysterious gardener. And yes, more: a bolted room harboring terrified men, Jewish all of them, betting and losing on the failed blasphemer and crucified criminal—Jesus of Nazareth as Messiah, fearing vengeance from their more orthodox religious compatriots. Then in that bolted room the presence of the wounded Jesus delivers a mandate. Some story! What is it about? A ghost? A resuscitated corpse? Is that why we sing and celebrate today? Is DNA reconstituting itself? The rising into the sky of the executed Jesus, as my grandfather used to say, "Body, boots and britches"? Is that what Easter is all about? Is that what Christ's Resurrection means? No way! For John, resurrection means a new community confronts our current communities. For John, himself writing from a tight, loving, persecuted commune, Easter—Resurrection—means a new realm of mutuality and trust making its way amid this world of brokenness and division. For John, Easter means breaking barriers.

I. **The event we celebrate this morning provides us not only with an announcement about unconquerable love binding us together and breaking barriers—reason enough for rejoicing—it challenges us to exercise loving and just community among ourselves.** Easter is not some mind-boggling event taking place in a Palestinian garden two thousand year ago. Easter affirms the ground of our hope today, the root of our future as a human community. It challenges us, you and me, to be resurrection-community barrier breakers, in and for the world. It challenges us to live differently for one another now.

Our question then, as we face the empty tomb, is this: Can we live this radical Easter hope? Can we signal resurrection community? Can we bear our discipleship as barrier breakers? Friends, living the Easter hope means, first of all, the possibility of healing—of barrier breaking—in personal relationships. When our Lord stands among those terrified disciples in that locked room and asserts, "If you forgive the sins of any they are forgiven"— if you retain the sins of any, they are retained—when John says that, he means that by living the Easter gift we can begin again with one another. No relationship is so injured, no tie so broken, no bond so mutilated that in the dimensions of unconquerable love it cannot be re-created.

Barrier breaking cleanses our relationships. It forges forgiveness. It heals the wounds bleeding the most among and within us. I will never forget a memoir that Alan Paton wrote after the death of his wife, Dorrie. Paton remembers a particularly painful occasion when Dorrie bluntly told him she could never love him as much as she had loved her first husband. Paton was crushed. But within the mysteries of human relationships and under no small duress, forgiveness for the injury was begged for and offered. And as Paton closes his reflection on that occasion, he writes:

> What strange creatures we humans are. Just how we come to love one another, and to care for one another for all of our common life and to grant one another territories on which the other does not trespass and to bear with one another's foibles and weaknesses and to grow closer and closer till we have but one mind on all the things that matter to us most and to have children and to put their welfare and happiness above all other things and to give them safety and security until it is proper for them to find these things for themselves—how it ever comes to happen in this imperfect world, only God knows.

Indeed! Only God, the truly miraculous barrier breaker, knows.

II. **But the barrier breaking of Resurrection goes beyond the personal walls we build between and among ourselves.** Easter proclaims the radical dissolution of social barriers as well. The powers of politics, commerce, religion—all those powers finally conspiring to nail Jesus to the cross on this Easter day—we confess the love of God in charge of them, too. The barriers we build, the structures we nurture, the ideologies we pursue, cutting us off from one another, marginalizing, dividing, or thrusting human beings into powerless, second-class, personally demeaning circumstances—have no place within the future of God. Do you remember John's Gospel telling us about Jesus confronting those disciples in a room locked against the world? Christ dissolves locked doors. Christ turns closed societies into open societies. To John, Christ bears the reality of peace born of justice.

To celebrate Easter's barrier breaker is to join, as we are now, and to sing the great Easter hymns; it is to rejoice together on Easter morn in the astounding good news of the empty tomb. But it is also to plow through the barriers killing other people. It is to stand for life, redemption, and justice, grounded in unconquerable love. We dare not sing Easter hymns celebrating barrier breaking without ourselves surrendering to and serving as ambassadors of the divine Barrier Breaker.

III. **And last, we confess on this Easter day a God who finally breaks those barriers splintering the human race into creeds and tongues, races and nations.** We reaffirm the glory of creation designed as rainbow. If the Easter promise and its barrier breaking mean anything, it transforms the human race into the human family.

Friends, I do not know a great deal about Ronald Brown, the former U.S. Secretary of Commerce who died in the plane accident outside of Dubrovnik, Croatia. I am unacquainted with the civil servants and business people who accompanied him on his trip to the Balkans. On this Easter day, one thing we can testify to is our conviction that he and his colleagues remain in the hands of One whose love, even under these random and tragic circumstances, will never let them go—One whose love breaks this ultimate barrier of death and who, on Easter day, we know affirms life. And even as we remember these American lives lost in the Balkans, we recall their mission, as President Bill Clinton said to mourners, "to use the power of the American economy to help the peace take hold in the Balkans, to help people in that troubled place, Bosnians, Serbs, Croats at each other's throats—to help the people in that troubled place have the kind of decent, honorable and wonderfully ordinary lives we American too often take for granted."

That effort to bring well-being, reconciliation, and peace with justice and integrity to the global village truly represents the taste of an Easter mission for all of us. Whether it be the welcoming of immigrants, the dissolving of racism, the tearing down of homophobia, the evaporation of nationalism, the honoring of all human beings, it is the promise of the Risen Christ—

this Barrier Breaker at Easter—confirms each of us, all of us, as children of grace.—James. W. Crawford

TOPIC: It's Back into the Fire!
TEXT: Luke 24:13–35

Our minds are full of questions. How in the world did they not recognize him? Why would they not know him? And who are these two disciples, anyhow? One name is given—Cleopas—and it's the only time his name is mentioned in the New Testament. I think it's the most dramatic Resurrection appearance by Jesus we've got.

I. **But they didn't recognize him. Why?** Emmaus is about seven miles west of Jerusalem; maybe they're walking into the sun on this first Easter afternoon, and their vision is not clear. Maybe Jesus looks different this day, is dressed differently. The grave clothes were lying back there in a Jerusalem tomb. Or maybe they are preoccupied with their grief, blinded by their fierce disappointment. "We had hoped," they said, "that he was the one to redeem Israel," but his death is a clear signal that Rome's yoke will not be cast off. Not this year, not the Passover. Hopelessness and disappointment again, and perhaps that's all they can see on this afternoon—that and a complete stranger who must've been the only person leaving Jerusalem who hadn't known all that had just happened around Jesus of Nazareth.

   They do know him later. Something about the way he blessed and broke the bread—a memory of how he'd fed five thousand? Maybe they'd been up close in the crowd that day. And when he was gone, they said, "Of course! The way he spoke of the Scriptures opened their meaning to us—that a servant Messiah would work and that suffering can have meaning. Of course! It's Jesus the Lord!" So in that same nighttime hour they rushed back to Jerusalem to tell the others—and have the others tell them—that by now there'd been other appearances as well.

II. **Down the years, of all the things replayed about this Easter afternoon, I suspect the main one was, "We could've missed him; we nearly did!"** He was going on. He wouldn't intrude on our schedule or our plans. We insisted that he stop and stay with us. Aren't you glad we insisted? There is nothing miraculous in Jesus' identifying behavior here—just some teaching and a table at the end of the day. But these two disciples and the eleven back in Jerusalem and all the rest of us disciples have lives that are radically changed because of his Resurrection.

What does it mean? Simply this, I think: our Risen Lord has given us a future. If he had died and stayed in the tomb, they would've known disappointment and grief. But they would've gotten over it. They'd had disappointments before. "We had hoped that he was the one to redeem," said the Emmaus Road disciples. They'd had loads of practice at being let down.

If Jesus is dead and done, they'll grieve, get over it, and get on with life. But if he is alive, we're in real trouble! That means he aims to finish what he started, and we are to be part of it! If he's dead, our hopes are dashed; if he's alive, his hope could be realized, and we are legitimately called to hope, as well. If he's dead, after a few weeks it's business as usual; if he's alive, everything is up for grabs! The Resurrection of our Lord is not just promise; it's demand! Easter not only rescues us, it delivers a challenge!

III. **So don't come here this morning to warm your heart over the coals of ancient history. It's back into the fire right now and for the rest of your days!** And being "in the fire" means now what it's always meant since Jesus: loving enemies, confronting pious phoniness, healing, teaching, feeding, clothing, preaching deliverance to all classes and kinds of captives, being community in a world of alienation and loneliness, laying out life—our influence, our resources, ours skills—to serve Jesus Christ.

Easter does not snatch us out of the fires and threats of living. But it does deliver us from hopelessness and powerlessness and, after a while, from our foolish fear. Because the thing is, now we are not alone—not now, not ever! Sometimes it's not that easy to spot his presence, but his Resurrection does guarantee that presence, even when we cannot touch it or hear it. You see, if he has beaten death, the final enemy, then nothing that can ever happen can separate us from our Lord.

Out of the fire? "No," says Easter, but into the presence and the hope and the future, because by faith in the Risen Christ, you have a future and a traveling companion along the way. Hallelujah! And thanks be to God!—William L. Turner

TOPIC: The One Who Goes Before Us
TEXT: Mark 15:47

Easter morning is the highest and holiest moment in the year. The Resurrection of Jesus stands as the centerpiece of our faith. The powerful poetry of Alice Meynell declares of it:

> No planet knows that this earth of ours.
> Bears as its chief treasure, one forsaken grave.

It was the day tragedy became triumph, when sadness became gladness, when doubt gave way to faith, when life overcame death! The first ones there were the women. The men fled and hid behind closed doors, but the women stayed. They saw the horror of the Crucifixion. They saw Joseph of Arimathea take down the body of Jesus from the cross. Then on the first day of the week, very early in the day, they went to the tomb to complete the burial rituals, as was their custom. They worried about the huge stone boulder that closed the entrance to the tomb and about the Roman soldier stationed there to guard it. To their surprise, when they arrived, the stone was rolled away and the guard was gone. There the angel met them and declared that Jesus had come back to life. It was then that the angel declared to them, "Don't be fearful. Simply know that he is not here. He is risen and will go before you into Galilee. There you will see him just as he said."

I. **There is a great amount of comfort in a statement like that.** "He'll go before you just as he said." Throughout the events of Holy Week, we have had the chance to think over and over, again and again, about the Resurrection promises. And what a difference they make!

In the past year, many of us have had an opportunity to dwell on the promises of the Resurrection. Dark days have descended on us in a variety of ways. Some marriages have ended. Some friendships have been dissolved. Tragic illnesses have risen up that refuse to go away. Death has come and claimed our loved ones. You have to think about the Resurrection when times like these come:

"I go and prepare a place for you so that where I am there you may be also."

"Because I live, you shall live also."

"Those who believe in me though they are dead, yet shall they live."

"Lo, I am with you always, even to the end of the world."

Honestly, I don't know what people with no faith do in the face of sorrow. Without the promise of Resurrection, all hope is lost. That awful plight is described by Eugene O'Neill in his play, "Long Day's Journey into Night." In his mind, it is at our birth that we have received the greatest amount of light that we will ever know. As we grow up and grow older, the shadows begin to surround us. The shadows darken as we move further into life. Finally, we come to darkness, and into total darkness we slip, at death. How very sad. Better that we should sing, "Light and life to all he brings; risen with healing in his wings." There's assurance within us when he goes before us.

II. **"Jesus is going before you to Galilee. There you will see him, just as he said." There is great confidence in a claim like that.** I think the greatest sermon I have ever read was Arthur Gossip's "When Life Tumbles in, What Then?" He preached the sermon the Sunday following the untimely death of his dear wife. In his sermon he said, "There are those of you who say that in turmoil we should fling away from our faith. I say, 'Fling away to what?' Those of you who live in the sunshine of life may believe. We who live in the shadow must believe. We have nothing else." How could he preach a sermon like that under such conditions? There's only one way: he was convinced of the Resurrection. Life lies beyond death.

Here is our faith. On it we stand. Our Lord has gone ahead of us, even in death, and has prepared the way. He has descended into death, conquered it, and come back from that dismal place with the keys of death and Hades dangling from his belt. One day we will see him face-to-face. He has gone before us and prepared the way.

God went before Moses and the people, a cloud in the day and pillar of fire in the night. God went before his people. God went to the tomb before the women. They went wondering about a stone that covered the entrance. But God went before them and rolled it away. The twelve were huddled in the upper room, fearful for their own lives, knowing at any moment that the hobnailed boots of the Jewish Gestapo might well be heard clicking on the cobblestone streets, locating them, breaking down the door to the place of their sanctuary, and carrying them off to die, just as they had done with Jesus. But the women came and told them the good news: "He's alive and has gone before you to Galilee."

We gather today, fully confident that not a day is lived, not a battle waged, not a headache felt, but that our Lord has been there already. I don't know who wrote this, but it captures my heart:

The road is rough, dear Lord, I said,
These are stones that hurt me so.
Yes, child, He answered, I understand,
For I walked this way long ago.
My burden, Lord, is far too great,
How can I bear it so?
Yes, child, I remember its weight,
For I bore my cross, you know.

He goes before us.

III. **We come now to the "so what?" of all this.** His "going before us" means this: What leads us to what and calls from us what? Look a bit further. The angel met the women at the tomb and gave them this message: "Now go and give this message to his disciples, *and to Peter.*" Be sure and not leave out Peter. And for our sakes, we ought not to miss it either. What of Peter? He's the one who loudly proclaimed on the morning of Jesus' arrest, "They may all leave you, but not me. I will stay with you even to death." In the garden he fell asleep three times when Jesus asked him to watch and pray. Then he denied Jesus three times. You might think he had worn out his welcome with Jesus. But no, the shocking truth is that Jesus wanted him included in the gospel message. "Go tell the disciples that Jesus is alive. Tell them all, but be sure you tell Peter." But even more shocking is this: God is always at work making disciples out of imperfect people, like us. That's the "so what" of it all.

In John Masefield's play *The Trial of Jesus,* Longinus, the Roman centurion, comes back to report to Pilate. Procula, Pilate's wife, asks, "Do you think he's really dead?" The centurion replies, "No, my lady, I don't." "Where then do you think he is?" "Let loose on the world, my lady, where no one will ever stop his truth." They thought Jesus could be held within the confines of death, but death wasn't big enough to hold him in. He defeated death. And today he is alive to walk before us.

They thought death would conquer Him;
They nailed him to a tree.
I know, I know He conquered death,
Because he lives in me.
—Lee McGlone

TOPIC: The Quiet Pentecost
TEXT: John 20:19–23

When we hear the word *Pentecost,* if we have any associations at all, the ones that come to mind usually come from the book of Acts, chapter 2. From that source we have a vision of the palpable power of the Holy Spirit as tongues—flaming tongues—poured out on the Church. We also hear rushing wind, giving the disciples the kind of power to do things they could not do before. So on the day of Pentecost, year after year, we talk about that vision of the Holy Spirit coming. But the coming of the Holy Spirit in the life of the Church and the lives of individuals is so important that the Scriptures talk about it more than once and in different ways.

John has this knack for seeing things a little bit differently. As I read this Scripture again, it dawned on me, for the first time, here is a "quiet" Pentecost. No flames, no wind, but *breath;* it is the same verb that is used in Genesis 2:7, when it says, "God breathed into us life." Here Jesus breathes the breath of the Spirit to quiet, to galvanize, to energize the disciples.

If you think because it is more quiet than Acts 2 it is any less powerful, look at this story. The disciples are given the power to do their job and we, as twenty-first-century disciples, are given the power to do our job. Given what that job is, this is no small feat. Our job is to be ministers of reconciliation. Now look around you. In nations, between ethnic groups, in families, in churches, there is a great need to be reconciled, to be set right with our true selves, with others and with God. That was the ministry of Jesus Christ, and it is the ministry of Jesus Christ through Christ's Spirit in us.

How is that power given, and how is it seen? It is given to us when we surrender our own wills and admit our own powerlessness to be filled with the power to do the things we want to do but can't do on our own. You remember Jesus telling about the person who would go to the altar to bring his sacrifice but says if you have something to work out with your brother or sister, go do it now. Remember also the passage in 1 Corinthians that says, "Be sure you discern the body of Christ before you come to this table." That's always confused me. There are at least three possible interpretations. One is that we discern how important it is that we take the body of Christ into us, and that certainly is a valid interpretation. Another is that we need to look to our own "body"—our own lives—and say, "Is there any sin that we have not confessed that we need to confess before we come to this table?" That is certainly possible.

But given the context, I think there is a third interpretation that rings true. To discern the body is to discern the community: your friends, neighbors, church members, family members. Is there someone I am withholding forgiveness from and through whom the power of the Spirit cannot flow? We discern the body by asking if there is anyone today we need to forgive. By asking that question, we might know this quiet revolution, this quiet Pentecost, this quiet power to forgive as we have been forgiven.—Gary D. Stratman

CHAPTER FIVE

Messages for Communion Services

Whether called Communion, the Eucharist, or the Lord's Supper—depending on liturgical background—this meal is the communal center of Christian faith. These sermons reflect historical and contemporary insights into the meaning of the Communion service from a variety of perspectives.

TOPIC: A Meal That Lasts
TEXT: John 6:30–40, 48–51

If you recall the story in the Gospel of John, Jesus had just performed a miracle in which he had fed five thousand men, women, and children. They were deeply impressed by someone who could feed them. So the scribes and the Pharisees came to him and said, "You have done this wonderful thing. Let us see if you can do something more spectacular. If so, we will know that you really are God. Prove to us that you are God's chosen one." In the light of this story, think with me about Communion around several themes.

I. **The first lesson we note in our text is the demand that Jesus prove God's existence in his life.** What sign would it take to convince you that God is real? Look around you at this fantastic, unbelievable universe! That is a pretty good sign of God. Did the universe just happen? There are some who say that it just happened. To me it takes far more faith to believe that the world just happened by chance than to say there was a source called God behind it as Creator.

What sign would you accept? Would you accept the sign of a hand, suddenly appearing and writing across the sky, "I am alive, I am real—signed, God"? Would that convince you that there is a God? Or do you think that a bunch of preachers have cooked up some scheme to convince you? We search for signs. Jesus said to the scribes and Pharisees, "You want me to produce bread like Moses produced in the wilderness? Hey, you are wrong. Moses did not give you bread. That bread came from God." The bread is only symbolic of the power of God. This whole universe—and you and I— are symbols or signs of the reality of the presence of God. Jesus was saying to them, "I am the central sign of the realness of God. When you see me, you know the realness of God. I am the one who makes God real." We always have Jesus around to prove to us that God is real.

II. **Then also as we gather at this table, remember that the Lord's Supper is a plentiful meal.** Yet some say, "How can this meal at the Lord's table be plentiful? How can this tiny piece of bread and this cup be a plentiful meal?" The Lord's Supper is plentiful because it gives us the presence of Christ. We receive Christ at the table. We are fed by him. We are nourished by him and sustained by the One who is the Lord of life. He is the One who reveals to us the meaning of life. He declares, "I am the bread of life and when you eat this bread you will not be hungry or thirsty again." Remember, at the Lord's table, there is always room for others. When we come to the Lord's table, the good news is that there is a chair for everyone to come and eat of the plenty of God's redeeming grace. No one is excluded.

III. **Then remember, we come to the Lord's table aware that we are taking the food that is perpetual.** It is lasting. When we eat of this bread and drink of this cup, we are taking in nourishment. It is nourishment that is the very Lord's presence. Some people stumble over the words of Jesus, "You have to eat my flesh, and drink my blood," because they want to take them literally. We use metaphors all the time about drinking and eating—we are drinking in someone's actions, we are devouring a book, we are devouring a tape, or we cannot swallow some story. All of these are figures of speech. So it is with the power of Christ. Christ nourishes you only as you allow him to come into your life and give you his presence. When you do that, you are satisfied. You are satisfied by the power and presence of a Christ that is perpetual. Christ continues to be there, to sustain you in all of your life. Jesus is telling us that the bread he gives is eternal, because it comes with the love, grace, and power of God's presence in and with us. Jesus Christ is the one who is life—life everlasting.

Whether it is on the moon, whether it is here on earth, in some remote place across this earth, or even on some distant planet, we know that God is there. We can commune with God, who is from everlasting to everlasting. What a marvelous sense of presence that is.—William Powell Tuck

TOPIC: In Remembrance of Me
TEXT: Luke 22:14–23

Today, we gather around the Lord's table to remember and to give thanks. Who of us has not done that in our families? We gather as family, pull out the old pictures, and sit around reminiscing. We remember, tell again our personal histories, and, having remembered, we can't help but give thanks. So as we approach the Lord's table, we hear Christ say, "Do this in memory of me."

I. **It may seem from the Bible that gratitude is another law to be fulfilled.** It comes at us as a command: "O give thanks unto the Lord, for he is good." And surely it is an appropriate response for believers. Its opposite—ingratitude—is no acceptable substitute.

Look at the story Jesus told of the ten lepers. Jesus meets ten of these social outcasts who are begging him to heal them. They stood far off, in compliance with the societal and health care customs of the day. To the ten, Jesus declared, "Go and show yourselves to the priests." Along the way to show themselves to the priests, the ten were cleansed. The story is quick to point out, however, that only one of the ten makes his way back to Jesus to express his gratitude. The one falls before Jesus, giving thanks. The penetrating question of Jesus follows: "There were ten cleansed, but where are the nine?"

There may be more than one answer to this query. It may be simply that they were the ingrates they seemed to be and, having received a healing, were so self-centered that they refused to return to say thanks. Or there is another option. It could be that they were doing just what they had been told. It could be that they were on their way to show themselves to the priest, just as they had been told. It could be they were simply doing their duty. But if so, they were missing the greater blessing. Doing duty is a grand thing, but living out of authentic devotion is even grander.

As we gather here around the table, we want to move beyond a sense of duty to the greater sense of devotion. When we hear Jesus say, "Do this in remembrance of me," we want to bow our heads and hearts and say, "Thanks be unto God from whom all blessings flow."

II. **The memory here is quite gruesome.** The Gospel writers were clear about it. Surely, there were many memories as the disciples gathered with Jesus that night. But one supreme, daunting thought rose above all others. It does us good to remember the Lord's miracles, but the miracles are not the central focus at the Lord's table. His challenging sayings, his eye-opening parables (surely, the most insightful in history), yet they are not at the center of this table either. That Jesus began the Church and empowered it with his Spirit is fundamental to our faith, but instituting the Church is not what we gather here to remember today. What then did Jesus intend when he said, "Do this in memory of me?" He meant one thing: the supreme act of laying down his life—of death on the cross. Here it is—that haunting, mysterious, mind-probing, heart-piercing recollection of a body broken and blood spilled out. And you see, when our thoughts linger there, our memories are jogged about the things that matter the most.

Here is the central thought of our faith. Here is our witness and the content of our proclamation. Enough cannot be said about its significance. Yet in doing so, we often are guilty of "assuming" Jesus' sacrifice for us—that he died to save us—but neglect to recall his word about a cross for us to bear. What was it? "If any one would come after me, let him deny himself, take up his own Cross daily, and follow me." It isn't just that Jesus died for us. In becoming his followers, we ourselves have died. We are dead to selfishness, dead to sin, dead to the world—dead to all this, but alive to God. How can we ever forget, when Jesus said, "Remember me."

III. **Something happens at the Lord's table, related to gratitude and to memory, that goes beyond both of these.** It's simply this: We can't come to this table and go away the same people we were before we came. The memory of the Crucified One, of his love invested in us, touches a deep chord within the believing heart. We will be touched deeply at the seat of our emotions. Hearts will mellow, minds will be challenged, grudges held for decades will melt away, anger that has seethed within us for years will fade away, faith will deepen, sins will be confessed, forgiveness will be experienced, giftedness will be clarified, calling will be encountered, strength will be reinforced, grace will be sufficient—all this, and more, here at the table, when we "remember him."

G. A. Johnston Ross told a remarkable story many years ago in a sermon. It seems that he was visiting in a small village church in New Zealand. As was their tradition, when time came in the service for the Lord's Supper, the worshippers rose from their seats and went to the front, knelt at the altar, and received Communion. Just as the group kneeled, a young man rose abruptly from the altar and made his way back to his seat. A few minutes later, the same young man made his way back to the altar and received the elements.

After the service, Dr. Ross asked the young man about his strange behavior. The man described how, as he went to the altar, he found himself kneeling by a man who, years earlier, had killed his father—a man he had himself vowed to kill. There he was, kneeling by his side. Unable to take the Lord's Supper with the man, he rose and returned to his seat. Yet he sat there; his mind went back to the Upper Room, with its table set and a voice saying, "By this all men shall know that you are my disciples—if you have love one for another." "I saw a cross," said the young man, "with a man nailed on it, and I heard him say to me, 'Father, forgive them for they know not what they do.' It was then that I arose and returned to the altar."

We simply can't remember what Christ has done and not be changed. The memory of Christ refuses to leave us alone. As we approach the Lord's table, we do so to remember and to give thanks. The scene appears gruesome, but our hope lies here: a Savior, crucified, dead, buried, yet arisen from the grave, and someday coming again to receive his own.—Lawrence Vowan

TOPIC: Finding the Landmarks
TEXT: Deut. 26:5–11

I. **A living faith is always more than memory.** In a recent visit to my home town, I decided to drive my wife around and show her my roots. The tour went something like this: "That is where my junior high school used to be. That is part of my high school. That used to be a drugstore where we hung out on Sunday afternoons before Training Union. That used to be our house." My home town is the same, but very different.

That statement would also apply to me. It also applies to my faith. Many of the people who helped to shape my early faith are now dead, the church is radically different, and times have changed. That takes nothing away from my roots. I still look with nostalgia at the old church that my family helped to build and the baptistery where I professed my faith in Christ. I still worship the same God and read the same Bible in a newer translation. Yet I no longer can hide in a naïve view of the world and of God with which I began. Since I first met Christ, my faith has confronted two major wars, racial and gender revolutions, an ecumenical revolution, parenthood, the death of a spouse and numerous mentors, and nearly thirty-nine years of viewing the church as a pastor.

II. **Simply repeating the answers of history or reciting a creed does not meet the challenge of this present time.** How shall we prepare our children for the world that is coming? If you think the Bible is just a rule book, look again. Jeremiah envisioned the day when the law will be written in the hearts of God's people, and Jesus rooted his concept of righteousness in seeking first the Kingdom of God. We have to give our children more than answers. They need to know the God behind the answers. We have to rise to face the questions of this present moment—some questions that our forebears did not know to ask. We owe to our children and grandchildren both a clear identity of their roots in the stories of our faith and the freedom and responsibility to hear a new word from God. The world needs to know the God of grace revealed in Christ. The gospel of Christ calls us to open the doors and hearts of the church to include all of God's children.—Larry Dipboye

TOPIC: Pass the Bread
TEXT: Matt. 14:13–21

Bread is the staff of life. Bread is basic to sustaining life. I have a nephew who has a gluten allergy that makes ordinary flour poison to him. The problem led to a series of crises, first with the diagnosis of the problem, then with the adjustment to a hard-to-follow diet. The diet is difficult at home and nearly impossible on the road. The family has gained a new appreciation for bread as the staff of life.

I. **We call grain one of the basic food groups, but in biblical times bread was so basic that it often represented all food.** *Bread* is still a colloquial expression for *money,* and we call the employed member of the family the breadwinner. When Jesus was pursued by the crowds, he had compassion on the mob, first by healing their sick and then by responding to their hunger. The disciples wanted to send them away, but Jesus commanded them, "You give them something to eat." When they could only find five loaves and two fish, he said, "Bring them here to me." Then Jesus took the bread and fish, looked up to heaven, blessed and broke the bread, and gave it to his disciples. Five thousand families ate, and twelve baskets of leftovers were collected.

II. **Bread in the Bible seems always to be a symbol of something more.** It always reminds us of the manna in the wilderness and the unleavened bread of Passover. "This is the bread of affliction which our forefathers ate in the land of Egypt." In John, Jesus said, "I am the bread of life," although he refused to turn stone into bread in the wilderness of temptation. Breaking bread together is a symbol of fellowship: "You prepared a table before me" (Ps. 23). We have to be careful not to spiritualize too much. Initially, bread is just bread. Jesus also saw bread as a necessity of life. Although the feeding miracle has layers of meaning, it begins with the compassion of Jesus for hungry people and a command for disciples to feed the masses wandering as sheep without a shepherd.

III. **Bread is the Body of Christ.** This is the only miracle of Jesus recorded in four Gospels. Add to the four the repetition in Matthew and Mark of the feeding of the five thousand, and the miracle is repeated no less than six times. Why? What is the importance of this story, as compared, for example, to the raising of Lazarus that is found only in John? Images of the Eucharist—the Lord's Supper—dominate the language of the miracle in every repetition, which probably explains the focus on bread in Matthew's telling of the story. The familiar verbs in the account of the Lord's Supper are repeated: he took, blessed, broke, and gave.

Fred Craddock has a theory about the importance of this miracle. He believes that it was so integrally connected to the Lord's Supper that it was told and retold every time the church gathered around the table of the Lord. Every time Christians gather around the table of the Lord, we are reminded that God provides our bread and feeds the world through us. We remember that this bread is more than bread. This is the bread of life—the Body of Christ that nourishes the soul, as well as the body.—Larry Dipboye

TOPIC: The Tie That Binds
TEXT: 1 Cor. 10:16–17

The cup of blessing which we bless, is it not a fellowship with the blood of Christ? The bread which we break, is it not a fellowship with the body of Christ? Because there is one bread, we who are many are one body, for we all partake of the one bread (1 Cor. 10:16–17).

There is a hymn we often sing around the Lord's table. It goes like this: "Blest be the tie that binds our hearts in Christian love; the fellowship of kindred minds is like to that above." It's a beautiful and noble hymn that recognizes our life together in fellowship. But I raise the question: What is the tie that binds? If indeed we are a fellowship of kindred minds, like to that above, how is it that we are so bound?

I. **Fellowship is quite an important matter.** At the heart of the brokenness of our world is the brokenness of fellowship. It goes all the way back to the very beginning, to that point where our primal ancestors gave in to a spirit of mistrust; the fellowship was broken, and the result was chaos. It's been with us since then.

I heard a story about a Midwestern merchant who had twin sons who were the best of friends. At their father's death, they took over the operation of his store. All went quite well, until one day, one of the brothers waited on the customer, laid a dollar bill on top of the cash register, and walked the customer to the front of the store. When he returned, the bill was gone. He asked his brother if he had seen the bill; the brother said he knew nothing of it. If the matter had been dropped there, all would have been well. But it wasn't dropped there. Later, and with a hint of suspicion, the brother asked again, "Are you sure you know nothing about this bill?" The other brother sensed the accusation and arose to his own defense.

As time went on, the breach became increasingly wider. Accusations were hurled. The animosity became intense. Eventually, they dissolved their business relations so that the store was divided down the middle. The personal warfare went on for twenty years. One day a car with out-of-state license drove up. A well-dressed man got out and went into one of the stores. He asked the owner how long he had been in business at that location. When he was told it was over twenty years, the stranger said, "Twenty years ago, I was out of work and drifting from place to place. I got off a boxcar in your town and had no money or food. I walked down the alley behind your store and saw on top of the cash register a dollar bill. I had been taught not to steal, but that morning I was so hungry. Everyone was in the front of the store, and I took that dollar bill. I decided that peace would never come until I faced you and made it right." The stranger was amazed to see the old man standing in front of him, weeping. "All I want," the store owner said, "is for you to go next door and repeat the same story you have just told me." The stranger did, only this time there were two old men standing before him, weeping.

Just imagine, how sad! Twenty years of hostility, anger, destruction—all rooted in a spirit of mistrust—a mistrust now shown to have no basis of truth. Even more sad is when we see that what happened in that Midwestern town lies at the root of our relation to God and to one another.

II. **You don't have to go very far in the Bible to see this.** How was it in the beginning? God understood the joy of existence to be too wonderful to keep alone, so he made a world and beings within it who could relate to him and to one another. And in the cool of the day, God would walk with them. I don't know all of what that means, but I suggest it means that in the beginning a strong sense of trust linked together the Creator and the creation. That's why Eden was called Paradise. But that place of paradise didn't last long. Something happened very soon to shatter trust. Genesis 3 describes what theologians call the Fall. Whatever that story is all about, it surely describes the breaking of trust.

Why did all that take place? I don't know, for sure. We could describe it as rebellion, arrogance, or disobedience. A close reading tells us it all came about as a result of basic mistrust. The creation no longer trusted the Creator. And the serpent said, "Are you sure God said . . . ? Did God really say. . . . ? Well, God probably meant . . . !" And they listened, and in the end they lost. And the story has been repeated in every human life since then. Chaos has resulted. Suspicion and mistrust, both of God and of those around us, has left us sadly broken.

III. **But God, being gracious and full of mercy, didn't leave us in that sad predicament.** He moved toward us again with the intention of restoring the broken relationship. That is what the Old Testament is about. Beginning with Abraham, with whom he established the Covenant, he reached out in love and affection. Through Moses, David, prophets, priest, and kings, he sought deliberately to destroy suspicion and to rebuild the trust. His final effort was the coming of his Son to be one of us. He was the supreme reconciler and has given to us the ministry of reconciliation.

Here is the tie that binds: the love of God poured out for us in the person of Jesus of Nazareth. His love heals our wounded spirits, breaks the bonds of suspicion, and establishes within us love of God and of one another. *Is not the cup we share a fellowship with the blood of Christ; is not the bread we break a fellowship in his body?* Yes. Indeed. Thanks be unto God for his everlasting mercy.—Lee McGlone

TOPIC: A Thanksgiving Communion
TEXT: Matt. 26:26–29

One of the unique customs of my home church was to end the Lord's Supper on a solemn note, then to sing a hymn, and then to exit the building in silence. It was my church's intention to follow the example of Scripture to the utmost. Does it not say, following the supper, that they sang a hymn and went out? I admire that little church's insistence on obeying the Scripture, but I don't think that's what the text means; after all, it says they sang a hymn and "went out to the Mount of Olives." Are we going to go all the way over there? I think not.

But there is something more here. The singing of hymns was a major part of worship around the Passover table. The hymns they sang were selected from among those *Hallel* psalms recorded in Psalms 113–118. *Hallel* is the root for our word *hallelujah*. These hymns—the ones sung at the Passover celebration—were songs of celebration and thanksgiving. They sang a hymn and went out, thus concluding their evening, the last they would have before Jesus would die. They sang a hymn of thanksgiving! It is a theme sounded throughout the Last Supper.

I. **I wonder, as we gather preparing to eat the holy meal, what emotions are inside us.** Probably, there are many, and appropriately so. There is *pathos* here. The very sight and the sounds of the table call out in us a sense of anguish, misery, woe, pity, sympathy, and tenderness. There is *fear* here. After all, the elements on the table (poured cup and broken bread) are reminders of the Lord's death and of our own mortality. There is *intimacy* here. Jesus gathered with the closest of his followers and ate with them. There is *mystery* here. What does he mean? This is my body. This is my blood. There is *holiness* here. We would do well to take off our shoes. Truly, we gather around the table, touched in our heart's deepest places.

There is one emotion, however, often overlooked: *thanksgiving.* But it should not be. Indeed, thanksgiving stands at the heart of our text. "On that night, Jesus took the bread and the cup, and he *gave thanks* for them." The Greek word for "he gave thanks" is *os euchasisto.* The word is used by some denominations to name the meal, the Eucharist. It's important that we, on the Sunday before Thanksgiving Day, sense before us the grand note of gratitude. We give thanks for this meal, even as we give thanks for the bounty of life.

II. **As a nation, we have celebrated Thanksgiving Day since October 3, 1863.** President Lincoln, after the two-decade-long urging of a certain Sarah Joseph Hale, declared Thanksgiving Day as a national holiday, to be observed "with one heart and one voice by the whole American people." An excerpt from the proclamation reads:

> We have been the recipients of the choicest bounties of heaven; we have been preserved these many years in peace and prosperity; we have grown in numbers, wealth and power as no other nation has ever grown.
>
> But we have forgotten God. We have forgotten the gracious hand which preserved us in peace and multiplied and enriched and strengthened us. We have vainly imagined . . . that all these blessings were produced by some superior wisdom and virtue of our own. Intoxicated with unbroken success, we have become too self-sufficient to feel the necessity of redeeming and preserving graced, too proud to pray to the God that made us.

I, for one, am grateful for the generous spirit of Mr. Lincoln but wonder how he would respond to the ingratitude of our day.

It ought to be said that gratitude is good for the soul. It is one of the enriching virtues that adds depth of character to human life. Thanksgiving removes our selfishness from the center of life and puts something there (mystery, if you will) that increases awareness and transforms one's outlook on life. Without having to be the eternal optimist, gratitude helps us to face every episode of life with adequate resources for success. Gratitude lifts the soul, and as it does, it turns our thoughts to God. Every good and perfect gift comes from above. We can't pass this week without saying, "Thank you, God."

III. **Notice that when Jesus gave thanks, he was gathered around the table with the closest of his followers.** The gratitude he expressed included them. It also includes us—all of us. The Lord's Supper is, in one respect, a fellowship meal.

Those with Jesus were not a perfect group. Already some had doubted; at least two had argued over who was the greatest in the Kingdom. None of them seemed to understand the gravity of the night. Soon one would betray him with a kiss, and another would deny him three times. They all seemed bewildered at best at the idea described in the broken bread and poured cup. This was a difficult group. But, most important, while they were not perfect, *they were with him!* And they were with each other. They needed each other but would not discover how much until later. In the end, they did. It was this very group that, for the most part, became founding fathers for the Lord's Church. Their love for one another and their ability to work together, worship together, live together—in short, their fellowship—proved to be their strength in the hard days to follow.

The same is true for us. Next to the gospel we believe and preach, nothing is as important as the fellowship we share. We must be family, if we are to be the people of God. Apart from the love displayed on this table, we are truly, of all persons, most to be pitied. As we eat today, join me in giving thanks for those by our sides.

IV. **But we must also express gratitude for the promise.** Jesus said, "I'll eat this meal with you now, but not again until I eat it anew in the Kingdom of God." In one swift sentence, our Lord lifted the discussion around the table to the realm of eternity. He proclaimed a day, yet to come, when the world as we know it comes to an end, and eternity, as only God knows it, begins. Today, we sit at a Messianic banquet proclaiming our belief in the living Lord Jesus as Savior and conquering King. It is a meal of anticipation. But in *that* day, we will sit at the great Marriage Feast, when the Groom, our eternal Lord, is united forever with his bride, the Church. Today, we honor him in untold varied persuasions, segregated by race and nationality, and cultural distinction. But on that day, all of God's children, of every race and tribe, of every continent, of every generation, of every denomination, of every theological persuasion or personal opinion, shall sit down together in the Paradise of God. And then we shall embrace, not only hand-in-hand but heart-in-heart and give thanks to God, our Maker.

On that day, I want to see my mother and my father, my brother and my sister—and my teachers, and those dear friends from our church who have gone on before. But most of all, I want to see the Savior. And when I do, I want to bow before him and say thank you. Thank you for loving us and dying for us and for preparing for us an eternal home.

Clifford Lewis said it this way:

For Christ who came from heaven above
For the Cross and His redeeming love
For His mighty power to seek and save
For His glorious triumph o'er the grave
For the lovely mansions in the sky
For His blessed coming by and by
I give thee humble thanks.

So must we. You know, if we ever stop to think more, surely we will thank more.—Lee McGlone

TOPIC: The Way of the Cross
TEXT: Luke 9:18–27

We gather this morning around the Lord's table to remember and celebrate. But our memory can't be altogether celebrative, for the scene we recall is gruesome at best. The elements on this table are the remnants of death: a broken body and blood poured out.

I. **Yet here it is, the central affirmation of the Christian faith.** Our Lord and Savior Jesus Christ, dead, on a cross. The cross of Christ is the central focus of all our preaching. There on the cross, the ultimate sacrifice of life and love was given. We'll never understand it all, but we can experience the awe-inspiring and life-changing focus of what God did through Christ, reconciling the world unto himself. Paul would say that in his preaching he sought to know nothing save "Jesus and him crucified." In the Supper, we not only read of it, we see it, and indeed we eat it; we experience it ourselves.

The cross is the central focus of all of life. Here in the text is the first description of the Lord's coming Passion to disciples and their revulsion at such an idea. As the episode begins, a question is asked about who Christ is. The truth is, one can't know Christ except as his follower. To others his work of grace is foolishness, but to us it is the power of God.

II. **Then comes the unfolding of the crisis.** He is to suffer and to be killed? What does this mean? And what of us? What does it mean—that we are to carry our own cross daily? And how are we to celebrate all this?

We begin by declaring that all of life is victory. Don't get me wrong. Not all of life is easy. Yet even in our despair and disappointment, our model of all Christian faith is Jesus. And how was his life lived in victory and fullness? Maybe we should commit this verse to memory: "Though he was God's Son, he learned obedience through suffering—and being made complete he became the source of eternal salvation to all who obey" (Heb. 5:8).

This well-known hymn declares the way of the cross: "Was it for crimes that I have done he groaned upon the tree?" Yes, indeed! "Amazing pity, grace unknown, and love beyond degree." "At the cross, at the cross, where I first saw the light, and the burden of my heart rolled away. It was there by faith I received my sight, and now I am happy all the day."—Lawrence Vowan

COMMUNION SERMON OUTLINES

These brief Communion outlines offer food for thought. Development of these ideas is unlimited.

TOPIC: God's Story Told

TEXT: 1 Cor. 11:23–26

Before us on the Lord's table is the sermon for the day. It tells

Of God's unconditional love.
Of our sin and disobedience.
Of Christ's sacrifice.
Of our joy in belonging.

—Lawrence Vowan

TOPIC: An Anticipation
TEXT: Isa. 50:4–7; Luke 22:15; Rev. 22:12–13, 20

"I will not eat this meal with you again *until* it is fulfilled in the Kingdom of God."

"Until" declares hope. There is a promise to which we look forward.
"Until" demands determination. There is a work we are to be doing.
"Until" fulfills a grand celebration. There is a joy we are to be experiencing.

—Lawrence Vowan

OFFERTORY PRAYERS FOR COMMUNION SUNDAY

Creator God, let these Communion elements, so reflective of our Savior, join with our offering to touch many with the presence of God. Amen.—E. Lee Phillips

As we come to the Lord's table this morning, Father, we come to give as well as receive. Remembering, we accept your sacrifice for us, but we also accept the responsibility that our commitment to you places upon us. Monetary gifts become one of our expressions of gratitude for all you have done on our behalf. Pray receive them and multiply them and use them for the ongoing of the Kingdom of Christ throughout the world, we pray in his most holy name. Amen.— Henry Fields

A PRAYER FOR WORLD COMMUNION SUNDAY

Eternal God, the One who by grace has brought us to this hour, we would now open wide the doors and windows of our souls to you. We hunger and thirst for the experience of your people, who so felt your nearness that they cried, "Where shall we go from your presence? Where shall we flee from your Spirit?" For in the beauty of nature, in the warmth of our relationships, in all things worthy and good, in courage and hope, in the victories of light over darkness, of love over hate, of good over evil—in these you have become real to us, for we have first come to know you through Jesus your beloved Son.

Through another week, you have led us. We've been tempted to be careless and ungrateful. You have been to us like a refreshing stream, your goodness richly given, and we have too often been thoughtless of the fountain. O God, today help us acknowledge you, thankfully, as the Friend who stands behind all friendships, as the source of all things good and noble and pure. Lord, help us this day to praise your holy name.

We pray today for world leaders; we pray for peace; we pray for each other. In times of need may we stand together and encourage each other. As we come to the table today, may we experience here once again the wonder of your grace. In the sights, sounds of the table of grace before us, may we experience you in this place. Lord, send us forth today as builders of a better world. Burden our hearts with the hurts that afflict your people. Teach us to be merciful, even as our Lord is full of mercy. May now the living presence of Christ our Lord stand forth in our midst and guide and guard and keep and encourage and challenge and correct us, all the days that we live.

Blessings and honor and power belong to you, O Lord. Before you we bow our hearts in submission and seek your way and will among us all. In the Spirit and the name of Jesus the Christ, we make our prayer. Amen.—Lee McGlone

CHAPTER SIX

Messages for Funerals and Bereavement

Preaching during times of bereavement rightly emphasizes the promises of faith on which we stand. These sermon summaries reflect hope born of memory, faith, and gratitude.

TOPIC: Music to God's Ears
TEXT: Psalm 92

I would dare to say that faith is the music of the believing heart. So while the rest of the world groans under the weight of discouragement, the voice of faith sings songs of hope in the promises of God. While other voices wail the mournful tune of death and decay, faith lifts up its voice with the triumphant cantata of Resurrection and God's coming Kingdom.

The Psalms sing with this kind of faith. And the music of such faith is first born in the faithful life. That is to say, long before the psalm was written on paper, it was written on the pages of life. The words were lived before they were sung. And the faith with which the psalmist sings was practiced in the world before it was penned as lyric.

I. **That's why I have selected Psalm 92 as a tribute to the memory of Miriam.** You see, I don't believe that you can separate the memory of Miriam's love for music from the memory of her love of God. Her music issued from her faith; it was nothing less than the harmony of her heart in union with the will of God for her life. That's what made Miriam special. She was first and foremost devoted to God and his church. And because of her devotion, her music has the quality of dedication and faith.

I remember a conversation in which I questioned Miriam about her busy schedule. I asked, "What in the name of God prompts you to go here, there, and everywhere, playing your music for this group and that group of people?" She gave me that impish little smile that she was famous for and said, "That's exactly right. I do it in the name of God!" Classic Miriam, isn't it?

II. **"The righteous shall flourish like a palm tree . . . they shall bear fruit in old age, they shall stay fresh and green . . . proclaiming, 'The Lord . . . he is my Rock!'"** Don't they sound like the words of some senior saint? They strike me as the words of a seasoned saint who has known the pitfalls of temptation and the power of God's salvation.

You know, you might have missed it. But there's a promise locked away in the words of this psalm—a promise that has been copied and rearranged in a thousand different hymns throughout the ages, a promise that will last beyond the shadows of time and into eternity, a promise embraced by Miriam and now is embracing her. The psalmist writes: "the righteous will stay fresh and green." More important, I think Miriam would encourage us to live lives harmonious to that hope. She would encourage us to live each day to the fullest and to do so for the sake of Christ and not for our own gain. I believe she would encourage us to teach this song of faith to others who know neither the melody nor the lyrics. And above all else, I believe Miriam would admonish us to invite them to join with us in this choir of faith we call the church.

III. **Which leads me to believe that Miriam's life was nothing less than music to God's ears.** Whenever God turned his ear to Miriam, I'm certain he heard a heart that was faithful and a soul wrapped in a song of praise to his name. I guess you could say that Miriam's life was a living psalm—a note of praise here, a short lament there, but always an underlying rhythm of thanksgiving.

The other night as I sat typing these words, I had an image. Maybe it was more than an image. Perhaps it was a small and personal revelation. I envisioned myself wandering around in the Kingdom of God like a lost and lonely lamb. And then this shadow appeared on the horizon. It was a small figure, with a steady gate, arms all wrapped around sheets of paper. And from a distance I saw the hand go up, and a voice said, "Hey, you! Wait a minute. I've just got one thing to tell you. Honest, it'll only take a minute." Anyone who knew Miriam knows that the minute hand of her watch never moved an inch! And here we were with an eternity of time!

Well, the image was comforting because someday we will see Miriam and sing with Miriam. Someday we will join voices and sing one mighty hymn of praise to the God who has promised us eternal life.—Albert J. D. Walsh

TOPIC: A Time for All Things: Funeral Sermon for Mildred Heard
TEXT: Eccles. 3:1–8

When death comes, we are forced to deal with matters of great consequence. Standing here, near this casket and soon preparing to move to the cemetery, we find ourselves on the edge of eternity. That may be a frightening place to be, but it is also a place of great joy, especially for those who find security in faith. Mildred is no longer with us, and we will throughout life miss her, but the full truth is this: Mildred has gone home to be with God. Death has taken her from us for a while but not forever.

It has been a joy to get to know Ed and Mildred over the years. I recall visiting several times in their home during Ed's illness and was impressed with their love and their faith. Over the years, one of the sure things around Parkview Baptist Church was Mildred's beautiful smile and her love of life. She was a faithful member of the Friends Sunday School Class and greatly loved.

I. **One of the fine things we bring to this day is our memory.** All of us gathered here have memories of being with Mildred. I suggest that we dwell on them, talk about them, because memory is a resource for great living. My wife, Brenda, told me just the other day of such a memory. She and our youngest son, Nicholas, who at the time was about ten years old, were having lunch at Aaron's Pharmacy. As they ate, Brenda noticed Mildred at another table, eating lunch with a friend and having a wonderful time talking and laughing. Nicholas looked to Brenda and said, "Mom, don't we know that lady?" "Yes," Brenda said, "That's Mildred Heard. She's a member of Parkview." To which our young son replied, "Well, I didn't know old people could have such a good time." He needed to know that, and Mildred taught him an important lesson. All of us have our memories.

II. **The Bible is also about memory.** The wisdom literature of the book of Ecclesiastes leaves us with a beautiful piece of poetry in chapter 3. It says, in looking back at life, that we can rejoice in the "times" of life. Look at them:

There is a time to be born. God, in eternal wisdom, brought us into being through a unique act of creation that we call birth. In truth, God made us. God made Mildred and us. And God made us in God's own image so that we may share in the joy of life that before the world began, only God knew. He created us for fellowship, for love, for sharing the very best in relation to himself and to those around us. There is a time to be born.

There is a time to live. There is a time to live with family and friends. Cherished are the memories of wonderful times together, Christmases, Thanksgivings, anniversaries, birthdays, graduations, births, marriages, and even other deaths. Those events, incorporated in the process of every day's labor, the work we perform, the service we render, the friendships we make, the laughter we share, the faith we engender—all become the foundation for the fullness of life. There is a time to live.

There is a time to die. We are reminded again today that life on this earth is never permanent. We all die. And death hurts. There is no way to dress it up and make it look good. Paul called death a sting. It hurts us, at times so deeply that our hearts almost break. Yet in faith we look to the truth that death is no victor, and we are no victims. We stand assured that though Mildred is gone from us, and we cannot see her or talk with her, she's not gone from us forever. We will one day stand together again. Her death, in a way, makes our own dying easier, for she is there waiting for us, just beyond the river. There is a time to die.

III. **Death is no welcome matter, but it's no cause for great fear either.** The Christian lives with hope that life never ends. We will live forever. Perhaps Tennyson's "Crossing of the Bar" says it best:

Sun set and evening star,
And one clear call for me!
And may there be no moaning of the bar
When I put out to sea.
But such a tide as moving seems asleep,
Too full for sound and foam,
When that which drew from out the boundless deep
Turns again home.
Twilight and evening bell,

And after that the dark!

And may there be no sadness of farewell

When I embark.

For tho' from out our borne of Time and Place

The flood may bear me far,

I hope to see my Pilot face to face

When I have crost the bar.

Mildred, you will be missed by us all, family and friends. We know that you are one of God's daughters, and we now will let you go and live with God. To God be the glory. Great things he hath done.—Lee McGlone

TOPIC: The Promise Fulfilled: Funeral Sermon for Mayme Scott
TEXT: Ps. 23; 2 Cor. 4:16–5:1; Rev. 21:1–8

Recent years have been difficult for Mayme and Tom. We've watched her handle a difficult disease, maintain her faith, and see her faith strengthened through it. The news that Mayme had cancer hit her hard. Such a word always does. Our visits during those first few weeks after the diagnosis focused on Mayme's concerns about her faith. I don't think Mayme ever doubted God or God's goodness, but she was concerned about herself. "I don't know if I've done enough," she would say. "I wish I could be sure." This was quite a quandary.

Here is what I said: "God loves you, more than you can know. God wants you, as much as you want it, to sense security in your faith. God doesn't want you to fear, especially right now." So we quoted some Bible verses, like John 3:16: "For God so loved . . ." whosoever believes! Another was Ephesians 2:8: "For by grace you have been saved through faith . . . and that not of yourselves; it is a gift from God, lest anyone should boast." Then I would say something like this: "Mayme, our salvation is not about us; it is about God. It is not about what we do but about what God has done for us. All we do is trust."

I'm so glad that in recent weeks, a true sense of peace came over her soul. The questions gave way to consolation. Fear seemed to pass away; hope and faith took its place.

I. **The two passages I read were special to us.** We read them together, time after time. Psalm 23 declares our assurance, God's guidance, comfort in death, and the heavenly home forever. Second Corinthians 4 says that in life we are "afflicted in every way, but not crushed, perplexed but not despairing, struck down but not destroyed. This outer body is wasting away but the inner being is renewed day by day." How is this so? "We are always carrying within us the death of Jesus—so that the life of Jesus will be real to us."

How welcome are these words when "our sad heart aches till it nearly breaks." Yet intermingled with the sadness is a holy gladness—the absolute assurance that life in faith does not end and that death does not win. God wins. God's Holy Spirit gives the victory.

II. **This third reading offers hope that lasts into eternity.** John is isolated on the island called Patmos, put there for a purpose other than his preaching of the gospel. He was separated by the sea in that small island prison. But there he had a vision. There was a new heaven and a new earth. And there was no more sea; that is, no longer was there any separation from loved ones, nor from God, nor from the labor of his ministry. God was there, and God's people were there. In that place there would be no longer any pain, or sorrow, or tears, or suffering, or death. For the former things all passed away; behold all things new! Here is the promise on which we stand today.

One of my favorite pieces of literature is John Bunyan's *The Pilgrim's Progress*. It tells in allegorical detail the story of its main character, Christian, who is traveling from this world to the Celestial City. Along the way he falls into any number of distractions that threaten to take him off course. He falls into the Slough of Despond, but by God's grace is lifted out and set on the road again. He arrives in the city of Vanity Fair and is almost overcome by its frivolous nature, but again God leads him out and sets him on his way. Finally, he arrives with his companion traveler at a giant river, the River of Death, which has to be crossed in order to reach the Celestial City. The companion steps into the river, first ankle deep, then knee deep, then waist deep. From the middle of the river, he turns to face Christian on the shores and shouts, "Be of good cheer, Brother Christian, I have found the bottom, and it is good." Indeed it is. Faith has made it so!

Prior to Mayme's death, she was reading a devotional book. The book-marker was at the reading for April 5. Here is what it said:

It is fitting that we reflect upon the resurrection . . . for apart from the resurrection there is no abiding purpose in life and no eternal hope in death. . . . Our birth was our entrance into this world; our living here is our schooling; and our death shall be our exit from it and our entrance into another one. So death has its kinder aspects. It was designed as gain; to bring relief to pain, to stop the flow of tears, to shorten the days of trial, to bid the soul go free.[1]

Then follows this line from the poet, Frederic Knowles: "The lordliest of all things!—Life lends us only feet, Death gives us wings."

Mayme, we will miss you. Please know that we love you and mourn your separation from us. But we know with abounding assurance that we will gather again in that far country, and there we will never know separation again.—Lee McGlone

TOPIC: A Faithful Servant: Funeral Sermon for John Mullens
TEXT: Ps. 23; John 14:1–7; 1 Thess. 4:13–18

Our first memories of Monroe, Louisiana, include John and Marj Mullens. His was the first voice I heard. Our first meal was with them. In fact, it was a conversation with these two in which the decision was made in my heart to come to Parkview Baptist Church. We shared worship together. We held warm and deep conversations in their home. Good memories like these, and thousands like them, make our hearts glad. We gather today to express our thanks to God for such a man as this. The city of Monroe has been fortunate to have a man of John's caliber. He was a leader, a friend, and a helper among us. Truly, John will be missed.

---

[1]Brownlow, Leroy, *Today Is Mine* (Fort Worth, TX: Brownlow Publishing Company, 1972).

I. **John was a great family man**. The children and grandchildren have wonderful memories to carry all their years—memories of many years of marriage, jobs, homes, graduations, their own marriages, children, grandchildren, Christmases, vacations—all memories to cherish. We can't forget that you, as a family, have been to this place before, to the funeral service and to the graveside—and you will go there again. But these memories make you who you are!

It was a wonderful occasion this past Sunday to spend time with John's children and to reminisce. Those years are blessed memories—Marj's great appreciation for music and John's inability to carry a tune and his habit of awakening the children in the morning by singing to them. Cherish these memories. Talk often about the joys of life with John as father, grandfather, and friend.

II. **He was also a great church man**. Those of us here have great memories also. John and Marj came to Parkview in April of 1951. They were here during the years of its most significant growth and the years of its greatest hurts. Marj served on the building committee that designed this beautiful sanctuary. Marj taught for a number of years in our Bible study ministry. John ably served in any number of leadership roles: deacon, teacher in the Friends Sunday School Class (I suspect that John, Marj, Miss Whitt, and others are having a grand celebration today), trustee, chairman of the stewardship team. And he was chairman of the pastor search committee that brought me to Parkview almost fifteen years ago.

III. **John was a man of great faith**. Recent years have been difficult for John and Marj. We've watched them handle almost overwhelming difficulties and do so in the strength of their Savior. These two taught us a great deal about grace and suffering and about how they are often closely intertwined. For those who knew them well, there's no surprise here. The God whom John and Marj loved and served had also known grace and suffering. They found their strength in following the Crucified One. Something the children said touched me deeply. Having a father like John—an earthly human father with such wisdom, patience, and love—is a vivid reminder of the far greater magnificence of the Heavenly Father.

IV. **The three passages we read speak pointedly to John's life of faith**. Psalm 23, the shepherd psalm, declares the deep, throbbing notes of assurance.

The hand of God leads us, as the shepherd guides the sheep. Needs are provided for—abundantly: the table overflows with grace gifts so that we sing, "Bread of heaven, feed me till I want no more." And when the walk of faith takes us through the valley of the shadow, whether the shadow of death or that of a difficult, disquieting, portion of life, we fear no evil. And in the end, we dwell in the Lord's house forever! John 14 is a portion of the Lord's farewell discourse. This parts reads, "Let not your hearts be troubled, neither let them be afraid." How welcome are these words on a day like this. Intermingled with the sadness of the hour is a holy gladness of eternity. The First Thessalonians passage affirms to Christians long ago, and to us today, that this is not all there is. Human life never was intended to be lived forever on planet earth. It is here for a while—a momentary flash in eternity's light—and then the earthly existence ends in death. But the promise of God is that life is lived on in the world that is yet to come. There the wholeness we seek, the peace for the nations, the righteous order—these are brought to completion in that great day.

I read at Marj's funeral a little poem that I believe is from C. S. Lewis, though I'm not sure. It sounds like him. It says,

If everything is lost, thanks be to God
If I must see it go, watch it go,
Watch it fade away, die
Thanks be to God that He is all I have
And if I have him not, I have nothing at all
Nothing at all, only a farewell to the wind
Farewell to the gray sky
Goodbye, God be with you October evenings.
If all is lost, thanks be to God
For He is He, and I am I.

John, we let you go, not easily but lovingly. Now to God's eternal hands and into his eternal home, we let you go. On another day, we will gather with you again and with all of God's faithful, heart touching heart, life touching life, hand-in-hand around the Great Throne of our Father Above. Now, dearest Lord, give us grace for the living of our days!—Lee McGlone

TOPIC: Standing on the Promises: Funeral Sermon for Greg Glover
TEXT: Rom. 8:37–39

Death under any circumstance is difficult. Yet when death comes at so young an age and with uncertainties, our time together is difficult. It is, then, our faith on which we stand. We turn today to look to the promises of God—the promises taught and lived out in the person of Jesus, our Savior.

We believe that our salvation is just as Paul described in Ephesians 2: "by grace through faith, and not of works." Years ago, Greg gave his life to Christ; he acknowledged that Jesus is the Son of God, that Jesus died on the cross for his sins, that Jesus was buried, and that on the first Easter morning, he rose again and later ascended into heaven. Because of that confession, we stand assured that, in this instant, Greg is at rest with God in heaven. "To be absent of the body is to be present with the Lord."

Today, we stand upon the promises. Let's hear the promise of God, both in Scripture, the Word of God, and in the words of our cherished hymns of faith.

"For God so loved the world that he gave his only Son so that whosoever believes in him will not perish but will come to everlasting life" (John 3:16).

"Therefore God highly exalted him and gave to him the name that is above all names, so that at the name of Jesus every knee should bow and tongue confess, of those in heaven and on earth, that Jesus Christ is Lord to the glory of God the Father" (Phil. 2:9–11).

"Salvation is found in none other, for there is no other name under heaven given to men by which we must be saved" (Acts 4:12).

"There is a fountain filled with blood, drawn from Immanuel's veins, and sinners plunged beneath that flood lose all their guilty stains. The dying thief rejoiced to see that fountain in his day, and there may I, though vile as he, wash all my sins away. Dear dying lamb, thy precious blood shall never lose it power. Till all the ransomed church of God be saved to sin no more. E'er since by faith I saw the stream, thy flowing wounds supply, redeeming love has been my theme, and shall be till I die . . . and shall be till I die."

"For God did not send his son in to the world to condemn the world, but that the world through Him might be saved. He who believes in Him is not condemned but he who does not believe is condemned already, because he has not believed in the name of the only begotten Son of God" (John 3:17–18).

"Just as I am without one plea, but that thy blood was shed for me, and that thou bidst me come to thee, O Lamb of God I come."

"Come unto me all ye who labor and are heavy laden, and I will give you rest. Take my yoke and learn of me, for I am gentle and lowly of heart, and you will find rest for your souls. For my yoke is easy and my burden is light" (Matt. 11:28–29)

"Whosoever shall confess that Jesus is the Son of God, God dwelleth in him, and he in God" (1 John 4:15).

"If we confess our sins he is faithful and just to forgive us our sins, and to cleanse us from all unrighteousness" (1 John 1:9).

"Create in me a clean heart, O God, and renew a right spirit within me. Cast me not away from Thy Presence. Take not your Holy Spirit from me. Restore to me the joy of thy salvation and up hold me with your Free Spirit. Have mercy on me, O God, according to the multitude of your tender mercies, blot out my transgressions" (Ps. 51).

Life for Greg was not easy, and he may not have known how to turn everything over to God for perfect healing. Yet we are assured that now he is at rest with God in perfect peace. Our promise of the heavenly reward is never based on our merit but on the commitment we have made to Christ. Salvation and the heavenly home is God's grace gift to us. We don't earn it. We would never deserve it. But God has graciously looked upon us and given us life eternal.

While our hearts ache, we are reminded that "we are more than conquerors through him who loved us . . . that neither life nor death, angels nor principalities, things present nor things to come, nor height nor depth, nor any other creature may be able to separate us from the love of God, which is in Christ Jesus our Lord" (Rom. 8:37–39).

The promise of God is that on one glad day all of God's children will be brought together in God's heaven. There will be grand family reunions. Loved ones that have gone on before us will know us, and we will know them. Around the throne, hand-in-hand with all of God's children, we will share and live and love forever. And then, those matters of earthly life that have caused us such grief will be cast away forever. There will be no more tears, no more sorrow, no more sickness, and no more death. Upon the promise of God we take our stand. Thanks be unto God and our Savior, Jesus Christ.—Lee McGlone

INVOCATION: Our Father who is in heaven and on earth, enshrined in the majesty of Creation yet ever present in the lives of your people, to you we come this hour to give honor and praise. Grant now the presence of your Holy Spirit that we may hear the quiet and gentle voice of eternity. Truly, our days are as grass, nourished and healthy in the morning but by day's end tired and worn. Yet our hearts hold dreams that time cannot quench. Upon the promise of your eternal Word, we take our stand.

May your holy name be forever praised! Great is thy faithfulness, O Lord God. Through the name of Jesus, the Son of God, we pray. Amen.

BENEDICTION: Father, let now the grace that has guided our lives to this point be forever our hope and shield. Grant your continued blessings on this dear family and hold them close to your side. Give to us all, loving Father, what you will, when you will, in whatever measure pleases you, and in all things have your way with us.

Now unto him who is able to keep us from falling, and to present us faultless before the presence of his glory with exceeding joy—to the only wise God our Savior, be glory and majesty, dominion and power, now and forever. In Jesus we pray. Amen.

PASTORAL PRAYER: Dearest Father, we gather in your name to offer praise and thanksgiving. As did the psalmist in days long ago, we cry out, "O, Lord, incline thine ear to us, for we are needy. . . . Give ear, O Lord, to our prayer. In the day of trouble, we call upon thee. . . . We give thanks to thee, O Lord our God, with our whole hearts . . . for great is thy steadfast love toward us."

Life is yours, O Lord. You created each of us in the beauty and glory of your own image. May we now celebrate the gift, give thanks for the gift, rejoice that the gift was ours—if only for a while. Father, help us to know that as we are reaching up to thee, thou art reaching out to us.

And now abide faith, hope, and love. And the greatest of these is love—the gift of your unending affection. Fix in our minds the noble truth that love is the greatest virtue, indeed, that you are love and that you give us the ability to love—and that your love is perfected in us, just as Jesus said.

Hold this dear family in your comforting hands. Give to all that assemble in this place the full assurance of your presence. We pray through Jesus Christ the Lord. Amen.—Lee McGlone

CHAPTER SEVEN

Messages for Evangelism and Missions

Inherent to pulpit ministry is the call to missions and evangelism. The gospel is to be preached—and it is to be preached to all the world. Clearly, persuasively, and biblically, the following sermons demonstrate a variety of approaches to authentic gospel proclamation.

TOPIC: The Ministry of Negation
TEXT: Acts 16:6–7

"Forbidden to preach" (from Acts 16:6)—that phrase suggests sinister opposition to the gospel. In our democratic society, the very idea of preventing anyone from proclaiming the Word is utterly repulsive. It comes as a shock to discover that the agent of hindrance in this instance was no atheistic persecutor but "the Holy Spirit of Jesus" (Acts 16:6–7).

Humanly speaking, there may have been geographical, political, or personal factors at work. But our passage is content to pass over all of them in silence, thereby forcing the recognition that sometimes our most earnest attempts to serve are frustrated, not by circumstantial factors or by human hindrances but by divine direction! How are we to understand the divine guidance whereby God himself sometimes thwarts the proclamation of his own Word?

I. **It must have been very difficult for Paul to accept the negative leadership of the Holy Spirit in his life.** Paul knew how to "press toward the mark" with intensity (Phil. 3:12–14). But once God had spoken, he also knew how to stop dead in his tracks and go no further. By experiencing with double force what we may call the Holy Spirit's "ministry of negation," the apostle learned a positive truth of great value for us today. God does not expect anyone, even an Apostle Paul, to do everything! At first, the Great Commission seems daunting in its universality: "Go make disciples of all nations . . ." (Matt. 28:19). Even the most intrepid missionary could be crushed trying to fulfill that mandate. But here we learn in concrete fashion that no one has to go everywhere and try to reach everybody. Sometimes God shuts more doors than he opens, simplifying our agenda by suggesting that we leave a few things for others to do!

The temptation to do too much may be just as dangerous as the temptation to do too little. Without some firmly closed doors, Paul could have spread himself too thin and been diverted from the one great task that God had given him to accomplish. How often, in the name of spiritual conquest, do we rush toward every opportunity that presents itself when we ought to be listening for the sound of doors being firmly shut by the Holy Spirit in an effort to curb our overcommitted lives! What a relevant truth for our church to remember during this missions emphasis. As we respond to the many needs all about us, no individual or group needs to carry the crushing burden alone. Even before accepting an assignment, it is well to remember that "others have labored, and we have entered into their labor" (John 4:38). Sometimes we try to start a new work that does not succeed. Rather than becoming discouraged, consider that God may have chosen someone else to fulfill that responsibility.

On a vaster scale, this insight also speaks to one of our nagging doubts about the world mission enterprise. When we measure the magnitude of that challenge against the meagerness of our resources, it is easy to experience a "failure of nerve." After all, we have no missionaries at all in many countries, and in others our presence is nothing more than a tiny beachhead. But here is the point: like Paul, we do not have to go everywhere in order to fulfill our mission. Many doors are now shut, and others may close in the future, but our task is to get busy going wherever the Spirit opens a door rather than worrying about avenues for service that are denied to us.

II. Proof that the Holy Spirit's "ministry of negation" is often preparation for an even greater opportunity of service was provided by the third divine intervention in our passage. An understanding of the geography involved will help us to appreciate the significance of what happened there. In order to travel "through the region of Phrygia and Galatia," Paul and his party were moving in a northwesterly direction with Asia to the southwest and

Bithynia to the northeast. Thus, to be doubly denied entry into either locale meant that the apostle could turn neither to the left (v. 6) nor to the right (v. 7). He was literally hemmed in on both sides by the Holy Spirit, which meant that his only viable option was to go straight on beyond Mysia to Troas and from thence into Macedonia.

By the time the book of Acts was written, its author realized that Paul's true destiny was to become a bridge between the Jewish and Gentile worlds. One major theme in Acts is the triumph of an "unhindered" gospel (Acts 8:36, 11:17, 28:31). Use of the same word in our text (v. 6) as in these other passages suggests that sometimes the Holy Spirit must "hinder" (that is, "prevent, forbid") certain strategies in order to implement an "unhindered" strategy in their place. There may be situations when God seems to be saying no twice as often as he says yes. In his stubborn determination, the Spirit sometimes has to shut two doors before we finally find the right one that he wants to open! Nobody likes a door slammed in the face but, by God's grace, this can force us to pursue new and higher priorities.

No one needs to learn this lesson more than those engaged in Christian service. At every moment there are pulls from all sides that offer valuable opportunities for service. How easy it is to fill every moment with activities that are self-evidently good and become so busy with religious work that we never stop to ask whether what we are doing is really what matters the most. Sometimes our highest priorities emerge, not out of a rational process of analysis but out of a trial-and-error struggle with the Holy Spirit. Filled with idealistic zeal, we virtually demand of God that the first thing we try will always work. Should there be an occasional setback, we impatiently insist that every precaution be taken to avoid a second failure. Yet Paul was mistaken twice before finally finding the better way. Really now, are we willing to be so open, so humble, and so daring that we will risk failing two times out of three in our search for the one thing that God most wants us to do?

This principle of paying any price to find and follow God's highest priority applies especially to our mission service. Always it seems more promising to stay put in one's own province. How many times have we heard this refrain: "There is so much to be done here at home. Someday we may get to the rest of the world, but meanwhile let us meet the pressing needs on our right and our left"? But Christ did not command us to stay close to home.

Rather, he bade us go into all the world, and until our gospel becomes truly global, we have not fulfilled our ultimate obligation. To be sure, I want to help Birmingham, and through it all of Alabama, but I must ask God to shut these doors in my face should such involvement cause me to take my eyes off a Troas waiting at the end of my little world. There are many valued things that we may want to do, but the one thing that we have to do is to get the whole world in our hearts for the sake of the gospel!

III. **That journey on to Troas, with the memory of twin frustrations still vivid in our minds, is always a daring act of faith in the Savior of surprises.** For remember, Paul did not embark upon this third alternative with any answers in hand. Rather, it was only when he got to Troas, after he had reached the end of the road with nowhere else to go, that he was given a vision of what to do next. It was not until he ran out of human plans and was ready to offer God, as it were, a clean page on his itinerary, that he received the divine plan that would lead him on to Macedonia.

How could Paul, like Abraham of old, venture forth "not knowing where he was to go" (Heb. 11:8)? There is one small clue in our passage that may point to a basic source of Paul's understanding, namely, the recognition that "the Holy Spirit" who guided their steps (v. 6) was none other than "the Spirit of Jesus" (v. 7). The more Paul brooded over his inability to get inward consent for either of his aborted itineraries, the more he may have come to realize that he was being treated by the Holy Spirit, just as the first disciples were often treated by Jesus when he was on earth. The Gospels abound with illustrations of how his followers wanted to go in one direction when their Master insisted on going in another. They wanted to stay in friendly Galilee, but he put them "amazed and afraid" on the road to Jerusalem (Mark 10:32). They wanted to seek security in Transjordan, but he wanted them to risk danger by going to Lazarus in Bethany (John 11:7–16). How insightful of Paul to realize that those who follow the "footsteps of Jesus" are always in for surprises.

What have we learned from this bit of text about the meaning of being "on mission" for Christ? We have learned that

Even our best-laid plans must be open to divine overruling from the very beginning.

We may fail twice as often as we succeed before we reach our goal.

Short-term frustration is often the prelude to long-term fulfillment.

The serendipities of the Spirit offer more promise than the strategies devised by human calculation.

It is better to follow divine promptings, however reluctantly, than it is to follow human preferences, however enthusiastically.

If we will walk God's narrow way to its very end, we will find a waiting world yearning to be helped.

—William E. Hull

TOPIC: The Clue to Authentic Evangelism

TEXT: Matt. 13:44–50

The reason we look at the church this morning arises from that trenchant little parable we read. Remember? It is the last of the three short parables following the images of a treasure in a field and a pearl of great price. We know the last one as the "Parable of the Dragnet." It sits there, a stick of spiritual dynamite, ending with threats of burning in a furnace or finding ourselves banished somewhere to weep and gnash our teeth. My soul! So unfriendly! Why those ominous threats? What is the point? It just does not sound like Jesus. Well, as Matthew says, the image of the dragnet attempts to illustrate the kingdom of heaven. It seeks to describe an agency in this world—an agency like an enormous dragnet, corks on top holding it up, lead weights on the bottom bearing it down, dragging through the river, the lake, the sea, sweeping up everything in its path, the flotsam and jetsam, flora and fauna, a wide variety of difference, a catholicity of diversity.

Now, I have to tell you, I love that dragnet image: the kingdom of heaven as a fisherman's net. When the net sinks beneath the waves, we know now what it will drag up—pan fish, game fish, food fish, and minnows. And along with some crabs, mollusks, and dog fish, we will find some cracked army boots, rotten tires, a rusted Prince Albert tobacco can, booze bottles, and miscellaneous seaweed. What an image! You see, I believe what that net drags up belongs in the realm of heaven. So it is with the church: a catch-all, a truly inclusive assembly. A dragnet!

I. **But then, what is this?** This is a fantastic, inclusive, wide-open dragnet—and then another image: the threat of burning in a furnace; banishment to the place of wailing and gnashing of teeth? Those images—severe, drastic, and fierce—those images signal the crucial nature of the choices we make regarding the kingdom of heaven. They tell us after we are swept up in the dragnet, the decisions we make about the realm of God and our participation in it, our readiness to build it, our eagerness to join with Christ in making this a better world—all signify life-and-death choices. The kingdom of heaven confronts us with matters of supreme urgency. When the fishermen in the parable make it with their dragnet to the beach and begin making selections among the catch, their choices do not distinguish between those who do evil and those who do good or between those who do wrong and those who do right. What they keep and what they throw out distinguishes between the sluggish and the committed, the apathetic and the earnest. This parable of the dragnet, with its embrace of everything and everyone, provides what seems to me to be an authentic clue to true evangelism: God's dominion embraces us all.

But more than that, it insists that the claim of God's realm and the choices we make represent the most vital, urgent, imperative decisions we face. Now, heaven knows we face a ton of tough decisions. The claims on our time, our incomes, our imaginations can nearly overwhelm us. Ask people how they're doing these days, and in most cases they will say, "about a C-minus"; they'll describe the stress they're under at the moment and apologetically comment that they are, at least, "surviving." Matters of cash flow, job security, personal relationships (or the lack of them) drain our energy and batter our spirits. Nonetheless, the Christian Church remains a body believing that the most important thing we do in this world resides in infusing it with the mind of Christ. The shaping of boys and girls, men and women who carry the common life of a community of character bearing the Spirit of Christ, praying and working for fairness, decency, and integrity—men and women who, where they find themselves, bend over backward, for God's sake, to make kindness, encouragement, and empathy a centerpiece in their approach to others. This—the Church's task—cries for implementation. And as the Parable of the Dragnet reveals, we church folk, invited by the gospel from North and South, East and West, can be claimed by no higher commitment.

II. **Now, the kind of world God wants for everyone lies behind the divine invitation to each of us; it represents the purpose of our calling and our mission.** It is why we are caught in the dragnet. You see, the New Testament's goal for us is not church membership; nor is it the building of big congregations; it is not the gathering of megachurches. The last thing God wants is the whole world in one great church. Our true goal is a world where the barriers of race and sex, the lines dividing us by clan, tribe, nation, and creed finally crumble. Our mission here is a public mission. Our calling is not to be a spiritual ghetto, a congregational club, a sectarian guild. The Gospel of John doesn't say, "God so loved the Church that he sent his only begotten son." It says, "God so loved the world." The realm of heaven, the Kingdom of God is the divine plan for the world.

Many of us are familiar with Walter Rauschenbush, who flourished at the beginning of the twentieth century. He lived his early years and took his theological training in my hometown of Rochester, New York. In one of his autobiographical reflections, Walter Rauschenbush describes the Christianity of his childhood—a highly personal and intense faith, he says, whose tenets consisted of "Christ died for the sinner; the sinner was saved by grace; the sinner can find new life, know the joy of Christ, and finally go to heaven." Rauschenbush stands grateful for that faith. He does not deny it. He cherishes it. But after spending his first pastorate in New York's Hell's Kitchen, he found his childhood faith somehow inadequate. What about the world, he asked? What about social, communal suffering? The question before him, as he writes, was how to find a place in the Christian faith "for this great task of changing the world and making it righteous, making it habitable, making it merciful, making it neighborly." "Somehow," he writes, "I knew in my soul that was God's work."

III. **And last, we hardly need be reminded in light of the life and death of the One who calls us and whom we serve, that our discipleship can be a constant challenge and perhaps get us into some trouble.** The Christian enterprise is a difficult, arduous, and expensive proposition. The dragnet does not sweep us into paradise. This is not a safe place. It is base camp. Church is not simply a place for us to come and hide from the challenges and difficulties of God's world. It is a place to get ourselves into spiritual shape to go meet the most troublesome and intractable challenges of our time.

And yet, let me say this to those of you who are visitors, to those of you who may come to this place occasionally to rest, to worship, to catch your breath, to mediate, to savor the music, to heal your wounds, to join in the hymns, to get your life in order: "Welcome!" Most of you know I consider this church a spiritual halfway house, and I am delighted you find this a place and a people where you can get your spiritual house in order. But let me tell you, just as I am jealous for your welcome here, just as I am eager to guard at every point your anonymity, just as I want you to be able to come and go without getting buttonholed, glommed onto, your arm twisted or in any way having your spiritual space invaded, I want you to know that Jesus Christ needs you to share in the saving of this world, and we need you here. We need you standing with us in our worship and in our mission. God needs your gifts; we need your gifts. We want your stumbling, incoherent, irresolute faith and wobbly discipleship to join ours with every confidence that makes this place and people far greater than the sum of all its parts. We want you to come and help heal us; we want you to join us in being claimed by a high commitment. We need you to join others in this house, as we seek to model and to build the Dominion of God in this world. We pray you enlist with us in a daring, dangerous, and world-changing enterprise. Swept into Christ's vast net, each of us, and as the closing words of our hymn begged, "On us let now the healing of your great Spirit fall, and make us brave and full of joy to answer to your call."—James W. Crawford

TOPIC: Unlocking the Secret
TEXT: Matt. 16:13–20

It was not intended to be a treasure hunt, and yet Peter found the secret wealth of eternity locked in Jesus—the "hidden chest" of inestimable values that the key of his faith readily opened. No "Open sesame!" or "Abracadabra!" Just, "You are the Messiah, the Son of the living God."

Men have dived deep into the swirling seas to find Spanish gold in long-sunken galleons. They have followed ancient maps purporting to lead to vast hordes of dazzling jewels and gleaming golden ingots buried by pirates long dead. They have ransacked ghost towns for the hidden caches of dust, flakes, grains, and nuggets of gold secreted by prospectors under cabin floors or near abandoned mines. Peter found his hoard of wealth, not in glistening coins and shimmering gems or raw ore, but in Jesus Christ, Savior of the world.

"You are the Messiah," he said, "the Son of the living God." Here is a treasure of greater value than all the gold and diamonds ever mined, greater than the crown jewels of all the kingdoms and the lustrous golden ingots in all the national treasuries of the world. And how did he unlock such vast riches?

I. **It was no simple matter, and yet it was not one so complex either.** Jesus asked his disciples a direct question: "Who do people say that the Son of Man is?" They responded with an array of famous names. "Some say John the Baptist, but others Elijah." They rattled off Jeremiah's name and included a generalized title—"one of the prophets"—for those who could not quite put their finger on who they thought Jesus was.

Then Jesus moved in. "But who do you say that I am?" It did not take Peter long to deduce that Jesus is considerably more than Elijah and John the Baptist. His brain shifted into reasoned speed. He had traveled with Jesus for some time. He had heard him preach and seen him still storms and heal disease-ridden bodies. The blind saw again at the command of Jesus. The Lord walked on water, and even Peter did for a while, until his faith faltered and he doubted. It did not take a genius with a rudimentary background in Jewish prophecy to realize that all of these factors indicated that Jesus was not just "one of the prophets," but the Messiah, the Christ, the Anointed One, the Son of God. He may not have understood all its subtleties, but Peter, the brash, blustery fisherman, brother of Andrew, resident of Capernaum, knew Jesus to be the world's greatest treasure. "You are the Messiah, the Son of the Living God," he said with deepest conviction.

To be sure, it was moments later—after this great confession—that Jesus gave Peter the "keys to the kingdom of heaven." Still it seems evident that Peter had found a key of his own to open the secret of salvation: it is to believe in Jesus, to accept him, to become his, and to trust him always; it is not only to be his student, a follower, a disciple, but an ardent believer.

Where this took place was one of the most pagan places in all of the Holy Land, about twenty miles northeast of the Sea of Galilee. Phillip the Tetrarch built the city and named it after the Roman emperor, Caesar Augustus—and himself, of course. He was not too modest to link his name with Caesar. Remnants of statues of Greek gods were there, as well as modern Roman ones; ancient temples littered the region. It had always been a pagan place, but it was here in the midst of all of the Greco-Roman fool's gold of faith that Peter found the real thing, the Jewel of God, the Messiah.

II. **Friend, open up the secret of the universe by letting your faith, small or large, be the key to turn the lock, for if you know Jesus to be God's Son, you will know him to be your Savior.** Your heart will sing, as it did for Peter, and it will sing joyously God's praises, lavishly praising him for the gift of life he grants the believing.

Upon the cross, Jesus died for us, carrying our sins for us. He ransomed us. He redeemed us. Jesus the Christ conquered earth so that we might live, not only now in the joy of his friendship but eternally in celebrative fellowship. Permit Peter to use the keys of the kingdom anew to open for you this great treasure, so that you, too, may echo his words concerning who Jesus is: "You are the Messiah, the Son of the living God." Amen.—Richard Andersen

TOPIC: Endurance and the Cross

TEXT: Heb. 12:1–12

Endurance is a commendable thing! The answer for those of us who are Christians is in endurance and the cross. We can endure because the saints endured before us. We can endure because we are disciples, disciplined by the Divine. We can endure because Jesus endured and did not falter.

I. **It is a gripping picture the writer to the Hebrews portrays.** He envisions a gigantic coliseum, filled to capacity. We are engaged in a great race. We are being cheered by our supporters who fill the bleachers, those who have preceded us in life and now dwell in eternity. Yet the race that is set before us is a fearsome one. All kinds of doubts creep up.

Our text encourages us: "Let us . . . lay aside every weight and the sin that clings so closely." He wants us to slim down to track-star sleekness so that we may accede to the thundering acclaim of the witnessing saints.

It is a lengthy roll call of faithful followers of God who persisted in the most trying of times under the most difficult of circumstances. They are the ones to whom we must look as we eye the race course ahead of us.

II. **Just as we need to stretch our muscles and exercise our limbs prior to the race to cast off burdensome sin and unnecessary spiritual obesity, so we must not fail to practice the divine disciplines.** Says the author of Hebrews, "Endure trials for the sake of discipline."

Parents "disciplined us for a short time as seemed best to them, but [God] disciplines us for our good, in order that we may share his holiness," writes the author of our text. Then he reminds us: "Discipline always seems painful rather than pleasant at the time, but later it yields the peaceful fruit of righteousness to those who have been trained by it." Isn't that the purpose? We need to be trained so that we can win the race.

III. **Which leads us to our final point.** We can endure affliction because the saints endured it before us and they cheer us on. We can endure affliction because we have been coached by God, who provides divine disciplines to enable us to endure trials by running the race as winners. But the pungent thought throughout the text is that we can endure affliction precisely because Christ endured it. The author to the Hebrews says it was "for the sake of the joy that was set before him." He "endured the cross, disregarding its shame and has taken his seat at the right hand of the throne of God."

Jesus had to endure hostility from soldiers and the chief priests, from common citizens and Roman authorities, but joy was before him! He endured the torment of the cross, knowing that its brutality would break his heart, despite its brevity, but the resulting joy would go on forever.

Friend, here is the underlying need of every Christian. It is to see the joy that warrants stretching muscles, applying discipline, and running the race, that urges us to follow Jesus fearlessly. Whatever circumstances daunt your path, look to Christ, who looked beyond the immediate distress to the joy that awaited him—and us. He is the pioneer and perfecter of our faith, who shows us how to run the race and claim the joy! Follow him! Endurance is the need if we are to bear crosses to their destinations! Faith and hope lead us on to joy.—Richard Andersen

TOPIC: Celebrating Faith: Our Intention
TEXT: Rom. 6:1–7

Here is the classic baptismal text. But it does more than provide words for the liturgy. It provides the larger picture of what it means to live the gospel.

Believers in each age, whether the first century or the twenty-first century, need to be reminded of the faith we celebrate.

I. **Our faith deals with sin.** "Shall we continue in sin that grace may abound? God forbid!" Some said it did not matter how the gospel was lived out or how one lived. God, after all, was beneficent—a cream puff—and would gladly forgive whatever. So live as you please. The distinction of Christian faith for this group was its indulgence. Here was their logic: If God glories in forgiving sin, then the more we sin, the more God is able to exercise forgiveness, thus the better off we all are. Paul said the logic was flawed. They had forgotten one thing. When they became Christians, they were buried with Christ, and the old within died away and a new life rose up. The hold of sin gave way also. The logic of disobedience was absurd. Our faith refuses to deny the sinfulness of the human condition. We are called not to deny it but to deal with it. And we do. The gospel offers a cure. We call it forgiveness!

II. **Our faith calls us to a high ethical lifestyle, "that we may walk in newness of life."** "Walking" in newness of life implies that we are going somewhere. There is a direction to life. Jesus said on one occasion that he was coming from the Father—and going to the Father. Celebrating faith is about going where God wants us to go. For Paul there was a lot at stake here. The gospel had finally reached Rome, the center of the empire. From there people traveled to every known destination in the world. If the gospel could work there, Paul believed, it could be carried everywhere. That's why Paul was so adamant here. There is simply too much at stake to remain sedate. Live any way? Continue in disobedience so God can indulge you? *No!* Absurd! Disobedience is behind us. We've died to sin and are now *walking* in newness of life.

Now the instruction is that the gospel is more than belief—orthodoxy; it is also about how we live—orthopraxis. The word *walk* has ethical implications. Theology and ethics are not separate fields of study. The thrust of the text is captured in the word of the black preacher who declared, "It doesn't matter how high you jump when you get happy, but how straight you walk when you hit the ground." Its one thing to talk the talk; it's another to walk the walk.

Elton Trueblood several years ago described a "vague religiosity" that comes about when one of us joins the church but has no real commitment to the message it preaches. He went on to say that this vague religiosity is the greatest threat to both the church and the nation. "We believe in God the Father, almighty, and his Son Jesus Christ, the fellowship of the saints." But the greatest joy is when belief makes itself known. Apart from obedience, sacrifice, commitment, witness, and testimony to our beliefs, the beliefs may well mean precious little. It can, however, call us to levels of high and authentic living.

III. **Our faith provides for purposeful living, "that we may walk in newness of life."** Walking in "newness of life" implies purpose. Our intention has to do with impact: "We're out to change the world." Nothing less is motive enough.

Karl Marx wrote in his Thesis XI, "The philosophers have only interpreted the world in various ways. The point is to change it." Marx was right in his intention, yet wrong in his methods. He believed it appropriate to manipulate genetics. By using the science of eugenics—encouraging the "better" elements of society so they would increase and discouraging the "lesser" elements so they would decrease—he planned to change the world. Where do you go with a philosophy like that? Straight to Adolph Hitler, and Beuchenwald, Dauchau, where the "lesser" elements—human beings by the thousands—were led to their deaths. Their starved and poisoned bodies were stacked like cord wood and burned—*ethnic cleansing* before the term was born. Marx was right. The point is to change the world. But the method was wrong.

And that is what Jesus Christ came to do. His message and methods were right. For Christ, there are no better elements, no lesser elements. We are all made in God's image and worthy of dignity and respect. We are also all sinners, having fallen short of the glory of God. But God showed his love to us, in that "while we were yet sinners Christ died for the ungodly." That's the message that Jesus preached.

And it happens through us. Consider the high honor it is to be a Christian. We're called to work right alongside God in his eternal task. That's a high calling. Annie Johnson Flint wrote it simply this way:

Christ has no hands but our hands to do His work today;

He has no feet but our feet to lead men on His way;

He has no tongue but our tongue to tell men how he died;

He has no help but our help to bring them to his side.

The only Bible some people may ever read is "us." It is the gospel "lived" that changes the world.

IV. **Our faith provides strength for the journey; "we are raised to walk with Christ—in the power of his Resurrection."** Charles Schultz's "Peanuts" cartoon captured me. Snoopy said of Woodstock, the rather frail bird of paradise, "Someday Woodstock is going to be a great eagle. And he will soar thousands of feet above the ground." Woodstock then takes off into the air, only soon to lose control and whirl about haphazardly. Snoopy declares, "Well maybe *hundreds* of feet in the air." Woodstock then falls to the ground with a crashing thud. He sits, looking bewildered, stars whirling around his head. Snoopy, in his rational wisdom, concludes, "Maybe he'd be one of those eagles who just walks around." Imagine that— an eagle that just walks around!

I don't want to be an eagle that just walks around. I'd rather be the eagle the prophet Isaiah talked about: "Do you not know, have you not heard . . . of course you have; the Lord is the everlasting God. . . . He doesn't grow tired or weary; but we do; even youth will grow weary, young men will stumble and fall . . . yes they do, as do we all; but those whose hope is in the Lord, who wait patiently for God's empowering direction, those Lord shall renew their strength, they shall mount up with wings, (strong wings), like Eagles; they shall run and not be weary, they shall *walk* and not faint."

The gospel is power to complete the task. That good work God has begun in you, he will bring to completion. God's goal for us makes all the difference. It keeps us going. Each person, family, and the church needs the vision, or else we may well give up too soon.

Listen to the text: dead to self; alive to Christ; something greater than ourselves that controls us, a magnificent obsession. That's the faith we celebrate. It gives us the right dreams and empowers us to follow those dreams to completion. And God shows the way. We are in his eternal care. "We're marching onward to Zion, the beautiful city of God."—Lee McGlone

TOPIC: Responding to God
TEXT: 1 Sam. 3:10–21

Can you remember when you first became aware of the reality of God in your life? Who helped you to understand? Did your community of faith affirm your awakening to God and encourage your continued growth in faith? We have a pretty good grasp of the stages of normal physical and mental development from birth, childhood, adolescence, youth, to adulthood. What are the stages of spiritual development? We claim no infallible answers, but biblical models of spiritual growth in dialogue with our personal experience of God inform our understanding.

I. **Spiritual development begins at the beginning.** Samuel was dedicated to the Lord from birth. In the dedication of her infant son, Hannah released possession of Samuel to the God by whom he was given, but that was not the end of the story. The boy grew in the service of God, with Eli the priest. A pattern in the spiritual development of Samuel is a biblical benchmark. Fred Craddock observes that the unique Gospel story, in Luke, of Jesus' visit to the Temple is modeled after Samuel, employing some of the same phrases and images like, "Samuel continued to grow both in stature and in favor with the Lord and with the people" (2:26). Luke wanted to show that Jesus was in harmony with Judaism throughout his life. He followed distinct steps of a Jewish male in the ritual moments of his spiritual development. Jesus was circumcised at the eighth day of life—a sign of the covenant of Abraham. He was dedicated or presented to God in the Temple at six weeks—the time of his mother's rite of purification. His childhood visit to the Temple corresponds to the rite of "bar mitzvah," reception as "Son of the Law" at age twelve. As the child grew into adult responsibility, a level of spiritual independence was acknowledged by family and friends.

Long before baptism, Jesus had awakened to the claim of God on his life, and Samuel was moving toward his prophetic mission with Israel long before the night of his vision of God's calling. This is not a terribly mystical process. We might ask when a child is ready to read. Formally, reading begins in first grade, but parents and extended family are introducing infants to books long before we expect them to read. For many parents these days, reading books to the child begins before birth. Children who grow up in a reading family are beginning to recognize words long before formal schooling begins. Faith development is no different. Children who grow up in an atmosphere where the reality of God, the importance of prayer, and the community of the church are among the basic necessities are ready to respond to the calling of God as they approach the age of bar mitzvah. Children begin to be aware of God as they observe the people of faith who help them to grow, yet all of us reach a point in life when we must begin to live out our own commitments in faith when we discover that God is not the private possession of the pastor or the church. God meets each of his children with expectation.

II. **Spiritual maturity turns on the commitment of faith.** Samuel is busy working with Eli in the Temple long before the turning point in his life and the life of Israel, yet, "Samuel did not yet know the Lord and the word of the Lord had not yet been revealed to him" (v. 7). Walter Brueggeman notes that this moment is the transition from Eli to Samuel as the spiritual leader to Israel. It is more than another personal experience of the calling of God. It is a national crisis that begins the new era of the Kingdom. The Bible dramatizes the calling of God with a voice in the night calling out, "Samuel," or a voice from heaven affirming baptism, "This is my son, the beloved." We often miss the description of Samuel's experience as a vision; we miss that some who witnessed the baptism of Jesus thought they heard thunder. If we had waited until we heard voices from the sky, I dare say that no one here would have come to commitment in faith.

The voice of God is often the sound of sheer silence, which Elijah heard in the cave, but we come to a point in life when we recognize the message of God, even in the silence. The spiritual dimension of life is in the unseen but very real inner world of every self. A basic human structure is common to all of us. The human self is more than a clump of organs hanging in a skeletal frame, covered with varying shades of pigment. We are the children of God from birth. The calling of Samuel is the rule rather than the exception. The differences among us are contextual. We are not all alike, and we do not have the same preparation for prayer, but the God who has made us loves every solitary child.

III. **Jesus described the moving of the Spirit of God as the mystery of the wind.** The wind blows where it will, and we see the effect, but we do not grasp the source or destiny of the wind. One day the wind blows, and we hear the sound, and we drop our nets in the water to follow Jesus. One day the voice of God sounds through the word of Scripture, the message of a teacher, the worship of the church, or the prayers of a parent, and the time comes to graduate to a new page in our life with God. No longer do we find God only through the intercessory work of Eli, but we discover that God speaks to us. Awakening to God is as basic to growing up as courtship and marriage.—Larry Dipboye

SECTION IV

A LITTLE
TREASURY OF
SERMON
ILLUSTRATIONS

I llustrations are like windows that open to allow in light—to illuminate. They come to the preacher from a variety of sources: literature, art, life, personal experience, and so on. A good sermon will become an even better sermon with appropriate illustrations that bring to life a biblical theme.

ADVENT. The movie *Cast Away,* starring Tom Hanks, is about a Federal Express employee named Chuck Noland, who is the sole survivor of a company plane that crashes near a South Pacific island. He is stranded for four years, hoping to be rescued. All he has beyond the few natural resources of the island are some flotsam from the plane—videotapes, a pair of ice skates, an evening gown, and a volleyball he calls "Wilson."

There is one package he never opens: a cardboard box with a pair of angel wings. He doesn't find out what is inside. Noland makes a raft, sails from the island, and is rescued by a ship. At the end of the movie he is back in America and hand delivers the unopened box of angel wings to a Texas farmhouse. He knocks, but no one answers. So he leaves the box against the door, with a note: "Thanks. This package saved my life." Somehow, in the unopened box of angel wings, Chuck Noland found hope in a desperate place. That's what Mary did with the angel's words. She could not fully understand all that was inside, but she found hope that got her through her troubles.—Leith Anderson

ANGER. Gordon MacDonald is a popular author and speaker. He and I have known each other most of our lives. Following a lecture Gordon gave, he was approached by a Nigerian woman who was a physician on the staff of a U.S. teaching hospital. She introduced herself with a familiar American name. Gordon asked her, "What's your African name?" She replied with several syllables that had an unfamiliar, although musical, sound to them. He asked her, "What does the name mean?" She explained that her name means, "Child who takes the anger away."

Then she explained: "My parents had been forbidden by their parents to marry. But they loved each other so much that they defied the family opinions and married anyway. For several years they were ostracized from both their families. Then my mother became pregnant with me. And when the grandparents held me in their arms for the first time, the walls of hostility came down. I became the one who swept the anger away. And that's the name my mother and father gave me."—Leith Anderson

ANGER. Frederick Buechner writes, in *Wishful Thinking:*

> Of the 7 deadly sins, anger is possibly the most fun. To lick your wounds, to smack your lips over grievances long past, to roll over your tongue the prospect of bitter confrontations still to come, to savor to the last tooth-some morsel both the pain you are given and the pain you are giving back—in many ways it is a feast fit for a king. The chief drawback is that what you are wolfing down is yourself. The skeleton at the feast is you.[1]

ASSURANCE OF FORGIVENESS. Wise counsel to the Christian pilgrim is this: *travel light!* Be rid of all excess baggage, for at times the way may be rocky and difficult, up steep slopes, and around dangerous precipices. Travel light! Do not carry the excess baggage of guilt, of regrets from the past, of unforgiven sin. Hear the assurance of God's own Word. As far as the East is from the West, so far have I removed your sins from you. Glory be to God!—John Thompson

CHOICE. The following poem is titled "The Ways," by John Oxenham:[2]

> To every man there openeth
> A Way, and Ways, and a Way
> And the High Soul climbs the High Way
> And the Low Soul gropes the Low

---

[1] Frederick Buechner, *Wishful Thinking* (San Francisco: HarperSanFrancisco, 1993), p. 117.
[2] John Oxenham, *Selected Poems of John Oxenham* (London: Ernest Benn Limited, 1924), p. 112.

And in between on the misty flats
The rest drift to and fro
But to every man there openeth
A High Way and a Low
And every man decideth
The Way his soul shall go.

CHRISTIAN LIVING. I heard my father tell, years ago, about driving the old Model T Ford on the rugged roads of southern Arkansas. The roads were unpaved, still dirt. There were deep ruts that you would either drive in or try to stay out of. When it rained, the roads were in such bad condition that the car would lunge forward, slipping and sliding from one side of the road to the other. Keeping the car straight in the road wasn't even an option. But as you bounced from one side of the road to the other, often in one ditch and out the other, you made progress along the way. That's the way of the Christian life. It's not interstate driving.—Lee McGlone

CULTURAL COMPARISON. Charles Dickens, in *Tale of Two Cities,* writes about comparing cultures:

It was the best of times, it was the worst of times, it was the age of wisdom, it was the age of foolishness, it was the epoch of belief, it was the epoch of incredulity, it was the season of Light, it was the season of Darkness, it was the spring of hope, it was the winter of despair, we had everything before us, we had nothing before us, we were all going direct to Heaven, we were all going direct the other way—in short, the period was so far like the present period, that some of its noisiest authorities insisted on its being received, for good or for evil, in the superlative degree of comparison only.

DEATH. Thomas Gray's "Elegy Written in a Country Churchyard":[3]

The boast of heraldry, the pomp of power
And all that beauty, all that wealth e'er gave

---

[3]Thomas Gray, "Elegy Written in a Country Churchyard" (Boston: Lee and Shepard, 1888), p. 81.

Await alike the inevitable hour
The paths of glory lead but to the grave.

DEFENSE. The Great Wall of China is a gigantic structure that cost an immense amount of money and labor. When it was finished, it appeared impregnable. But the enemy breached it. Not by breaking it down or going around it. They did it by bribing the gatekeepers.—Harry Emerson Fosdick

DESIRE. Sin comes when we take a perfectly natural desire or longing or ambition and try desperately to fulfill it without God. Not only is it sin, it is a perverse distortion of the image of the Creator in us. All these good things, and all our security, are rightly found only and completely in him.—Augustine

EASTER. I've always admired the early pioneers of our country's history. They were adventuresome and courageous. "Trailblazers" they were called, as they struck out from their homes in the relatively safe eastern colonies to explore the unknown territories of the westward expansion. They were the ones who went before us, faced the dangers, and paved the way for the rest of us. Jesus has become the trailblazer for us, and the word was declared by the announcing angel to the women: "He is risen, and has gone ahead of you and will see you in Galilee." Our Savior is always the One going ahead of us.— Lee McGlone

ENDURANCE. Admiral Jim Stockdale was a prisoner of war in North Vietnam. He was the highest-ranking officer in the "Hanoi Hilton" POW camp for eight years (1965 to 1973). He had no POW rights. He never knew if or when he would be released. He was tortured over twenty times. How did he endure? Stockdale says, "I never lost faith in the end of the story. I never doubted not only that I would get out, but also that I would prevail in the end and turn the experience into the defining event of my life, which, in retrospect, I would not trade."—Leith Anderson

FAITH. Understanding is the reward of faith. Therefore seek not to understand that thou mayest believe, but believe that thou mayest understand.— Augustine

FELLOWSHIP. I can't recall where I came across this story, but it is a modern parable of heaven and hell. The description of hell is given. A table is spread with a sumptuous meal. Yet around the table sits a host of sad, dejected, angry, growling people. They are starving. They sit at a table of plenty but can eat nothing. The problem: they can hold a fork but their elbows will not bend, so there they sit, forever, with a bounty of food before them but unable to eat. Their famished bodies wither away.

Next is the image of heaven. It also is a table running over with delicious food. Around the table, however, sit happy and healthy people, laughing and loving one another. Oddly enough, their elbows will not bend either. So how do they solve the dilemma? They feed one another.—Lawrence Vowan

FORGIVENESS. Edwin Lutzer writes, in *Putting Your Past Behind You:*

> In the 14th century, Robert Bruce of Scotland was leading his men in a battle to gain independence from England. Near the end of the conflict, the English wanted to capture Bruce to keep him from the Scottish crown. So they put his own bloodhounds on his trail. When the bloodhounds got close, Bruce could hear their baying. His attendant said, "We are done for. They are on your trail, and they will reveal your hiding place." Bruce replied, "It's all right." Then he headed for a stream that flowed through the forest. He plunged in and waded upstream a short distance. When he came out on the other bank, he was in the depths of the forest. Within minutes, the hounds, tracing their master's steps, came to the bank. They went no farther. The English soldiers urged them on, but the trail was broken. The stream had carried the scent away. A short time later, the crown of Scotland rested on the head of Robert Bruce. The memory of our sins, prodded on by Satan, can be like those baying dogs—but a stream flows, red with the blood of God's own Son. By grace through faith we are safe. No sin-hound can touch us. The trail is broken by the precious blood of Christ. "The purpose of the cross," someone observed, "is to repair the irreparable."[4]

---

[4]Edwin Lutzer, *Putting Your Past Behind You* (San Bernardino: CA: Here's Life Publishers, 1990), p. 42.

GENEROSITY. The story is told that one day a beggar by the roadside asked for alms from Alexander the Great as he passed by. The man was poor and wretched and had no claim upon the ruler, no right even to lift a soliciting hand. Yet the emperor threw him several gold coins. A courtier was astonished at his generosity and commented, "Sir, copper coins would adequately meet a beggar's need. Why give him gold?" Alexander responded in royal fashion, "Cooper coins would suit the beggar's need, but gold coins suit Alexander's giving."

GRACE. Brennan Manning writes, in *The Ragamuffin Gospel*:[5]

> A story is told about Fiorello LaGuardia, who, when he was mayor of New York City during the worst days of the Great Depression and all of WWII, was called by adoring New Yorkers "the Little Flower" because he was only five foot four and always wore a carnation in his lapel. He was a colorful character who used to ride the New York City fire trucks, raid speakeasies with the police department, take entire orphanages to baseball games, and whenever the New York newspapers were on strike, he would go on the radio and read the Sunday funnies to the kids. One bitterly cold night in January of 1935, the mayor turned up at a night court that served the poorest ward of the city. LaGuardia dismissed the judge for the evening and took over the bench himself. Within a few minutes, a tattered old woman was brought before him, charged with stealing a loaf of bread. She told LaGuardia that her daughter's husband had deserted her, her daughter was sick, and her two grandchildren were starving. But the shopkeeper, from whom the bread was stolen, refused to drop the charges. "It's a real bad neighborhood, your Honor," the man told the mayor. "She's got to be punished to teach other people around here a lesson." LaGuardia sighed. He turned to the woman and said "I've got to punish you. The law makes no exceptions—ten dollars or ten days in jail." But even as he pronounced sentence, the mayor was already reaching into his pocket. He extracted a bill and tossed it into

---

[5]Brennan Manning, *The Ragamuffin Gospel* (Colorado Springs, CO: Multnomah Publishers, 2005), pp. 91–92.

his famous sombrero saying: "Here is the ten dollar fine which I now remit; and furthermore I am going to fine everyone in this courtroom fifty cents for living in a town where a person has to steal bread so that her grandchildren can eat. Mr. Baliff, collect the fines and give them to the defendant." So the following day the New York City newspapers reported that $47.50 was turned over to a bewildered old lady who had stolen a loaf of bread to feed her starving grandchildren, fifty cents of that amount being contributed by the red-faced grocery store owner, while some seventy petty criminals, people with traffic violations, and New York City policemen, each of whom had just paid fifty cents for the privilege of doing so, gave the mayor a standing ovation.

HARDSHIPS. Max Lucado writes, in *In the Eye of the Storm*:[6]

Chippie the parakeet never saw it coming. One second he was peacefully perched in his cage. The next he was sucked in, washed up, and blown over. The problems began when Chippie's owner decided to clean Chippie's cage with a vacuum cleaner. She removed the attachment from the end of the hose and stuck it in the cage. The phone rang, and she turned to pick it up. She'd barely said "hello" when "ssssopp!" Chippie got sucked in. The bird owner gasped, put down the phone, turned off the vacuum, and opened the bag. There was Chippie—still alive, but stunned. Since the bird was covered with dust and soot, she grabbed him and raced to the bathroom, turned on the faucet, and held Chippie under the running water. Then, realizing that Chippie was soaked and shivering, she did what any compassionate bird owner would do . . . she reached for the hair dryer and blasted the pet with hot air. Poor Chippie never knew what hit him. A few days after the trauma, the reporter who'd initially written about the event contacted Chippie's owner to see how the bird was recovering. "Well," she replied, "Chippie doesn't sing much anymore—he just sits and stares." It's hard not to see why. Sucked in, washed up, and blown over . . . That's enough to steal the song from the stoutest heart.

---

[6]Max Lucado, *In the Eye of the Storm* (Dallas: Word Books, 1991), p. 11.

HOLINESS. Here is Elizabeth Barrett Browning's poem, "Aurora Leigh":

> Earth's crammed with heaven
> And every common bush afire with God
> But only he who sees takes off his shoes
> The rest sit round and pluck blackberries.

HONESTY. I am not bound to win, but I am bound to be true. I am not bound to succeed but I am bound to live the best life that I have. I must stand with anybody that stands right and part from him when he goes wrong.—Abraham Lincoln

HOPE. Henri Nouwen wrote a book called *Sabbatical Journeys*,[7] in which he describes the relationship between the "flyer" and the "catcher" in a circus trapeze performance. The flyer lets go of the trapeze and flies high above the audience in moments of frightening danger. He does nothing more to get himself caught than hold his position as still as possible. One of the Flying Roudellas told Nouwen, "The flyer must never try to catch the catcher."[8] The flyer just trusts and the catcher will catch. It is like that with us and God. We let go and fly through danger, filled with trust and hope. It is not our job to catch the Spirit of God. The Holy Spirit will catch us.—Leith Anderson

JESUS. He began his ministry by being hungry, yet he is the Bread of Life. Jesus ended his earthly ministry by being thirsty, yet he is the Living Water. Jesus was weary, yet he is our rest. Jesus paid tribute, yet he is the King. Jesus was accused of having a demon, yet he cast out demons. Jesus wept, yet he wipes away our tears. Jesus was sold for thirty pieces of silver, yet he redeemed the world. Jesus was brought as a lamb to the slaughter, yet he is the Good Shepherd. Jesus died, yet by his death he destroyed the power of death.—Gregory of Nazianzus, A.D. 381

JOY. *The Progress Paradox* by Gregg Easterbrook[9] has been widely reviewed. It documents the enormous improvement in American lives over

---

[7]Henry Nouwen, *Sabbatical Journeys* (New York: Crossroad Classic, 2000).
[8]Nouwen, *Sabbatical Journeys*, pp. 81–82.
[9]Gregg Easterbrook, *The Progress Paradox* (New York: Random House, 2004.

recent generations. Average life expectancy has doubled since 1900. Undernourishment was a major problem in our country, and now we are "overnourished." Central heating was unusual and air conditioning unknown. Medical care is much more sophisticated and available. Easterbrook says that if ever the Western world has had a Golden Age, it is "right here, right now."[10] Yet we are not happier. If anything, Americans are less happy than we were fifty years ago.—Leith Anderson

JOY. The Thirty Years War was one of the worst in human history, spanning an entire generation, from 1618 to 1648. It was the worst of times, with disasters and deaths through war, epidemics, and economic depression. In 1636, during the worst of those times, there was a godly pastor named Martin Rinkert. In one year he conducted five thousand funerals for his parish—about fourteen per day. In the midst of the misery, he wrote a table grace for his children that became a familiar hymn.

> Now thank we all our God
> With hearts and hands and voices,
> Who wondrous things has done,
> In whom his world rejoices.

—Leith Anderson

LIFE. The 1947 Frank Capra film, *It's a Wonderful Life,* starring Jimmy Stewart and Donna Reed, touches life with its characters. The story is about the Bailey Building and Loan Company, where business is not all that matters; it is about a miser named Mr. Potter, who wants everything he can get his hands on; it is about love, family, trouble, and, finally, triumph; it is about duty and love.

Above all, it is about one life and how Bedford Falls would have become Pottersville had it not been for George Bailey. It is about his wish that he had never been born coming true for long enough for him to see how he had touched the lives of many others and how they had touched him. He saw how his entire community would have forever changed had he never been born. He saw that the greatest gift of all was his life and that if he lived it to the fullest, unselfishly, he would live with the angels. When he saw how wonderful life was, he chose

[10]Easterbrook, *The Progress Paradox,* p. 39.

to come back to it, regardless of its difficulties. It really is a wonderful life.—
Lee McGlone

MINISTERIAL MISCONDUCT. From Shakespeare's *Hamlet,* I, 3:

> But, good my brother
> Do not, as some ungracious pastors do
> Show me the steep and thorny way to heaven
> Whilst, like a puffed and reckless libertine
> Himself the primrose path of dalliance treads.

PEACE. I rest beneath the Almighty's shade, My griefs expire, my troubles cease; Thou, Lord, on whom my soul is stayed, Wilt keep me still in perfect peace.—Charles Wesley

PEACE. In the great depths of the oceans the pressure is enough to crush a submarine like a can of Coke. In order to explore down deep, the oceanographers have built bathyspheres. They are like miniature submarines constructed out of steel plates that are several inches thick. They have thick "skins" to stop the crushing power of the pressure on the outside from getting to the scientists on the inside. When those bathyspheres finally settle on the ocean floor and turn on their lights for exploration, the scientists see fish—fish with very thin skins. Why don't they implode? Those fish have pressure inside them equal and opposite to the pressure outside. They are able to swim freely and easily where we would be destroyed. That is what peace is like. Peace on the inside is equal and opposite of all the stresses and pressures crushing us from the outside.—Leith Anderson

PERSEVERANCE. John Bunyan writes, in *Grace Abounding:*[11]

> Often when I had been making to the promise, I have seen as if the
> Lord would refuse my soul for ever. Then I would think of Esther, who
> went to petition the king contrary to the law. I thought of Benhadad's
> servants, who went with ropes upon their heads to their enemies for
> mercy. The woman of Canaan, that would not be daunted, though

---

[11]John Bunyan, *Grace Abounding* (London: Penquin Classics, 1987), p. 21.

called a "dog" by Christ; and that man that went to borrow bread at midnight, were also great encouragements to me.

PRIDE. Be not proud of race, face, place, or grace.—Charles Haddon Spurgeon

PROBLEM SOLVING. While traveling out west on our family's summer vacation, we saw the snow-capped Rocky Mountains in the distance. They looked frightening. Our first response was, "We can never get across those mountains. They're too high, too steep, too treacherous." But of course, we did cross those mountains, all 12,000 feet of them. We are glad we did. Crossing Bear Tooth Pass in northern Wyoming was one of the highlights of our trip. We did it by understanding the route we had to travel and taking it slowly, a little bit at a time.

That is the way it can be with our problems. Our problems often look like mountains. Our first response is, "We can never overcome them. They are too difficult, too enormous, too complicated to ever be solved." Problems are a lot more frightening when we do not understand them, their extent, and their root cause. We must size up our problems and understand them and then begin to address them a little at a time.—Randy Hammer

PURE HEART. Some years ago there was an Ivory Soap commercial on television that showed a baby being bathed in a bathtub. The commercial contended that Ivory Soap was 99.99% pure. The sponsors did not claim that their product was 100% pure, only 99.99% pure. So it may be with our hearts. We will never reach complete perfection and purity in this life. In spite of our best efforts, there will probably be a trace of impurity in our hearts. Nevertheless, we can still strive toward perfection. We can make a 99.99% pure heart our goal.—Randy Hammer

REJECTION. Max Lucado writes, in *God Came Near*:[12]

In 1858 the Illinois legislature—using an obscure statute—sent Stephen A. Douglas to the U.S. Senate instead of Abraham Lincoln, although Lincoln had won the popular vote. When a sympathetic friend asked

[12]Max Lucado, *God Came Near* (Colorado Springs, CO: Multnomah Press, 2004), p. 57.

Lincoln how he felt, he said, "Like the boy who stubbed his toe: I am too big to cry and too badly hurt to laugh."

RELIGION. Thomas Carlyle writes, in *Signs of the Times:*

Religion more or less in every country is for the most part a wise prudential feeling, grounded on mere calculation; a matter, as all other now are, of expediency and utility; whereby some smaller quantum of earthly enjoyment may be exchanged for a far larger quantum of celestial enjoyment. Thus religion, too, is profit, a working for wages.

REMORSE. Lord Byron writes, in *On the Day I Complete My Thirty-Sixth Year:*

My days are in the yellow leaf
The flowers and fruits of love are gone
The worm, the canker, and the grief
Are mine alone!
The fire that in my bosom press
Is like to some volcanic isle
No torch is kindled at its blaze
A funeral pile.

RESURRECTION. One of the most emotional memories of my life came at a graveside when I was four years old. The day before Christmas, I stood with my family as we buried my twenty-one-year-old brother. It was a dismal day, cold and rainy. But what I remember most was the soldier who stood in the distance and played "Taps." That memory was replayed not long ago, when I read of a soldier who had written a request to the military concerning his own death. "When I die," he wrote, "do not sound taps over my grave. Have someone play reveille, the morning call, the summons to rise." How could such a request be made? Confidence in the Resurrection makes such a request appropriate.—Lee McGlone

SIN: John Milton writes, in "Paradise Lost," Book I:

"What though the field be lost?
All is not lost—the unconquerable will
And study of revenge, immortal hate
And courage never to submit or yield . . .
To bow and sue for grace
With suppliant knee . . .
that were low indeed
That were an ignominy and shame beneath
This downfall."
. . . So spake the apostate Angel, though in pain
Vaunting aloud, but racked with deep despair.

SOCIAL CONCERN. William Cowper writes, in *The Task:*

I would not have a slave to till my ground
To carry me, to fan me while I sleep
And tremble when I wake, for all the wealth
That sinews bought and sold have ever earned
No: dear as freedom is . . .
I had much rather be myself the slave
And wear the bonds, than fasten them on him.

SORROW. Robert Browning Hamilton writes, in *Along the Road:*

I walked a mile with Pleasure,
She chatted all the way;
But left me none the wiser,
For all she had to say.
I walked a mile with Sorrow
And ne'er a word said she;
But, oh! The things I learnt from her
When Sorrow walked with me!

SORROW. Alfred Lord Tennyson's poem, "In Memoriam":

That loss is common would not make
My own less bitter, rather more
Too common! Never morning wore
To evening, but some heart did break.

SPIRITUAL GROWTH. Philip Yancey writes, in *Disappointment with God:*[13]

Human beings grow by striving, working, stretching; and in a sense, human nature needs problems more than solutions. Why are not all prayers answered magically and instantly? Why must every convert travel the same tedious path of spiritual discipline? Because persistent prayer, and fasting, and study, and meditation are designed primarily for our sakes, not for God's. Kierkegaard said that Christians reminded him of schoolboys who want to look up the answers to their math problems in the back of the book rather than work them through. We yearn for shortcuts. But shortcuts usually lead away from growth, not toward it. Apply the principle directly to Job: what was the final result of the testing he went through? As Rabbi Abraham Heschel observed, "Faith like Job's cannot be shaken because it is the result of having been shaken."

SPIRITUAL INVESTMENTS. A bank teller once shared with me that a lady had come to the bank with a stack of savings bonds; she wanted to know how much they were worth. The bonds had been purchased thirty or forty years past, put in a vault, and forgotten about. The bonds were so old and there were so many of them that it was going to take a good while to calculate their worth. The teller said, "She is going to be pleasantly surprised; her bonds will be worth a small fortune."

So it is with righteous living. We do not expect an immediate return on our spiritual investment. But if we are diligent to "lay up treasures in heaven," as Jesus put it, our investment will come back to us. We will surely be pleasantly surprised. When we are diligent and faithful in making spiritual investments,

---

[13]Philip Yancey, *Disappointment with God* (Grand Rapids, MI: Zondervan, 1988), pp. 207–208.

whether it be doing good deeds and righteous living or spreading the good news of God, a return on our investment is sure to eventually come. We will, in time, receive the rewards of righteousness. In due season, we shall reap the fortune if we are faithful and do not lose heart.—Randy Hammer

THANKSGIVING. Matthew Henry, the great commentator of an earlier day, told of an encounter in which he was robbed. A friend later questioned him about how he could square this sad ordeal with Henry's preaching that said we are to be thankful in all things. Henry responded by saying, "First, let me be thankful that I have never been robbed before; second, that though they took my purse, they did not take my life; third, that though they took everything, it wasn't much; and fourth, that it was I who *was* robbed and not I who robbed." Gratitude may well depend on our point of view.— Lee McGlone

TRAGEDY. A General Electric ad raises the question: "What was Thomas Edison's biggest blunder?" To our surprise, we learn that Edison opposed the theory of alternating current that had been developed by Charles Steinmetz. We also learn that Steinmetz, an immigrant, was almost denied admission at Ellis Island. Some thought him to be unfit. "One of the men most responsible for the electrification of America was almost turned away at its gate." That would truly have been a tragedy. Yet another tragedy, a greater one, takes place frequently—when people deny Christ admission to their lives. How very sad that darkness is so often chosen over light, hatred over love, despair over hope. Jesus said, "I have come that you may have life, and that you may have it abundantly!" That's the promise. Let's not miss it.—Lee McGlone

TRUE RICHES. In Patrick Henry's words:

> I have now disposed of all my property to my family. There is one thing more I wish I could give them and that is faith in Jesus Christ. If they had that and I had not given them a single shilling, they would have been rich; and if they had not that, and I had given them all the world, they would be poor indeed.

TRUST. Tim Hansel writes, in *Holy Sweat:*[14]

> One day, while my son Zac and I were out in the country, climbing around in some cliffs, I heard a voice from above me yell, "Hey Dad! Catch me!" I turned around to see Zac joyfully jumping off a rock straight at me. He had jumped and then yelled "Hey Dad!" I became an instant circus act, catching him. We both fell to the ground. For a moment after I caught him I could hardly talk. When I found my voice again I gasped in exasperation: "Zac! Can you give me one good reason why you did that???" He responded with remarkable calmness: "Sure. Because you're my Dad." His whole assurance was based in the fact that his father was trustworthy. He could live life to the hilt because I could be trusted. Isn't this even more true for a Christian?

WAITING FOR GOD. Waiting for God is not laziness. Waiting for God is not going to sleep. Waiting for God is not the abandonment of effort. Waiting for God means, first, activity under command; second, readiness for any new command that may come; third, the ability to do nothing until the command is given.—G. Campbell Morgan

WALK OF FAITH. The Resurrection is the antidote to hostility, to hopelessness, and to melancholy. The Resurrection brings death to life. Someone has said, "The stirring wildness of God calls brittle bones to leaping and stone hearts to soaring." But it's not about being in church on Easter morning. It's about a living, vital, walk of faith with the One who lives forever.—Lee McGlone

WORSHIP. James Packer writes, in *Your Father Loves You:*[15]

> To worship God is to recognize his worth or worthiness; to look Godward, and to acknowledge in all appropriate ways the value of what we see. The Bible calls this activity "glorifying God" or "giving glory to

---

[14]Tim Hansel, *Holy Sweat* (Dallas: Word Books, 1987), pp. 46–47.
[15]James Packer, *Your Father Loves You* (Colorado Springs, CO: Harold Shaw Publishers, 1986), p. 15.

God," and views it as the ultimate end, and from one point of view, the whole duty of man (Ps. 29:2; 96:6; 1 Cor. 10:31). Scripture views the glorifying of God as a six fold activity: praising God for all that he is and all his achievements; thanking him for his gifts and his goodness to us; asking him to meet our own and others' needs; offering him our gifts, our service, and ourselves; learning of him from his word, read and preached, and obeying his voice; telling others of his worth, both by public confession and testimony to what he has done for us. Thus we might say that the basic formulas of worship are these: "Lord, you are wonderful"; "Thank you, Lord"; "Please Lord"; "Take this, Lord"; "Yes, Lord"; "Listen everybody!" This then is worship in its largest sense: petition as well as praise, preaching as well as prayer, hearing as well as speaking, actions as well as words, obeying as well as offering, loving people as well as loving God. However, the primary acts of worship are those which focus on God directly—and we must not imagine that work for God in the world is a substitute for direct fellowship with him in praise and prayer and devotion.

CONTRIBUTORS

Anderson, Richard. Pastor, The International Church of Copenhagen

Carter, Terry. Professor of Christian ministries, Ouachita Baptist University, Arkadelphia, Arkansas

Cox, Ken. Pastor, First Baptist Church, New Boston, Texas

Crawford, James. Pastor Emeritus, The Old South Church, Boston, Massachusetts

Dever, John. Professor of church and society, Southern Baptist Theological Seminary, Louisville, Kentucky

Dipboye, Larry. Former pastor, First Baptist Church, Oak Ridge, Tennessee

Faszer, Ted. Professor, North American Baptist Seminary, Sioux Falls, South Dakota, and minister of music, First Baptist Church, Sioux Falls, South Dakota

Fields, Henry. Pastor, First Baptist Church, Toccoa Falls, Georgia

Hammer, Randy. Pastor, First Congregational Church, Albany, New York

Hollon, D. Leslie. Pastor, St. Matthews Baptist Church, Louisville, Kentucky

Huffman, John. Retired Baptist minister, Louisville, Kentucky

Hull, William E. Research professor, Samford University, Birmingham, Alabama

Hunt, Lizette. Writer of children's material, Dickinson, North Dakota

Lovette, Roger. Pastor, Baptist Church of the Covenant, Birmingham, Alabama

McGlone, Lee. Pastor, First Baptist Church, Arkadelphia, Arkansas

Paine, Roger. Senior minister, First Parish in Lincoln, Lincoln, Massachusetts

Phillips, E. Lee. Minister and freelance writer, Norcross, Georgia

Pope, W. Gregory. Pastor, Crescent Hill Baptist Church, Louisville, Kentucky

Redding, Gary C. Pastor, First Baptist Church, North Augusta, Georgia

Sisk, Ronald D. Professor of homiletics and Christian ministry, North American Baptist Seminary, Sioux Falls, South Dakota

Stratman, Gary. Minister, Hollywood Presbyterian Church, Hollywood, California

Thompson, Marcia. Author of children's material, Sioux Falls, South Dakota

Tomlin, Carolyn. Writer specializing in church curriculum materials, Jackson, Tennessee

Tuck, William Powell. Former professor of preaching, Southern Baptist Theological Seminary, Louisville, Kentucky, and retired Baptist pastor, Richmond, Virginia

Turner, William L. Retired pastor, South Main Baptist Church, Houston, Texas

Twyman, Louis. Administrator, Broadway Baptist Church, Louisville, Kentucky

Vinson, Richard. Dean, Baptist Theological Seminary of Richmond, Richmond, Virginia

Vowan, Lawrence. Retired Baptist pastor, Cabot, Arkansas

Walsh, Albert J. D. Pastor, Heidelberg United Church of Christ, Heidelberg, Pennsylvania

West, Danny M. Associate professor of preaching and pastoral studies, M. Christopher White Divinity School, Boiling Spring, North Carolina

INDEX OF CONTRIBUTORS

SERMON TITLE INDEX

Children's sermons are marked as (cs).

INDEX OF SERMON TEXTS

INDEX OF PRAYERS

INDEX OF MATERIALS USEFUL AS CHILDREN'S STORIES AND SERMONS

INDEX OF MATERIALS USEFUL
FOR SMALL GROUPS

TOPICAL INDEX